A CHRISTIAN THEOLOGY OF THE OLD TESTAMENT

Authors in the Biblical and Theological Classics Library:

A CHRISTIAN THEOLOGY OF THE OLD TESTAMENT

George A.F. Knight

paternoster
press

Reprinted in 1998 by Paternoster Publishing
as part of the Biblical and Theological Classics Library series

04 03 02 01 00 99 98   7 6 5 4 3 2 1

Paternoster Publishing is an imprint of Paternoster Publishing,
P.O. Box 300, Carlisle, Cumbria, CA3 0QS, U.K.
http://www.paternoster-publishing.com

British Library Cataloguing in Publication Data
A catalogue record for this book is available from the British Library.

ISBN 0-85364-879-4

Cover design by Mainstream, Lancaster
Typeset by WestKey Ltd, Falmouth, Cornwall
Printed in Great Britain by
Caledonian International Book Manufacturing Ltd., Glasgow

Contents

PART THREE
God and Israel

PART FOUR
The Zeal of the Lord

Introduction

This is *a* Theology of the Old Testament. *The* Theology of the Old Testament will never be written. Each generation sees new vistas within the Scriptures of which earlier generations were unaware. Thus the Theology of the Old Testament has to be represented to each generation in the language and thought of that new generation. He who seeks to represent it thus must also take into account the ever-growing heritage both of the world of science and of the world of biblical studies.

This is *not* a study of the religious ideas of ancient Israel. There is now a number of excellent works of such a nature. This Theology is written with the deliberate presupposition – and none of us can escape our presuppositions – that the Old Testament is nothing less than Christian Scripture. Therefore it is what the Germans would call a *Kirchliche Theologie* of the Old Testament. It is written by one who assumes that the Church believes the Old Testament to be the Word of God, just as surely as it believes it of the New Testament. A Theology of the Old Testament must arise out of the combined thinking of the Church, and not merely from the disciplined studies of scholars who may not necessarily be committed to a Christian obedience. Actually, as Professor N.W. Porteous, of Edinburgh, has said: 'For the Biblical theologian neutrality would be unscientific'.[1] The Old Testament is a book that must be read within the walls of the Christian Church,

---

[1] OS, Deel VIII. *Semantics and Old Testament Theology, 1950,* pp. I ff.

since 'the Church has received the Old Testament from the hand of Jesus'.[2] Therefore an exposition of the Old Testament cannot confine itself merely to a critical and historical analysis either of its books or of its teaching.

The assumption that the Old Testament is the Word of God to the Church, however, is not the same thing as the inference that may be drawn therefrom, viz., that the Old Testament must be understood christologically. We are not meant to assume that we merely search its pages for intimations of the (future) Messiah of the New Testament. The Old Testament is, rather, Revelation, in the same sense as the New Testament is, for it brings to man the revelation of God's mighty acts and purposes, just as the New Testament does. The faith of the Church Catholic has ever been that the Old Testament is revelation of the same God as that revealed in the pages of the New Testament. The New Testament shows us the God and Father of our Lord Jesus Christ active in the Son for the redemption of the world. The Old Testament must therefore declare and reveal to us the same God active to the same end, since the God of the New Testament is the same God as the God of the Old Testament. This does not mean merely that the New Testament 'fulfils' the Old Testament. The God of both Testaments is declared to be the 'living' God. His relationship with Israel in the pages of the Old Testament must be a growing and a dynamic one, issuing, in the New Testament story, in something which is therefore really new, yet organically related to the old. In the New Testament God acts through his Son. In the Old Testament he also acts through his Son. In fact, we might employ St Paul's declaration in II Cor. 5.19, and with the alteration of two words, use it to show forth the essential contents of the Old Testament, and thus phrase the quotation: 'God was in Israel, seeking to reconcile the world unto himself'. 'In Israel' God did not succeed in redeeming the world. It remained for him to act 'in Christ' in order finally to draw all men unto himself.

---

[2] A statement subscribed to by nine leading Continental Old Testament scholars in *Evangelische Theologie*, July/Aug., 1952, Heft 1/2, on back of the cover paper.

In the Epistle to the Hebrews in the New Testament, the writer places an Old Testament quotation in the mouth of the New Testament Son. It runs: 'A body hast thou prepared me. In burnt offerings and sacrifices for sin thou hast had no pleasure. Then said I, Lo, I come (in the volume of the book it is written of me) to do thy will, O God' (Heb. 10.5). By these words of deep insight the writer has given us a key to a Christian understanding of the Old Testament. The Old Testament tells us of God's relationship with Israel, and through Israel, of his relationship to the world. Israel in the Old Testament is called to be 'The People of God'. Now this same People of God finally gives birth to him whom we call the Son of God, by means of the body of the Blessed Virgin Mary. 'The People of God' in the Old Testament period are therefore no less than the 'body' which 'thou hast prepared me'. But the body is the body of a Son. 'Israel is my son', God had said to Moses (Ex. 4.22). It is only natural, then, that we should find in the Old Testament that God deals with that Body, viz., his Son, Israel, in the same way, and to the same purpose, as he deals with the Son, Jesus, who also came in a body. Moreover, since this is the case, God will surely continue to deal with the People of God, the Church, to the present day, still in the same manner as he has done in the past, since the Church comprises the members of the body of Christ.

The Theology of the Old Testament must be viewed in its totality even though the Old Testament contains many theological ideas separable from one another. If we do so, then we discover that the central theme of the Old Testament is nothing less than the revelation of the redemptive activity of God in and through the Son, Israel. This means that the Covenant, for example, is not the primary issue of the Old Testament. It can only be secondary, since the Covenant is merely given to Israel in order to be a means to this greater end and purpose of God. So too with such themes as the giving of the Law, the contribution of the great Prophets, the teaching of the Sages, and so on.

We are therefore challenged to discover a 'whole' view of the meaning of the Old Testament. This is true especially when we are confronted with a passage such as the following from the pen of St Paul: ' . . . how that Christ died for our sins according to the scriptures; and that he was buried, and that he rose again the third day according to the scriptures' (I Cor. 15.3–4). Or again, we are challenged to discover a 'wholeness' in the Old Testament revelation when we notice that random texts or passages taken from the Old Testament itself, and possibly written at widely different periods of Israel's story, often most surprisingly agree in their general interpretation, provided they are seen in the light of the Old Testament revelation as a whole.

This Christian *Theology of the Old Testament* is consequently an attempt to discover and present the total meaning of the Old Testament. It does not attempt to analyse the progressive thought of Israel about God and about God's mighty purposes. But it does seek to discover what the Old Testament has to say to the twentieth century in the light of the Christian revelation as a whole.

The book is written in non-technical language, as far as possible. A 'Church Theology' is naturally meant for the ordinary churchman to read. The narrative form that is used has been adopted at the suggestion of the publisher. The reader will not find the sectionalized method of exposition that is customarily employed in a Theology of any nature. Biblical references are to the Authorized or King James Version of the Scriptures (AV). These do not always coincide with the versification of the Hebrew Massoretic text, far less with the Greek of the Septuagint (LXX) Version. The linguist, however, with his Hebrew and Greek texts before him, knows how to overcome the discrepancies in versification. To give the references to both the English and the original text would be an annoyance to the general reader, and at the same time a work of supererogation for the biblical scholar. Hebrew words, again, have been transliterated, both for the sake of economy in publishing costs and for ease of understanding by the non-Hebraist. While the transliteration has been made to give as close a rendering as possible of the original sounds, it has not always been consistent, especially in those cases where a Hebrew word, like 'adam', is known in English already. Greek words, however, have been retained in their original alphabet. Again at the suggestion of the publishers, footnotes have been used sparingly. Accordingly, when references are made to other works, it is usually in order that the point in question may be studied more fully in the books suggested at the foot of the page.

I wish to express my warm gratitude to several good friends. To the Rev. James G. Matheson, M.A., B.D., of Dunedin, and formerly of Edinburgh; and to the Rev. J.M. Bates, M.A., also of Dunedin, who have read through the original typescript with an eagle eye. Also to Rev. Fr A. Gabriel Hebert, S.S.M., and to Rev. Fr Antony Snell, S.S.M., both of St Michael's House, Crafers, South Australia, who have read the MS carefully and made many helpful and constructive suggestions. Finally also to my wife, not only for typing out the MS, but also for bearing with me while I wrote the book.

November, 1957
Knox College,
Dunedin,
New Zealand

Abbreviations

ANET   Ancient Near Eastern Texts, ed. J.B. Pritchard.
ANH   Dalman's Aramäisch-Neuhebräisches Handwörterbuch.
ARSV   American Standard Revised Version of the Bible.
AV   Authorized, or King James, Version of the Bible.
BJRL   Bulletin of the John Rylands Library.
BO   Bibliotheca Orientalia.
BZAW   Beiträge zur Zeitschrift für die alttestamentliche Wissen-
        shaft.
DBS   Dictionnaire de la Bible, Supplément.
DSD   Dead Sea Scrolls, The Manual of Discipline.
DSS   Dead Sea Scrolls.
EB   Enctyclopedia Biblica.
ERE   Encyclopedia of Religion and Ethics.
ET   Expository Times.
GK   Gesenius-Kautzsch, Hebrew Grammar.
HDB   Hastings' Dictionary of the Bible.
HTR   Harvard Theological Review.
ICC   International Critical Commentary.
JBL   Journal of Biblical Literature.
JNES   Journal of Near Eastern Studies.
JQR   Jewish Quarterly Review.
JSS   Journal of Semitic Studies.
KB   Köhler-Baumgartner, Lexicon in Veteris Testamenti
        Libros.
KZNT   Strack-Billerbeck, Kommentar zum Neuen Testament.

LXX   Septuagint, the Greek Version of the Old Testament.
MS(S)   Manuscript(s).
MT   Massoretic Text, the traditional Hebrew text of the Old
        Testament.
OHL   Oxford Hebrew Lexicon, by Brown, Driver and Briggs.
OS   Oudtestamentische Studien.
OT   Old Testament.
RTR   Reformed Theological Review.
RV   Revised Version of the Bible.
SJT   Scottish Journal of Theology.
TS   Theologische Studien.
TWB   Theological Word Book of the Bible, ed. Richardson.
TWNT Theologisches Wörterbuch zum Neuen Testament, ed.
        G. Kittel.
TZ   Theologische Zeitschrift.
VT   Vetus Testamentum.
ZAW   Zeitschrift für die alttestamentliche Wissenschaft.

Part One

God

One

How God Makes Himself Known

One of the possible ways of translating the first few verses of Genesis is as follows: 'When, in the beginning, God created the heavens and the earth, and the earth was without form and void, and darkness was upon the face of the deep, and the spirit of God was brooding over the face of the waters, GOD SAID, Let there be light, and there was light'. If we follow this way of translating, as is vouched for in a footnote to the ARSV, then the verb SAID becomes the first finite verb of the first sentence in the Old Testament.

In that first sentence, at any rate, no matter in what order we take the clauses, we are given the key to much that follows in the OT.

When were these words first written? There seems little doubt that they first saw the light, not in the land of Israel at all, but in the land of Mesopotamia, which was so far off to the Jews; also that they were written by an exile from his native land, who was living under the hated yoke of the Babylonian conqueror of Jerusalem and of the people of Judah. Jerusalem fell finally to Nebuchadnezzar in 587 B.C. It was not merely the fact that he belonged to a defeated people that would continually gall this unknown writer. Rather he was oppressed by a consciousness that the very people whom he believed had been chosen by his God to be the divine instrument in a cosmic plan was now no more – it was no longer an independent political unit, a nation amongst other nations. Our writer could look back upon a long history of his people. The historical facts were no doubt available to him, preserved as they would be on scrolls and originating from the historical memory of both the northern and the southern branches of his people, that of Ephraim in the north and Judah in the south. This people of Israel, that had been chosen and nurtured by God 'since the land of Egypt' (cf. Ps. 81.10, etc.) was now come to an end, and was now no more a people, but merely the slave of a haughty power. And in being no more a people, in being a fugitive and a slave in a foreign land, Israel was demonstrating to a sneering world (as its more sensitive members imagined, cf. Lam. 1.7, 21) that its God was no more a god than any of the other gods of the nations. It was now patent that all its vaunted faith in a purpose running through its history, as its God was working out his plan, not only for Israel, but for the whole world, was just so much national egotism and egregious folly.

Yet it was just at that period of degradation, both national and personal to the writer, who in the year 587 B.C. may have seen his beloved city of Jerusalem go up in flames before he was carried into exile, that he penned what is for us now the first chapter of Genesis. And if it is the case that we are able to see a depth of understanding of the purposes of God in the opening words of the Old Testament as we have it today, then we are to remember that those words were wrung from the heart of a man who became the interpreter of God's ways *par excellence* just because he lived through that moment in Israel's story which was obviously the decisive experience in its history for an understanding of the ways of God and man.

The OT is a book about God. But the OT is also a book about God and Israel. Yet the OT is understandable only when we discover that it is about God and Israel as they confront each other in a special relationship and for a special purpose. The theology of the OT is thus observable and discoverable as we watch the historical unfolding of the purpose of God which becomes 'incarnate' in, with, and through the working of God's Spirit upon that one nation, which in his wisdom God chose to use for his mighty purposes.

If then we wish to discover what the theology of the OT really is, it will not be sufficient merely to pick various ideas out of its pages, and then piece them together, in order to form some kind of a systematic presentation of theological ideas. We must rather seek to follow in historical sequence the development of the relationship between the *living* God who is spoken of so frequently in the OT, and that empirical People whom God has chosen to become his instrument for the attaining of his cosmic purpose. Or, in other words, we shall require to seek to glimpse that which may well appear to be impossible for mortal eye to view: the pattern of a vital, ever-changing, ever-evolving response of a People, under the influence of the Spirit of God, to the ever-developing, ever-deepening self-revelation of that People's God as he makes himself known to them in and through his peculiar relationship to them in the Spirit.

The OT gives us no description of God. It tells us nothing of what God is like in himself. It tells us only of what God is like as he meets with, confronts, and thus reveals himself to, his people, Israel, in the action of his Spirit. Thus what we shall be required to do if we would seek to discover a theology of the OT will be to listen while we hear the God of this people, Israel, reveal himself through his confronting them with his Word, with his very self; and only then shall we be in the position to make any attempt to systematize such knowledge as we shall have gained. But we shall have to remember that it will not be possible to produce a system from the knowledge we shall have gained by this process of listening to the encounter of Israel with her God. The reason for this is that the moment we seek to tabulate and to systematize that living experience of encounter between Israel and her God, its reality will grow cold and dead to our touch. What we shall have to attempt to do is rather to put ourselves alongside the people of Israel of old, and thus seek to enter ourselves into their experience of meeting with the God whom they had come to know and trust 'from the days of Egypt'. St Augustine's insight, '*credo ut intelligam*', must be followed by anyone who hopes to understand the OT. He must remember that only he who believes can ever hope to understand.

However, we must begin somewhere if we wish to study the theology of the OT. Therefore, even before we analyse the significance of the story of the people of Israel, we shall find ourselves forced to make certain arbitrary statements about the nature of God and his chosen relationship with Israel. Only later shall we be in the position to see how that relationship has produced the ideas that we are handling. We shall find that we must begin this study by asking ourselves what the God of the OT is like who is thus so concerned to reveal himself to Israel. Thereupon we shall next find ourselves asking what is the nature of this purpose of God's self-revelation which he is making through Israel, as it is recorded in the pages of the OT.

It was just such a question that the unknown priestly writer (as we are in the habit of calling him) sought to answer when he was faced in Babylon with the final collapse of all his hopes and beliefs. And it was then, despite the crashing of his world about his ears, that he confidently uttered that fundamental statement on which so much of the faith of both the Old and the New Testaments rests: 'GOD SAID'.

The conception that God could reveal himself in speech and action is an anthropomorphic one. That is to say, Israel's experience of God as a living Person is understood by Israel's thinkers almost wholly in terms of what it means to think, speak and act as a man. In himself God is unknowable. He is the 'God who hides himself' (Isa. 45.15; Job 11.7; Ps. 97.2; Ex. 33.20). He is Spirit and not flesh like the Egyptians (Isa. 31.3). On the other hand, since the OT does not so much tell us *about* God as relate what God says as he speaks in the first person singular, e.g. 'I, the Lord, have called thee in righteousness', 'I am the Lord', 'I form the light', 'I have made the earth', and many such expressions, we are presented in the OT with the speech of a God who addresses men in the same kind of way as man himself addresses his brother. Nowhere in the OT is God called by the descriptive epithet of Person. In fact, the Hebrew equivalent of such a word does not exist. But everywhere it is taken for granted that God addresses man in personal terms, and by the same means as one man addresses another. The person of Man himself is a mystery. Man is fearfully and wonderfully made (Ps. 139.14). How much more then is the Person of God a mystery, especially when the attempt to understand him is made in language that man uses of his brother man. Thus we may say by way of introduction that the God of the OT is never described in terms of himself. Rather he is known to Israel just in those forms of thought that are available to man, as one man seeks to reveal his mind and heart to another; in other words God is known by his speech and by his acts. Thus he is known by man to be a Personal Being, not because he can be described as he is in his essence, but because he can be known as he reveals himself to hearts and minds which, in their turn, in some sense are describable in terms of God's heart and mind.

Two

God Known From His Image

If God said, then he is understood to have spoken through a mouth. 'For the mouth of the Lord hath spoken it' (Isa. 1.20) is a constantly recurring phrase of the great prophets. But the mouth implies a head. All the parts of the human head are envisaged as belonging to God. He has eyes (Isa. 1.15), ears (Isa. 5.9), a nose ('The Lord's nose grew hot', Ex. 4.14), and so also all other parts of the human frame. God can walk (Gen. 3.8), sleep (Ps. 44.23), and breathe (Job 4.9). His hands (Ex. 7.17) act for him, his nostrils smell the sweet savour of sacrifices (Gen. 8.21). But the sacrifices of Israel were also regarded as God's food (Num. 18.17). We find again that God uses his eyes to read (I Sam. 10.25).

Before we can begin to understand, then, how God can be said to communicate of himself to man, we shall have to discover, paradoxically, how Hebrew man thought of himself in OT days. We shall have to examine something of the anthropology of the OT if we wish to know how the Hebrews understood the conception of communication and revelation between even man and man. Anthropology and theology are mutually relevant studies in connexion with the OT. This same first chapter of Genesis, with which we began, believes that the God who has spoken, first made man in his own image (Gen. 1.26). This can only mean that, since God is not knowable in himself, God is revealing himself to one who in some sense must be capable of understanding his Word. What is this man, therefore, to whom God, in the OT, communicates his Word?

In the first place, man is not merely male. The true meaning of
the word *'adham* (Adam) comprehends both male and female as
one (Gen. 1.27; 5.2). Those two passages from the priestly writer
are supplemented by a pictorial image from the earlier writer J.[1]
In the latter's story of the creation of man as we have it in Gen.
2, the unity of male and female is clearly demonstrated by means
of the figure of woman being formed from the rib of the male.
The union of male and female, which J thus pictorializes, P
declares to be 'in the image and likeness of God'. The Hebrew
words *tselem*, 'image', and *demuth*, 'likeness', are not quite
identical. The latter means something like 'copy', 'resemblance'.
The word *tselem*, on the other hand, may represent something
very concrete. It is one of the words that is used of a graven or
molten image (e.g. Num. 33.52; II Kings 11.18), or of a plastic
copy of an object to be worshipped (I Sam. 6.5). It is also the word
used to describe wall-paintings, or murals (Ezek. 23.14). In one
instance at least (Ps. 39.6) it may even mean 'silhouette'. The two
words, therefore, supplement each other's meaning.

Now, in another section attributable to the priestly writer (Gen.
5.3), we find that a human son, in his turn, is engendered, after the
image and likeness of his human father, so that he is in the 'form'
of his father. Of course, the image in this case is not necessarily a
physical one. Gen. 9.6 will help to make this clear. There the

---

[1] The letters J E D H and P used throughout this book refer to the various
writers, or possibly to the oral traditions finally set down in writing, that
are to be found within the Pentateuch, or Torah, two names for the first
five books of the OT. J's material seems to stem from the Southern
kingdom of Judah, E's from the Northern kingdom of Ephraim, or Israel,
while D is otherwise the writer(s) whom we call the Deuteronomist. H,
or the Holiness Code, comprises material inset within P. The letter P is
the symbol used for the material supplied by a Priestly group of writers,
who edited and finalized the Pentateuch during and after the Exile. See
one of the many 'Introductions' to the OT, e.g., that of R.H. Pfeiffer,
British edition, 1952, or that of W. O.E. Oesterley and Th. H. Robinson,
1934, reprinted 1946; or H.H. Rowley, *The Growth of the OT*, 1950.
For the early chapters of Genesis, here and in Part Two, a simple
introduction is that by D.M.G. Stalker, *Genesis i–xii*, 1950.

shedding of a man's blood is forbidden on the ground that God has made man in his own image. Naturally, there is no suggestion in this verse that man's physical body and blood are a copy or an image of anything in the being of God. Conversely, however, it is the image of God in man that distinguishes man from the animals. Gen. 1.20, 24 reveal the belief of the writer that the animals were one with the elements, the waters and the birds being classified together. We would illustrate such a conception today possibly with a definition like the following: 'The butterfly is an animated leaf in the wind'. On the other hand, man is set over the animal creation to 'rule' it (Gen. 1.28) and to control it (2.19).

On this ground, we might say that in some sense of the term the OT regards man as the 'son' of God. Yet it does not make explicit use of the term. Its writers know full well the danger of being misunderstood by the ancient world with its polytheistic preconceptions, and its crassly materialistic views of the relation between the gods and man. But we have seen from the juxtaposition of Gen. 5.3 with Gen. 1.26 that the priestly writer must have had this conception in mind. To quote L. Koehler: 'The son represents the father, man represents God. Man occupies the place of a son of God'. Yet man is only the *representation* of the form of God; he is not the form itself. The formlessness of the 'image' of God is expressed elsewhere in words which we can apply in our present context: 'Ye heard the sound of the words, but ye saw no form; only ye heard a sound' (Deut. 4.12). Yet, as we shall see later, God has indeed a form, even though it is invisible to the eye of man, so that man can speak of that form only with words that demand a comparison. So Ezekiel speaks in his great vision: 'I saw, as if . . . ' Perhaps, by the way, this 'as if . . . ' qualification is the function of the word *demuth*; the latter serves as a weakening of the comparison between God and man that is made by the conception of 'image', *tselem*. Man is made *like* God, but is certainly not God.[2]

---

[2] See L. Koehler, 'Die Grundstelle der Imago-Dei-Lehre, Gen. 1.26', *TZ*, 4. Jahrgang, Heft 1, Jan.–Feb., 1948, pp. 16 ff.

C. Vriezen, 'La Création de l'Homme d'après l'Image de Dieu', OS, Deel II, pp. 87 ff. D.P. Volz, 'Die Wuerde des Menschen im AT', in *Glaube und Ethos*, Festschrift Wehrung, 1940, pp. 1–8.

Now, since it is possible to suggest the paradox that the formless God of the OT does yet indeed possess a form, then the paradox extends to man as well. Man, made in the image of the formless God, certainly possesses a form himself Not only so, but this form of his is that to which we have now referred. Not only does man possess a human body; man, created in the image of God, is to be understood as having the form of a union of male and female.

It is no accident that Plato's 'Symposium' accepts the myth of Androgyny.[3] This is a word used to represent the idea that man and woman are essentially one person. The myth is made clear to us when we remember how Narcissus fell in love with his own reflexion in the pool. Narcissism is self-love. The biblical myth, on the other hand, presents us with a picture of sexual polarity: 'It is not good that the man should be alone; I will make him a helper fit for him' (Gen. 2.18, ARSV). Narcissism presupposes the elimination of anything in the nature of opposites; it looks for the identity of subject and object. The biblical picture of Adam and Eve, however, implies what Martin Buber has taught us to call the 'I-thou' relationship between two equal persons. Yet, in the biblical view, these two persons are one flesh (Gen. 2.24). That is to say, while man is two, yet he is one. Nay more. The word *'adham* comprises the conception that man is perhaps at least three before he is fully man. Adam and Eve are not complete in the biblical story until Adam really 'knew' *yadha'* his wife (Gen. 4.1; 5.3), and a child is born of that knowledge.[4] Both the knowledge, and the child which results therefrom, are therefore necessary aspects of that total complex of being which receives the name of *'adham* or *'adam* in Hebrew thought.

---

[3] E. Brunner, *Man in Revolt*, 1937, p. 348.
[4] I Levy, in *VT*, 1956, p. 430, translates it as 'Adam made love to his wife'. Ten times in the OT clearly, and seven times doubtfully, the verb *yadha'* refers to coitus. R. Gordis, in 'The Knowledge of Good and Evil in the Old Testament and the Qumran Scrolls', *JBL*, LXXVI, June, 1957, p. 131, shows how this verb is a universal euphemism for sex relations.

There is a further aspect of the Hebrew noun, *'adam*, which we must also take into account, as we seek to understand what man made in the image of God can be. And here again we are presented with another polarity of thought. We are now to deal with the two conceptions, (*a*) that the word *'adam* means all humanity as such, and (*b*) that *'adam* may be used of an individual man (or woman, for that matter), belonging to the genus man. For example, in the priestly legislation we read that if an *'adam* shall have a skin disease, he shall show the diseased limb to the priest (Lev. 13.2). Man is thus both the individual and the race. Man is both one, and he is many. Thus man is not merely a number of isolated individuals. Men are somehow interrelated with one other. They have a common ancestry in one particular Adam, and they have a common flesh (Job 14.22), and a common destiny in death (Isa. 40.7). Yet each individual man or woman in the OT is truly an individual person. We have no doubt of this when we see the originality of outstanding personalities such as David or Jeremiah. Therefore a man is like a finger on a hand. Each finger is an individual finger. Yet all the fingers have a common root in the hand that carries them.

This paradoxical oneness yet plurality of man, which we have now observed from two angles, we must constantly bear in mind if we would know something of the nature of God as the OT reveals him. For it is this individual, yet *'organic'* creature who is made in the image of God.

Virtually all the older commentators and theologians have taken it for granted that the plural form 'us' when used by God of himself is a mere relic of the polytheistic thinking of early days. 'And God said, Let us make man in our image . . . ' (Gen. 1.26); 'Let us go down, and there confound their language . . . ' (Gen. 11.7). Writing as he did in the tenth century B.C., so the argument runs, our author J could not have been influenced by the great eighth century prophets. The latter were virtually monotheists in their view of Israel's God. Living in what was still the 'henotheistic' period of Israel's development, J was of the opinion that Israel's God, though supreme amongst all gods was yet but ruler over the pantheon that he controlled. On the other hand, it is conceded, J may have come to believe that the gods of the nations were now of so little account that they could be thought of as 'no gods',[5] or else they were relegated to the position of a subsidiary court of angels (e.g. Ps. 82.1). Yahweh, Lord of the pantheon, therefore spoke for all the gods, or angels, when he used the pronoun 'we'. This theory may indeed represent a factual description of the development of the relationship of Israel's God to the gods of all the nations, or to the angelic host. (We examine this conception in Part I, chap. 5.) But that is not to say that the priestly writer accepted such a view, living as he did after the great prophets had made their particular contribution. A much more likely hypothesis is that he consciously used the words he did, and that when he spoke of man as created in the image of God, he intended us to understand that the nature of God was 'organic' and complex, just as is the nature of man.

Although the individual in the OT could be as truly an individualist as any twentieth century personality, the very conception of individuality was foreign to his thought. To be alone, to be separated from one's kind, and to live without contact with other men, that was the ultimate fear of OT man. Even for a nation to live alone meant that in the end it became a 'non-people' and perished off the earth (Deut. 32.21). All Hebrew adults seem to have married. The early polygamy of which we read was a valuable means of bringing into a family group the unmarried woman or widow. The so-called 'levirate law' (Deut. 25.5–10, cf. Matt. 22.23–33) laid the requirement upon Israel that when a man died, his brother was to marry the widow of the deceased; failing him, another *go'el* or 'redeemer' was to step in and offer the helpless, homeless woman a place within his home. The little book of Ruth tells us of an actual example of the action of a *go'el*.[6] On the other hand, the word of the Lord to Jeremiah, ordering him not to take to himself a wife (Jer. 16.2), marked Jeremiah off

---

[5] For example, the Hebrew word *'elil*, used of a worthless divinity, may have been employed as a play upon the name Enlil, one of the important gods of the Assyrio-Babylonian pantheon.

[6] See G.A.F. Knight, *Ruth and Jonah*, second edition, 1956.

to be quite different from other men. Furthermore, Jeremiah, being unmarried, would not be able to have children as his heritage (Jer. 16.2), and so would remain like the outcast and the eunuch (Isa. 56.3). To be one with one's children, just as to be joined with one's fathers, even if it be in death (Gen. 25.8), was surely better than living as a solitary, or than dying without the comfort of knowing that others had gone to the same unknown destination as oneself.

It is understandable then to discover that the people of the OT are to be found living in organized groups. There was of course the nation, the whole '*am*. It is interesting now at this point to realize that the whole '*am*, as one unit, was regarded as possessing a corporate personality in itself. This was true of Israel, just as it was true of the other contemporary nations.[7] 'The soul of the people was discouraged' (Num. 21.4). 'And Moses sent messengers from Kadesh unto the king of Edom, Thus saith *thy brother Israel*, Thou knowest all the travail that hath befallen us, how *our* fathers went down . . . And Edom said unto *him*, *Thou* shalt not pass through *me* . . . '[8] (Num. 20.14, 18). In this case the whole nation can be addressed as 'thou', and yet at the same time the speaker may be aware that the nation is a plural entity, SC. 'our fathers'. More thanonce we find Moses addressing Israel in this strain in the singular and in the plural within the one sentence. Thus: 'I have led *you* forty years . . . *your* clothes are not waxen old upon *you*, and *thy* shoe is not waxen old upon *thy* foot' (Deut. 29.5). When the Psalmist speaks in the first person singular, it is seldom possible to declare whether he speaks for himself, or whether all Israel is speaking through his voice (cf. Ps. 4.7–8). Isaiah can refer to the whole nation as one unit when he says: 'But Israel doth not know, my people doth not consider' (Isa. 1.3). In the book of Numbers again, there is a daring anthropomorphism which brings out clearly the 'unity in diversity' of this People of

[7]   H. Wheeler Robinson, 'The Hebrew Conception of Corporate Personality', in *Werden und Wesen des Alten Testaments*, 1936, pp. 49 ff.
[8]   This important concept is discussed fully by A.R. Johnson in *The One and the Many in the Israelite Conception of God, 1942*.

God, this *'am 'elohim*, or, more commonly, this *'am yahweh*, the People of the Lord, the nation which God had brought up out of the land of Egypt. In Num. 11.11 f. we read 'And Moses said unto the Lord, Wherefore hast thou evil entreated thy servant? And wherefore have I not found favour in thy sight that thou layest the burden of all this people upon me? Have I conceived all this people? Have I brought them forth, that thou shouldest say unto me Carry them in thy bosom, as a nursing-father carrieth the sucking child, unto the land which thou swarest unto their fathers?' These verses lead us to a fuller understanding of another similar verse to be found in Exodus. There it is implied that while it was not Moses who begat this people, God indeed had conceived and brought forth a son, and was carrying them in his bosom as a nursing-father. In Ex. 4.22 God says to Moses: 'And thou shalt say unto Pharaoh, Thus saith the Lord, Israel is my son, even my firstborn'.

The use of the word 'Israel' in such a context makes it clear that all Israel could be known under the name of its eponymous ancestor, Jacob. 'How goodly are thy tents, O Jacob' (Num. 24.5); 'Jacob shall rejoice, and Israel shall be glad' (Ps. 14.7), etc. This usage did not die out even in the post-exilic period. Mal. 3.8–12 speaks of a national crime that will be visited on the people as one unit. In the last book of the OT to be written, viz., Daniel, we are perhaps rather shocked to learn that the wives and children of those men who have accused Daniel falsely are cast into the lions' den to be devoured along with their guilty menfolk (Dan. 6.24); perhaps we imagined that the conception of corporate guilt was held only in the early period. We recall how all Achan's family suffered with him for his individual greed and disobedience (Josh. 7.16–26), and how the penalty for idolatry in the Second Commandment involved the punishment of God upon the third and even the fourth generation (Ex. 20.5). Consequently we are led to the interesting conclusion that right till the closing of the OT canon the OT writers themselves held this 'corporate' view of the people of Israel.

The fact that Israel, throughout the whole OT period, from its beginning to its end, forms not only a unit, but a unit specially related to God as one entity, is made clear in a number of vivid metaphors. These will be the subject of a later inquiry.[9]

Within Israel as a whole there were the various well-known 'tribes'. Hebrew has two words for tribe, *matteh*, and *shebhet*. Both words come from roots that mean 'staff' or 'sceptre', and consequently represent the symbol of the unifying influence of the leader of the group. Each tribe was bound up in a corporate manner with the ancestor who had given it birth. In the poem known as the 'Blessings of Jacob' (Gen. 49), each of the tribes in turn is addressed by the very name of its eponymous ancestor. In Deut. 33.8, again, the whole tribe of Levi is referred to under the description of 'thy holy one'.

Then there were clans, *mishpahoth* (Gen. 24.38), similarly organized. And finally there was the family unit, comprising the larger family of three or even four generations that is customary in the east to this day. Parallel again to this devolution of groups within Israel, we find that all the nations of the earth were imagined to be united in one great family group, since all could trace back their ancestry to their common progenitor, Noah (Gen. 10).

Each of those groups, however, whether tribe, nation or family, was regarded in still another light. Not only could the group be considered both as a unit in itself, as a corporate entity comprising all the individuals who made up its wholeness, the whole group could also be *represented* by the personality in the leading position 'at the top'.[10] In the case of the nation, the king could represent the whole of his people to a degree that was almost mystical. He could be thought of as 'the breath of our nostrils' (Lam. 4.20), and might even be addressed as if he were God himself (Ps. 45.6). He was the 'father' of his people (I Sam. 24.11), and he was 'fairer than the children of men' (Ps. 45.2). In the same way, the head of the family stood in a special relationship to the other members, as if he were the apex of a triangle, whose base was the slaves and even the domestic animals that lived within the sphere of the

---

[9]   See Part Three, pp. 157–184.
[10] Cf. I Cor. 11.3; Eph. 4.15; 5.23; Col. 1.18; I Peter 2.7.

family. The master, the husband, the head, of such a family group
was its *ba'al*. The *ba'al* was first of all the husband of his wife or
wives. They were *ba'aled* by him (Gen. 20.3). As such he was also
their 'lord', *'adhon*. We read that Joseph considered himself both
'father' and 'lord', *'adhon*, of Pharaoh's household (Gen. 45.8).
But Sarah could also address her husband, Abraham, by this same
title of *'adhon* (Gen. 18.12). The word *ba'al*, however, makes
clearer than the more neutral word *'adhon* how the whole family
group was subject to the master, who was its directive spirit and
representative (Ex. 21.4–5). The fourth commandment is obviously addressed to such as he. Every member of his household,
down to the dumb brutes in the stable, had to obey his will and
command 'Thou shalt not do any work, thou, nor thy son, nor
thy daughter, thy manservant . . . ' He was indeed 'pater familias',
and the will of each member of the family was controlled by his.
On the other hand, ideally speaking at any rate, the members of
each of these social groups showed to each other a mutual respect.
Each group indeed had a head. The king was head of the realm,
the husband was head of the wife and slaves; yet we find that
members of a group could address one another as *'ah*, 'brother',
or *rea'*, 'neighbour', 'fellow-citizen' or in the case of a woman, as
'amith. In the early period of Israel's story, the members of a group
were very closely bound up with each other, just as was the case
with any of the eastern peoples who were Israel's neighbours. We
must not forget that pure individualism is a modern phenomenon.
Abigail declared that all Israelites were 'bound in the bundle of
life' together (I Sam. 25.29). The whole tribe or group stood or
fell as one. Perhaps the most outstanding example of this conception of group solidarity is made patent to us in the story of Achan,
to which we have already referred. Joshua had put the city of
Jericho under a ban (Jos. 7). The totality of life in that city had to
be made over from the god of the city to Israel's God, Yahweh.
It was to be made holy to Yahweh (*hiqdish*) by being totally
destroyed and sent up in smoke (*heherim*). To omit to do so even
in minute detail would demonstrate disloyalty to Yahweh. Everything in the city of Jericho, men, women and children and
domestic animals, was thus to be offered to Yahweh. This was

because the whole city was one psychical entity. But one warrior of Israel, Achan, through mere personal greed, kept some of the booty for himself. Just as the city of Jericho was one psychical entity so too was the family of Achan. When the latter was finally found guilty and condemned to be stoned, his whole family had to be stoned along with him, 'and his sons, and his daughters, and his oxen, and his asses, and his sheep, and his tent, and all that he had . . . ' The sin of the *ba'al* at the head of the family group had evidently pervaded the whole membership of the group, and had contaminated even his inanimate possessions. It was therefore imperative that the infected part of the 'body' of Israel should be wholly cleansed of the diseased member; for even those at the 'base' of the 'triangle', had been affected, and indeed infected, by the strength of the personality of the *ba'al* at the apex.[11]

A similar psychic relationship between the High Priest in Israel and the nation as a whole is the mature outcome in the post-exilic period of this unformed concept. A sin committed by the High Priest reacted on the whole community. That was why special expiatory offerings were made for the High Priest alone (Lev. 4.3 ff.; 16).[12]

Within the group, then, there was spiritual and moral leadership by the 'lord'; but though his will was law within that psychic community, there was, paradoxically, a mutual fellowship and a real sense of freedom between those who comprised the group. In later years, when strong individualists like Jeremiah and Ezekiel pondered the significance of the ties that bound man to man, and each declared in turn (Jer. 31.29–30; Ezek. 18.2) that individual people were to be held responsible for their own actions, their judgement in no sense invalidated the Hebraic understanding of communal relationships within Israel which they had inherited from the past. Jeremiah himself was a product of his people and of his age, as he was evidently well aware himself. He would not have been Jeremiah as we know him if he had been born in Athens or in Rome. Though an individualist, he was bound by invisible

---

[11]   See J. Pedersen, *Israel*, I–II, 1926, pp. 61 ff.
[12]   J. Pedersen, *Israel*, III–IV, 1940, p. 190.

ties with his parents, his city of Jerusalem, and with his nation's past and future.

One of the fundamental conceptions to be found in the Old Testament, and one which we shall seek to substantiate as we proceed, is that the world of nature, the world of human nature, and everything else that is conceivable in the universe is to be understood in terms of unity. This conception is in contradiction to that held by that representative philosopher of Greece, Plato. His view of reality, that it was to be understood in terms of ideals, while earthly shadows merely reflected those ideals, is not evident anywhere at all in the works of any Old Testament writer.

Perhaps the clearest analogy we can use in order to understand the Hebraic approach to the unity of all things is to suggest that the Hebrews pictured reality in the shape of a coin. A coin has two sides. Reality, similarly, may be conceived as a two-sided whole. Ideally speaking, a coin cannot be set on edge and split down the middle. The two sides are each but an aspect of the total oneness of the coin as such. When we in our day see the figure of Britannia inscribed on one side of our coin, we know at once that the whole coin, back and front taken together, is a British penny. The one side of our coin then, according to OT thought, is the world of matter, in which man lives and moves and has his being. But that fact does not render the significance of the other side of the coin remote from this life of men. The world of the spirit, represented by the other side of the coin, is wholly involved in and is at one with the world of things. In other words, this life here is significant, not just for time and space, but also for eternity, the world of the spirit; in fact, time and eternity, matter and spirit, are so far mutually dependent that they cannot be separated each from the other. Or to put it in still other words 'matter' and 'spirit', the OT contends, are wholly integrated, and cannot be separated the one from the other. However, as in the analogy of the coin with its two faces, each of the two may be considered by itself merely for the sake of convenience, though never the one apart from the other, or out of relationship to its fellow.

With this general statement we shall have to remain content at the moment. The substantiation of such a bald description of the

Hebraic approach to reality can only be made as we touch upon concept after concept in the thought-world of the OT. At the moment we shall use this general principle which we have enunciated to enlighten another aspect of the personality of man in the OT, ever keeping in mind that we are thereby gaining an insight into what the Hebrews believed to be a vision of the nature of God himself.

The Greeks have been accused by generations of scholars in the western world of cutting the personality of the individual man into two, and of calling him an amalgam of body and spirit, or body and soul. It is only a century and a half since a group of doctors attempted the experiment of weighing a dying man, and then of repeating the weighing immediately after his death. They sought thereby to discover how heavy his 'soul' weighed that had just departed his body. The Hebrews, on the other hand, would never have made such a mistake. They thought of the personality of man as an indivisible whole. In their view body and spirit are each fully representative of a man, just as are the two sides of the coin of our analogy.

The 'J' narrative of the creation of man, as we have it in Gen. 2, makes clear in pictorial language what is the relationship between the body and the spirit of man. There we read (v. 7) that 'the Lord God formed man of the dust of the ground, and breathed into his nostrils the breath of life; and man became a living soul'. The significance of each of the terms used in this sentence we must now examine.

In the first place we read that God 'formed', that is, fashioned out of something already there. The verbal root *yatsar* is here accepted by the editor in contradistinction to the verb *bara'* which the priestly writer had employed in the first chapter. The latter verb emphasizes the creativity of the action, rather than the results of the manipulation of the material.[13] So God formed *'adam* (this

---

[13]   Paul Hymbert, 'Emploi et portéee du verbe bara' (créer) dans l'Ancien Testament'. *TZ*, 3. Jahrgang, Heft 6, Nov./Dec. 1947, pp. 401 ff. L. Koehler, *Theologie des Alten Testaments, pp. 68 ff.* W. Eichrodt, *Theologie des Alten Testaments*, II, pp. 45 ff. W. Foerster, *TWNT*, III, article κτίζω.

'plurality in unity', this genus man whose composition we have examined) out of dust from the *'adamah*. The latter word seems to be the feminine form of the word for 'man'. The connexion therefore between man's body and the ground is obviously in the mind of the writer, even though etymologically speaking the words may possibly have had different origins. Man is dust, and to dust he shall return (Gen. 3.19). But the result of God's action was not a soul within a body, one that could later be extracted from that body and which could then continue to exist apart from the body, when the body finally crumbled in the dust. Man is not an amalgam of two separable entities, dust and the breath of life. He is one entity.[14] 'And man became, turned into, a living *nephesh*'. Thus it is *basar*, his flesh-substance, that actually unites man with man, not separates him, as we moderns tend to imagine.

We have not translated the word *nephesh* by the word 'soul', as the AV does here. We have refrained from doing so because our Western 'Greek' heritage of thought invites us to read into the word 'soul' a meaning which the Hebrew does not convey. The Hebrew word *nephesh* is actually translated by some forty different words in the AV, a fact which will prevent us from hastening to render it by any one English equivalent. For the moment we shall translate it by the word 'person', but be on our guard, remembering that we must not bring to our aid any of our modern presuppositions. Yet even to use the word 'person' is to be unfaithful to the text. This is because even the animals are considered to be a *nephesh ḥayyah*, even though in no instance does the word *nephesh* by itself refer to animals in particular.[15]

In the first place the human *nephesh* is regarded as the seat of all our human emotions and appetites. It is the seat of physical

---

[14] Cf. with a NT reference 'To Paul, man does not have a body, he is one', from Kendrik Grobel, 'Σῶμα as Self, Person, in the LXX', *Studien für Rudolf Bultmann*, 1954, p. 52 ff. He also quotes Karl Barth, 'Man ist leibhafte Seele, beseelter Leib'.

[15] Cf. A.R. Johnson, *The Vitality of the Individual in the Thought of Ancient Israel*, 1949, p. 23, n.

hunger (Ps. 107.9) or of physical thirst: 'as cold waters to a thirsty *nephesh*' (Prov. 25.25); or again of moral desire: 'What his *nephesh* desireth, even that he doeth' (Job 23.13). But then the word is used also of the seat of the intellect, and so as a substitute for the word 'brain', for which Hebrew has no equivalent: 'And that my *nephesh* knoweth right well' (Ps. 139.14). But once again it may stand for the life force in man as such that can ebb and flow in potentiality according to whether the person is sick or well.

We read that God 'breathed' the breath of life into man's nostrils. This God did not do for the animal world. Animals are alive in an automotive manner that does not apply to man. The Targum of Onkelos, a Jewish paraphrase of Genesis, whose oral sources go back to late OT times, makes the interesting differentiation between them by declaring that man is a 'talking spirit'. The word *neshamah*, breath, is a typical Hebraic pictorial concept. By means of it the idea is conveyed that God has transferred from himself into man the life force which God alone can give. The idea of 'breathing into' is exactly translated in English by the Latin root 'inspire'. The concepts of 'breath' and 'wind' are closely related. In fact, the Hebrew words *neshamah* and *ruah*, wind or spirit, may on occasions be used interchangeably. Isa. 30.33 speaks of the *neshamah* of the Lord kindling a wood-pile. But Ezek. 37.1–10 uses *ruah* of a like conception, of the breath of God coming into man, not this time, as in Gen. 2., to create man or blow the flame of his being into life, but now to recreate him: 'Say to the wind, (*ruah*) Thus saith the Lord God, Come from the four winds, (*ruhoth*) O breath (*ruah*) and breathe (*pehi*, the verb used in Gen. 2.7) upon these slain, that they may live' (v. 9).

This noun *ruah* frequently occurs as a substitute for the noun *nephesh*, and can actually be used as a pronoun just meaning 'self'. 'My *ruah* is strange to my wife' complains Job (19.17). Here Job obviously makes use of our noun in place of the pronoun 'I'. So *ruah*, being a substitute for *nephesh*, can really therefore be a parallel term. This is true even though ruah is only part of the whole person who is the *nephesh*. Thus we have ' . . . the spirit of Jacob their father revived' (Gen. 45.27); 'when he had drunk, his spirit came again, and he revived' (Judg. 15.19). That is to say in contradistinction to the animals which are merely animated bundles of life, man can be described in terms of either category. He is a living *nephesh*, as is the animal world; but he is also *ruaḥ*, which the animals are not. And this is because man's *ruaḥ* is that aspect of him which is not of this world at all (Zech. 12.1). In this latter respect the word *ruaḥ* is frequently employed to represent the more unusual elements in human character with which God has 'inspired' man. Thus Saul's abnormal psychological state is attributed to a *ruaḥ* from the Lord (I Sam. 16.15); 'it shall come to pass, when the evil spirit from God is upon thee . . . '; so too the peculiar ability of those who are clever with their hands is attributed to a similar endowment from God in terms of *ruaḥ*. So it was with Bezaleel who was called to decorate the Tabernacle (Ex. 35.31). Samson's unusual strength, again, originated in the spirit of the Lord coming mightily upon him (Judg. 14.6); while of course human wisdom was naturally understood to be grounded in the wisdom of God (Prov. 1.23). But the various appetites, for which the word *nephesh* is normally used, may also be attributed to the *ruaḥ* in man, especially in post-exilic books (cf. I Chron. 5.26; II Chron. 21.16, where we have instances of an appetite for war; or Hos. 4.12, which speaks of an appetite for fornication; or Num. 5.14, where we read of an appetite, or spirit, for jealousy).

But most important of all is the association of the *ruaḥ* in man with the very *ruaḥ* of God. God himself is *ruaḥ* (Isa. 31.3), so that God imparts something of himself when he 'inspires' man. On occasions, owing thus to its higher associations, the word ruaḥ is employed in the OT almost in the manner that we speak today of a man's character. Man receives his character from the 'character' of God. 'Thus saith the high and lofty One that inhabiteth eternity, whose name is holy; I dwell in the high and holy place, with him also that is of a contrite and humble spirit' (Isa. 57.15). This immediate contact of God's spirit with man's is sometimes described in remarkable language – but then it is a remarkable truth. In Judg. 6.34 we read that 'the spirit of Yahweh clothed itself with Gideon'. Gideon thus wore upon himself the spirit of the living

God! The mighty action which he then performed in saving Israel was not just his own action; it was God's saving action as well. Of still deeper significance, however, is the manner in which the prophets applied this conception to their own calling. 'But truly I am full of power by the spirit of Yahweh' exclaimed Micah (3.8); thereupon the 'character', or moral content of that *ruah* is made clear: 'and of judgement, and of might, to declare unto Jacob his transgression, and to Israel his sin'.

To repeat, we have numberless instances in the OT of the word which we translate as 'spirit' being used to represent the whole man, in the same way as the word *nephesh* is used of the whole man in Gen. 2.7, *after* the breath of God has entered into the clay effigy and man becomes alive. This means, of course, that the idea of spirit in man is virtually synonymous with the idea of man himself. From our discussion of the relationship between the spirit of God and the spirit of man, however, we are not to be misled into imagining that the spirit of man may be likened to a divine spark, a *scintilla dei*, set within a clay body, which will one day return to the source of that flame in the event of the death of the body. Man is an entity, quite indivisible into his various elements, even though aspects of his personality, such as his appetites, his affections, his moral purposes, may be examined and handled one by one, just as we can look at each side of a coin in turn.

This 'wholeness' of man becomes even more strikingly clear when we examine the various uses of the word for 'body' in the OT. Man is not only spirit, he is also flesh, *basar*. We have just seen that OT man could not conceive of separating his ruah from his whole or total being. Now, exactly the same phenomenon is recognizable in the case of the words that describe the various parts of the human body. Each part curiously enough could represent the whole *nephesh*; and contrariwise, the personality of the whole person could be 'expressed' by any one of the body's constituent parts. That part of the body which we call the heart is an obvious example of this truth. In the OT the heart is virtually a synonym for the *nephesh*, from the earliest days of Hebrew literature to the latest. The Hebrews had little knowledge of the physiological functions of the anatomy of the human body. They did not know that the seat of thought is in the brain; in fact they imagined that man thought and felt with his heart. One can, of course, feel the heart responding to the various emotions, as it palpitates with excitement or fear. One experiences no physical sensation or emotion taking place within the skull. Accordingly, it is hardly necessary to refer to a concordance to discover how often the word 'heart' is used to represent the wholeness of an individual's life and experience. What is surprising, however, is that the more obscure bodily organs can represent for their owner the wholeness that one knows the total personality to possess. When Jeremiah exclaims (4.19) 'My bowels, my bowels, I am pained at my very heart', he is acknowledging that the moral and spiritual experience of desolation which a whole personality can undergo may be objectified for him who experiences it primarily in those organs of the body which he can feel actually physically reacting to the stress of the spiritual emotion. So too with the various other organs. The author of Lam. 2.11, who is in anguish at the fate that has befallen his beloved city of Jerusalem, employs the words 'my liver is poured upon the earth' to express the experience of horror which has gripped his whole being. It is an experience which can actually be felt physically through the channels of his interrelated psycho-somatic being. The old English word 'reins' obscures the meaning of the Hebrew word *kelayoth*. Its modern equivalent today would be 'kidneys'. Prov. 23.16 has it thus: 'Yea, my kidneys shall rejoice, when thy lips speak right things'. Ps. 73.21 parallels two organs of the body, both of which obviously represent the whole of the speaker's person or *nephesh*: 'Thus my heart was grieved, and I was pricked in my kidneys'. Other organs similarly can represent the whole person who owns them, the belly (Prov. 20.27), the bones (Ps. 6.2; 51.8), the eye(s), the hand, the ear, the mouth, and so on, all of which act in this way as representative of the whole personality. So integrated is the whole person, according to OT thought, so representative of each other are the flesh and the spirit of the man whose total being is regarded as his *nephesh*, that the OT can even speak of the *nephesh* of a man who is dead (Lev. 21.11; Num. 5.2), and whose body is lying under the ground.

The pattern of thought, then, which the Hebrews entertained when they considered the relation of the various organs and limbs of the human body to the total personality of their owner, was a pattern very similar to that which they entertained when they envisaged the relationship of individual persons to the group in which they lived. They envisaged one physical organ at a time as the possible *ba'al* of the whole, and they recognized that the whole of an individual's personality may be expressed in but one or two of those same physical organs. In other words, they recognized that each individual personality was a complex entity, just like the society in which he lived. Moreover, man is both the individual and the race. And it is this 'man' who is made in the image of God! In the light of the above, then, we see why the OT can make two complementary statements about the nature of God. It can speak of God in the singular number, and say that God is one (Deut. 6.4; Zech. 14.9). But it can also use the plural form of speech (Gen. 1.26; 11.7; Isa. 6.8) when it seeks to express that aspect of the divine nature in the image of which this corporate entity known as Adam has been made.

Three

God Known in His Self-Revelation

As we have said, nowhere in the OT are we provided with a description, or the attempt to make a description, of the essence of God as he is in himself. But in a remarkable passage from the early history of Israel we are given words of a self-revelation by God to Israel which provide us with the nearest equivalent of a description of what God is in himself that the OT has to offer. The passage in question is to be found in Ex. 3.11–18). Moses has just undergone the experience of witnessing in the wilderness the bush burning (yet the bush was not consumed), and of becoming aware by means of that experience that he was in the immediate presence of the God who had been the God of his fathers, the God of Abraham, Isaac, and Jacob (Ex. 3.1–6). Thereupon he feels the constraint of God's presence. He believes that God is urging him to return to his brethren in Egypt and bring them forth from the bondage of slavery under the hand of Pharaoh. But then he asks the question: 'Who am I that I should go unto Pharaoh, and that I should bring forth the children of Israel . . . ?' (v. 11). To this question he hears a reply from God, an utterance which is introduced by the same words as in the Creation narrative in Gen. 1, GOD SAID.

The English of the AV does not make clear that there are two separate sentences in the words that follow that ought to be closely related. The AV has set the words I AM THAT I AM of v. 14 in capital letters; but it has omitted to do so for the identical verb that occurs in v. 12 of the same passage of self-revelation, where

we have 'Certainly *I will be* with thee'. First let us examine the
words that follow from Moses' request for the name of the God
who has spoken to him. The Hebrew for those capitalized words
is *'ehyeh 'asher 'ehyeh*. The verbal form of *'ehyeh* is the third
person singular masculine 'imperfect' of the verb *hayah*. This verb
hayah does not mean 'to be'. It is more nearly understood by the
verb 'to become' in English, or the verb γίγνομαι in Greek, though
we cannot totally exclude the idea of 'being'. The LXX (Greek)
translation of these three Hebrew words, ἐγώ εἰμι ὁ ὤν, cannot
thus be a true representation of this self-revelation of God. God
is not ὁ ὤν, the 'self-existent one' of the philosophers. Moses has
just understood that he is the God of Abraham, Isaac and Jacob,
men over against whom God has stood in some degree of personal
relationships. God had not been utterly remote from Abraham.
He had 'become' something to Abraham. The phrase as it appears
in Hebrew, 'the God of Abraham', is expressed by what the
grammarians call 'the construct state'. Hebrew does not employ
a preposition for 'of' in such a phrase. The words 'God' and
'Abraham' are instead so closely bound together that they are
virtually pronounced as one. If we then translate the words by the
English phrase 'I become what I become', we are drawing nearer
to its meaning in the original than if we abide by the translation
'I am that I am'.[1]

But again, the Hebrew language does not contain the idea of
verbal tenses as we know them now. The description of that part
of the verb which we call the Imperfect does not explain to us
what it would if we were handling the verbal 'imperfect' in a
modern language. The Hebrew imperfect is strictly what the Latin
word 'imperfectus' implies; it is the 'uncompleted' form of the
verb, whether that verb could be said to bear a past, a present, or
a future significance. The word *'ehyeh* is in this imperfect form of
the verb. *'Ehyeh* is just as rightly translated by our future tense as
by our present tense. Therefore it is just as correct to translate it

---

[1]   The Latin rendering in the Vulgate, viz., EGO SUM QUI SUM has also
misled many theologians in the past who were unacquainted with the
original Hebrew.

by 'I shall become what I shall become', as by the phrase 'I am becoming what I am becoming'. Now, there are two verses that we ought to bring into close juxtaposition. In the first place, Ex. 3.7–10 tell us of the concern that God feels for Israel, suffering as they are in Egypt. He declares that he is about to act to save them from their pain and suffering. Moreover, he declares what the future holds for them. He is purposing to 'bring them up out of that land unto a good land and a large . . . ' As the story is told, of course, the entry into the land of Canaan is still a far off future event. And so we come to the former of the two verses (v. 12). Then Moses asks: 'Who am I, that I should go . . . ?' And God replies: *Ki 'ekyeh 'immach*, 'Indeed I shall be (or, better, become) with thee'. This Word of God is thus clearly to be linked with that uttered later, in v. 14, the second of our two, viz.; *'ehyeh 'asher 'ehyeh*. God is offering to 'become' to Moses, by being 'with' Moses.[2] God is offering to make himself increasingly known to Moses through personal nearness to him. And being 'with' Moses, the *ba'al* of Israel, God himself will share in all that is to come, i.e., in the redemption from Egypt, the Covenant of Sinai, the entry into the Promised Land, and the whole future development of Israel.

Along with those twin utterances let us set a third. 'AND GOD SAID, I (am) the God of thy father, the God of Abraham', *'anochi 'elohei 'abhicha* (v. 6). Here no use is made of the verb *hayah*. Instead we have the frequently recurring 'I AM' (the 'am' being understood in English) of the great self-manifestations of God that we find, for example, in Deutero-Isaiah. There we have expressions like *'anochi, 'anochi Yahweh* (Isa. 43.11), or, making use of the other pronoun for 'I', *'ani hou*, I AM HE (Isa. 43.10, 13). Later we shall note that these declarations of God's name and person in Deutero-Isaiah are accompanied by many active participles. Active participles describe the actions of living beings. The conception of God as the 'living' God is actually the characteristic conception which the OT holds. But secondly, we shall see that the participles which many passages in the OT choose to describe

---

[2]   Cf. Matt. 28.20.

the living God in action are those which express his loving concern for the Israel whom he has adopted. For example, the same Isa. 43.11 which we have quoted continues: '*'anochi, 'anochi Yahweh*, and beside me there is no *saviour*.' Or v. 13 reads: 'I am he, and there is none that can deliver out of my hand: I will work, and who shall let (prevent) it?'

In the early days of Israel's story, a name was sometimes given to a child in order to be an exact description of the child's personality.[3] The name was then a kind of label. Nabal, the 'fool' who did not buy off the outlaw, David, with offerings of food and drink, bore a name which truly described him (I Sam. 25). The Hebrews were not necessarily good philologists. We see today that they made frequent mistakes in the etymology of names. Thus the explanation of the name Moses in Ex. 2.10 is obviously incorrect; it was the assonance of two words that pleased the Hebrew ear, and assonance sometimes took priority over both philology and exegesis. But it is surprising how many proper names in the early period were evidently given to represent an idea that the parents hoped would be embodied in the children. Thus, in the case of the eponymous fathers of the Israelites, we find that Abraham is a form of word play on '*abh*, meaning 'father', and *ram*, meaning 'exalted'. Later, after he had heard the promise that he would be the father of many nations, his name was lengthened to '*abh-ra-ham* the 'father of a multitude' (Gen. 17.5). If Naomi, who plays a part in the book of Ruth, is a historical character, her name must have been given her in good faith. It means 'happy', 'lovely', 'beautiful'. But it did not remain a true description of that originally lovely maiden. She lost by death, not only her husband, but also her two sons. Thus when she returned home to Bethlehem from Moab, she exclaimed 'Call me not Naomi, call me Mara, for the Almighty hath dealt very bitterly with me' (Ruth 1.20). The word *mara*' just means 'bitter'. Now she needed a new name to describe the essence of her personality, because her whole person had changed with her changing circumstances.

---

[3] J. Fichtner, 'Die Ätiologie in den Namengebungen', *VT*, 1956, pp. 372 ff.

A large number of OT names is compounded with the syllable 'jah', a shortened form of the name *yahweh*. In the days of King David, it was primarily the aristocracy who bore such names. But as the history of Israel unfolded, there was a continually growing tendency to give children of all classes a name with the prefix or suffix 'jah' added to it; in fact a name came to be a whole sentence, expressing either a fact about or a wish for the child and his relationship to his God. In David's day fewer than half of the extant names had a religious character about them, but in the post-exilic period more than half of the laity and every single member of the priesthood in the lists supplied in the books of Ezra and Nehemiah are compounded with a name of God.[4] Such a man as Isaiah (*Jesha' jah*) grew in the knowledge of God as saviour as he walked with God throughout his life. This fact was made plain both to himself and to his neighbours from the name he bore. Like Moses, every true OT man hoped to find that God was 'with' him, as the future 'became' out of the present moment of his experience of life.

That is why even Israel's God needed to have a name.[5] 'And Moses said unto God, Behold, when I come unto the children of Israel, and shall say unto them, The God of your fathers hath sent me unto you; and they shall say to me, What is his name? what shall I say unto them?' (Ex. 3.13). It is in reply therefore to this question that God gives Moses an astounding answer. In the Egypt of Moses' day, each Pharaoh possessed a secret name as well as a throne name. The Egyptians, just like the Hebrews, believed that the name, whether secret or public, ought to be an exact revelation of the essence of the person bearing it. But concurrent with that belief was another, one that naturally was closely allied to it. The peoples of the ancient near east all believed that since the name, ideally at any rate, was the exact representation of its owner, to know the name of the owner was actually to know his very essence. And to know the essence of a man or a king was to know *him*, to know him wholly and utterly, and so was to have complete

---

[4]   G.B. Gray: *Studies in Hebrew Proper Names*, 1896, p. 243.
[5]   See O. Grether, *Der Göttliche Name im Alten Testament*, 1933.

power and authority over him. That is why the Pharaoh's secret name was wisely kept secret. But the foolishness of God is wiser than men. Moses has the temerity to ask God for his name, for the exact and total description of his very essence – and God gives him it. We can therefore draw no other conclusion but that in giving his name God put himself in total humility into Moses' hands, that in a sense which is certainly no exaggeration of language, God 'emptied himself' before Moses his sinful creature. Thus God, whose name was now known to be I WILL BECOME WITH YOU, was offering to go forward into the unknown future continually unfolding his nature and purpose to the people of Israel, that people which at that very moment was a mere slave nation in the alien land of Egypt. The identity between God's 'goodness' and God's 'name' is made in Ex. 33.19. 'And he said, I will make all my goodness pass before thee, and I will proclaim the name of Yahweh before thee.' Thereupon this divine utterance continues: 'and I will be (*'ehyeh*) gracious to whom I will be gracious, and will shew mercy on whom I will shew mercy'.

There is a sense in which the book of Exodus really precedes the book of Genesis. This is because Israel's true history begins at that moment where we are introduced to a people swarming like flies in Egypt, waiting for a Moses to come and lead them forth from the hand of their oppressor. The first chapter of Genesis deals, not with an historical incident like the Exodus, but with a theological description of the origin of the universe. As we have said before, the first chapter of Genesis was written, not in the land of Israel itself, but when Israel the people were in exile in the alien land of Babylonia. The book of Exodus is compounded of at least two main strands of tradition. There is the so-called narrative, which possibly, along with others which various scholars call by various names, such as E, E', etc., traces the true historical memory of the mighty events at the time of the Exodus out of which the people of Israel were born. The priestly writer we know as P, on the other hand, was one who had known the horror and the fear and the desolation of soul that overcame his people when the nation was destroyed by Nebuchadnezzar in 587 B.C., when there came upon that people the seeming end of all their national story. We can see distinctly as we read the book of Exodus that the editor of the book as a whole, as we have it now, one of the P school himself, undoubtedly saw the events recorded by J and others in the light of his own and his people's contemporary experience in exile. At that time they were in a plight comparable with their earlier experience as slaves under the hand of Pharaoh in Egypt. God had at that earlier period acted as Saviour of Israel, and had brought his people, not merely out of Egypt, but actually into being as a nation. Before that mighty event, then, naturally Israel did not really *know* his God. Thus we may say that anything that happened to Israel before God revealed himself to Moses as the Saviour of his people must belong to a different area of revelation. In fact, Israel could not have supposed that Yahweh was the Creator-God before he knew him as his Saviour. Until God had revealed himself as '*ehyeh 'asher 'ehyeh* no Israelite could have speculated that his 'god' could have been the author of all things any more than any of the other gods of the nations could have been. The Exodus event was thus *the* great creative act of God, for it was that moment when God revealed his inner essence as that of compassion and saving power and purpose.

We must at this point ask ourselves if there could be any relationship between Moses' objective experience of seeing a natural phenomenon, and his subjective experience of hearing the Word of God. What the natural phenomenon was that tradition-ally has been called the Burning Bush we are no longer in a position to say. The country known as the Negev is bituminous in many areas. The *fata morgana*, frequently visible on the great Hungarian plain, for example, may therefore have been a feature of that district also. But we are not primarily interested to know what the phenomenon was. The all important matter is that Moses was clearly convinced that he had met, at the Burning Bush, with nothing less than the Word of God, both then and again later, when at the same spot, the 'Sinai Covenant' was sealed.

That the Word impinged itself upon his consciousness as he gazed at the objective phenomenon is a conception which we can well accept. We are aware ourselves how an objective vision can produce a subjective image in the mind. At the very beginning of his career the youthful Jeremiah found himself gazing, obviously in deep thought, at the branch of an almond tree in spring. In Hebrew, the consonants for the word 'almond tree' are *sh-q-d*. (In those days Hebrew used no vowels.) The pronunciation of the word would have been *shaqedh*. Now the actual Hebrew consonants must have formed themselves objectively before the eye of his mind. He saw the word, in fact, and not the tree. And as he saw the consonants thus objectively forming before his mind's eye, he must have read them off in an alternative manner, as *shoqedh*. Understood as such the word now means 'watching over'. Then a third step took place in this objective-subjective relationship between Jeremiah's seeing a natural phenomenon and his hearing the Word of God. God used the second pronunciation of the word to bring it home to Jeremiah's consciousness that God himself was 'watching over' his Word to perform it (Jer. 1.11–12). Later in his chequered career Jeremiah was able from his own experience of life to validate the truth of this 'word' of God to him as a youth (Jer. 31.28).

Somewhat similarly, though not in an identical manner, Moses must have discovered that the physical phenomenon before his material eye was the objective sign of his own subjective experience of the Word of God forming within his inner consciousness. That he took time to make this identification is clear since he did not at first believe that he had met with the Word of God. In Ex. 4 we are told of two experiments that Moses had to perform in order to confirm his own faith, one being an experiment with his rod or staff, the other being the trial of leprosy. These incidents are called by the name of 'sign', *'oth* (Ex. 4.8, 9, 17) and later the word is coupled with another, 'wonder', *mopheth*.[6] The *'oth* in the OT was undoubtedly considered to be an empirical event which carried in itself its own eschatological significance, i.e. an event with a meaning beyond itself. The ten so-called 'plagues' are known both as *'oth* and as *mopheth*. This word *mopheth*

---

[6] See S.H. Hooke, 'The Sign of Immanuel', in *The Siege Perilous*, 1956, p. 223.

particularly emphasizes the event as being a special display of God's power (Ex. 7.11; 11.9; Ps. 105.5), an event that produces awe and wonder in the beholder. Thus Moses' call, his testing, and the 'mighty acts' of the Exodus story and of the giving of the Law are all of one piece in this respect. Each subjective experience which Moses underwent was accompanied by a parallel physical phenomenon. The subjective experience by itself it might be possible to explain away; so too might the physical phenomenon be declared to be a 'mere' natural event (as critics have frequently done!). Again some scholars have suggested that the whole series of events recorded in the early chapters of Exodus are the product of a later generation, who inevitably wrapped their heroic early leader in layers of myth and legend. It is possible for us to go a long way with those who declare such an interpretation of the Exodus to be the truth of the matter. Thus the birth story of Moses and his discovery in a basket floating on the Nile may be based on a legend similar to that told of King Sargon,[7] the first king of ancient Babylonia, and similar to that told of many great men of the past. But on the other hand such tales were told of great men simply because these men were great. And Moses was a great man. And one aspect of his greatness was just his ability to see subjectively the shattering implications of the various *mopheth* of the Exodus event and to see them each as an *'oth*. That is to say, Moses had sufficient insight to regard each and every incident in the Exodus nexus of events as meaningful in the sight of God. He saw each incident as it took place, not only as a 'sign', but also as a 'seal' that the historical happening in question was originated and controlled by God himself. For example, Moses became finally convinced that when the shepherd's crook in his hand became a serpent (Ex. 4.3) or a monster, *tannin* (7.9), such as inhabited the primal ocean, and returned to become a crook again, the power of Yahweh over the monster Pharaoh had been demonstrated.[8]

---

[7] A. Jeremias, *The OT in the Light of the Ancient East*, II, 1911, pp. 92–96.

[8] See further p. 99 below.

The word *'ehyeh* is the first person singular imperfect of the verb *hayah*. At Mount Sinai Moses was immediately confronted by the living God. His person was directly addressed by one whom he knew to be accosting him as one person accosts another person. At that moment Moses knew that God was saying to him 'I am', 'I shall become'. 'I shall become with you'. Now throughout the whole of Israel's subsequent history this great moment of God's self-revelation in the first person singular was naturally referred to in retrospect by means of the third person of the verb. 'What is his name?' asked Moses (Ex. 3.13). This question is recorded in the original narrative of J. The priestly editor in Ex. 6.2–3, however, states the belief of Israel that the name by which they knew their God thereafter was Yahweh. Ex. 6.3 puts it this way 'And I appeared unto Abraham, Isaac and Jacob by the name Shaddai, but I was not known to them before by my name Yahweh.'

The literature available on the origin of the 'sacred tetragrammaton' (so-called because the divine name is written with four Hebrew consonants) is very extensive. Yet it would seem that the divine name in Exodus ought to be understood in terms of its context rather than in the light of extra-biblical categories.[9] How the third person of the verb *hayah* was pronounced in the days of P we cannot now tell. The ancient Hebrews adopted an attitude of reverence to the NAME, and thus early took to using a substitute for it. They adopted the word *'adfon*, meaning 'lord' and frequently put it in place of the NAME. And on this word were appended the vowel sounds of the word *'elohim* (God), so as to produce the pronunciation *'adhonai*. As to the 'sacred tetragrammaton', if and when it was ever uttered in post-exilic years, we have the statement of Theodoret that the Samaritans (not the Jews) pronounced it as Ἰαβε, and we have the statement of Clement of Alexandria that it was pronounced Ἰαουε or Ἰαουαι. Last century the scholar Ewald affirmed that the rhyme in Samaritan poetry required this particular pronunciation, viz., *yahweh*.

---

[9]   L.M. Pákozdy, 'Die Deutung des Yahweh Namens in Exodus 3.14', *Judaica* II, 1955, pp. 193–208.

On the other hand, the imperfect 'Qal' of the verb *hayah* would by rights be the form *yihyeh*. At least that is the form found in the classical Hebrew of the OT. However, this difference in form is certainly explicable, since from earliest times the consonants *yodh* and *waw* were frequently interchanged; and at the same time the vowel-sound 'a' of the first syllable of the NAME may have been the original vowel used in still earlier times in the imperfect of the verbal form. But again, we do not need to postulate a transposition of the two consonants.[10] A verb *hawah* exists, though it is rare, which may have been a dialectical variant of *hayah* (cf. Gen. 27.29; Isa. 16.4; Neh. 6.6; Eccles. 2.22; the imperfect form occurs in Eccles. 11.3 as *yehu*, though it might equally have been written in the form *yahweh*). Still another factor to note is that the name *Jah* may pre-exist the period of Moses, and may even be the name of the God of Moses' father-in-law Jethro.[11] In that case, the editors of Ex. 3 and 6 have skilfully woven the existing name into the syllables of the divine self-revelation in the two passages. Jethro may well have been virtually a monotheist himself, and a kind of 'priest-king' of the God of the Kenites, who in turn may have been a sept of the larger Midianite clan. Moreover, we know that the Kenites continued for centuries in friendly relationships with the Hebrews (cf. Judg. 1.16; I Sam. 15.6; etc.). When Moses told Jethro of the experience he had undergone at the Burning Bush, Jethro, with good sense, may well have invited Moses to recognize that the one God in whom he himself believed was the same God by whatever national name men gave him.[12]

Yet one thing is sure, that the name Jehovah is not biblical at all. It was invented by one Galatinus in A.D. 1520 on the basis of the vowels which the Massoretes had placed on *'adhonai*.

A number of modern scholars would prefer to pronounce the NAME as *Jahu* instead of as *Yahweh* (or *Jahweh*). They too would

---

[10] Cf. Oskar Grether, *Name und Wort Gottes im AT*, 1934, pp. 3–17

[11] Cf. G.R. Driver, *OT Essays*, pp. 18 ff.

[12] Cf. Chr. H.W. Brekelmans, *OS*, Deel X, pp. 215 ff., 'Exodus XVIII and the Origins of Yahwism'; also article 'Israel (Histoire d')' *DBS* IV. Paris, 1949, col. 736.

relate the interpretation of the name to the Exodus events, and look for its origin in either the sound that Moses heard reverberating round the mountains when thunder rolled[13] or the sound that Moses himself uttered in awe at the experience. Thus Martin Buber suggests that the name has its origin in the words *ya-hu'*, 'Oh, he'. He makes the suggestion on the grounds that the modern Mohammedan utters just such an exclamation when confronted with the unknown and the numinous. But that is not to say that the priestly writers would think of such an etymology. After all, they were not writing in the immediacy of experience themselves, but in the tranquillity of historical recollection.[14] We should not forget, however, that the schismatic Jews who have left us the Elephantine papyri in Egypt also pronounced the name as Yahu.

However the name may have been pronounced,[15] it was evidently regarded as a description in the third person of the essential Being of Israel's God. This description is therefore not accurately carried over into the Greek in the LXX version of the OT. There we find that the form *Yahweh*, or *'Adhonai*, is rendered by the Greek word κύριος, or Lord. The form LORD, in capital letters in the AV, however, has certainly come to stay in the English language.

'By my name *Shaddai* . . . ' (Ex. 6.3). The discussion that has been carried on to elucidate the meaning of this other divine name has been lengthy but inconclusive. No one has yet produced a satisfactory derivation of the word. Most interpreters have been compelled to rest upon the traditional meaning of 'Almighty'. Yet we should not neglect the manner in which the unscientifically minded Hebrews of the late OT period explained the word to their

[13]   H. Torczyner *Die Bundeslade und die Anfänge der Religion Israels*, 1922, p. 76. See also W.A.L. Elmslie, *How Came our Faith*, 1948, p. 120.

[14]   Martin Buber, *Moses*, 1946, p. 50. For a full discussion of this question see D.B. Eerdmans in *OS*, Deel V, art. 'The Name Jahu', pp. 1 ff. See also W. Eichrodt, *Theologie des ATs*, I, 1948, p. 92.

[15]   The vowelling *Yahweh* may possibly imply a Hiph'il imperfect form of the verb, in which case the word may mean 'He will cause to be'. But the Hiph'il of the very *hayah* is otherwise unknown.

own satisfaction. They read the Hebrew letters as if they were Aramaic, and so obtained the translation: 'He who belongs to me'. Such etymology is impossible, and we cannot accept it. But we are bound to accept the spirit of it. We are bound to recognize that by such an etymology post-exilic Jewry was equating the meaning of the name *Shaddai* with the significance of the divine words of self-revelation which also could mean: 'I shall become with you'. Moreover, this semi-Aramaic rendering of the name may be what lies behind the rendering of the word *Shaddai* by the Greek word ἱκανός of Aquila, Symmachus, and Theodotion, all three of whom rendered the OT into Greek in the second Christian century. The word ἱκανός 'sufficient', is otherwise a mystery in this context.[16] Meanwhile, let us note that the LXX by the second century B.C. had already lost the true meaning of the original Semitic word (cf. the LXX of Num. 24.4, 16; Isa. 13.6, where Θεός is the translation used, and Ezek. 10.5, where the word is merely transliterated as σαδδαΐ).

---

[16] See C.H. Dodd, *The Bible and the Greeks*, 1935, pp. 13 ff. But as 'sufficient' it reminds us of the highly personal sense of the Hebrew original.

Four

God's Further Self-Manifestation

It is the verb in any language which declares the action of the subject. The active-participle is a form of the verb, and in Hebrew it frequently represents continuing action. What are some of those participial phrases to which we have referred as descriptive of the living God in action?

God is he who 'sitteth on the circle of the earth' (i.e. on the inverted 'bowl' of the heavens visible from earth, Isa. 40.22); God is he who is the 'creator of the heavens and the stretcher-out-of-them', and 'the hammerer-out of the earth' (42.5). The prophet has already described (41.7) the hammering work done by a living, human goldsmith, who is actively creating something with his hands. But now he employs the same active-participles of the living God.

Deutero-Isaiah refers indubitably to the Exodus name for God. He evidently sees the name as a self-revelation of the divine Being made in the first person singular of the verb. In the lines of his great poems he makes God exclaim more than once *'ani hu'*, 'I am he'. So we find 'I am he who hath wrought and done it' (41.4), who was there before the day was (43.13), or who has SAID, and creation came into being (45.11, 12). Moreover, not only did God create in the beginning, he continues to create. As we said, such is also the force of the Hebrew active-participle. Thus, for example, 45.7, 18 should be translated as: 'He who fashions light and creates darkness, and makes peace, and creates evil; I am Yahweh, doing all these things' (sc. continually), and 'He who creates the heavens, he is God, who fashions the earth and makes it' (sc. continually). A century or so later than Deutero-Isaiah the following words were penned about Yahweh's creative activity: 'Thou, even thou, art Yahweh alone; thou hast made heaven, the heaven of heavens, with all their host, the earth, and all that is upon it, the seas, and all that is therein, and thou *keepest them all alive* (or) *in being*' (Neh. 9.6). That is to say as the 'living' God, Yahweh did not merely create the universe in the beginning; he recreates all life each new day.

The first few verses of Isa. 43 reflect a further interpretation of the Exodus passage. In v. 3 we have the great statement *'ani yahweh*, 'I am Yahweh'. That is immediately coupled with further descriptions of God as he manifests his self. It runs: I am 'the Holy One of Israel, thy Saviour'. That is to say, God manifests himself as more than creator; he declares himself to be the Saviour of Israel. Not only so, he is Saviour, not from afar, but by immediate contact with his people Israel. Although he is the Holy One, the utterly other, the Creator who shapes the clay as he will, and who is as different from his creation as the potter is from his clay (Isa. 64.8; Jer. 18.4), yet he is the Holy One of Israel. He is in some strange manner the Holy One[1] because he is the Holy One of Israel!

The Hebrew construct state, bringing two nouns into such close relationship that the two together form one new idea, is again employed (viz. *qedhosh yisrael*) to demonstrate the paradoxical union of God, in his utter holiness, with Israel in her sin and weakness. This involvement of God with Israel is expressed once more in vv. 3 and 5 in terms reminiscent of the 'Certainly I will be with thee' of Ex. 3.12. There God's 'being for Israel' is expounded by God himself in the words *'ani 'ittecha* 'I will be with thee'.

A century had well nigh gone by since the prophet Jeremiah had been called to what seemed as impossible a task as that to which Moses had been ordained. 'I have ordained thee a prophet unto the nations . . . to root out, and to pull down, and to destroy, and to throw down, to build and to plant' (Jer. 1.5, 10). But along with the seemingly impossible command had gone the further words *ki 'ittecha 'ani* 'certainly I will be with thee' (Jer. 1.8). Thereafter Jeremiah had received an outward and visible sign of this inward and invisible call (1.9) when God had touched his mouth. His experience reminds us of the curious words recorded in Ex. 7.17. There God says to Moses: 'I will smite with the rod that is in mine hand . . . ' when it was really Moses' hand that held the rod. Or again, in the heroic past of the nation there had been an indubitable case of God's 'being with' another individual Israelite. This had been made clear in the truly Hebraic manner of presenting truth, viz., in story form. In the story of Joseph, we see his complete certainty of God's developing purpose in his life (Gen. 45.5–8; 50.20).

Writing from the agony of the Exile in Babylonia, the prophet is now able to recognize how God had kept his promise to Moses, and had 'been with' both individuals and Israel as a whole. Even as he spoke he knew from his own experience the truth of what he said, 'When thou passest through the waters, I will be with thee' (Isa. 43.2); 'Fear not, for I will be with thee' (v. 5). God's 'being with Israel' had indeed been summed up in the name he had revealed to Moses.

It was in the agony of the Exile, then, that Israel heard the words 'fear not' even as she learned to know that Yahweh was with her. The priestly editor of the Pentateuch is able to assure us then quite naturally that the Yahweh who had 'become with' his people thus far, even when they were passing through the waters and the fire, had said the same of old to those he had been 'with'. The awe that all men feel for the 'beyond' and all that is strange and uncanny, is an awe compounded with horror and fear. Yet it is in answer to this natural horror of the human soul in the presence of the numinous in all its forms, that this truly biblical phrase resounds. 'Fear not' says God to Abram, when the latter's human consciousness begins to comprehend the immensity of the divine plan that is to work out *through* him and his faithfulness in days to come (Gen. 15.1). 'Fear not' exclaims the weird and inexplicable voice to Hagar (Gen. 21.17), coming, as it seemed, out of the sky where all divinity dwells. And similarly with other 'numinous' experiences that men had undergone when face to face with the horror of the 'other world'. Thus Judg. 6.22–23 runs: 'And when Gideon perceived that he was an angel of Yahweh, Gideon said, Alas, O Lord God! for because I have seen an angel of Yahweh face to face. And Yahweh said unto him, Peace be unto thee; fear not'. Faced with the mystery of death at which all men fear and quake, Elijah commands the widow of Zarephath with the words 'Fear not' (I Kings 17.13). Overwhelmed by the mysterious vision of the heavenly host, Elisha exhorts his frightened servant with the same words 'Fear not' (II Kings 6.16). Moreover, if we so desired, we could exemplify the use of those heartening words from the NT just as frequently as from the OT (e.g. Matt. 1.20; 28.5; Mark 4.40; Luke 1.13; 1.30; 2.10; 5.10; 8.50; Rev. 1.17).

Returning finally to the Exodus narrative we see how the picture of the nature of the God who had promised to 'become with' his people is 'filled out'. Ex. 34.5 is a passage that is probably from the hand of a later redactor. If that is so, then it was written by one who could look back through Israel's history and declare that, despite all the trials and troubles of life, all the wars and diseases and pains to which the human flesh is heir, 'Certainly I will be with thee' was a truth now more fully explicable than it ever could have been to Moses. And so we read: 'And Yahweh descended into the cloud and stood *with* him (Moses) there, and (Moses) called upon the name of Yahweh'. That is one possible way of reading the verse. No subject is given to the verb 'called' in either the Hebrew or the LXX version. But the translation common to the AV and to the ARSV, where the subject is taken to be Yahweh, is both permissible and actually more probable than the above, since it makes Yahweh the subject of the verb. In that case the verse declares that it was Yahweh who proclaimed his own name. Yahweh thereafter expounds the significance of his name in the words 'Yahweh, Yahweh, a God compassionate and gracious, slow to anger, and plenteous in loyal-love and reliability; keeping loyally-in-love with thousands, forgiving iniquity and rebelliousness and sin; certainly not letting off the guilty; visiting the iniquity of fathers upon sons and grandsons, to the third and even the fourth generation' (Ex. 34.6, 7).

These particular words of God's self-manifestation contain material which we must eventually examine. Yet is it justifiable to attribute to Yahweh a description of his very Being that was made centuries after Moses' experience of God's call upon Mount Sinai? The answer surely lies in the fact that these particular words had become part of the very woof and web of Israel's consciousness of God. Israel had continued to learn the truth and reality of them, as she journeyed 'with' God down the years. This we know, because the phrases we have quoted come to be repeated in many forms and by various kinds of writers. Yahweh is the God who is 'with' his people because he is in their midst (Deut. 7.21; 31.17, D; Num. 11.20; 14.9, 14; 16.3, P; Josh. 3.10; 7.12; Hos. 11.9). He is 'with' his people in loyal-love, in graciousness and with forgiving power, for many of the Psalmists, and for many others of the OT writers (cf. Pss. 86.15; 103.8; 111.4; 112.4; 116.5; 145.8; Joel 2.13; Jonah 4.2; Micah 7.18; Num.; 14.18; II Chron. 30.9; Neh. 9.17). Jeremiah is sure that God's promise to be the God of Israel in the sense that Israel will know his presence intuitively in their hearts is bound one day to be fulfilled (Jer. 31.33). Actually, his promise to 'become with' Israel is fulfilled within the context of a relationship so deep and so profound that, in the end, it involves the actual entry of God himself into the life of man in space and time.

Five

The Unity of God

We have seen that man in the OT regarded himself as a 'unity-in-diversity', and not merely as an individual integer in the modern sense. His personality was of a unified nature, body and soul together being one entity. This fact we must remember as we recall that man was made in the image of God.

Again, OT man was not fully man when he was alone. He was only truly man when he was 'man-in-society'[1]; the word Adam means the whole genus man as well as each individual of the various species. This fact too we must keep in mind as we recall that man was made in the image of God.

But another important aspect of man which we must also bear in mind as we search the OT for a doctrine of God in his 'being with man' is that man, whether individual or corporate, is inconceivable as man apart from the earth on which he stands. Originally man was made from the dust (Gen. 2.7), and to dust he must return (Gen. 3.19). Consequently we must be awake to the fact that the OT writers are unable to separate their conception of the final state of man from that of the final state of the earth. Nowhere in the OT can we discover a doctrine which declares that man must needs be saved *from* the earth. Such an idea would be really inconceivable, since man himself is 'earth'. If man needs saving and recreating, then the earth will have to be saved and recreated along with man.

---

[1] See G. Ernest Wright, *The Biblical Doctrine of Man in Society*, 1954, *passim*.

We now ask ourselves how these three points about man can in any way reflect the nature of the God of the OT revelation.

It is a mistake to read into the OT our modern views of what God must be like in his own Person, views arising from our modern conceptions of individuality. It is true that throughout the whole OT God is spoken of in terms of personality. But personality, humanity, and individuality are three quite different concepts. The essence of God is certainly divinity; while the essence of man is just as certainly humanity. On the other hand, since man is made in the image of God, God's 'divinity' must therefore be understandable to man in terms of 'personality', and of that kind of 'person' 'with' whom God has promised to be and to become. God is person himself since he behaves as a person. He thinks, he acts, he creates; he is long-suffering, faithful and loyal. Chronologically speaking, Hosea may have been the first OT thinker to speak of Yahweh as the living God, and thus regard him in terms of Person; but he was certainly not the last to do so (cf. Hos. 1.10; Ps. 42.2; 84.2; Josh. 3.10; etc.). In fact the OT presents us with many pictures of Yahweh, each of which expounds in a 'human' manner what it means by the adjective 'living'. God is, of course, Father, but he is also Husband (Isa. 54.5), Friend (Ex. 33.11; Isa. 41.8), Judge (Gen. 18.25), Shepherd (Ps. 80.1), King (Ps. 10.16); in like manner God heals (Ex. 15.26), works as a Potter (Jer. 18.3), as a Fuller (Mal. 3.2), as a Builder (Ps. 51.18), and so on.

The Person of God, however, must not be conceived in modern individualistic terms. God is no mere monad, the mere 'oneness' of being, in the mathematical sense of the word 'one'. He is a 'unity-in-diversity' as Adam is, Adam who is both male and female, both an individual and a corporate being, a union of both matter and spirit, a spiritual being, who is at the same time a part of the physical world. Just as man can express his essential being through his bodily organs, so too can God express his Being in similar ways. Such a conception will seem strange to us only if we have approached the biblical picture of God with the preconceptions of a scientific schooling in our mind.

OT man was aware that he possessed physical organs. Through these organs he 'expressed' his personality to others. When then he declared that God possessed hands, eyes, ears, or mouth, it is obvious that he was declaring in picture language that the living God expressed himself in like manner to himself. The Hebrews could not conceive of the abstract idea of 'man'. They could only speak of Adam, the man they knew themselves to be. In the same way, they could not conceive of God as naked Spirit, as the merely Existent One. They had to speak of God as they knew him in action, raising his right arm, writing with his finger, making Jerusalem his footstool. Thus even the crash of thunder was the physical expression of the voice of God, and the glories of nature were the hem of his garment.

With his voice, then, God SAID. He said a Word. The Hebrews, in company with other peoples in the ancient Near East, attached great potency to the spoken word. Idle chatter may signify little, but certainly words spoken with intent are in another category. They are effective. We may perhaps most easily envisage how the Hebrews thought that the word spoken with intent could have effect by recalling the manner in which characters are made to speak in a modern newspaper comic strip. There the words of the actors are ringed around and connected by a line to the speaker's mouth. Their words have a very solid and objective look about them. Before they were uttered the words were hidden in the speaker's heart. But now that they are clearly enunciated, they have become an object, a thing, and are now separate from the person who uttered them; yet they express the speaker's heart or purpose. It has now become impossible to push the words back into the speaker's mouth. They are uttered and out, and are so potent in themselves that in the next picture frame we are shown their effect upon the other characters in the comic strip. Now, the Hebrew word *dabhar* bears just this double sense of both 'word' and 'thing'. Once a word, *dabhar*, is uttered with intent, it has effect once again in *dabhar* – it becomes a thing.

An English version of the Bible is not able to bring out clearly this inalienable relation between 'word' and 'thing'. Joshua's valedictory speech runs thus in our AV: 'And behold this day I am going the way of all the earth: and ye know in all your hearts and in all your souls, that not one thing (word?) hath failed of all the good things (words?) which the Lord your God *spake* concerning you' (Josh. 23.14). From I Kings 11.41 we see that history could be regarded by the Hebrews as *things* done at the *word* of a king. Thus a man's word, if spoken with intent, was always becoming 'incarnate', so to speak. In contradistinction to this conception, then, an idol was a *lo'dabhar* (cf. Isa. 41.24; 44.20), that is, not only a 'non-thing', but also 'that which has not been spoken' by the true God.

Cursing and blessing are two obvious ways of speaking 'with intent'. Travellers in the East last century have written of how an Arab would duck if another cursed him, to let the curse travel harmlessly over his head like a bullet. Pedersen[2] has drawn attention to the fact that when Isaac blessed the wrong son (Gen. 27.28–29) he was unable to recall his words. All he could do was to give another blessing to Esau. The so-called 'Blessings of Jacob' (Gen. 49) and 'Blessings of Moses' (Deut. 33) were regarded as being effective in their results. The word spoken with intent could not return unto the speaker 'void', that is, without effecting what it was meant to perform by the speaker. But more; since the word came forth from the heart of a living person, the word itself was also alive in a real and vital sense. Taken thus the word was not only objectively separable from the speaker, it also conveyed the living will and purpose of the speaker to the one addressed.

As with man, so with God. 'For as the rain cometh down, and the snow from heaven, and *returneth not thither*, but watereth the earth and maketh it bring forth and bud, that it may give seed to the sower and bread to the eater, so shall my word be that goeth forth out of my mouth: it shall not return unto me void, but it shall accomplish that which I please, and it shall prosper (i.e. be effective) in the thing whereto I sent it' (Isa. 55.10–11). The living God must surely speak with intent every time he utters his Word. 'I have sworn by myself, the word is gone out of my mouth in righteousness, and shall not return, that unto me every knee shall bow . . .' (Isa. 45.23). Such an utterance could mean for the

---

[2] *Israel*, I, p. 182 ff. Cf. also A.R. Johnson, *The Vitality of the Individual in the Thought of Ancient Israel*, 1949, p. 6.

Hebrews no less than the eventual 'incarnation' of that Word in history. They believed that in God's good time every knew shall therefore bow to him.

In Ex. 3.13 we read that Moses posed to God the fundamental question 'What is thy name?' We saw moreover on page 44 how God answered Moses in all humility, putting himself in Moses' power, so to speak, by revealing to him the essence of his being.

Now since the name of a man or God was regarded as an exact picture of the one who owned it (p. 43) the name came to be accounted as virtually a projection of its owner. This projection was thus an entity existing in its own right, summing up in itself all that its owner was. To use the language of the theologian Karl Barth,[3] the Hebrews regarded the name as a kind of *alter ego* of the man whose nature it described. Such a view of the vital identity of the name was naturally applied to the name or names of God. In Lev. 24.11, e.g., we read that to 'blaspheme the Name' was equivalent to blaspheming against the Lord God himself.[4] Again Ps. 20.1 expresses the wish 'The name of the God of Jacob defend thee'. From this it would appear that God's name could virtually act on God's behalf for the reason that his personality was in some sense expressed in his name. In the same sense we have 'The name of Yahweh is a strong tower' (Prov. 18.10). 'The name of the Lord cometh from far' (Isa. 30.27). Thus it is quite logical for an OT writer to declare that God may act, not for his own sake, so to speak, but for his name's sake (cf. I Sam. 12.22; Ps. 23.3; 106.8).

More striking still is the extent to which the Name of God can represent the living God in certain passages connected with the cult. For example, in the so-called Book of the Covenant we find the following: 'An altar of earth shalt thou make unto me . . . in all places where I record my name I will come unto thee, and bless thee' (Ex. 20.24). The Deuteronomic Code repeats and develops this concept. Thus Israel is commanded to worship in 'the place

---

[3] *The Doctrine of the Word of God*, trans. by G.T. Thomson, 1936, p. 365.

[4] Cf. *KB*, p. 984a: 'The *shem yahweh* means not only the name, but the full being and power of Yahweh'.

which Yahweh thy God shall choose to place his name there' (cf. Deut. 12.5; 12.11; 14.23–24; 16.6; 26.2). This place where God chose to put his name was thus his 'habitation on earth' (Deut. 12.5). Historically speaking, this 'place' may have been in the first instance one of the northern sanctuaries (e.g. Jeremiah suggests that it was Shiloh, Jer. 7.12), but in later years it was certainly identified with the Temple Rock of Jerusalem.

One of the strongest impressions about God one receives in the OT is that he is depicted as utterly transcendent. He is, in fact, the LORD. He is the Maker and Creator of the ends of the earth; he is the Ruler of history. 'But will God indeed dwell on the earth? behold, the heaven and heaven of heavens cannot contain thee; how much less this house that I have builded? Yet have thou respect unto the prayer of thy servant . . . that thine eyes may be open toward this house night and day, even toward the place of which thou hast said, My name shall be there' (I Kings 8.27–29). From these words attributed by the historian to Solomon at the dedication of the Temple we see a second emphasis however. God is immanent as well as transcendent. This he had promised Moses he would be; and now he was immanent through his Word and through his Name, and the latter was actually to be found at one spot on earth.

In OT thought it would seem that the Name of God and the Word of God developed separate identities of their own. Yet it would be absurd to suppose that by the use of such terms the Hebrews destroyed the unity of God. The Word of God continues to be God, in that it is *his* Word; yet it can act for God in the realm of 'thing'. However, both Word and Name remain pictorial expressions. They are not to be conceived as hypostases or meta-physical entities existing in their own right apart from God. If there is no man to utter a word, then there is no word; and if there is no man, the very idea of name cannot arise. There are no such things as flames without the parent fire. Yet grant the existence of the fire, and the flames must act on its behalf, conveying, as it were, the fire's purpose of burning. In the same manner the Word and Name of God may indeed act as God's *alter egos* without disturbing the unity of his being.

The unity of God is nowhere more explicitly emphasized than in the important verse which Judaism has isolated and called the *Shema'*. It runs 'Hear, O Israel, Yahweh our God is Yahweh, one' (Deut. 6.4). Now, that Yahweh was 'one' in the sense that there is no other God, all the prophets agreed. Amos, for example, insisted that it was Yahweh, the God of Israel, who had brought up his people out of Egypt (Amos 3.1; 9.7). But Amos was equally insistent that Yahweh had brought up the Philistines from Caphtor and the Syrians from Kir (9.7); and that he was Lord of Damascus (1.3–5), Tyre (1.9–10), and all the surrounding nations. Thus Amos offered Israel a new depth to the so-called First Commandment: 'Thou shalt have no other Gods before me', without anywhere explicitly declaring that Yahweh was the only God. The gods of the other peoples slowly receded before the logic of such a universalistic faith: 'For all the gods of the nations are idols: but Yahweh made the heavens' (Ps. 96.5). Yet it was not until the post-exilic period began that the prophets finally won the loyalty of Israel to Yahweh alone. In fact, the question of idolatry, and with it an ever possible apostasy from Yahweh, is the supreme question before the People of God until the Exile in Babylon. Indeed, Ezekiel's vision in Chapter 8 of that book presents us with what may be regarded as the acme of Israel's apostasy. This vision came to him in the period between the two sieges of Jerusalem. It was only when she had to remain in far-off Babylon that Israel finally came to understand that the gods were really 'no-things', *'elilim*, 'worthlessnesses', a word which, though coming from the period of the eighth century prophets, may have been a pun upon the name of the Assyrian god, Enlil.

The battle of the prophets for a true monotheism was thus a battle for faith in and loyalty to Yahweh as the 'unique' God. Hebrew has a word for unique. It is used in Gen. 22.2 in God's command to Abraham: 'Take now thy son, thine *only* son . . .' *Yaḥidh* means 'only' again in Amos 8.10 and Jer. 6.26, while in Ps. 25.16, and Ps. 68.6, the meaning is rather 'solitary' or 'isolated'. But the biblical understanding of the word 'one' is not exhausted by the conception of 'unique'. In the Shema which we quoted the adjective used for 'one' is not *yaḥidh*, but the normal cardinal number, viz., '*eḥadh*. Since 'one' in this sense does not refer to the uniqueness of God we shall require to discover its significance from other passages. And at once we are reminded of the words which the final editor of J's narrative has inserted to describe the significance of the oneness of the male-female relationship: 'Therefore shall a man leave his father and his mother, and shall cleave unto his wife, and they shall be one, '*eḥadh*, flesh' (Gen. 2.24; cf. Ex. 36.13). And man was made in the image of God!

If the OT is in any sense the Word of God, then that Word has come to us, not only through the people of Israel as a nation, but also through Israel's language and thought processes. We are thus bound to take seriously the psychology of the Hebrews; and if we would learn how the living God revealed himself in and through his association with the OT 'People of God', then we must most certainly seek to think their thoughts after them.

Six

God Known Through His Family

Yahweh is the most important name by which Israel's God was known, but the OT offers us a number of others. In Ex. 17.15 he is called *nes*, Standard; in Gen. 31.42, 53 (E) he is the *pahadh* or Dread of Isaac, while in Gen. 49.24 he is the Mighty One, *'abhir*, of Jacob. The God of Israel was evidently known by more names than one before his self-revelation at Sinai, as the priestly editors knew (Ex. 6.3). These are but isolated names, however, and tell us little about the nature of the God of the OT. Again the general epithet for the idea of divinity, viz., the word *'el*, though frequently used of Israel's God, also tells us little. The word is ancient. It appears, for example, in the Ras Shamra documents of the fifteenth pre-Christian century as the name of the chief divinity of the Canaanite pantheon. With the exception of Ethiopic, all the Semitic languages employ this word as the root form of their word for God, and it is known to the general public even today in the Arabic name for God, Allah. The word may derive from the root *'ul*, meaning 'to be strong';[1] others suggest that it meant originally 'to excel', 'to be in the forefront'.[2] A likelier suggestion is that it has developed from the root *'alal*, to bind.[3] Yet how it originated is not so important as what it meant for the Hebrews in OT times. Although the word *'el* occurs on 217 occasions yet

---

[1] Cf. *OHL*, p. 41.
[2] Cf. Nöldeke, in *Elohim El.* 1882.
[3] O. Proksh, *Theologie des Alten Testaments*, 1950, p. 444.

in the great majority of instances it does not stand alone. Normally it is conjoined with another expression bringing out the 'living', 'active' nature of Israel's God, such as '*el gibbor* (mighty warrior), or '*el hai* (the living God). It is also frequently coupled with the name Shaddai which we have seen occurs in Ex. 6.3, as well as commonly in the book of Job. It is these additional terms, then, which give the word a fuller meaning for the writers of the OT.

The word '*elohim*, however, is the standard and normal OT word for the divine Being. The noun as it stands is plural in form. A plural verb is occasionally construed with it, though it is normally found with a singular verb. The fact that '*elohim* as a word for God is in the plural in Hebrew, when the other Semitic languages have retained a singular noun, has been an object of remark throughout the centuries to Jews and Christians alike. Many have been the suggestions put forward to explain the anomaly.

Some have suggested that the plural is a plural of majesty. But that is to read into Hebrew speech a modern mode of address. So far as our biblical records can help us, the kings of Judah and Israel are all addressed in the singular. Even less worthy of consideration is the suggestion that here we are confronted with the 'we' of the newspaper editor.

Again it has been suggested that the plural form was employed by Israel as a parallel to a Canaanite practice. The goddess Astarte frequently appears in the plural, as Ashtaroth, in the Ras Shamra literature. Gradually she came to be known under slightly different guises at different local shrines, just as each local *baal* bit by bit developed local characteristics, even though each was originally a manifestation of Baal-Hadad of the Canaanite pantheon. Possibly the theologians of Canaan used the device of the plural name in order to keep Astarte one, despite the fact that she was worshipped under many forms.[4] This explanation leads us to approach the problem of the Hebrew word '*elohim* from within the grammar and thought of the Hebrews themselves.

The nouns *mayim*, water, *shamayim*, heaven, and certain other plurals built from a singular root, such as *ne'urim*, youth, form a

---

[4]   G.E. Wright, *Biblical Archaeology*, 1957, p. 109.

possible category where we may place '*elohim*. Grammarians have called the plural they express a quantitative plural. Now, there is no reason why we should not add our word '*elohim* to this particular list. Water, for example, is a peculiar substance. It can be conceived in terms of individual rain drops, or it can be envisaged in the form of the mass of the ocean. Yet in both cases it is equally water. So here we have in a natural phenomenon an instance of what we have already called 'diversity in unity'. Water is both singular and plural at the same time. Water is distinctly one particular entity, and so is unique. It is not soil or any other substance. It is *yaḥidh*, might we say. But at the same time water may be observed in movement in a plurality of ways. Keeping such an analogy in view, then, we note from the first chapter of Genesis that it is '*elohim* who says: 'Let us make '*adham* in our image' (Gen. 1.26). We have already noted that '*adham* is both singular and plural at the same time, both representative and comprehensive, the whole of the concept of man plus the sum of all the parts that make him up. Now in Gen. 11.7, in the story of the Tower of Babel, we find that it is the singular name Yahweh of whom a plural verb is used: 'Let us go down, and there confound their language'. So both *yahweh* and '*elohim* are found speaking in the plural as 'we'. In Isa. 19.4 we have an instance of a parallel usage, not uncommon. There the term '*adhon* in the plural is employed of human masters, but is construed with an adjective in the singular. On the other hand, in Isa. 6.8, a verse which belongs to the story of the call of Isaiah, we discover that Isaiah hears from the lips of Yahweh pronouns in the singular and in the plural simultaneously: 'whom shall *I* send, and who will go for *us*?' (In this case we should note that the word which is used as a circumlocution for the divine name, '*adhon*, bears the plural vowelling that derives from the noun '*elohim*.) But after the Exile the tendency is to employ a singular verb with '*elohim* even when, in a corresponding passage, a plural has already been used. Thus Neh. 9.18 is a quotation from Ex. 32.4, Nehemiah employing a singular verb when Exodus uses a plural. Evidently the later writers did not wish to give the impression that the noun '*elohim* was to be understood to mean the idea of 'gods'.

That it could be so understood, is, of course, self-evident, and the OT writers were compelled to use the word *'elohim* when they wished to express the idea of gods in the plural. Thus the first commandment (Ex. 20.3) runs: 'Thou shalt have no other *'elohim* before me'. Let us note the relationship, then, that obtained in the thought of early Israel between Yahweh and the gods.

Israel learned to put her trust in Yahweh alone only slowly and after much 'going awhoring after other gods'. The gods of the neighbouring nations remained real gods for a long time. By the time that they were looked upon with scorn they had receded into the background of Israel's thought and had fallen to the level of angels created by Israel's God. The 'sons of God' or 'sons of the gods', *benei 'elim* (Ps. 89.6), were now a great host on high doing the will of the Creator of all things.

It is natural then that a new name should arise for Israel's God. Beginning with Amos and Hosea the title 'Lord of Hosts', *yahweh tsebhaoth*, grew to be a commonly used description of the God of heaven, though the name does not occur in the Pentateuch, in Trito-Isaiah, Ezekiel, Ezra-Nehemiah or Job. On the other hand Isaiah, Jeremiah and the immediate post-exilic prophets greatly favour its use: and it occurs in Samuel in connexion with the cult attached to the Ark.

Who then were the hosts of whom Yahweh was accounted as Lord? Yahweh was certainly Lord of the hosts of warriors of Israel who crossed the river Jordan and fought to gain the Promised Land (Ex. 7.4; 12.41, 51: 'I will lay mine hand upon Egypt, and bring forth my hosts'). We should note that *'elohim* could be used in a similar way to Yahweh. In I Sam. 17.45, for example, *yahweh tsebhaoth* is called *'elohim* of the armies of Israel.

But Yahweh with equal certainty was Lord of another kind of host. The stars which sprang to view as evening fell were also Yahweh's hosts. He called them forth by number, and none was missing when he counted them nightly (Jer. 8.2; Ps. 33.6; 147.4). The stars were no mere dead matter. They were an aspect of the living hosts of heavenly beings, the angels. These too were creatures who performed the will of God. Israel never fully learned to distinguish between what we regard as the separate realms of the material and the spiritual. It is thus quite in accord with such a unitary view of the universe that the 'visitor' whom Joshua encountered at Gilgal turned out to be 'Captain of the host of Yahweh' (Josh. 5.14), 'above', and thus a counterpart of Joshua himself, who was captain of the host of Yahweh, down below. And in other places the word which we translate as angels, *mal'achim*, is so employed that we cannot clearly see whether it is divine or human messengers that are in question (cf. Isa. 44.26).[5]

Yahweh's name, 'the Lord of hosts', then, serves to strengthen still further the emphasis of the OT writers upon the uniqueness of their God. No matter that, probably under Persian influence, the Israelites in the post-exilic period interested themselves more and more in the question of the individual identity of many of the angels, their thoughts on the nature of angels could not affect their monotheistic view of Yahweh. It would be absurd to suggest that that 'captain of the host', whom Joshua met, in any sense broke up the unity of the Godhead, because it would be equally absurd to postulate such a notion of the human Joshua on earth.

In the sixth chapter of Isaiah, where Isaiah receives his call, we are introduced to the heavenly host, who are there clearly understood to be in the form of angels. In this inaugural vision, Isaiah comprehends that Yahweh is utterly and completely separate and distinct from the angelic host. He sees that the host *serves* Yahweh and ministers to him as the veritably Holy One. This conception is, of course, fully echoed in many of the Psalms, for example, in Ps. 148.2: 'Praise ye him, all his angels, praise ye him, all his hosts'. There he is indeed LORD of hosts, as he is also Lord of all creation. And yet this conception of otherness than, and lordship over, the angels is only one aspect of God's relationship to his angels.

The other rests upon the conception that the God of the OT is unspeakably humble, if we may use the phrase. With perhaps the one possible exception of Ezekiel's conception of God, that of the great OT prophets is of a God who does not grasp at his Godhead and cherish it simply because it is his by right. In the OT God

---

[5] For parallels, see *KzNT*, II, pp. 124–6.

stoops to share his very Godhead with the created beings that he has called into existence. And among them are his angels. There is no other way in which we can understand God's dealings both with his heavenly host, the angels, and with his earthly host, the people of Israel, unless we keep this essential truth of the divine humility firmly in mind.

We may illustrate this relationship of humility from some usages of the word *'elohim*. For example, there is a number of passages where the Person of the living God is linked, by means of this word *'elohim*, with the persons of sinful men. In Ex. 21.6; 22.8, and in I Sam. 2.25 the AV translates *'elohim* by the word 'judges'. The first of these instances runs: 'His master shall bring him (his slave) unto the judges'. When a man is brought before his judges, he is evidently brought before God present in the judges. Instead of saying, as we might do today, that the judges mediated (at least ideally) divine justice, the Hebrew language implied the thought that God's very Person was present in the perfect justice dispensed. In another content, the witch of Endor declared that she saw *'elohim* coming out of the earth (I Sam. 28.13). Again, the Person of God must have been in some sense present in the human Moses. God explains to that hesitant and doubting creature: 'See, I have made thee *'elohim* to Pharaoh'! (Ex. 7.1, P). Moreover, we can define this last occurrence of the word *'elohim* with more precision because in the parellel passage from the pen of J we find 'I will be with thy mouth' (Ex. 4.12). In other words, Moses was meant to become the instrument of the living Word of God, perhaps even its vehicle.

A good example of the close relationship that obtains between God and his angels, on the other hand, is to be found in Ps. 82.1–6. There we discover the following words: ' *'Elohim* stand(s) in the congregation of *'el*; in the midst of *elohim* he judges', and again 'I have said, ye are elohim, and all of you are sons of *elyon*'.[6]

Scholars today are being led to the conclusion that there is no means of explaining the phenomenon of Moses without conceding

---

[6] This less frequently occurring divine name is evidently connected with the root 'to be lofty', and from that idea we obtain the translation 'the Most High'.

that he was as truly a monotheist as was Amos centuries later. But such a belief cannot be postulated of the majority of the leaders of Israel in the period in between those two prophetic figures. Men in that period were rather what we would call today, henotheists, and not monotheists. That is, Yahweh was only one God amongst many in their eyes. It was not possible to worship him outside the land over which he held jurisdiction (cf. I Sam. 26.19). But as time went on, and under the influence of the great prophets (and possibly the priests, and the sages as well – cf. Jer. 18.18, where the three classes are mentioned together), Yahweh undoubtedly becomes predominant over all the other gods. This new relationship is shown in such a statement as: 'For Yahweh is a great 'el, and a great king above all 'elohim' (Ps. 95.3).

We have used the expression 'family relationship'.[7] In the primitive prose narrative forming the basis of the poem of Job these heavenly beings are known as 'sons of' 'elohim (Job 1.6). Another ancient passage, at least as old as the reign of David, tells how 'the sons of the 'elohim saw the daughters of men' (humanity) (Gen. 6.2), 'and they took them wives of all which they chose'.

Now, such is the Hebraic mind, with its delight in pictorial rather than in formal and speculative thought, that these sons of God are never strictly defined. When the LXX translation was made in the second and first centuries B.C. the word normally used in the Greek for 'sons of God' was ἄγγελοι or angels (cf. Ps. 138.1 LXX 137.1). However, more impersonal words were sometimes used, one of which, for example, was δυνάμεις or 'powers' (cf. Ps. 89.8 = LXX 88.8). Perhaps they had in mind the Hebrew 'abhir, used of God in Gen. 49.24, and quoted therefrom elsewhere (e.g. Ps. 132.2; Isa. 1.24; 49.26). It is applied to 'mighty' men (e.g. Judg. 5.22; Ps. 68.31), horses (Jer. 8.16), and to the bulls

---

[7] We have taken the title of this chapter from a concept to be found in the Talmud. In Hag. 13b the phrase *Familia shel me'olah*, 'the family above', occurs as a description of the angels. Today we tend to equate the members of a family, and regard them as a team; we exalt the status of the children. But in olden days there was no equality in a family. Father was quite clearly 'Paterfamilias'.

that symbolized the kings of Assyria (Isa. 10.13; cf. Ps. 50.13). Whatever descriptive term was employed, however, the close relationship between the Person of God and the heavenly beings was still displayed no matter how the latter was envisaged. Thus Ps. 68.17 runs: 'The chariots of *'elohim* are twice ten thousand, thousands upon thousands; the Lord is among them (as) in Sinai in the holy place (or), in holiness (or), in the sanctuary.' In this case we would agree that the host of the Lord were the hosts of Israel whom he had brought up out of the land of Egypt. But the LXX (LXX Ps. 67.17) interprets those hosts in another light. It speaks of the thousands of εὐθηνοῦντες or 'rejoicing ones', a word which in the context of the Greek text is to be understood to mean the angelic host. The Greek word reads like a translation of a Hebrew active participle in the plural, such as we saw Deutero-Isaiah delighted to employ when he described the living God in action. Again, the words 'in the *qodhesh*' (holy place) with which Ps. 68.17 concludes, remind us that the 'sons of God' are sometimes known as the *qedhoshim*. Now the consonants of this Hebrew word may represent three different conceptions. Firstly, the word may be construed, not as a noun, but as an adjective in the plural, agreeing with the plural noun *'elohim*; e.g. in Hos. 11.12 (Hebrew text 12.1) it probably means 'the Holy One' himself. Secondly, the word may be understood as a noun in the plural, so that we may translate it as 'holy ones'. It obviously means as much in Ps. 34.9; 89.7; Job 5.1; 15.15; Zech. 14.5; Dan. 8.13. These 'holy ones' are clearly the 'family' of the angels in heaven. Yet thirdly, the *qedhoshim* are sometimes as evidently the loyal members of the house of Israel, who keep the Covenant that God has made with Israel at Sinai. In this case the AV usually translates the word by 'saints', e.g. in Ps. 16.3. Naturally this extraordinary intermixture of usages will affect the OT doctrine of redemption and so we shall be compelled to return to it later. At the moment, however, we note that the word for 'holy', whether in singular or plural, may refer (*a*) to God, (*b*) to an angel, or (*c*) to a human saint.

Let us now put together various expressions that represent in some manner the heavenly hosts of whom Yahweh is Lord. The very looseness of the expressions represents a fluidity of thought that is characteristic of the Hebraic approach to the nature of God:

(a) *Benei 'elim* 'sons of the mighty', or, 'of the gods' (plural in Hebrew) (Ps. 89.6), translated in the LXX (Ps. 88.6) as Θεοῦ the word for God being in the singular.

(b) *Benei 'elohim* 'sons of God' (Job 1.6) translated in the LXX as 'angels of God'.

(c) Yahweh's 'hosts' are often translated as 'powers', δυναμεις (Ps. 89.8; 103.21; 148.2, etc., Heb.).[8]

(d) God's 'angels' may be equated in poetic language with the winds (Zech. 6.5) or, as his heavenly 'ministers', with flames of fire (Ps. 104.4)

(e) Since the word *ruah* means both 'wind' and 'spirit', the angels too may be conceived simultaneously as winds and spirits (Ps. 104.4).

(f) *Qodhesh* (the abstract noun meaning 'holiness') is actually translated in the LXX by ἄγγελοι 'angels' (Deut. 33.2).[9]

(g) Angels are the will of God in action (Ps. 103.21).

(h) The word *'elohim* may be identified either with angels (Ps. 8.6 LXX) or with human judges (*vide supra*).

The above list does not claim to be an exhaustive survey of the many fluid expressions which the OT writers employed as they sought to describe the relationship of God to the angels. But an examination of them leads us to two contrasting statements. (i) God is Creator of the angels, and is thus wholly other than them.

---

[8] O. Cullmann has pointed out that the 'powers' spoken of in Rom. 13.1 are both heavenly and earthly at once. It is not possible to distinguish between them. TZ, 10. Jahrgang, Heft 5, Spe-Okt 1954, *Zur neuesten Diskussion über die* ἐξοσἴαι *in Röm.*, 13.1.

[9] Here the Hebrew is obscure. *q-d-sh* may be read as Kadesh. *'esh-dath* is obviously corrupt. The important point, however, is that the translators give the general sense when they picture the 'holy myriads' as angels, who themselves are rays of light and flames of fire, but 'following at God's foot'. See S.R. Driver, *Deuteronomy*, I.C.C. 1895, ad loc.

(ii) God condescends to make use of the heavenly host, and stoops to reveal his will by means of his messengers in both earth and heaven. In a real sense, God who is LORD identifies himself with the angels that he has created. As part of his creation they sing his praise, yet when he acts to attain his loving purposes he limits himself to act through them. This latter truth is made plain to us in those passages where the angels are envisaged as flames of fire (cf. Ps. 104.4).

A flame has no root of existence in itself. It is born from the glowing mass of burning timber, or it is seen to emerge from the radiant ball that is the sun. As the flame leaps forth from out of the fire, however, it actively bears the power of the fire, which is the will to burn. The flame is identical with the fire, yet the flame is not the fire in itself. In doing the 'will' of the fire, the flame is compelled to separate itself from its source, and continues to perform its task in this state of separation. Yet when its task is done, the flame ceases to exist as an entity in its own right. While it was in action as a flame, however, there was a species of family relationship between it and the other flames, and between it and the parent fire.

This potent analogy gives content to the many so-called theophanies that are recorded from the pen of OT writers in both the early and the late period of Israel's story.

The following passages describe for us what happens when any particular angel performs a 'mission' for God. (The root of the word for angel, *mal'ach*, means 'to send'.)

In II Sam. 24.16 the angel is the ambassador of God's purpose to destroy: 'And when the angel stretched out his hand to destroy (Israel), the Lord repented him of the evil, and said to the angel that destroyed the people, It is enough'.

In II Kings 19.35 it is 'the angel of the Lord' who smites the Assyrian camp outside Jerusalem with death. So too in the story contained in I Chron. 21, where sin brings a pestilence upon Jerusalem, which God sent by the hand of an angel. Compare also II Chron. 32.21; Dan. 3.28 (where both the LXX and Theodotion agree in rendering the Aramaic equivalent of the Hebrew by ἄγγελος); Dan. 6.22 (where we have 'angel' in both the Aramaic and Theodotion, but not in the LXX). In II Sam. 24.17; I Kings 13.18; Zech. 1.9, the angel is the instrument by which the Word of Yahweh is conveyed to man. We have already noted that God's Word could be alive and perform its function independently of God, although, paradoxically, God was in his Word, in the same way as the fire may be in the flame.

There is no evidence in the OT that the conception of angels is a late one. Some scholars have maintained that in the post-exilic period the God of the Hebrews grew more and more remote from Israel and finally became transcendent alone. The conception of intermediaries between God and man, they maintain, had therefore to be introduced. It is true that a proliferation of angels is a mark of the period of the apocryphal books, and that the hierarchical ranks and even the names of leading angels may have entered Judaism from the east through Persian influence, as we have said. But the conception that God could be represented on earth by an angel is as old as some of the oldest extant literature of the OT that we possess, and is indeed a marked feature of both the J and the E documents of the Hexateuch.

Let us now make a list of the various OT theophanies seriatim, and as we do so take note of the continuing fluidity of thought that marks them all.[10]

(*a*) Gen. 16.7–14 (J) The passage begins with 'the angel of Yahweh' finding Hagar, and in v. 10 the angel actually addresses her. In v. 13, however, Hagar recognizes that it is Yahweh himself who speaks to her, and therefore gives him the title of 'the God who sees'.

(*b*) Gen. 18.1–22 (J). In v. 1 the LXX renders 'Yahweh' by Θεός v. 2 records a visit of 'three men', and we are given to suppose that they were as human as were the judges of Ex. 21.6 (*vide supra*). But in the next verse all three are addressed by the title 'My Lord', in the singular, as if they were one personality. Thereafter the Hebrew uses the plural, but the LXX continues to use the singular.

---

[10] For an analysis of the OT theophanies and of their significance see A.R. Johnson, *The One and the Many in the Israelite Conception of God*, 1942.

(c)   Gen. 19 (J), the story of the fall of Sodom. In v. 1 we are told that two *mal'achim came* to the city. This noun may, of course, represent either human or divine messengers. The LXX translates by the word ἄγγελοι In v. 13, however, we learn that Yahweh had sent them (cf. the root meaning of the word *mal'ach*). Then in v. 17 we read 'When *they* had brought them forth, *he* said . . . ' v. 18–19 read 'And Lot said unto them Oh, not so, my Lord(s) (the plural is the plural form used when the epithet applies to God); behold now *thy* servant . . . ' And in v. 21 we have the reply of the three men 'See, *I* have accepted thee . . . that *I* will not overthrow this city . . . '

(d)   Gen. 21.17–19 (E), the story of Hagar's heavenly visitor. In v. 17 the word 'angel' is employed as a parallel to the word 'God'; but in v. 18 the angel is actually identified with God; 'for I will make him a great nation' he says, yet in v. 19 God acts without the angel's help.

(e)   Gen. 22.11–18 (J), the story of the sacrifice of Isaac. In vv. 11–12 the angel summons Abraham as if he were God himself speaking; in v.14 Abraham accepts the fact that it had indeed been Yahweh who spoke to him. The words of blessing that follow however come through the mouth of an angel (vv. 15–18).

(f)   Gen. 31.11–13 (E), a dream of Jacob. In this case the angel actually says 'I am the God of Bethel' (v. 13). The LXX translators noted this difficulty and paraphrased rather than translated by saying: 'I am the God that appeared to thee in the place of God'.

(g)   Gen. 32.24–30 (E), the 'Peniel' incident, referred to in Hos. 12.4. The story begins with Jacob wrestling with a man (*'ish*), but it ends with his exclamation 'I have seen God face to face'. Hosea interprets the story by saying that 'he had power over the angel', though the word 'angel' does not occur in the Genesis text.

(h)   Gen. 48.15–16 (E), Jacob blessing his sons. Here Jacob declares that it was an angel who had redeemed him from all evil. However, several hundred years later, the tension behind such a pictorial expression comes to a head. Deutero-Isaiah repeatedly declares that it is God alone who is the Redeemer of Israel (cf. Isa. 43.14; 44.6; 44.24; 47.4; etc.); yet again it was actually a disciple of his who exclaimed a few years later: '(Yahweh) was their saviour . . . the angel of his presence saved them' (Isa. 63.8–9).

(*i*) Ex. 3.2–6 (J and E), the call of Moses. In the Burning Bush it was an angel that appeared to Moses (v. 2), but in v. 4 we read 'When *Yahweh* saw that he turned aside to see, *'elohim* called unto him out of the midst of the bush'.

(*j*) Ex. 14.19–22. In this passage the angel of God is clearly differentiated from God himself. His function is to go before the camp of Israel. Yet in Ex. 13.21 we were told that it was Yahweh who went before the camp of Israel by day in a pillar of a cloud . . . and by night in a pillar of fire. Moreover when we read on in chap. 14, at v. 24 we find that it was actually Yahweh himself who was in the pillar of fire and the pillar of cloud. Yet the Priestly author of Num. 20.16, writing centuries later, prefers to say that it was an angel who brought the Israelites out of Egypt, rather than boldly to declare that it was God.

(*k*) Josh. 5.13–16. Joshua encounters a man (*'ish*) who later declares himself to be 'captain of the host of Yahweh'. But in some sense this 'man' bears within him the presence of Yahweh, because he adds: 'Loose thy shoe from off thy foot, for the place whereon thou standest is holy'.

(*l*) Judg. 2.1–5. The angel of Yahweh again declares: 'I made you to go up out of Egypt', and continues as if he were actually Yahweh himself: 'I will never break my covenant with you'.

(*m*) Judg. 6.11–14, Gideon's heavenly visitor. In v. 12 the angel is separate from Yahweh, and speaks *about* Yahweh; but in v. 14 he becomes Yahweh himself. In v. 22 we have both truths placed in juxtaposition: 'and when Gideon perceived that he was an (the) angel of Yahweh, Gideon said, 'Alas, O Lord! for I have seen an angel of Yahweh face to face'. However, in the following verse it is Yahweh who replies

'Peace be unto thee'. The LXX in vvs. 14 and 16 reads ὁ ἄγγελος for the Hebrew *Yahweh*.

(n) Judg. 13.2–23, Manoah's heavenly visitor. The story begins (v. 3) with an angel visiting Manoah. Manoah's wife, however, (v. 6) thinks that he is a man (*'ish*) of God who looks like an angel (or messenger) of God. Manoah (v. 8) employs her description of the visitor in a prayer to Yahweh. Thus he does not identify his visitor with God. Yet at the end of the story (v. 22) Manoah says to his wife, 'We shall surely die, because we have seen *'elohim'*.

(o) It is an angel that guides Ezekiel in his vision of the restored Temple. Sometimes it is *Yahweh* who speaks, however, (cf. Ezek. 44.2) and at other times, without any hint of a change of speaker, it is obviously the angel who calls upon Ezekiel to note the details of the edifice, just as if he were the very Person of God himself.

(p) Zech. 1–6. In this post-exilic book, separated from J and E by nearly half a millennium, the same fluidity of thought is maintained. In 1.12–13, for example, the angel of Yahweh addresses Yahweh, and Yahweh replies to him. In 3.6–10, however, the angel becomes the mouthpiece of Yahweh himself, and can say (v. 9) 'For behold that stone that I have laid before Joshua'. But in Deutero-Zechariah Yahweh himself performs the function which elsewhere he delegates to an angel (Zech. 9.8).

The person of 'the Angel of the Covenant', who appears in the book of Exodus, forms a convenient figure on which to focus our attention. We have seen that Ex. 13.21 declares that it was Yahweh who went before the travelling Israelites, but have noticed that Ex. 14.19 prefers to say that it was an angel of *'elohim* who preceded the host. After the narrative of the giving of the Law, thereafter, the E document continues: 'Behold, I send an Angel before thee, to keep thee in the way, and to bring thee into the place which I have prepared. Beware of him, and obey his voice, provoke him not; for he will not pardon your transgressions: for my name is in him' (Ex. 23.20–21).

This is a remarkable utterance. We have seen earlier that the 'name' was the description of its owner's essential being, and that as such the name could virtually be considered as an entity separate from its owner; we saw indeed that the owner's personality was present in his name. From the passage in question we now understand that the Hebrews envisaged God's essential nature to be such that he could extend his being 'from heaven' to earth. When he did so, God set amongst the Israelites an 'alter ego' of himself; It was the angel whom they were to obey, we read, not God himself. Yet how better could the priestly writer have expressed himself striving as he was to express a theological concept in pictorial language? The God of the OT can never wholly reveal himself or his will to man. He is indeed the *Deus Absconditus* of the theologians. 'Verily thou art a God that hidest thyself' (Isa. 45.15); 'I will wait upon Yahweh, that hideth his face from the house of Jacob' (Isa. 8.17). 'Awake, why sleepest thou, O Yahweh? arise, cast us not off for ever. Wherefore hidest thou thy face?' (Ps. 44.23–24). But God is at the same time the *Deus Revelatus*. Such terms as these would of course be inconceivable to the writers of the OT. What to us are abstract theological conceptions could occur to the Hebrew mind in pictures alone. Unfortunately, however, the picture of an idea does not delineate that idea with the exactitude of analytical language.

The Hebrews carried in their hearts the faith that God is wholly other than man, who in his turn is God's finite, mortal and fallen creature. The Hebrews believed, therefore, that it is inconceivable that mere man could ever 'know' Almighty God. On the other hand, they were equally aware that Almighty God had indeed spoken to them words of love and mercy, and that the essence of that Word of God was his action in leading them out of Egypt, in bringing them through all kinds of dangers, and in guiding them into and settling them in their Promised Land. This spoken and then acted Word of God, moreover, was virtually a revelation of God's very heart and purpose, although, paradoxically, as we have said, man cannot 'know' God in any real sense of the word.

God's action began in the mind of God. Thus it was not even necessary for God to speak. It was sufficient for him just to think his plan! (Jer. 29.16). Yet, since God is the living God of history, that thought of God became at once an action, expressed in living forms and images.

How better then could the Hebrew mind in its turn express the paradox of revelation than by using pictorial forms and images after God? They thereby found a means of presenting the truth of God without seeking to reconcile what is beyond the logic of the human mind. Our writers were certainly not consistent in their exegesis of the concept of God's self-revelation. For example, Ex. 23.21, which, as we have said, seems to come from the pen of E, says one thing about the Angel of the Covenant: 'Provoke him not, for he will not pardon your transgressions; for *my* name is in him'; whereas Ex. 32.34, a passage probably written by J, but of course edited as a whole by P, makes the following statement about the coming punishment: 'Behold, mine Angel shall go before thee: nevertheless in the day when *I* visit, *I* will visit their sin upon them'.

We dare not dismiss such pictorial thinking, on the ground that it is 'early' and 'primitive'. Pictorial thinking is the essence of the whole biblical revelation. It is employed in the NT just as much as it is in the OT. The Gospel parables represent truth delivered in picture form. The book of Revelation represents the attempt of the finite human mind to express in pictures what is too wonderful for mortal man to conceive in any other form. One might expect the last book of the OT to be the most developed in its theology. Yet, the OT, in the Alexandrian order of its canon, actually ends with a reference to the Angel of the Covenant. 'Behold, I (will) send my angel, *mal'ach* , . . . even the angel of the covenant' (Mal. 3.1). Thus even in this post-exilic period when, with the help of the prophets and the priestly writers, the thought of Israel has now fully matured, the same dialectical contrast is maintained in picture language, as was evident in the earlier period, between God as he is in himself, and God as he is represented in the person of his messenger.

The final passage we might adduce for study when examining how God reveals himself through his 'family' is Isa. 63.1–9.

The first six verses of this passage paint a terrible picture of Yahweh as the God of wrath. 'He is trampling out the vintage where the grapes of wrath are stored; He hath loosed the fatal lightning of his terrible swift sword', in the words of Julia Ward Howe's well-known hymn. 'And I looked, and there was none to help; and I wondered that there was none to uphold, therefore mine own arm brought salvation unto me; and my fury, it upheld me' (v. 5). The God of Israel, says the writer, is the only God. There is no other god; therefore there can be no other saviour. 'So he was their Saviour' (v. 8). But then we read on: 'In all their affliction he was afflicted, *and the angel of his presence saved them*: in his love and in his pity he (God or the angel?) redeemed them' (v. 9).

Two facts about v. 9 should be noted: (1) The text is not wholly clear. The LXX reads οὐ πρέσβυς οὐδὲ ἄγγελος, ἀλλ' αὐτὸς κύριος ἔσωσεν αὐτούς (not an old man (messenger?) nor an angel, but the Lord himself saved them). The word κύριος is present only in some manuscripts. The word πρέσβυς moreover, must render an original *tsir* (another word for messenger) where the Hebrew now reads *tsar* (affliction). But the significance of the theological ideas involved does actually become clear, even though we cannot establish the text wholly to our satisfaction. (2) The meaning of the word 'presence' is important. The English represents the Hebrew word for 'face'. The verbal root from which it is built, viz. *panah*, means 'to turn'. The noun 'face' comes from the turning of one person to another in recognition. In Hebrew the noun is used in the plural, probably because one can see various aspects of the face from different angles. However, when the noun is conjoined with a preposition (e.g. *lephenei*), the new form is weaker in significance, and usually means 'in the presence of . . . ' or such like. But here no weakening has taken place; it still means 'face' and nothing less. We can therefore translate the Hebrew by the concrete term as boldly as in the phrase where we are told that Jacob saw God *panim 'el panim*, face to face (Gen. 32.30).

Hebrew man, however, employed a like fluidity of thought when he considered his own human nature as when he attempted to describe the nature of God. The face is that part of the human anatomy by which we distinguish one man from another. We are able to do so, because a man's personality and character are made visible on his face. His face, in fact, 'represents' his character, or his 'heart' to use the word an OT writer would have preferred. No man knows the essence of another's being. Each man is *homo absconditus* to his brother man. Yet, paradoxically, a man can 'know' his friend by studying his face. It is through his face, and from the word issuing from his mouth, that a man expresses his true heart, and becomes *homo revelatus* to his friend. For all practical purposes, then a man's face is the man, and his face is all that a man need show the world. His heart is in his face, so to speak, even when the heart, the inner man, remains invisible to the eye.

Now, *panim* may be used in like manner in Hebrew as a substitute for the person himself. An example is to be found in the story of Ahithophel. The latter counsels Absalom with the words, literally 'thy face going into battle' (II Sam. 17.11), where the ARSV paraphrases with 'in person'. God, of course, has a face as well as man. That is how our passage can speak of the 'angel of his face'.

Here then we have a concept used in a manner parallel to that of Name. We recall how God, though remaining hidden 'in heaven', had put his Name at both Shiloh and later at the Temple in Jerusalem. It is interesting now to realize that the Hebrews must have believed that the Sanctuary was the place of God's Face as well. We read that bread was set out daily in the Sanctuary, in the preTemple period (I Sam. 21.6), in the period of Solomon's Temple (I Kings 7.48), and in the post-exilic period alike (Ex. 25.30; 35.13; 39.36, all of which are passages from the hand of the later priestly writer). Now, this bread bore several titles, but one of them was 'the bread of (for) the Face'.

Returning to Isa. 63.9, after this necessary excursus on the significance of the word for 'face', we find that we have obtained a new and fuller content to the phrase 'the angel of his face saved them'.

The phrase 'the angel of his face' is unique in the OT. We cannot dogmatically declare that the reference is to the angel of the Covenant in the book of Exodus. Yet when we remember that the construct relationship between two Hebrew nouns may be translated in many ways, we recognize that the phrase may mean 'the angel who is his face'. And since this angel 'saved' them as 'the angel' did in Exodus, it is highly likely that our writer intended to make the identification.

In the first strophe of the poem God had been trampling out the grapes of wrath alone (v. 3). Yet it was not 'God' but 'mine own arm' that had brought salvation then – surely another picture of God, hidden, yet revealed on the level of the understanding of the human mind. 'His own arm' was that part of God which he normally manifested to men when he acted for their salvation (cf. Deut. 5.15; Job 40.9; Ps. 44.3; Isa. 33.2; 40.10; 51.9; 53.1; etc.). What our poet now goes on to do in the second strophe is to personalize and thus render much more potent this agent of God's redemption. He names him as one of the members of the heavenly family.

The act of God which the poet thus describes in the second strophe is an act of love and redemption (vv. 7–9). The angel had been the instrument whereby that redemption had been wrought in days of old. But God, in his great humility, had at that time been 'in' his creature, the Angel of the Covenant. Thus it was that when the angel suffered with his people Israel it was actually God who had been sharing their pains with them. For 'in all their affliction he was afflicted' (v. 9), and *yet*, it was his Face that saved them!

It will be obvious to the reader that the profoundly important truths lying behind such picture language will demand full treatment at that point in our discussion where God's relationship with Israel is under study.

Seven

God Known Through His Spirit

The pictorial theology which we examined in the chapter above affords us help once more when we seek to understand the OT conception of God's Holy Spirit. We may take up an examination of the doctrine of the Spirit in the OT at that point where we left off our exegesis of Isa. 63. In vv. 10–11 of that chapter we read: 'But they rebelled, and vexed his holy Spirit: therefore he was turned to be their enemy' (cf. the picture of the grapes of wrath at the beginning of the chapter). Then we are told that Israel remembered the days of old, that is to say, the mighty acts of God which he had performed in bringing his people out of Egypt, that people in whom God had put his holy Spirit.

The Hebrew word for spirit is *ruah*. However, this Hebrew word originally meant wind, the ordinary physical wind that blows from off the sea. Man can create wind by blowing. Therefore so also can the living God.

The poem is Ex. 15, which proclaims the wonder of the Exodus of God's people out of Egypt, affirms: 'Thou didst blow with thy wind, the sea covered them: they sank as lead in the mighty waters' (v. 10). But man cannot see wind. He can, of course, see the effect of wind, in the great waves which can sink a ship (Jonah 1.4). The effect of the blowing of the wind is the effect of the will of God as God blows upon the sea, and upon the land, and upon man. In the same way that the Word does not return unto God void, neither does the Spirit of God blow without effectively bearing the will of God. Though man cannot see wind, yet he can breathe out on a cold and damp morning, and see his breath congeal as cloud; and the cloud can descend as damp air upon the soil. He sees his breath, in other words, becoming effective. So it is with the Spirit of God in the OT. The Spirit of God may be the agent of creation (Job 26.13) in exactly the same manner as the Word by which the heavens were created (Ps. 33.6); in fact, as we shall see, the Spirit may be the agent even of judgement and of mercy to men (cf. Gen. 6.3). The Spirit blowing as the wind is thus yet another theological picture of the activity of the *Deus Revelatus* in the midst of Israel's life.

The great eighth century prophets Isaiah and Micah speak of the *ruah* of God only very rarely, Hosea not at all. When they do, they have of course broken with the earlier physical connotations which the word had borne before. Jeremiah, like Hosea, makes no use of the concept of God's Spirit at all. But in both Deutero-Isaiah and Ezekiel it becomes a major term. Both of those great exilic writers use it to describe God's intelligible, purposeful, effortlessly powerful activity with which he continues to maintain and nurture the life of his people. 'He that giveth *breath* unto the people, and *spirit* to them that walk therein' (Isa. 42.5).

However, as we have said above, in its early days the word *ruah* bore no moral significance. It merely signified power. Thus when the *ruah* of God 'leaped' upon King Saul (I Sam. 18.10) he received a sudden accession of vehement power. This power showed itself in the manner in which he 'prophesied' *hithnabbeh*, probably falling into some kind of an ecstatic state. Even Jeremiah, some four centuries later than Saul, is tempted to believe that the power of God is nothing less than shattering and overwhelming strength: 'O Lord, thou hast deceived me, and I was deceived; for thou art stronger than I, and hast prevailed' (Jer. 20.7). Accordingly it was only when men came to recognize that the power of God must be consistent with his holy nature that the phrase 'the Holy Spirit' could possibly come into use. The phrase occurs indeed only twice in the whole OT – once in Isa. 63.10–11, where it is repeated as we saw when we examined the passage, and once in Ps. 51.11.

Now, since the Spirit of God is no less than God himself acting in accordance with his essential nature, Spirit actually comes to be pictured in a manner that is virtually parallel to the pictorial concept of the angelic activity which we have now examined. We find, for example, that it is the Spirit of God which conveys God's will to his messengers, and gives them the power to obey him: 'Thou sendest forth thy spirit, they are created' (Ps. 104.30). In early times the spirit in man had represented those higher elements in his character which God had 'inspired', or breathed, into him. Thus Samson's unusual strength had come straight from God (Judg. 14.6), and Bezaleel's craftsmanship likewise (Ex. 31.3). But as man's understanding of the ways of God increased with the passage of time, ever more facets to the meaning of the power of the Spirit of God were revealed to his growing understanding. Micah is sure that he is 'full of power, and of judgment, and of might, by the spirit of Yahweh' (Micah 3.8) 'to declare unto Jacob his transgressions, and to Israel his sin'. In other words, the prophet had become aware that since the Spirit came from God it conveyed to him a moral judgement upon events, simply because God himself is a moral Being. The Psalmist expresses the prayer 'Take not thy holy spirit from me' (Ps. 51.11) for this reason too. Knowing that God is holy, he knows that, as a sinner himself, he cannot live in the presence of God without the aid of God's Holy Spirit.

Trito-Isaiah and Haggai, both post-exilic prophets, possibly lay the emphasis rather upon the continuing presence of God through the indwelling of his Spirit, while Pss. 51 and 139 reiterate the depth of understanding attained by the prophet Micah. What they do is to claim the presence of the Spirit for individual men and women. And yet those two post-exilic writers realize that the fullness of the knowledge, and of the presence, of the Spirit of the living God would be known only in the future, and not in the period of their lifetime. The day was still to come when the fullness of the giving of the Spirit would take place: 'And it shall come to pass afterward, that I will pour out my spirit upon all flesh . . . ' (Joel 2.28), a faith which was wholly homologated by the writer of Isa. 59.21. Although God had put his Spirit within Israel, and although Israel had not yet understood the significance of God's mighty gift, yet one day Israel would do so, and to that end God would not take away his Spirit from them, 'for henceforth and for ever'.

Although this work does not pretend to make a systematic presentation of the full development of all the doctrines to be found in the OT, yet we cannot leave the question of the doctrine of the Spirit without noting that after the time of Trito-Isaiah there appears a reversion to the language used about the spirit that is characteristic of the early historical narratives. This is true of the post-exilic books of Chronicles, while Ecclesiastes adopts what is almost a non-Hebraic view of the nature and function of the human spirit. In contradistinction to the teaching of all the documents that comprise the book of Genesis, he so thinks of the union of matter and spirit in man that at death 'the spirit shall return unto God who gave it' (Eccl. 12.7; cf. Ps. 104.29–30). A true understanding of the relation between the spirit in man and the Spirit of God was in danger of going into eclipse in the thought and experience of the postexilic community of the Greek period. It will only be when we reach that part of our study which is contained in Part III that we shall come to understand how this tendency could have come about.

Each of the pictorial terms which we have now examined, because they illumine for us the creative and redemptive activity of the God of the OT, viz., God's Name, Word, Face, Angel, and Spirit, represents the genius of the people of the OT for presenting theology in picture language. Not one of these pictorial concepts, let us recall, acts as a kind of intermediary, a hypostasis, between the life of God and the life of man. God's assuming a form, whether that of Angel or as his own Holy Spirit, has no meaning apart from God himself. Revelation does not mean that the hidden God is resolved into the revealed God in any form whatever. The *Deus Revelatus* actually remains the *Deus Absconditus* throughout the whole OT from the earliest forms of expression to the latest and profoundest writings in the exilic and post-exilic periods.

Eight

The Holiness and the Glory of God

Two frequently recurring Hebrew words must now come under review. Firstly we shall examine the word 'holy' as it is used in the OT of God.

Up to the present, in our discussion of the significance of the biblical statement that man was made in the image of God, we have not as yet touched upon the heart of the matter. Our study so far has been a study of the various metaphysical conceptions of the nature of God that were held by the OT writers. Man made in the image of God, however, is a moral being as well as that kind of creature whose ontological nature can be discussed in terms of both matter and spirit, of unity and diversity. The anthropomorphic thinking of the OT represents a kind of two-way traffic in this regard. Man learns to know what God is like because he knows in his own life on earth something akin to the family relationship that obtains in the heavenly places, to which we have alluded. Man comes to know about this 'family relationship' for the reason that he is God's creature, nay, he is God's child, and therefore, in some sense of the word he is part of the family of God.

But on the other hand, God reveals to man, by means of the family relationship in the heavenly places, what he, God himself, is like. In this way, man comes to discover that he in turn is a moral creature too because the author of his life in the first place is moral in his relationships with his family.

A generation or two ago it was customary to speak of the 'attributes' of God. It seemed possible in those days to abstract from the pages of the OT certain qualities of God's character and nature, and to examine them in detail, in much the same manner as a botanist examines the petals of a rose. Thus OT theologians would speak of the 'holiness' of God, of the 'righteousness' of God, of the 'natural' divine attributes, such as God's omnipotence, omniscience, omnipresence, and so on, of his 'redemptive' attributes, such as his saving love, and of other 'attributes' as well. Our understanding of the thought of the Hebrews in this regard, however, is very different today. As we have seen earlier in this study, there is no suggestion in the OT that its writers present us with any 'propositions' about the living God. Nor does the OT provide us with any speculative ideas about him at all. Rather it presents us with a record of the initiative taken by God, as he seeks to show his love to man, and of certain great acts which God performs to the end that mankind might be saved both from the state of sin in which he finds himself, and into a new fullness of life which it is God's good pleasure to give him.

Now, we are not given to know from the pages of the OT what is the nature of God as he is in himself. But we are given to know him as we see him in his actions, and as he performs his righteous will. To this statement we must add another, viz., that God's righteous will is not made known in merely abstract form. It is made known through his continued relations with one particular, historical people, whose political and social life we can date and study and criticize, this time not in the manner that the botanist studies the rose. None of the so-called attributes of God is therefore really such at all. Abstract nouns such as holiness, righteousness, love, etc., are really only concepts in the mind of man. Rather we must look for verbs or active participles, derived, it may be, from the same roots as those very nouns, if we would find human words fit to describe God as he reveals himself in the pages of the OT. We do so because, as we have already noted, it is just such verbs or active participles which reveal to us what God is like in his living contact with this particular people.

Yet at once we are faced with a difficulty. It is that the OT writers are aware that the nature of God is beyond what can be described even by those verbal forms by which his relationship with Israel is set forth. The essence of God is divinity, as we have said, and God was there 'in the beginning' before ever he created either the universe or that particular people with which he becomes involved.

Fortunately there is one Hebrew word which, once it has developed to the fullness of its meaning, seeks to represent just this conception that God is wholly other[1] than man and the universe that he has made. It is the Hebrew root *q-d-sh* which we translate by the verb 'to be holy'.

The origin of this verbal root is lost in antiquity. But in Israel's early years the root indicated to the hearer something like the Maori conception both of *tapu* and of its opposite at once, that of *mana*. In Hebrew, the opposite of the noun or adjective *qadhosh* is the word *ḥol*, meaning 'profane'. We may illustrate this curious interchange of usages with the following picture. Let us imagine two squares each representing the walls of a house, each of which contains a harem of wives. Harem A is the property of its *ba'al* or lord, whom we shall call X. Harem B is the property of husband Y. Husband Y has no right whatsoever to enter the precincts of harem A. Harem B alone is his domain. Since this is so, then the wives within its walls are *qadhosh* to him as their lord, but *ḥol* to husband X. On the other hand the wives in harem A in their turn are *qadhosh* to husband X. However, since he is jealous of husband X, husband Y might conceivably invade the walls of harem A and destroy all the women therein. If he were indeed to do so, then he would do what the AV calls 'devote' them; or more lamely 'utterly destroy' those unfortunate wives. Now the two latter English expressions represent the *hiph'il* (transitive) form of the verbal root *ḥ-r-m* from which, oddly enough, through the cognate language Arabic, the English word 'harem' has come to be (cf. Josh. 8.26; I Sam. 15.18). The consonants of the noun

---

[1] The words 'wholly other' represent, however, but one horn of a paradox. The God of the OT is primarily he who 'becomes with' man. Therefore he must be such that man, made in his image, can know him who thus meets him in historical situations.

derived from the verb, it is interesting to note, are actually identical with the name of an Egyptian goddess who personified the fertility process.[2]

In the early days of Israel's story, Yahweh himself was known under the name of *ba'al*. While this word meant 'husband' or 'lord', it was also the generic title for the local fertility gods of the Canaanites. It is clear that in the period of the monarchy the use of the name Baal for Yahweh was dropped. It had become too dangerous a name to use. The uneducated masses obviously could not differentiate between one Baal and another (cf. I Kings 18). Consequently Israel's historians altered the syllables *ba'al*, if they formed part of a person's name, into the syllables *bosheth*, a word which simply means 'shame'. For example, Saul, the Yahweh worshipper, had evidently called one of his sons *'ish-ba'al*, 'man of Baal' (II Sam. 2.8), but the historian at a later date evidently altered that name to Ishbosheth (cf. I Chron. 8.33 with II Sam. 2.8).

We can observe how Yahweh was once in fact a Baal in the sense which we have suggested above. Joshua, the warrior leader, 'put to the ban', or 'utterly destroyed', or 'devoted', the whole city of Ai, since he believed that, as the instrument of Yahweh-Baal , he must needs destroy the inhabitants of a city of whose Baal Yahweh was evidently jealous (Josh. 8.26–8).[3]

This conception, that one could utterly devote an object to Yahweh, continued to obtain for centuries. The late priestly regulations even incorporated it into the rules for sacrificial worship. Thus Lev. 27.28 now runs: 'No devoted thing (*herem*) that man shall devote unto Yahweh . . . shall be sold or redeemed; every devoted thing is most holy (holy of holies) unto Yahweh'.

Following upon this line of thought we notice that the conception of holiness slowly deepened and became more moralized. Many departments of Israel's life had to be made holy unto the

---

[2]　J.B. Pritchard, *The Ancient Near East in Pictures*, 1954, pp. 183–4 and p. 304.

[3]　See N.H. Snaith, *The Distinctive Ideas of the Old Testament*, 1944, pp. 21–50.

Lord; that is to say, they were set apart, or sanctified (hiqdish), and thereby regarded as belonging to Yahweh. Thus, in early Israel, there were holy men and women (*qedheshim*), 'temple prostitutes', to be found in many sanctuaries (cf. Deut. 23.17). In this case the conception of morality has scarcely been attained. One day in the week also was set apart for Yahweh; thus it was that the Sabbath day could also be regarded as holy (Ex. 16.23; 20.8).[4] The first born of every animal and human parent, again, was regarded as holy, since it too belonged, or was to be set apart to, Yahweh (Ex. 13.2). The instances we have cited are all from the hand of the priestly writer, who multiplied regulations of this nature to a degree where we need not follow him.[5] Suffice it to say that it was the ultimate hope of Israel that all aspects of her life, even the work done in the kitchen by the housewife, and in the open by the warrior-horseman, should become as holy to Yahweh as were the specially sanctified vessels to be found in the post-exilic Temple at Jerusalem (Zech. 14.20–21).

Thus far then little moral content to the word *q-d-sh* has been suggested. In its early usage it bore virtually none at all. Yet, when it was later applied to God, as well as to things divine, the word became an attempt to express the conception of that total otherness which is the mark of what is neither mortal nor created. When, for example, Moses sought to approach the Burning Bush, he heard the words: 'Draw not nigh hither, for the place whereon thou standest is holy ground' (Ex. 3.5). Moses was a human creature, the mountain was *tapu*, and so it was filled with the *mana* of God. Moreover, when it was the turn of the Israelites as a whole to approach this 'holy' mount, Yahweh then commanded Moses: 'Go unto the people and sanctify (*hiqdish*) them . . . for Yahweh will come down in the sight of all the people unto mount Sinai' (Ex. 19.10–11). The instructions continue (v. 12) 'And thou

---

[4] See Ernst Jenni, *Die Theologische Begrundung des Sabbatgebotes im AT*, 1956.

[5] See Johs. Pedersen, op. cit., III–IV, 1940, pp. 264 ff.; A. Richardson, *A Theological Wordbook of the Bible*, 1950, art. 'Saint' by O.S. Rankin; etc.

shalt set bounds unto the people round about saying, Take heed to yourselves, that ye go not up into the mount, or touch the border of it, whosoever toucheth the mount shall be surely put to death'. The mountain carried a high electric charge, as it were. To put foot on it would give a man, or even a domestic animal (v. 13) a shock sufficient to cause death.[6]

But God could be present, not only at Sinai; he could be anywhere else that he made his name to dwell. Thus when Uzzah touched the Ark, in all innocence, as it seems, he too was immediately 'electrocuted' (I Sam. 6.19; II Sam. 6.6–7). That structure belonged to God, therefore it was filled with Yahweh's *mana*, and thus was utterly 'holy'.

The story of Jacob's dream (Gen. 28.10–22) demonstrates a development in content of the word *qadhosh*. The story cannot of course show any greater seriousness in regard to the idea that God and man are wholly other than does the story of Moses' encounter with God upon the mount. We read that when Jacob awakes from his dream, he exclaims: 'Surely Yahweh is in this place, and I knew it not. And he was afraid, and said, How dreadful is this place! this is none other but the house of God, and this is the gate of heaven' (vv. 16–17). Here then we have the element of 'exaltedness' added to the concept of 'otherness', and thus by complementing it, giving the word 'holiness' a new depth of meaning. The writings of D and P in particular ever seek to show the moral excellence of God. They at least are fully aware of this profounder nuance borne by the idea of holiness.

A deeper significance still, however, is traceable in the use of the word in such a passage as Josh. 24.19. There Joshua declares: 'Ye cannot serve Yahweh: for he is an holy God; he is a jealous God; he will not forgive your transgressions nor your sins.' Holiness here, then, is separation, not only from man as man, but also from man as sinner.

We have no right either to despise the ancient stories of the early books of the OT or to imagine that the ideas represented therein about the holy God may be dismissed as 'primitive'. It is

---

[6]   See W.A.L. Elmslie, *How Came Our Faith*, 1948, p. 66.

the religious content of the stories that is vital for an understanding of OT theology, and not their simple form. Too lightly
and easily men speak today of the Creator of the heavens and the
earth in chatty terms. They speak of God as the kindly Friend in
heaven, or as the Big Brother at their side. In thought and prayer
they approach him with careless irreverence. No stories could
express more clearly the awe-ful otherness of God from man than
the Sinai stories or that of the destruction of Uzzah. So we set
aside the significance of those stories at our peril, even though we
would express the reality of God's holiness in other forms today.
Right throughout the OT, in fact, God is regarded as wholly and
utterly distinct from his universe. Never is there the least suggestion in it of pantheism; God is never identified there with the
universe he has made. In the biblical view, God is ever and always
LORD. 'The heaven and the heaven of heavens is the Lord's thy
God, the earth also, and all that therein is' (Deut. 10.14; I Kings
8.27; II Chron. 2.5; 6.18). He sits *above* or *upon* his creation
(Ps. 24.2), and sees the nations beneath him as a drop of a bucket
(Isa. 40.15).

Finally and last in our ascending order of understanding of
God's holiness, we turn to Isaiah's great vision of God recorded
for us in Isa. 6. Here the word 'holy' represents a conception for
which there are really no human words available. As the angels
chant in chorus: 'Holy, holy, holy, is the Lord of hosts', they use
the word to represent what we try to understand when we speak
of God's total perfection of being. Now, though God is here
utterly other than his created world, he is not 'other' in the sense
of transcendence alone. God is not separated from his world by
distance, i.e. by what we know either as space or time. He is
separated from it by the sin with which it is diffused.[7] And yet
there immediately follows a paradox in the wording chosen to
represent God's relation to this sinful world. Despite the fact that
the whole earth lies in sin, Isaiah becomes aware that the 'glory'
of God suffuses and pervades that same sinful universe (Isa. 6.3).

---

[7]   Cf. I. Efros, 'Holiness and Glory in the Bible', *JQR*, April, 1951,
p. 365.

Not only so, but he learns that that glory becomes known to sinful man as forgiving, creative, purposeful action. Thus once again we have reached a matter with which we cannot deal until on a later page we discuss the relationship of Israel to her God.

Isaiah's vision now leads us to examine the second great word used in the OT to describe what God is like in himself, viz. 'glory'.

The Hebrew root *k-b-d* meant 'heavy', in a literal sense.[8] But it was used as well of a man who was heavy with possessions, and who was therefore 'rich'. In the East a rich man received honour. A noun from this Hebrew root can therefore mean 'honour' as well. But if he received honour, the rich man also received 'glory' from his neighbours; in fact his possessions were his glory. His possessions were not, of course, the man himself. Rather, they were the outer aspect of his inner character. We can usually make some judgement upon the character of a man or woman from the clothes they wear, or from the manner in which they furnish a room. The 'successful' man is certainly known from the kind of possessions which he values. These represent their owner, in other words. Their owner's personality is made visible by this 'hem of his garment'. Now, this is just the kind of thinking that the OT employs when it applies the word 'glory' to God. Thus it is that 'the heavens declare the glory of God' (Ps. 19.1); 'let all the earth be filled with his glory' (Ps. 72.19); 'in his temple doth everyone speak of his glory' (Ps. 29.9); he is in fact the 'King of glory' (Ps. 24.7–10).

The idea of glory, translated as it is by several nouns, covers many aspects of God's self-manifestation to man of his essential nature. (*a*) Certain physical phenomena are spoken of in this light. The pillar of fire and cloud, for example, are said to contain God's glory, *kabhodh* (Ex. 16.10; Lev. 9.23–24). (*b*) Certain of the Psalms on occasions use the parallel nouns *hodh* and *hadhar*, with *kabhodh*, and speak of God's 'clothing himself' in the beauty or glory of the heavens (Ps. 93.1; 104.1). (*c*) The glory of God's self-manifestation in the heavens is understood under what is almost a quasi-metaphysical term, viz. 'radiance', *nogah*: 'At the

---

[8] See *OHL*, ad loc.

brightness that was before him his thick clouds passed' (II Sam. 22.13 = Ps. 18.12). (*d*) The glory may even manifest itself in signs and wonders, as at the time when Israel came out of Egypt (Ex. 16.7). (*e*) But the idea of glory may abandon all physical and material associations and represent nothing less than the ethical nature of God. 'The Lord of hosts shall be exalted in judgement, and God that is holy shall be sanctified in righteousness' (Isa. 5.16). (*f*) Finally, God's ethical nature as *kabhodh* may be conceived as objectively separable from God himself, and as residing in the Tabernacle (Ex. 40.34, P), and later in Solomon's Temple (I Kings 8.11, D)[9] even though of course, God himself dwelt 'in heaven'.[10]

In chapter 2 we saw that man's physical organs may express in action the totality of the will and purpose of his *nephesh*. Now, nowhere in the OT is it explicitly stated that Yahweh is, or has, a *nephesh*, like man. Yet on several occasions a possessive adjective is added to the noun *nephesh* to form a kind of substitute for the idea of 'self'. As we must keep reminding ourselves, God's essence is divinity, while man's is only personality. However, the '*imago dei*' language of the early chapters of Genesis implies that God must be conceived as *nephesh*, even though the phrase 'God's *nephesh*' never occurs as such. Let us now look at the actual uses of the word that do occur, with Yahweh as subject. In Judg. 10.16 we find the phrase: 'His *nephesh* was grieved'. I Sam. 2.35 runs: 'According to that which is in my heart and in my *nephesh*'. Job 23.13 says 'What his *nephesh* desireth even that he doeth'. Jer. 9.9 has: 'Shall not my *nephesh* be avenged on such a nation as this?', and again Jer. 12.7 runs: 'I have given the dearly-beloved of my *nephesh* into the hand of her enemies'. Amos 6.8 exclaims: 'The Lord Yahweh has sworn by his *nephesh*'; while in Isa. 42.1 the word seems even more explicitly to mean God's 'self' even though it carries the suffix 'my': 'Behold my servant . . . in whom my *nephesh* delighteth'. The fact that in Isa. 46.2 the word is used of the false gods of Babylon only adds to the force of the argument

---

[9]   Efros, ibid., p. 367.
[10]   J. Abrahams, *The Glory of God*, 1925, p. 26. He insists, with Bennett and Driver, upon the original ethical nature of Glory.

that the nature of any divinity could be considered in terms of personality. A justifiable translation of this last verse would then be 'their persons have gone into captivity'. This is just the language used elsewhere of the Spirit of God, when the word Spirit is employed virtually as a substitute for the divine name. This practice is particularly apparent in the post-exilic writings: cf. Ps. 51.11; Isa. 61.1; 63.10; Hag. 2.5; Zech. 4.6; 6.8; 7.12; etc. In the case of the passage Isa. 63.10, the phrase 'the Spirit of God' is exactly paralleled by that other 'the Face of God', which has been before us already.

Since Yahweh had hands, eyes, arms, and so on, the Hebrews were naturally compelled to picture him as a man writ large. The Ancient of Days, the old man with the long white beard, is naturally by no means the only such picture of God with which the OT presents us (Dan. 7.9, 13). Thus it is understandable when men say that God *acts*, and that he acts in the same way as a human *nephesh* acts, although we may not feel inclined to press the relevant Hebrew instances to form the conclusion that God is a *nephesh* himself. Yet we possess an instance where the verb built from the noun *nephesh* is used of God as if he were man. 'For in six days Yahweh made heaven and earth, and on the seventh day he rested, *way-yinnaphesh*, and he "took-a-deep-breath-and-was-thus-refreshed-in-his-*nephesh*".'[11]

In the case of man, it is the organs of flesh, his *basar*, which express his inner being and will. What then can the OT say of God, who is Spirit, and who cannot by the very nature of things be said to have a body? Actually, the OT does picture God as having a body, though of course that body cannot be composed of what man knows as *basar*. It is just here that the concept of glory is employed, for it is through his glory that the hidden God of the OT principally expresses his essential Self to man.

There are instances where even man's body is his glory. It so happens that the consonants for 'liver' and 'glory' are identical, so that even from the context it is not always clear which is meant.

---

[11] One meaning of the verbal root of the word, cognate with the Assyrian usage, is 'to get breath'. The reference is to Ex. 20.11.

Ps. 16.9, e.g., presents us with a strange parallel, 'Therefore my heart is glad and my glory rejoiceth: my flesh also shall rest in hope'. Instead of 'glory' we would be justified in reading 'liver', and thus be able to refer to three organs of the human body in succession. On the other hand, the Psalmist, conscious of the ambiguity of the consonants *k-b-d*, may have indeed intended a *double entendre* when he penned his line.[12] In the case of the divine Being, however, his 'glory' is certainly that metaphysical entity in the realm of spirit which is the counterpart of what man knows as flesh. Yet God's glory is not the equivalent of his Spirit. Glory is the outward manifestation of Spirit, *as if* (cf. Ezek. 1.28) God wore Glory as his apparel.

Once again the argument from the adjective 'living' as applied to God obtains. Glory must be as truly living as the human flesh which clothes a living man is living. We have seen that the angels bore a relation to God analogous to that which flames bear to the fire. Angels are, of course, living beings. So then the glory of God is living in the sense that they too are living. They have their source in God, as the flames have their source in the heart of the Fire: 'Who maketh his angels spirits, and his ministers flaming fire' (Ps. 104.4). Similarly, God's Glory is described by the device of paralleling it with the noun *nogah*, 'brightness', 'brilliance' (Ezek. 10.4); cf. Isa. 60.3 (= 'light'); Heb. 3.4. See p. 95.

A.M. Ramsey has pointed out[13] that nowhere are the *tensions* of biblical theology greater than in the concept of glory. On the one hand, glory represents, metaphysically speaking, the invisible and omnipresent God: 'The glory of Yahweh filled the house' (II Chron. 5.14); 'The whole earth is full of his glory' (Isa. 6.3). On the other hand, glory is characterized as a meteorological phenomenon: 'The glory of Yahweh abode upon mount Sinai' (Ex. 24.16); 'All those men which have seen my glory' (Num. 14.22). At times again the concept of glory seems to be a mixture of the two. Thus Ezekiel seems to feel that when the glory of God

---

[12] The consonants *may* be wrongly vowelled in Gen. 49.6; Ps. 7.5; 30.13 (Heb.); 57.9 (Heb.); 108.2 (Heb.).

[13] *The Glory of God and the Transfiguration of Christ*, 1949, p. 22.

departed from the Temple (Ezek. 10.4) it 'went up' and away as if it had the very wings of an angel. Just as the holiness of God is understood in the last resort in terms of God's saving purpose, so too is his glory. This is because Yahweh is actually accounted to be 'the Glory of Israel'! (Jer. 2.11; Ps. 106.20; cf. Isa. 60.1–3; Micah 1.15; Ps. 3.3; Hab. 2.14; I Chron. 16.24).

We have now handled two great OT words, viz., Holiness and Glory, both of which represent aspects of a conception which, paradoxically speaking, human words cannot describe, viz., the inscrutable God who reveals himself. We shall do no more at this point therefore than draw attention to another important biblical picture-concept, one which unites as one the two great words we have examined, particularly when we find the OT speaking of God's Being in terms of flesh or matter. It is the frequently recurring figure of Light or Fire. But since the primary use of this figure is to be found in connexion with God's redemptive purpose for Israel, we shall require to return to it later. At the moment, however, we may observe how the double figure of Light – Fire is often able to pictorialize the more abstract conceptions covered by the words Holiness and Glory. 'The Lord is my light' (Ps. 27.1); 'O send out thy light' (Ps. 43.3); 'Who coverest thyself with light as with a garment' (Ps. 104.2) – these are all examples of the first half of the double figure. In examples of the second half of the figure, however, we are undoubtedly aware of the tension caused by the intrusion of the meteorological element. 'The Lord thy God is a consuming fire' says Deut. 4.24; this is no surprise, since 'the mountain burned with fire' (Deut. 4.11). Mount Sinai was possibly a volcano in eruption in Moses' day. Many biblical scholars believe this, and place the mount to the east of the Gulf of Aqaba, where the region is volcanic.[14] The concept of fire, as we shall see however, developed greatly in the sweep of its meaning.

Fire, then, is made visible in the form of flames. 'The angel . . . appeared . . . in a flame of fire' (Ex. 3.2). Here then we have the

---

[14] See W.J. Phythian-Adams, *The Call of Israel*, 1934, pp. 140–54; A. Lods, *Israel*, 1932, pp. 79–80; W.A.L. Elmslie, *How Came our Faith*, 1948, p. 207.

effective will of God now made manifest to human consciousness. 'The angel . . . ascended in the flame' (Judg. 13.20). 'Yahweh shall cause the glory of his voice to be heard . . . with the flame of a devouring fire' (Isa. 30.30). Now, one Hebrew word for angel is 'seraph'. The root *s-r-p* means 'to burn'. The noun from this root, however, was used also of two kinds of serpent. It was the name of a particularly venomous serpent, whose poisonous bite 'burned' its victim (Num. 21.8); and it was the name of a flying serpent or dragon (Isa. 14.29; 30.6), an animal that was evidently equally venomous! Yet this very word which he uses elsewhere for a flying fiery serpent is the word which Isaiah employs to describe the angels whom he sees in his inaugural vision (Isa. 6.2, 6). Before Isaiah's adoption of the word in this way the seraph was probably a serpent deity. Actually, the instigating factor in his vision may have been the brazen serpent which seems to have been preserved in the Temple right up till a period in Isaiah's lifetime subsequent to his vision (II Kings 18.4). The word may be related both to an Egyptian and an Assyrian root. But it is not important where Isaiah found the idea. What is important is the use he made of it in the description of his vision. In Gen. 3.24 it is Cherubim who guard the Garden of Eden with swords of fire. But here we have the related angelic beings known as Seraphim virtually pictured as the flames of God's glory themselves, performing his will, and rejoicing, within the 'family relationship' of the heavenly places, at the wonder and mystery of the holiness of God.

The contents of the last few paragraphs may have added little to our understanding of the significance of the two great Hebrew words for Holiness and Glory. We have introduced them here, however, since the concept of the Fires of God is a vitally important figure for an understanding of God's redemptive activity in and through his people Israel. Consequently we shall be led to return to the figure at a later point in our inquiry.

Nine

The So-Called 'Natural' Divine Attributes

We dare not evade the real issues of OT theology and seek to escape exact definitions by taking refuge in the fluidity of its picture language. It is one thing to say that we can no longer speak today of the separate 'attributes' of God, as men did till a generation ago; it is another thing to deny that the God of the OT is described in terms of what we would term his 'natural divine attributes'.

On the one hand, nothing exists apart from God (Isa. 45.6), only *'ephes*, 'lack', 'negativity', 'non-existence'. Yet, on the other hand God, if he wills, can be anywhere. That, of course, means that there is only one God. Yet the one God is not necessarily to be understood as omnipresent. Abstract terms such as omnipresence, omniscience, and so on, are, indeed, foreign to the OT world of thought, and do not exist in the Hebrew language. Instead of such abstractions what we find expressed in the OT is just what we would expect to find, viz., descriptive terms of God in action. Psalm 139 uses language more closely allied to our modern conception of 'natural divine attributes' than any other passage in the OT. Yet even it confines itself to picture language, and to descriptions of God in action. 'If I ascend up into heaven, thou art there: if I make my bed in Sheol, behold thou art there' (Ps. 139.8). This is the Psalmist's way of saying that God can be anywhere he wishes at any time. That is to say, he is not *every*where, because there is no*where* apart from him. But he can be *effectively* present *any*where; and this paradoxical truth is evident even though God himself fills heaven and earth (Jer. 23.24). Thus he may reveal himself specially to individual men, even while he hides himself from them. So he may be both near and far at the same time (Jer. 23.23).

Let us list a few commonly accepted 'natural' divine attributes, and see what descriptive passages the OT can produce to cover such ideas.

God is eternal. 'Before the mountains were brought forth, or ever thou hadst formed the earth and the world, even from everlasting to everlasting thou art God' (Ps. 90.2). But as in the case of God's omnipresence, so here again we are presented with a paradox. The essence of the paradox lies in the meaning of the Hebrew phrase 'for ever'. Although God is 'eternal', he lives 'for ever', *le 'olam*, e.g. Deut. 32.40: 'I lift up my hand to heaven, and say, I live for ever'. Expressed as it is thus in English, 'eternal' and 'for ever' would seem to be identical notions. But in Hebrew this is not so. The expression *le 'olam* (for ever) does not contain within it the conception of eternity as distinct from immensity of time. By the use of the noun *'olam* men sought rather to describe the longest duration that the human mind could conceive. The word could point in both directions, both backwards and forwards in time. Thus, *min 'olam* means virtually 'from the beginning of creation'. It is applied therefore to God's promises to man on this earth, which have stood ever since God created man; and it is applied equally to the duration of man's existence on the earth in days to come: 'I will cause you to dwell in this place, in the land that I gave to your fathers, for ever and ever' (Jer. 7.7). The OT has nothing specific to say about the divine activity before creation and after the end of this world of space and time. Yet the noun *'olam* embraces the ideas both of space and time. Time only began to be meaningful at that point in history when God brought his people out of Egypt (this is the subject of a later section); so too when God's plan and purpose shall reach fruition then both time and this world will cease to have the significance that they bear today. It is for this reason, then, that God's words 'I live for ever', although true in an absolute sense, are here to be understood in the context of God's self-emptying, in that he should have dealings at all with his own creation inside space and time.

God is unchanging. 'A thousand years in thy sight are but as yesterday when it is past' (Ps. 90.4). 'I, the Lord, the first, and with the last; I am he' (Isa. 41.4). 'I am the Lord, I change not' (Mal. 3.6). Yet, here again, the God who does not change may, paradoxically speaking, both (*a*) 'become with' his people (see chap. 3), and (*b*) change his mind or his plan. Such is the meaning of the verb 'to repent', *niham*, when applied to God: 'The Lord repented of the evil which he thought to do unto his people' (Ex. 32.14). In this case, again, it is obvious that the question of the unchanging God changing must be bound up with his self-emptying in his relationship with his people Israel.

God is transcendent. He is *ram*, high, above his whole creation (Ps. 99.2). 'He that sitteth upon the circle (vault) of the earth' (Isa. 40.22).

God is omniscient. 'Thou knowest my downsitting and my uprising, thou understandest my thought afar off' (Ps. 139.2); 'There is no searching of his understanding' (Isa. 40.28).

God is omnipotent. 'The darkness and the light are both alike to thee' (Ps. 139.12); 'he taketh up the isles as a very little thing' (Isa. 40.15). He can do what he pleases (Ps. 115.3; Dan. 4.25, 35), even with the beasts of the earth (Jer. 27.5–6).

God is creator. 'Lift up your eyes on high, and behold who has created these things, that bringeth out their host (the stars) by number: he calleth them all by names by the greatness of his might, for that he is strong in power; not one faileth'. (Isa. 40.26). 'In the beginning, when God created the heavens and the earth . . . ' (Gen. 1.1). Yet not only did he create in the beginning, he keeps his creation continually renewed: 'Thou, even thou, art Lord alone; thou hast made heaven, the heaven of heavens, with all their host, the earth, and all that are therein, the seas, and all that is therein, and thou *preservest* them all' (mehayyeh 'keep in life' Neh. 9.6; Ps. 66.9). And what God does for the earth and the beasts he does for man as well: 'The people which shall be created (*'am nibhra'*) shall praise the Lord' (Ps. 102.18). Even more, as Sovereign Lord of all, God can, if he wills, bring to an end the universe he has created and which he now keeps in being: 'Of old hast thou laid the foundation of the earth: and the heavens are the work of thy hands. They shall perish, but thou shalt endure' (Ps. 102.25–26).

God is described in the OT, then, as Sovereign Lord of all, as King and Creator of the ends of the earth. He is recognized to be omnipotent, omniscient, unchanging and eternal. On the other hand, there are other categories by which God is described in the OT, some of them aspects of the categories we have just examined, which are so searching and so profound that the mind of men could never have imagined them. Yet, if *per impossibile* he had indeed done so, he would never have dared to apply them to Almighty God. This is because they are categories, not of might, but of humility. Indeed, they refer to a humility so deep that they are beyond the grasp both of man's intellectual powers and of his moral understanding. So deep are they, in fact, that 'natural' man does not observe that they exist for him or present him with a problem at all. It is only those whose hearts are enlightened by the Holy Spirit who can even begin to penetrate to them, and to see what they mean for a sinful world.

Part Two

God and Creation

Ten

The Primal Chaos

We began Part One of this Theology of the OT by quoting the first verses of Genesis, thus: 'When, in the beginning, God created the heavens and the earth, and the earth was without form and void . . . ' The English words 'without form and void', however, are a poor substitute for the finely alliterative Hebrew words in the original – *tohu wa-bhohu*. What is the significance of those curious terms, and why should the Genesis narrative continue with the words: 'and darkness was upon the face of the deep'?

It was a great gain to theology as a whole when last century parallels to the Genesis stories were discovered. The archaeologist at that time gave the world the literature of other ancient Near Eastern peoples. These supplemented what we have in the OT of the early literature of the people of Israel. This other literature must have been known to some at least of the thinkers of Israel. On the one hand, Abraham had reached Palestine originally from Babylonia, and on the other hand, Israel had dwelt for long in Egypt. Again, she was a near neighbour to that civilization which has left us the so-called Ras Shamra documents, which were discovered only at the end of the nineteen twenties. Thus the early writers of the Pentateuch would surely know the stories of Creation, of a Garden of Eden, of a Flood, and so on, that were the common property, in various forms, of the nations in the midst of whom Israel dwelt. Moreover, Israel was forcibly returned to the land of Abraham. In the Exile in Babylonia Israel met with the legends and lore of the East at that point in her life when she had reached maturity of thought. However, it is not the relationship of Israel's version of those stories to the versions of the other nations which is our immediate concern. It is rather the use made by Israel of those stories, stemming as they do from a common stock. The Hebrew people borrowed much from neighbouring lands. But in everything that they took over from others they effected a radical transformation.

According to the religious thought common to the peoples of the Mesopotamian plain, 'in the beginning' the divine parents Apsu and Tiamat, and their son Mummu existed. 'Apsu was the primeval sweet-water ocean, and Tiamat the salt-water ocean, while Mummu probably represented the mist rising from the two bodies of water and hovering over them . . . These three types of water were mingled in one, forming an immense, undefined mass in which were contained all the elements of which afterward the universe was made'.[1] As the myth is passed down over the centuries, however, we find it difficult to differentiate between Tiamat the chaotic watery ocean itself, and Tiamat the monster that dwelt in that salty sea. Thus when we compare the several forms of the myth as it was recounted in Israel's day by Israel's neighbours, we are confronted with a fusion of ideas.

Common to them all is the conception that there was in the beginning of time a Monster of Chaos. In Babylonia he was named Tiamat, in Indic he was known as Vrta, while amongst the Greeks he took the form of the monster Typhon.

The genius of the Hebrews, on the other hand, was to moralize this mythological concept. It would be entirely natural if in those pre-scientific days they thought as the rest of the world thought about the origin of the earth and the continued working of the heavenly bodies. But one important difference that marked the Hebrews off from all other peoples of ancient times was just the use they made of this and other common stocks of mythological material.

---

[1]   A. Heidel, *The Babylonian Genesis*, second edition, 1951, p. 3. For the text of the myth, see E.A. Speiser, *Ancient Near Eastern Texts relating to the Old Testament*, ed. J.B. Pritchard, 1950, pp. 60–72.

We must make it clear to ourselves what the Hebrews actually did in this regard. It is not sufficient for us merely to suggest that our priestly writer changed the idea of a god of chaos into a concept of chaos as such; it was not just that he changed a primeval battle of the gods into an orderly creative act by the one and only God who manipulated for his own ends and purposes the dead matter (and not living gods) which he had at his disposal. So far as the priestly writer did make such changes he produced great and significant differences from, for example, the Babylonian version of the myth. The great contribution of the priestly writer, however, was nothing less than to remove the whole conception of creation out of the realm, not only of myth, but also from the concepts of space and time, and to tell the mighty story of the beginning of all things in terms, not of time, but of purpose. The first chapters of Genesis do not relate a series of early cosmogonic myths now spiritualized, and made to subserve an early theory of the origin of the world. These chapters are a theological exposition, in picture language, such as the Hebrews have always excelled in creating, of the reason for the call of Israel out of Egypt at a historical moment occurring within this very flesh and blood world of space and time. Consequently we do not find in the OT any discussion of 'creation' in the sense in which modern scientific man is interested.[2] The book of Genesis is no scientific textbook dealing with the creation of matter or of time. On the other hand it is with the moral purpose of God that the OT is deeply concerned, and with God's relation to that humanity whom he has, indeed, created. So it is that through humanity, and through God's relation to that humanity, the very idea of 'creation' alone takes on meaning and design.

The Biblical Narrative

Let us now turn to the biblical story. The first chapter of Genesis has nothing whatsoever to tell us about God and what God was

[2]   The verb *q-n-h* is only an apparent exception. It is as vague in meaning as is the English verb 'to get'. So it can mean 'get', 'beget', 'buy', 'possess', etc. Cf. Deut. 32.6; Prov. 8.22; Ps. 78.54; or Gen. 4.1. The problem of its meaning therefore arises in Ex. 15.16 and Ps. 74.2.

doing before he began to create. The verb *bara'* (create) itself (Gen. 1.1 tells us little that the modern scientifically minded person seeks to know. We do not know, for example, whether *bara'* means '*creatio ex nihilo*' or not, or whether its chief emphasis is upon the fashioning of something new. It occurs in parallel with the every-day verb '*asah*, 'to make', and elsewhere in parallel with *hotsi'*, 'to bring forth', and with *yatsar*, 'to fashion'. But the verb *bara'* always has God as subject, and represents an act proper to divinity alone. Moreover, its subject is almost always Yahweh, except in Gen. 1 and in a few passages that have been retouched in the course of transmission such as the so-called Elohim Psalms (Pss. 42–83). Then again, it is a verb which is hardly found till the Exile experience interpreted the ways of God to Israel. Thereafter it bears a nuance covering the conception not only of the creation of Israel but of its recreation, a conception which will demand our attention in a moment (cf. Isa. 48.7; 65.17; Ps. 51.10; 104.30).[3]

The primary emphasis of the word in Genesis, however, is that God produced order out of chaos, and light out of darkness. That is to say, we are not given an explanation of the source of Darkness and Chaos; but we are told that God is in control of both, and can use them for his purposes. We are not told that God created Darkness, but he grants it the right to exist by giving it a name. We are told that God's Spirit, that is to say, his creative purpose in action, in a form conceivable by the thought of man, 'brooded' (not 'moved', *r-ḥ-p*, v. 2) upon the surface of the primal chaotic watery mass. The only other occasion when this verb occurs is in Deut. 32.1. There it is used of an eagle hovering or brooding over her young. The mother eagle has a loving purpose in so doing. She is doing no less than fostering new life by her loving act.

And God SAID: 'Let there be light – and light *became*' (Gen. 1.3). The Word became flesh. The Word is that which issues from the heart of God, and the heart of God is no less than God himself; the Word of God is thus the Will of God in action. Something that

---

[3]   See Paul Humbert, 'Emploi et porteé du verbe bara' (créer) dans l'AT', *TZ*, 3. Jahrgang, Heft 6, Nov./Dec. 1947, pp. 401 ff. II Macc. 7.28 is the first passage to express explicitly the conception of *creatio ex nihilo*.

proceeded from God therefore became a thing, became a portion of God's created matter. God who is high and lifted up, God who is LORD, and who is holy, and whose glory he will not give to another, that God created from his own being a 'thing'. That thing was now, paradoxically, no longer God, though it had issued from him, and was originally 'with' God; for it was now standing over against God, separated from his holy self. This thing, though, this Light, was a good thing (Gen. 1.31), because it had emanated from the heart of the good God.

Once more the mystery of the unexplained Darkness confronts us. The Light was good. But God divided the Light from that other thing, that thing which God called Darkness. For Darkness is not good. Darkness must be kept distinctly separate from Light, which is altogether good. Just as we are not told where Darkness comes from, so we are not told where *tohu* and *bohu* come from, nor the formless chaotic watery ocean over which God's creative purpose brooded in the beginning.

We must keep reminding ourselves that Gen. 1 does not contain any analytical description either of a physical entity known as Darkness or of a metaphysical one summed up thus pictorially. Rather it offers a description of a theological reality. No more does the Bible tell us where the Darkness and Chaos come from that reside both in the human soul and in the corporate life of nations. But what the Bible goes on to describe is that at a point in history from which Gen. 1 takes its meaning, Chaos ruled in a land called Egypt, where a people called Israel was forced to make bricks without straw.

Israel's Identification of Chaos[4]

'And the Lord spake unto Moses and unto Aaron saying, When Pharaoh shall speak unto you saying, Shew a miracle for you: then

---

[4] For the manner in which some other nations identified it, see T.H. Gaster, 'The Egyptian "Story of Astarte" and the Ugaritic Poem of Baal', *BO*, IX, 1952, p. 82.

thou shalt say unto Aaron, Take thy rod, and cast it before Pharaoh, and it shall become a serpent' (Ex. 7.9). This last word, serpent, is *tannin* in Hebrew.[5] *Tannin* is our monster or dragon of chaos common to the various mythologies of the ancient Near East. He went under other names as well. He was sometimes equated in Israel's thinking with the chaotic ocean itself, as if he personalized it, in the same way as the Babylonians thought. We find such an equation in Job 7.12 and Ps. 74.13. In those passages, and perhaps also in Job 3.8,[6] *yam*, the Sea, is paralleled with tannin, the personified Deep. This is the same word as *yammu* of the Ugaritic myths.[7] Again, he bore the name of Leviathan. 'There is that leviathan, whom thou hast made to play' (in the sea) (Ps. 104.26); 'Thou breakest the bands of leviathan in pieces' (Ps. 74.14). In the previous verse our monster had just been called *tannin*, in its plural form, evidence both that tannin and leviathan were two names for the same creature, and that the concept of Chaos was conceived as both one and many at the same time, in the manner true to Israel's thinking to which we have already referred. This is true also of another word for 'monster', viz. *behemah*, as in Ps. 73.22. Isa. 27.1 shows that our monster could be *visualized* as a serpent: 'In that day the Lord with his sore and great strong sword shall punish leviathan the piercing serpent, even leviathan that crooked serpent; and he shall slay the dragon, tannin, that is in the sea'.

So it was that Yahweh commanded Moses to let Pharaoh discover that he, Yahweh, was in control of all things, even of the primal Deep, whether personified as Leviathan, or pictured as a Dragon, or merely envisaged as a chaotic Ocean. But Pharaoh

---

[5]   Though *nahash* in J's narrative (Ex. 4.3).

[6]   See G.R. Driver, 'Problems in the Hebrew Text of Job', in *Wisdom in Israel and the Ancient Near East*, 1955, p. 72.

[7]   Th. Gaster, op. cit., BO IX, 1952, p. 82, believes that in that ancient myth about the god who defeated the marine monster and installed himself in a newly-built palace we have 'a kind of undertone' to the Song of the Sea in Ex. 15, especially vv. 8–10 See also J.B. Pritchard, *ANET*, 1950, pp. 42 ff.; and C.H. Gordon, *Ugaritic Handbook*, 1947, III, 34, for *tannin*.

would not heed the demonstrated Word of Yahweh. In consequence there took place the Exodus of the People of God from the land of slavery, the land of Darkness, of evil and chaos. It is interesting to note what happened thereafter in the thinking of Israel. The Pharaoh himself later became the Dragon, and the land of Egypt the Monster whom God must overwhelm. As well as the name of Leviathan, Isaiah uses the West-Semitic form of the name for Leviathan, or for the Babylonian Tiamat (the latter being visible in the Hebrew word for 'deep', *tehom*, Gen. 1.2), viz., Rahab. 'For Egypt's help is worthless and empty, therefore I have called her "Rahab who sits still" ' (Isa. 30.7 ARSV). Egypt is like a great, fat, blubbery whale, or some other monster of the Deep, stranded helpless at the mouth of the Nile.

The destruction of the Egyptian army, then, with Pharaoh at its head, was the actuation on earth, at a specific moment in space and time, of God's victory over the Deep and the darkness of night: 'Awake, awake, put on strength, O arm of the Lord; awake, as in days of old, the generations of long ago. Was it not thou that didst cut Rahab in pieces, that didst pierce the dragon, *tannin*? Was it not thou that didst dry up the sea, the waters of the great deep, *tehom*; that didst make the depths of the sea a way for the redeemed to pass over?' (Isa. 51.9–10 ARSV). It is obvious to us that this passage from the pen of Deutero-Isaiah is a conscious piece of theological writing. His material comes down to us from the same generation as the priestly editor of Genesis. It is evident that both he and P must have had before them the more 'factual' story left them by J, in which the latter described how the wind (and perhaps an earthquake) rendered the shallow Reed Sea (*yam suph*) crossable by the People of God on foot. But Deutero-Isaiah speaks, not of *yam suph*, but of the primal Ocean. The crossing of the Red (or Reed) Sea and the defeat of Pharaoh were nothing less than the revelation of God's primal victory over the chaotic Ocean which he had already won in the beginning'. It was not only a 'negative' victory however of which the OT speaks. God's action represented not only the conquest of evil. It was also a positive victory. Out of the waters of the Red Sea came forth a People redeemed and blessed: 'O Lord God of hosts, who is a mighty one like thee, O Yah . . . thou rulest the raging of the sea: When the waves thereof arise, thou stillest them. Thou hast broken Rahab in pieces . . . thou hast scattered thine enemies with thy strong arm . . . Blessed is the people that know the joyful (trumpet) sound; they shall walk, O Yahweh, in the light (cf. Gen. 1.3) of thy countenance' (Ps. 89.8–10, 15). The great poem in Ex. 15 which rejoices in the redemption of Israel from Egypt, expresses itself in the same vein as our Psalm. For we read in v. 8 that what congealed in the heart of the Red Sea was no less than the primal ocean, *tehom*, itself. The passage in Isa. 63, which has already been before us in Part I, makes the same claim for the nature of the waters through which Israel passed (v. 13); and so too in the case of the poem interpolated in the book of Habakkuk, as it sings of God's mighty acts.

In the beginning, then, God overcame the powers of Darkness and of the Chaotic Ocean. This primal victory of God, however, was not understood by Israel thus theologically till later years. It was only when Israel was well and truly settled in her promised land that she could look back upon God's redemptive act in bringing his people out of Egypt and see it in the light of what the priestly writer later expounds as he speaks of the beginning of all things. It was left to Deutero-Isaiah and the priestly school, speaking out of the 'existential' experience of the Exile that Israel went through, out of the depths of the horrors of being overwhelmed in the deep, to present in verse and to sing for the first time in the world's history a new and profound meaning to the creative activity of Israel's God, 'in the beginning'. He it was who linked up the creation of Israel with Israel's redemption (Isa. 43.1; 44.24). On the other hand, the great prophets both before and after the Exile were fully aware that, though God had undoubtedly overcome the forces of evil and though the victory had truly been won 'in the beginning', yet those forces still pressed in upon Israel and her life (cf. Isa. 17.12–13). The whole ordered world could possibly return to chaos, as Jeremiah saw in a vision (Jer. 4.23–29; cf. Isa. 34.11). In fact the individual souls of men and women within Israel knew what it was to dwell within the chaos of primal disorder, and to harbour the deeps of *tehom* within their hearts. If to walk in obedience to the will of God was to walk within the Light (Ps. 27.1; 43.3; 119.105), then to rebel against God was to go down into the depths of tehom. It is obvious from the contents of the book that bears his name, that Jonah the prophet is to be understood as the personification of the people of Israel as a whole.[8] When Jonah, we recall, refused to do the will of God, he left the light, and went down into the depths of *tehom* (Jonah 2.5). There the waters invaded and overwhelmed his very soul, his *nephesh* (v. 5)[9]

Chaos and the Individual

The chaotic waters of *tehom* which lay above and below the visible firmament (Gen. 1.6–7; 49.25; Ex. 20.4; Deut. 33.13) at its creation, are therefore still present in the life of man. They not only overhang and undergird the earth; they do the same with the souls of men. God is undoubtedly in control of the chaotic ocean, yet just as undoubtedly he permits it to remain as part of his created universe. At any moment the 'windows of heaven' could open, and the fountains of the great *tehom* (Gen. 7.11, not 'sea') could well up from below and the whole world of men could be overwhelmed as in the days of Noah. It is only of the mercy of God that this catastrophe does not recur (Gen. 9.8–17). God is able at any time to contend finally with the 'great *tehom*' and burn it up with the fire of his zeal (Amos 7.4). That is why, when the waters close over his head, the individual Israelite, crying 'out of the depths' (Ps. 18.16; 130.1), is fully aware that he can have no help save in God who controls those very waters.

We might note how frequently the Psalmist prays to God to be rescued from 'many waters', the waters that come in unto his

---

[8]   For a full discussion, showing that the name 'Jonah', meaning 'dove' in Hebrew, is applied to the people as a whole, see G.A.F. Knight, *Ruth and Jonah*, Torch Commentary, sec. ed., 1956.

[9]   Though the Psalm in chap. 2 may have had a separate origin, and been used liturgically, yet it forms a unity with the book as a whole as it was finally edited.

soul (Ps. 18.16; 46.3; 69.1, 2, 14, etc.). These waters become symbols of the enemies from whom the Psalmist craves to escape (Ps. 69.14; 88.17; 124.2–5; 144.7). They thus represent in the experience of individuals the 'war' which God has waged from the beginning with Darkness or the Deep, and which became visible in the history of the nation of Israel when Yahweh overthrew mighty Pharaoh at the Red Sea (Ps. 89.8–10). Yet all the time the waters are God's waters, and God can handle them as he will. He may use them to discipline his children (Jonah 2), or he may use them to refresh his people and renew their drooping spirits. In the wilderness God refreshed his people with 'many waters' gushing out from the rock which Moses struck (Num. 20.11). Those waters had, of course, burst up through the ground from 'the water under the earth' (Ex. 20.4), in other words, from the chaotic waters of *tehom*. Then, in the end of the days, the kingdoms of the earth which have warred against God, and which have emerged from the sea of chaos, God will finally overthrow and cast down (Dan. 7.1–9). This is naturally to be expected of Almighty God, who created Darkness as well as Light because 'thy way is in the sea, and thy path in the great waters' (Ps. 77.19). If once it could be said of God 'thou didst divide the sea by thy strength, thou breakest the heads of the dragons, *tanninim*, in the waters, thou breakest the heads of leviathan in pieces' (Ps. 74.13–14), or if 'the channels of the sea appeared, the foundations of the world were discovered' (II Sam. 22.16), then God can do the same again at any time. 'Many waters cannot quench love' (S. of Sol. 8.7). 'The Lord on high is mightier than the noise of many waters' (Ps. 93.4)[10] There is every reason to believe that the great Brazen Sea (II Kings 16.17; 25.13), which stood in the precincts of Solomon's Temple, and for whose *raison d'être* the OT gives no sufficient explanation,[11] may well have

---

[10] See Herbert G. May, 'Many Waters', *JBL*, Vol. LXXIV, March 1955.
[11] II Chron. 4.6 (evidently on the basis of the use made of the laver in Ex. 30.19) says it was for the priests to wash in. But its rim was above their heads!

served to remind Israel of this great truth about which so many Psalmists sing.[12]

Other Aspects of Chaos

But *tohul wa-bhohu* was envisaged, not only as watery chaos, but also as (*a*) Desert, and (*b*) Abyss.

(*a*)   There is a phrase in the first chapter of Genesis that keeps recurring like a refrain, viz., 'And God saw that it was good'.

---

[12]   See W.F. Albright, *Archaeology and the Religion of Israel*, 1942, pp. 148 ff.

It is interesting to note that the figure of the Dragon has continued to be used till the present day to express an understanding of the power of God over the forces of evil. The fact that it has done so is evidence that even in those centuries before the dawn of the scientific era when the Church could not have been expected to realize that the first chapter of Genesis represents not a cosmogonic fact but a theological truth, it held fast to that essential theological truth which the picture language of Genesis conveys.

Ezekiel gives us a picture of a later Pharaoh, one who epitomizes all the Pharaohs of history under two forms (a) as the enemy of God, and (b) as the Dragon of the deep (Ezek. 29.3): 'Behold, I am against thee, Pharaoh king of Egypt, the great dragon (*tannim*) . . . ' The dragon of the modern children's tale is a development of this essential biblical picture, and preserves the shape in which evil has continued to present itself to the imagination of man. The story book dragon is always pictured with a long tail like a serpent's, and at the same time it can shoot flames from its mouth (Isa. 27.1; 51.9). Moreover, the biblical dragon could symbolize the powers of pride and self-sufficiency (Job 26.12). This idea too is carried on in the folk tales of many nations. It is inherent in the allegory which the medieval Church wove round the manger at Bethlehem. It saw the latter as Noah's Ark, or as Moses' Ark, which floated on Pharaoh's river (the word *tebhah* is used for both these receptacles, and occurs in those two places alone); and the Church believed that it was guarded by the God who ruled over Chaos.

But that it saw Herod as the Dragon is of still greater interest to us as we watch the myth develop. Dragons have always been pictured to be

Each creative act of God produced another area of an ordered and integrated universe. As Deutero-Isaiah comments upon God's primal creative-act: 'For thus says the Lord who created the heavens (he is God!), who formed the earth and made it; (he established it; he did not create it to be a chaos (*tohu*), he formed it to be inhabited!)' (Isa. 45.18 ARSV). Not far from the doorstep of the ordered world of every Near Eastern civilization there always lay the desert. The desert, like the unstable ocean deep, was not for human habitation; it was not even part of the ordered world. In the OT therefore we are asked to look forward to the day when the desert, just like *tehom*, will finally be overcome. As a mark of that final victory, the desert will then blossom as the rose (Isa. 35.1), and will thus evidence the accomplishment of God's mighty plan (Isa. 40.3); (cf. also Isa. 13.20–22; 34.13–15; Mark 1.13).

(*b*) As Abyss the Chaos figure is correlated with the conception of Sheol, the underworld of the departed from this life.[13] Since it is this inhabited world of earth where men, under God, can regulate and rule, then the world below this earth must be quite unlike the earth we know. There man has no longer any purposeful activity (Job 3.13–22) and there Yahweh's rule

---

red in colour; that is why the Pharaoh of the medieval painter was normally decorated with a red beard. And that is why both the beard and the clothing of Mephistopheles have traditionally been coloured red. Two other NT interpretations of the Chaos symbol may still in a word be adduced. The motif of the Ark occurs in I Peter 3.20–21 where the fragile earthly abode of God's advancing purpose becomes the Church afloat on the stormy seas of chaos. The other is a direct quotation from a verse to which we have already referred (Ps. 89.9). When Jesus stilled the waves on the Lake of Galilee (Mark 4.35–41), he referred essentially to that verse. Thereby he made the claim that he was Lord, not just of the Sea of Galilee, but rather of the Chaotic-Deep over which the Spirit of God had brooded as an eagle broods over her young (Ps. 24.2; 93.3–4). Finally the NT asserts that in the end God will do away with *tehom* and its monster in all its forms and threats for ever (Rev. 13.1; 21.1). See K. Grayston, 'The Darkness of the Cosmic Sea, A Study of Symbolism in St. Mark's Narrative of the Crucifixion', *Theology*, April, 1952, pp. 122 ff.
[13] Cf. *KB*, ad loc.

does not even reach (Isa. 38.11). This sombre world is described in terms of this whole area of thought with which we have been dealing: 'Before I go whence I shall not return, even to the land of darkness and the shadow of death; a land of darkness, as darkness itself; and of the shadow of death, without any order (i.e. chaotic) and where the light is as darkness' (Job 10.21–22; cf. Prov. 27.20 *kethibh*; Luke 8.31).

But it was the experience of the Exile, down into which Israel had to go, that enabled her thinkers to make the fullest interpretation of the meaning of death; for it was in the Exile that they learned that they were not alone, but that God was with them in all the pain and sorrow that marked the 'death' of their nation as an entity (Dan. 3.25). Only so did they come to believe as the years went by that this same God must be in control of the Abyss, of the shadowy land of departed spirits, as well as over the world of men (Ps. 139.8, 11–12).

The OT, then, can draw no line between the divine activity as God reveals himself in creation, and the divine activity as God reveals himself in redemption. Since it was Light which *became* when God first began to create, and which issued from God's very heart and became a 'thing' objectively separable from God himself, then that Light was as much God's great redemptive purpose as it was the foundation of all creation. God must know what will be the outcome in event of each of his spoken Words. Thus God's spoken purpose must have been from the beginning 'with' God; the purpose must be 'alive' even as God himself is alive. The 'purpose' in the shape of Wisdom can thus speak in the first person singular: 'The Lord possessed (*q-n-h*)[14] me in the beginning of his way . . . when he prepared the heavens, I was there . . . then I was by him, as one brought up with him' (or, 'like a master workman', ARSV) (Prov. 8.22, 27, 30).

Now, God's purpose, in the form of Wisdom, rejoiced particularly in his inhabited world and 'delighted in the sons of men' (Prov. 8.31). God's relationship to his creature, man, must therefore form the next subject of our inquiry.

---

[14] Cf. footnote 2.

Eleven

The Significance of Man

Although it is true that the OT does not differentiate between God's creative and redemptive activities, yet the OT naturally recognizes as a basic hypothesis from which to understand his redemptive purpose that God created man. Yet, since the mythological language used in the early chapters of Genesis is obviously not meant to represent mere factual event, the 'other side of the coin' (the significance of those events) must also just as obviously be taken into account. The book of Genesis, in both its J and P accounts, is telling us about the *significance* of God's creature man even more cogently than it tells of man's original state and man's original being.

When, then, we read that God created man, we are to keep the question firmly in mind as to why God created him at all; and we are to continue to ask the question 'why?' at every point in our inquiry.

It was on this ordered, upper world, the world which God saw to be good, that God set man to live. God 'breathed' *naphah* into the clay which he had taken up in his hands, and from which he had made a human shape, 'and man became a *nephesh hayyah*' (Gen. 2.7). Now, the brute beasts, as well as man, were formed by God to be a *nephesh hayyah* (Gen. 1.24). What then was the difference between man and beast? The difference is made clear at once. In the first place we read that man is given authority to rule over all the animal creation and to control and use for his own ends all the produce of the earth (Gen. 1.29–30); thus man cannot be identical with the beasts over which he rules. On the other hand, man shares his physical form with the beasts over which he has authority to rule; they too are formed by God out of the dust of the earth.

Is it then merely his authority to rule creation that differentiates man from the beasts? Here again we turn to the great and decisive redemptive activity of God in rescuing his people from the darkness of Egypt in order to provide an answer to our question. The man whom Israel knows as man is the man whom God has redeemed. God has not redeemed the animal creation, but he has redeemed his 'son'. God has other sons, too, the 'seventy' nations of the earth (Gen. 5 and 10), all of whom owe their origin to one common ancestor. What then of these other sons?

Amos can stand upon his mountain-top at Tekoa, and see in imagination the nations all around him being moved about the earth as a player would move his pawns upon a chessboard (Amos 9.7; cf. Isa. 37.29). But God, who is the God of purpose, would not move them thus in vain. Even the pagan nations of the earth are to be understood as living within God's plan, and in the end his redemptive purpose will be known to all the earth (cf. Isa. 2.1–4; 19.18–25, etc.). Those other nations, on the other hand, will know the meaning and purpose of their very existence only if they learn it from the lips of Israel (Isa. 49.6; 50.4), God's first born son (Ex. 4.22). Israel is one in blood with all the races of men (Gen. 5; 10), therefore it is incumbent upon Israel to tell the other peoples what it means to be the kind of creature of God whom God believes it possible and worthwhile to redeem. Man is not a creature who exists in his own right, ontologically speaking, in any sense other than does the animal creation. Man exists only as a creature of grace. He was not created for any merit he might have in himself (Hos. 9.4). Made in the image of God, he is fashioned so as to be able to respond to 'every word that proceedeth out of the mouth of God'. On the other hand, if God, so to speak, but 'holds his breath', then man ceases to be (Ps. 104.29–30; Job 34.14–15). The God who thus sustains him in being has become known to Israel in the redemption from Egypt as 'merciful and gracious, longsuffering, and abundant in goodness and truth' (Ex. 34.6). Since Israel is able to appreciate this action of a God of such a nature and to understand its significance for her own life in turn, then man must be a moral being – not, again, moral in his own right, but a being who knows what it is to be 'merciful and gracious . . . ' himself, on the ground that he has learned to be like that from God alone. Living as a social being on earth, man who is both an individual and the race at once, comes to learn as a result of God's primal act of grace how to reflect within his own life what we have called the life of the 'family relationship' known to the heavenly host.

There is a degree to which man can indeed turn (*shubh*) and go back to God, although even here he cannot turn unless God first turns him (Jer. 31.18). There is a degree to which he can still enjoy the fellowship of God, even in his 'fallen' state. In Israel's early period man's sense of individual responsibility may indeed have been small. In common with all ancient nations Israel held a highly communal view of society.[1] Yet we must not forget that the great prophets taught Israel the reality of individual responsibility before God (cf. Jer. 31.29–30; Deut. 24.16; Ezek. 18.1–4), even when the individual, as we saw in Part One, consciously remained a member of that nation with which God dealt as a whole. 'Wash you, make you clean . . . Cease to do evil: learn to do good; seek justice, relieve the oppressed, do justly by the fatherless, stand up for the widow' (Isa. 1.16–17 ARSV). The attractively written little 'historical novel' about the person of Joseph in the book of Genesis (37; 39–50) demonstrates to us how even a sinner (note Joseph's self-righteousness and egotism as he recounts his dreams in chap. 37) can indeed meet every vicissitude of life with a high and gallant heart. Or again, the figure of Abraham is another example of a sinful man, who, although subject to the wrath of God, is able to experience the fellowship of God. In Isa. 41.8 and II Chron. 20.7 we meet with the moving description of Abraham as the friend, nay, indeed, the lover of God. Thus Jeremiah the prophet, sinner though he was, believed that he actually 'stood in the counsel, *sodh*, of the

---

[1]   See G. Ernest Wright, *The Biblical Doctrine of Man in Society*, 1954.

God of all the earth' (Jer. 23.18). Both man and angels knew the experience of *sodh*. Human friends could take 'sweet counsel together' (Ps. 55.14); the *benei 'elim*, the 'family fellowship' of the angelic beings, could do so too (Ps. 89.7). Yet both Abraham and Jeremiah, whom J would say had 'fallen' and who thus lived in a state of rebellion, could possess that kind of fellowship with the living God which the angels know!

There is another aspect of the meaning of sin which we must face, however, before we can answer the question 'What is man?'

The Fall of Man

The story of the Fall of man, as we have it in Gen. 3, is not told by the writer as a narrative of historic fact any more than is the creation narrative in the first chapter of Genesis. No chapter in the whole Bible is a better example of the ability the Hebrews showed of presenting truth in picture form. In fact, without the existence of this important chapter, much of the remaining portions of the Bible would be unintelligible to us today. Gen. 3 does not tell us that at some calculable date in the world's history, palaeolithic man, or the missing link, or man at any other stage of his evolution, suddenly fell into sin. Let us see what the story does actually say in the picture language it employs.

The priestly writer has already informed us that God had given man responsibility to rule over the world he had created. That is to say, it was not the intention of God that man should live in idleness. Man was meant by God to tend the garden in which God had placed him (Gen. 2.15; cf. Ps. 104.23). Again, not only was man to rule over the beasts, in J's incomparable phraseology, man was instructed to give the beasts a name. The name, we recall, was to the Hebrews, at least ideally speaking, the exact description of its owner. Thus to know the name was to know the essence of its owner. And to know the essence of man or beast was to have power over him (Gen. 2.19–20).

But merely to exercise control over the animal creation was not a satisfying outlet for the vital nature of man. In no sense could the animals be companions to one who was made in the image of God. Man is not fully man, as both J and P declare, when he lives alone, as a single unit. 'It is not good for man to be alone'. God therefore ordains that the male should find the fulness of his being when he regards the female of the human species as his true 'opposite number'. Eve is not Adam's 'help-meet', his aide-de-camp to serve him, and merely execute his will. The word 'help-meet' has actually entered the English language from this verse (Gen. 2.20) of the AV, yet is a mistranslation of the original Hebrew. Eve is Adam's '*ezer kenegdo*, his 'help, corresponding to him'. Eve thus complements Adam, just as Adam complements Eve, with the result that it is the two together, man and woman, who form what the priestly writer has called by the name of Adam (Gen. 5.2).

We have declared that Adam is able to respond to the grace of God's primal act of redemption and so to build up a cultural life upon earth (Gen. 4.19–21). What is this element within man, however, which can make a response of gratitude, when the animals, who are one with him after the flesh, are unable to do so at all? The answer comes from J's narrative again (Gen. 2.7) where we read that God himself has set within man that which can make the response, viz., his own 'breath'.[2] The 'vision of the valley of dry bones' reads almost like a commentary upon this verse in Genesis (Ezek. 37). Even when the bones of the dead of Israel, we read there, had once again received their flesh, and were covered with skin once more, those bones had certainly not yet become man again. 'There was no breath, *ruah*, in them' (v. 8). It was only when, finally, the third element, the *ruah* of God 'breathed upon these slain' that they lived, and stood up upon their feet (v. 10).

In Part One, chap. 2 we looked at the manner in which God created man as an ontological being. Now we have returned to examine the same passages, because we have had to review them in a new light. Now we are able to understand more fully how the

---

[2]   The word used here is *neshamah*, a parallel to *ruah* when the latter means 'breath'; cf. Isa. 30.33; II Sam. 22.16; Job 4.9; 32.8; etc.

spirit which God has added to man represents those higher elements in his composition which God has 'breathed' into his *nephesh* as a whole.

In the beginning God created an image of himself. What could have happened to destroy this plan of God, so that the image he had made in man should have become defaced? What power could possibly exist in the universe which God has created that could frustrate the plan of God himself? It was not the serpent. Man had already given the serpent its name. That is to say, man ought by rights to have had power over the serpent himself. We are not given the answer to this fundamental question. But we recall that 'in the beginning' there was chaos, and there was 'darkness upon the face of the deep'. That deep was God's deep, so that it was he who allowed the chaos and the darkness to continue to exist. Consequently, the darkness must be contained within the overruling plan and purpose of God.

That is why man, too, knows both God's light and God's darkness.[3] We have seen that Isa. 45.18 declares that God intended his world to be orderly and inhabited, like the Garden of Eden, and not be *tohu*. *Tohu* thus represents the opposite of orderliness and creative purpose; it is what we today would call the tendency to disintegration. Adam and Eve ought to have led an integrated and purposeful life. But Adam (and Eve) carry in their heart the tendency, *yetser* (wrongly translated as 'imagination' in Gen. 6.5, but cf. I Chron. 29. 18) towards chaos or disintegration, a tendency which is the reverse of the will of the Spirit of God (Gen. 1.2). Why this is so, we are not told. Man possesses free-will sufficient to enable him to turn a deaf ear to the serpent's wiles; but in practice he does not do so. The tendency to destroy, to corrupt, to disrupt relationships between man and God (Gen. 3.10), between man and woman (3.12), and between man and his brother (4.8), represents a true picture of the nature of man as he actually is.

---

[3]   See G. Pidoux, 'Encore les deux Arbres de Genèse!' *ZAW*, 66, 1954, Heft 1/2, pp 37 ff.

The Reality of Sin

The OT has many terms for evil, sin, and wickedness. Thus there is *ra'*. This term means 'bad' in the general sense that something is not good. It is used of bad fruit (Jer. 24.2), or of unpleasant experiences (Gen. 49.7); of objects of little value (Lev. 27.10), or of a 'sad' heart (Prov. 25.20). But it can also cover any calamity, such as famine, earthquake or war (Amos 6.3), and since it includes all the evil in the human heart it covers the whole conception of moral evil. In this way, we can say quite simply that Haman was a *bad* man (Esth. 7.6).

Rasha', again, is a general word for 'wicked', or 'criminal' (Ex. 2.13; Deut. 25.2, etc.); it is always used in a moral sense. 'The wicked' as the word occurs in the plural, becomes a collective term for the 'adversaries' of God (cf. Ps. 3.7). Yet each individual Israelite knows the 'plague' of his own heart (I Kings 8.38).

The result of wickedness is the experience of guilt, *'asham*. This is the name in Hebrew of a particular kind of sacrifice that came into use rather late in Israel's story. The AV usually translates it by 'trespass-offering'. (See its use in Lev. 5.14–6.7.) But the essential idea is the sense of guilt which the *rasha'*, the wicked man, experiences in his heart, and which he knows to be caused by the disruption of relations with God which he ought to have valued and cherished.

There are many other terms used for sin. Thus there is *het'*, in the sense of failure or of missing the mark (e.g. Deut. 21.22; Ps. 51.9).There is a noun from the same root with a feminine suffix (e.g. Ex. 32.30). This noun appears also in a slightly different form (e.g. Ex. 34.7); and it occurs again in still a third form (e.g. Gen. 4.7). Then there is the noun *'awon*, usually translated 'iniquity', and often used in parallel to *hattath* (e.g. I Sam. 20.1); and there are less frequently used terms, like *'awel*, 'unrighteousness', *'awen*, 'trouble', 'wickedness', and others. Perhaps the most important root to note, however, is that of *p-sh-'*. Often wrongly translated as 'transgress', its primary sense is that of 'rebel', 'revolt', since it puts the emphasis upon the disruption of personal relations between God and man through human folly and pride.[4]

The great eighth century prophets lay little emphasis upon sin as a breaking of the moral law that is enshrined in whatever codes of law were available in their day to Israel. Those occasions when they do speak of Israel's having 'despised the law (Torah) of Yahweh' (e.g. Amos 2.4) may enshrine a later point of view than that of the great prophets themselves; or at least this emphasis takes a subsidiary place in their teaching (cf. Isa. 1.10; 5.24; Hos. 4.6). The primary emphasis of the great prophets on the other hand is made with the aid of just such a verb as *p-sh-'*. They look upon sin, not primarily as a breaking of the moral law, but rather as a breaking off of relations with the living God (e.g. Isa. 1.28; Hos. 7.13; Amos 4.4).

This innate tendency on the part of man to disrupt relationships between himself and God is a conception presented now as our 'theological picture' develops. God created man to be nothing else than his creature, and as such to possess a limited range of experience. But man ever seeks 'to be as God', 'to know good and evil' (Gen. 3.22), that is, to know the whole sweep of knowledge as if from the positive to the negative pole of its totality.[5] But 'knowledge' here does not comprise merely intellectual knowledge; rather the emphasis of the story is upon moral knowledge. As rebellious youth in every generation expresses the temptation here depicted: 'We ought to try everything once'.

The happy fellowship with God which man is intended to live is thus a lost ideal. Accordingly, it is a fact of experience that he is now 'shut out of the garden'. Man cannot regain the fellowship with God which he has lost by his rebellious independence and pride. Outside the gate of the garden of Eden God has placed 'cherubims, and a flaming sword which turned every way, to keep

---

[4] See C. Ryder Smith, *The Bible Doctrine of Sin*, 1953, pp. 15–21.

[5] R. Gordis, 'The Knowledge of Good and Evil in the OT and the Qumran Scrolls' *JBL*, LXXVI, June 1957, pp. 123 ff., has recently made an interesting case for the phrase to mean 'knowledge of sex, natural and unnatural'.

the way of the tree of life' (Gen. 3.24). In other words, man cannot return to the garden of his own volition. Whether he is ever to enter the garden again will depend now upon an act of God.

It is not that man has wholly lost the image of God. The image is now only defaced by sin, not totally destroyed (Gen. 9.6). In his mercy God set his mark upon Cain, the murderer, so that even the perpetrator of the most heinous sin into which man can fall is still able to respond to God's Word and still pursues his ends under God's care and protection (Gen. 4.9–15). But man now lives (a) with a sense of shame in the presence of God, and (b) in fear of the living God (Gen. 3.10). Again, wholly unlike the animal creation, man is conscious that he is mortal and knows that he must die (Gen. 3.19). Meanwhile, life for him outside the Garden can only be hard and vexatious, and he must earn his daily bread by the sweat of his brow (Gen. 3.19). God is now faced with a problem. If he were merely to condone man's rebellious pride, and offer an oral forgiveness, man would neither understand the heinousness of his 'tendency' nor appreciate the majesty of God's offer of fellowship. Therefore God has to employ a plan different from that which he had entertained as his original intention for man. To further that plan, God chooses and adopts the People of Israel as the necessary instrument for the attainment of his new purpose.

The rest of the OT thereafter deals solely with God's loving effort to attain the end that he had in view from the beginning.

The Fall of the Angels

But before we give a final answer to the question 'What is man?' and before we leave the early chapters of Genesis to examine the manner in which God's purpose of saving love did finally work itself out through his relationship with Israel, we must turn to yet one more pictorial representation of the nature of evil that the book of Genesis provides.

The first four verses of Gen. 6 comprise an ancient 'erratic boulder' embedded in the final narrative. These verses obviously contain elements of an ancient legend. 'There were giants in the earth in those days'. Perhaps the legend arose through the need to express mythologically the significance of the natural phenomena we know of as falling meteors. The word used for giants is *nephilim*, a word which could mean both 'fallen creatures' and 'abortions'.[6] How to choose between these two meanings it is hard to say. However, it is not the origin of the story which is primarily important, for it is not the origin which is significant for a theological understanding of the OT. The importance of the story lies in the use made of it by the final editor of Genesis, co-ordinating his material as he did in the period of the close of the Exile. What he quotes from his early source is this; 'The sons of God(s), *'elim*, saw the daughters of men that they were fair; and they took them wives of all which they chose' (Gen. 6.2). Our priestly writer, it would seem, carried in his mind some of the pictorial representations of the 'heavenly family' which Israel employed to expound her thought on God. By including in his narrative a story which our exalted theologian might well have excluded if he had seen it in the light merely of a silly popular tale, P was seeking to express yet another aspect of the Fall. J had written of the Fall in the form we have it in chap. 3, the story of the Garden of Eden. But now, by making use of this other popular story, P sought to express the faith that the Fall is a reality, not only in the heart of man, but also in 'the heavenly places'.[7] In other words, it is not only man who is alienated from God and his loving purpose, the whole universe is riddled with evil and the spirit of rebellion. God created the whole universe to serve him, man on earth, the angels in heaven, but both earth and heaven have rebelled against the

---

[6]   L. Köhler, *Hebrew Man*, English transl. 1956, p. 51.

[7]   That there had been a Fall amongst the angels as well as a Fall of man became a commonly accepted doctrine n the post-OT period. Dan. 8.10 may thus be understood; but the doctrine is clearly held in Enoch 91.15, and in *The Admonition*, the Zadokite Documents III, 18 (ed. Chaim Rabin), 1954. R. Gordis refers to Ps. 82.6 f. as a biblical instance where both 'Falls' are mentioned together, *JBL*, op. cit., p. 127. He reads *sarim* as equal to 'angels'; cf. Dan. 10.13, 20, 21; 12.1. See also Jer. 12.4.

plan of the living God. This is why some of the angels, in OT thinking, were actually regarded under the term of 'abortions'. Belief in this rebellion is held throughout the whole OT period. One of the latest chapters of the OT to be written is Isa. 24, coming possibly from the late fourth century B.C. There we read in v. 21: 'And it shall come to pass in that day, that the Lord shall punish the host of the high ones that are on high, and the kings of the earth upon the earth'. The OT writers sufficiently understood the significance of life to realize that since God is one, his universe must be one too. The heart of man is tainted with evil. Therefore the whole universe, of which it is a part, is tainted along with it.

When we remember this Hebraic unitary view of creation we can better understand the significance of the 'curse' lying upon the world both animate and inanimate (Gen. 3.14–19). The very ground which, when God created it, ought to have 'brought forth grass, and herb yielding seed after his kind, and the tree yielding fruit . . . and God saw that it was good' (Gen. 1.12), does in fact produce but 'thorns and thistles' (Gen. 3.18). Man ought to have found creative joy in tending the garden (Gen. 2.15). In actuality he does not live in Eden at all. The way back to God's original plan for both man and Garden is barred by the cherubim who are in themselves the living representation of the execution of God's will. And so the whole of God's unitary universe is infected with sin and is lying in a state of rebellion. It remains then for God to act in such a manner, if he is indeed to pursue his plan of redemption, that both 'heaven and earth', spirit and matter, shall be rid of the curse that rests upon them. When then we follow the plan of God, as we read of it beginning at Gen. 12, we are always to keep in mind that even though the drama that is being enacted takes place on one spot upon this earth below, yet it is effective throughout the whole of the cosmos, even to 'the waters under the earth'.

The task God has before him is one that brooks no delay. The power of sin is such that it grows, snowball like, from generation to generation. The very first son of Adam and Eve commits the terrible sin of murder (Gen. 4.8); yet only a few generations thereafter his descendant Lamech not only commits the sin of murder, he boasts of what he has done, and exults in the horror of it, defying the world at large (Gen. 4.23–4). Three times over our editor, in chap. 6, in the strongest language he can find, some of it ostensibly from the mouth of God, declares that 'every tendency of the thoughts of [man's] heart was only evil continually', and that 'the earth was corrupt; for all flesh had corrupted his way upon the earth', and 'the earth is filled with the violence of them'. We left Amos gazing at the movements of the nations, as God moved them over the chessboard of history. But we also find him gazing from his hill-top towards those of his immediate neighbours, whose sins he knew only too well. Damascus, or Syria, had 'threshed Gilead with threshing instruments of iron' (Amos 1.3); Gaza had 'carried away captive the whole captivity' (1.6); Tyre had 'delivered up the whole captivity to Edom, and remembered not the brotherly covenant' (1.9); Edom in its turn 'did pursue his brother with the sword, and did cast off all pity . . . ' (1.11); Ammon had 'ripped up the women with child of Gilead, that they might enlarge their border' (1.13); Moab had 'burned the bones of the King of Edom into lime' (2.1); Judah in her turn had 'despised the *torah of yahweh*, and have not kept his commandments' (2.4); and Israel had 'sold the righteous for silver, and the poor for a pair of shoes . . . and a man and his father go in unto the same maid . . . ' (2.7).[8]

Amos is not the only prophet so to speak. The consciousness of Israel's sin is overwhelmingly evident in all the prophets as we turn from one to the next. 'Turn ye every one from his evil way, and from the evil of your doings' (Jer. 25.5), is an oracle typical of their reiterated message.

Who then is Man? The OT does not give the kind of analysis and description that satisfies our questions. But he is shown to us as a creature capable of knowing God and of responding to him in gratitude, so that he could have walked with God in the Garden. Yet, in the depths of his inner consciousness, he knows that sin is crouching at the door (Gen. 4.7), so that in consequence he is ever

---

[8]   These quotations are made without prejudice to the question of Amos' authorship of them all.

ready to fall into that profound Darkness which is in the background of all his thoughts. Made a little lower than *'elohim* (Ps. 8.5), yet he has hopelessly rebelled against him in whose image he was fashioned. But the saving purpose of God for man has been there from the beginning, just as has the darkness. 'In thy light shall we see light' man then exclaims. The OT does not tell us who man is. But it is only the OT, of all the world's literature, which tells us what is the significance of man.

Twelve

The Wrath of God

The OT entertains no illusions, either about the lack of loyalty on the side of Israel towards Yahweh, or about Yahweh's attitude in consequence towards his sinful people. The OT repeatedly emphasizes that God has singled Israel out for special blessing, and at the same time for special responsibility (cf. Deut. 1–11 *passim*; Amos 3.2). Psalms 78 and 106, for example, are poems which recount the whole story of Israel's relationship with God till the time of writing. But this story comprises no lyrical description of the life history of a merely privileged people, even though 'we will not hide them (i.e. what we have heard and known) from their children' (Ps. 78.4). The story is told rather that those very children 'might not be as their fathers, a stubborn and rebellious generation' (v. 8). In fact, the fathers 'kept not the covenant of God, and refused to walk in his *torah*, and forgat his works, and his wonders that he had showed them' (vv. 10–11).

Even though Yahweh 'divided the sea and caused them to pass through' (v. 13), 'they sinned yet more against him by provoking the most High in the wilderness' (v. 17); 'they tempted God . . . they spake against God' (vv. 18–19). Though he gave them food from heaven 'they were not estranged from their lust' (v. 30) . . . 'for all this they sinned still, and believed not in his wondrous works' (v. 32). Even when trouble made them remember that God was their Rock, 'nevertheless they did flatter him with their mouth, and they lied unto him with their tongues . . . ' (vvs. 35–36) . . . and so the sins of Israel are recounted right till the period of the establishment of the line of David (v. 70). In consequence, what the Psalmist must now go on to declare is that 'the wrath of God came upon them' (v. 31; cf. also Ps. 106.23, 40); 'he cast upon them the fierceness of his anger, wrath, and indignation, and trouble, by sending evil angels (angels of evil) among them' (v. 49).

Hebrew possesses more words than English does to represent the conception of the Wrath of God – *haron*, *'aph*, *'ebhrah*, *za'am*, *'abhar*, *qeseph*, *ka'as*, *ragaz*, and *hemah*. As we have seen, God does not 'possess' 'attributes'. Therefore the Wrath of God must be an aspect of the living God as a whole as he makes himself known to his people. The Wrath of God is the positive attitude that God takes in response to the sin of man. Yet, just as wrath is not an attribute of God, so sin is not an attribute of man. Wrath is not a metaphysical entity apart from God himself. Nor is sin an entity apart from the man who sins. The OT therefore, in its usual pictorial manner, makes clear that the attitude of the all-holy God to sinful Israel is that of wrath against, not the sin, but the sinner. 'I have seen this people, and behold, it is a stiff-necked people: now therefore let me alone, that my wrath may wax hot against them, and that *I* may consume *them*' (Ex. 32.9–10; cf. Jer. 12.8). This is in contradistinction to much modern preaching when it is said that God hates the sin, but loves the sinner. The Psalmist can say: 'Thou, O God, *hatest* all workers of iniquity' (Ps. 5.5; cf. Hos. 9.15; Mal. 1.3). It is true, of course, that wickedness as such God may overtly condemn (cf. Ps. 45.7; Amos 5.15). Yet the essential understanding of what it means to be a sinner displayed by another Psalmist has led him to exclaim, to the astonishment of many today, 'Do not I hate them, O Lord, that hate thee? . . . I hate them with perfect hatred' (Ps. 139.21–2).

Nowhere is the Wrath of God more significantly pictorialized than in the story of the Flood. There we see what it means for the whole world to lie under God's 'curse'. The story of the Flood is composite, as we see from a comparison of passages such as Gen. 6.19 and 7.2. It is, however, based on legendary material, deriving from what was evidently a historical flood or floods in the lower Tigris-Euphrates valley.[1] The story would certainly have come

---

[1]   C.L. Woolley, *Ur of the Chaldees*, 1929.

down over the centuries in oral tradition.[2] The local flood in
Babylon, however, was a historical phenomenon. The Flood in
Genesis was not. In picture language it represents to us the truth
that the Deep is still present everywhere throughout the whole of
God's creation. God has only to say the word, as it were, and the
fountains of *tehom* (Gen. 7.11) will break through and burst up
from 'the waters under the earth' (Ex. 20.4), where the monster
Rahab or Leviathan, or the whale, or the dragon, is playing even
now. And at the same time the waters which lie above the
firmament (Gen. 1.7) could come crashing down and overwhelm
the life of man, beast and bird. The Wrath of God is such that the
whole of God's creation ought to be blotted out, both the heavenly
beings who have rebelled against their God (Gen. 6.1–4),[3] and
man on earth who has done the same (Gen. 3.14), with results
that have affected even inanimate nature (Gen. 3.17–19). 'It
repented Yahweh that he had made man on the earth, and it
grieved him at his heart. And Yahweh said, I will destroy man
whom I have created from the face of the earth; both man and
beast, and the creeping thing and the fowls of the air; for it
repenteth me that I have made them' (Gen. 6.6–7). So runs this
strongly anthropomorphic declaration of the significance of the
wrath of the living God.

Unlike human anger, which fluctuates with the passing mood
and whim, the Wrath of God is permanent, unswerving, and
undeviating. God must necessarily hate the evil which is the
opposite of his holy love. The great thinkers of the OT accept this
fact without any hesitation whatsoever. 'We are consumed in thine
anger, and in thy wrath are we troubled' (Ps. 90.7). The most
profoundly significant event in all Israel's story, after the People of
God was called into being by God himself, was the destruction in
587 B.C. of the city of Jerusalem and of the people of Israel as a
political entity. The prophets who lived before that event saw
clearly that, God's nature being what it is, his wrath must eventu-

---

[2]   For such language, see E. Nielsen, *Oral Tradition*, 1954.
[3]   See K.L. Schmidt, 'Lucifer als gefallene Engelmacht', *TZ*, 7 Jahrgang
Heft 3, Mai/Juni, 1951, pp. 161 ff., with reference to Isa. 14.12.

ally declare itself upon Israel's sin. Israel, they knew, stood under the judgement of the living and holy God. 'Hear this word that the Lord hath spoken against you, O children of Israel . . . you only have I known of all the families of the earth: therefore I will punish you for all your iniquities' (Amos 3.1–2). Next in point of time comes Hosea: 'Hear the word of the Lord, ye children of Israel: for the Lord hath a controversy with the inhabitants of the land, because there is no truth, nor mercy, nor knowledge of God in the land . . . Therefore shall the land mourn, and everyone that dwelleth therein shall languish, with the beasts of the field, and with the fowls of heaven; yea, the fishes of the sea also shall be taken away' (Hos. 4.1, 3). The contemporary prophets, Micah and Isaiah, both begin their utterances in the written form in which we have them, by declaring in vivid pictures the wrath of God against human sin. Micah shows us the mountains melting beneath God's feet, and the valleys cleft, as wax before the fire . . . 'for the transgression of Jacob (i.e. the people of Israel) is all this, and for the sins of the house of Israel' (Mic. 1.4–5). Isaiah (chap. 1) first calls heaven and earth to witness that Israel is rotten 'from the sole of the foot even unto the head', and then continues: 'If ye be willing and obedient, ye shall eat of the good of the land: but if ye refuse and rebel, ye shall be devoured with the sword: for the mouth of the Lord hath spoken it'. The warnings of Jeremiah, a century later, in the same strain, are frequent and equally incisive (e.g. Jer. 1.16; 4.27–31, etc.). Finally, Ezekiel can express the mind of God in this regard in the most matter-of-fact language: 'I have not said in vain that I would do this evil unto them.' (Ezek. 6.10).

So terrible is the sin of man that there can come a point where God ceases to strive with man any longer (Gen. 6.3). This does not mean that God desires the destruction of mankind. On the contrary, God 'doth not afflict willingly, nor grieve the children of men' (Lam. 3.33). 'As I live, saith the Lord God, I have no pleasure in the death of the wicked' (Ezek. 33.11). On the other hand God's justice must demand the death of the sinner. This is because God is true, *'amen*, true to himself, true to his nature as holiness and goodness. God's abandonment of sinful man must proceed, therefore, not from himself, but from the effect of the corruption in man.[4] A case in point is God's response to the sin of adultery. God's original plan for man was that one man and one woman should live together as one flesh (Gen. 2.24). 'For all professed abhorrence of adultery, the sin of David with Bathsheba stood as a standing record of the fact that the best of Israelites had committed the sin which was recognized as a characteristic sin of heathendom; and because he had given great occasion to the enemies of the Lord to blaspheme David had inevitably incurred his wrath' (II Sam. 12.14).[5] Jeremiah makes the same point (Jer. 5.7–9): 'How shall I pardon thee for this? . . . When I fed them to the full, they then committed adultery, and assembled themselves by troops in the harlots' houses. They were as fed horses in the morning: everyone neighed after his neighbour's wife. Shall I not visit for these things? saith the Lord'.

The verb 'to visit', *paqadh*, is a strongly anthropomorphic verb representing the sudden 'coming' of God in wrath. In its ordinary uses the verb has a variety of meanings, but all are connected with the same central picture. We can imagine a company of soldiers awaiting their inspecting officer. First the company is 'mustered', or 'passed in review' (Ex. 30.12; I Sam. 11.8). Thereupon they are 'numbered off' (I Sam. 13.15). Officers are 'appointed' or 'assigned' to their task (Num. 3.10), and 'put in charge' of their men (II Kings 25.23). Then comes the inspecting officer, 'seeking' (Isa. 26.16) to discover if all is in order; he may even 'look for trouble' (this is the meaning of 'call to mind' in Ezek. 23.21), or 'look in vain' ('miss') for what he seeks (I Sam. 20.6). So he makes a 'visitation', as he comes with all the authority and prestige that attach to his office as inspecting officer. For a general has the right and the duty to inspect his troops. It is in just such terms as the above, then, that God himself is coming to *paqadh* his people. He too has the right to do so. And since he will undoubtedly find that his people have failed the purpose for which they were enrolled in his 'army', *tsabha* (Num. 2.4, etc.), he is therefore bound to punish his people for their sins (still another meaning of the verb *paqadh*, cf. Jer. 9.25; 11.22; Hos. 12.2).

---

[4] R.V.G. Tasker, *The Biblical Doctrine of the Wrath of God*, 1951, p. 14.
[5] Ibid., p. 17.

The Instruments of God's Wrath

Just as the saving purpose of God is made concrete for our understanding in the form of angels who execute his will, so too the wrath of God is shown to be executed by means of similar 'living' creatures. The Hebrews were able to express the conception, within the framework of their total view of creation, that God may make use of angels of destruction as well as of angels of construction. Writing from Babylonia, where Zoroastrianism was then spreading, Deutero-Isaiah needed but one sentence to refute that faith. Zoroastrianism was a religion with a high moral tone; but it differed from the faith of Israel in that it held a dualistic view of the universe. It believed in a Power of Goodness and a Power of Evil, represented by Light and Darkness respectively.[6] Isa. 45.5–7 sweeps aside such dogmas in a few mighty utterances: 'I am Yahweh; there is no other; no god exists but I; it was I who was girding thee, though thou didst not know me . . . I form light and create darkness; I make peace (*shalom*, i.e. wholeness, integration, completion), and create evil; I Yahweh do all these things'.

In Num. 21.6 we read: 'And Yahweh sent fiery serpents, *seraphim*, among the people, and they bit the people'. In Isa. 14.29 also we learn that the seraph is reported as being able to fly. The word *seraph* is, of course, the name used elsewhere of a kind of angel. Israel possibly adopted the concept of an angel pictured as a flying dragon from the solar fire-god worship of her neighbours.[7] But in Isa. 6, in which Isaiah recounts his vision of the holiness and glory of God, the *seraphim* are clearly creatures of God, who minister to his will and declare his glory. The root of the word, however, demands attention. The verb *saraph* means 'to burn', and we have seen that the glory of God is conceived under the potent image of fire. If then the seraph is an ambassador of God, it is natural that he should execute the fire of God's wrath.

---

[6] See A.J. Carnoy, art. 'Zoroastrianism' in *ERE*, Vol. 12, 1921, pp. 862 ff.

[7] See T.K. Cheyne, art. 'Seraphim', in *EB*, one-volume edition, 1914, col. 4374.

The following verse is thus in full accord with the rest of the OT thought in this regard: 'He cast upon them the fierceness of his anger, wrath, and indignation, and trouble, by sending evil angels' (Ps. 78.49). Such angels are not morally evil creatures, they are angels who convey the evil which is the expression of God's wrath. One may convey a plague (II Sam. 24.15–16 = I Chron. 21.14– 15); another may be an angel of death (II Kings 19.35), as was the angel who destroyed the Egyptians' first-born babies (Ex. 12.23). If 'the wrath of the king' could be envisaged as 'angels (messengers) of death' (Prov. 16.14), it was natural that the messengers of the God of Fire should be given the name of *methithim* ('those who put to death', Job 33.22).

The Figure of Satan

It is very difficult to make categorical statements about the appearance of the figure of Satan. He occurs in only three places in the whole OT, and all these three are late passages.

(*a*) The first two chapters of the book of Job form a prologue in prose to the poetic drama which begins in chap. 3. The prologue may well be older than the poem. In Job 1.6 we read that 'when the sons of God came to present themselves before Yahweh, the Satan came also among them'. The word *satan* means in Hebrew 'adversary'. Here he is *the* adversary, and is singled out from the rest of the angelic host and given special mention. Clearly, however, in this prologue, the Satan is as much the 'living' execution, or executor, of the will of God as is the destroying angel in the days of Egypt. He is given the task of becoming 'the fire of God' upon the family of Job (1.16). The portrait here drawn of this special angel, however, is that of a creature with a sneer upon his face (1.9–11). The Satan seems to enjoy the very possibility that Yahweh may be wrong in putting his trust in Job. And Satan is shown to be just as cynical about man as he is about the will of God (2.4–5). Yet God here has 'stooped' to use Satan just as humbly as when he used his angels.

(b) His character as the adversary is still more clearly drawn in Zech. 3.1–3, a passage which we can date almost exactly at the year 520 B.C. (see Zech. 1.1). Here God's wrath against the 'filthiness' of sin is seen once more in the form of fire (3.2–3). The Satan, however, whose essence as an angel should be a flame of fire, seems to have developed by now a will of his own, and to have opposed the redemptive plan of Yahweh. And so Yahweh has now to say to Satan:'Yahweh rebuke thee, O Satan'.

(c) The post-exilic author of Chronicles has obviously not appreciated the words of II Sam. 24.1, where we read: 'And again the anger of Yahweh was kindled against Israel, and he moved David against them, saying, Go, number Israel and Judah'. According to ancient thought it was foolish to hold a census. Knowing a people's number was like knowing his name – one gained power over him by knowing it. An enemy could come to know a nation's military strength if the latter allowed its numbers to be known. Yahweh had once been 'angry' with his 'good' king Hezekiah for a similar offence. Hezekiah had showed the ambassadors of the king of Babylon the contents of the royal armoury (Isa. 39). For this act of folly and of pride Isaiah had had to rebuke his king. The Chronicler, then, cannot believe that the idea of holding a census should originate in King David's mind from Yahweh. He writes: 'And Satan stood up against Israel, and provoked David to number Israel' (I Chron. 21.1).

In this third, and probably latest passage, the word Satan no longer carries the definite article. The word has now become a proper name; and Satan's will is clearly depicted to be in opposition to the will of God. This, however, is as far as the OT goes in the matter of the development of the personality of Satan. He is not again mentioned in any canonical book. Yet in these three passages we see the growth of a doctrine of the existence of an Evil One sufficient to form a satisfactory basis for its development in the NT.[8] In the meantime we must rest content with the unitary view

---

[8] E.g. Rev. 12.9 identifies Satan with 'the Devil', and calls him both 'dragon' and serpent.

of all things which is integral to the OT conception of creation, and recognize that the Hebrews were able to keep the personality of Satan subordinate to him who is LORD of all. 'I the Lord create Light and Darkness; I make peace and create evil' (Isa. 45.7). The writer of Isa. 14 thus presents us with a picture true to the essence of the faith of a thousand years of Hebrew thought when he says of the earthly king of Babylon: 'O Lucifer, heilel, son of the morning! how art thou cut down to the ground, which didst weaken the nations!' (Isa. 14.12; cf. Ezek. 28.16; Job 9.13; 26.12). The name 'luci-fer', 'light-bearer', which the AV has accepted from the Latin Vulgate, is a close enough translation of the Hebrew word, which means 'shining one'. But the latter is not a name, except that it may have been used outside Israel as the name of a heavenly body, such as Venus, or perhaps the new moon.[9] The word *heilel* is here applied to the earthly power of Babylon. The latter had exhibited the ultimate sin of hybris, and had sought to outdo the God of heaven himself (vv. 13–14). Therefore, said our writer, his 'star' would fall, and God would overthrow him down to the pit of the underworld. God lets evil run its course till it exhausts itself, or even turns and rends itself (Isa. 14.19).

In using such language our author was asserting that the sin of Babylon had 'total' significance in the eyes of God. Its sin had 'reached above the stars'; it had pervaded earth and heaven. Yet the light with which this 'shining one' shone at all was only reflected light (as is the light of the moon), and was not derived from any innate possession of its own soul. Even mighty Babylon on earth, conceived as a Satan to other nations, was kept in life and being by the grace of God alone. The fall of Babylon, represented by the fall of 'Lucifer', was thus 'totally' involved in that reality which the OT calls the Wrath of God.

Non Posse non Peccare

The Wrath of God is immutable. Thrice God commands Jeremiah not to pray for Israel (Jer. 7.16; 11.14; 14.11), 'for I will not hear

---

[9] See J. Skinner, *Cambridge Bible*, ad loc.

thee'. Israel had now gone too far. According to the OT it is possible to reach a position of *non posse non peccare*, to be unable not to sin (Isa. 6.10; II Chron. 36.16). The obverse of that belief is that the judgement of God must fall. Ten years before the first fall of Jerusalem, Jeremiah declares that its fall cannot now be revoked (Jer. 26.6). Twenty years later, again, when it seemed that the great final siege of the city by Nebuchadnezzar of 588–7 B.C. was about to be lifted by the fortuitous movement of an Egyptian army (Jer. 37.5), Jeremiah raises the issue again, and makes it this time crystal clear: 'Deceive not yourselves, saying, The Chaldeans shall surely depart from us: for they shall not depart. For though ye had smitten the whole army of the Chaldeans that fight against you, and there remained but wounded men amongst them, yet should they rise up every man in his tent, and burn this city with fire' (Jer. 37.9–10).

Yet this doom took what must have seemed to Jeremiah's hearers a long time to fall. In the previous century the fall of the Northern Kingdom of Israel is 722 B.C. had been regarded by the contemporary prophets as only a kind of 'first-fruits' of God's wrath. 'Who is a God like unto thee, that pardoneth iniquity, that passeth by the transgression of the remnant of his heritage?' had asked the writer of Micah 7.18 (i.e. possibly not Micah himself). Isaiah had believed that the reform undertaken by King Hezekiah had averted for the time being that doom which God had pronounced through his lips (Isa. 37.22–9). But the moment was bound to come when the doom would finally fall, since at no point in her history had Israel ever turned back to God with her whole heart. She had not, because she could not – such is the ultimate insight of the prophets; their conclusion was therefore expressed in the comprehensive picture language of the Genesis writers, who knew full well that the gates of Paradise are barred by the agents of the living God himself (Gen. 3.24). And so, in the end, Ezekiel, who lived through those agonizing years in Israel's story, has finally to declare that the wrath of God has rendered the defence of Jerusalem futile (Ezek. 7.14). *Deus dixit: Delenda est Jerusalem.*

The outstanding example in the OT of the manner in which even an individual can go 'too far' in resisting the will of God is shown us in the story of Pharaoh.[10] Since the book of Exodus is composite, it is difficult to establish with confidence a sequence in the narrative where we read of the hardening of Pharaoh's heart. There several words are used to describe the action of hardening. In Ex. 7.14 (J we read that 'Pharaoh's heart is heavy' (the Qal of the verb *kabhedh*). The tradition known as E prefers the verb *ḥazaq* (to be strong), and uses it in the same sense as J uses the verb 'to be heavy' (Ex. 9.35). Yet Pharaoh's heart 'grew hard', because Yahweh actually rendered it hard: 'for I have hardened his heart' (Ex. 10.1, where the verb is the Hiphil (transitive) of *kabhedh*, a Redactor's word); and again we find the Piel (also transitive) of the verb *ḥazaq* in Ex. 10.20 (E). P employs the transitive form of the verb qashah (to be hard) (7.3) along with the more usual Piel of hazaq (9.12) which is his standard usage; (cf. Isa. 63.17).

Hosea analysed the nature of sin with a shrewd insight. He spoke of it from three points of view. (i) Sin is that titanic element in man, that hybris, that insolence, which encourages him to imagine that he can live independently of his Creator. His figurative language described this action of rebellion as adultery. Accordingly, when Israel 'offended in Baal, he died' (Hos. 13.1). *Beth-el*, the House of God, has become *Beth-awen* (Hos. 4.15). The root of '*awen*, viz. '*on* is connected with procreative 'power' (12.3), but in the titanic sense. It is also conjoined with the idea of 'false gods' (10.5, 8). Thus it conveys the sense of 'emptiness' (Isa. 1.13; 10.1), of a false strength bringing unhappiness in its train (Num. 23.21; Jer. 4.15; Amos 5.5). (ii) Sin is a 'state' into which man has come (Hos. 4.6), a kind of bog in which his feet are stuck so that he cannot free himself. Since all mankind is one, and the generation contemporary with Hosea was all bound up in the bundle of life with the fathers of old, then sin was not so much inherited as shared. A child could thus naturally enter into the effects of his grandfather's sin (Ex. 20.5; cf. 34.7; Jer. 31.29; Ezek. 18.2), even though each individual within Israel must be

---

[10] Franz Hesse, *Das Verstockungsproblem im Alten Testament*, 1955.

responsible for his own sin (Deut. 24.16).[11] The whole northern Kingdom in Hosea's day, the descendants of the patriarch Jacob, thus shared in the sin of him who 'took his brother by the heel in the womb' (Hos. 12.3). In other words, all Israel (or 'Jacob') in their ancestor Jacob, was fundamentally selfish. The embryo has no sentient life of its on, *yet* is bogged in sin – but then the embryo is one in being with the mother whose blood flows in its veins. However, a possible resolution of this difficult contradiction seems to be hinted at in Jer. 39.18: 'Thou shalt not fall by the sword, but thy life shall be a prey unto thee, because thou hast put thy trust in me, saith the Lord' (cf. Isa. 65.6 f.). (iii) Sin is also a power that pervades man's environment. It can be 'caught' like a disease. It was a 'spirit' of whoredoms which was abroad in the midst of Israel's life (Hos. 5.4). It could thus even grip a whole nation that might otherwise have remained rational and sane. Hosea thus declares sin to be a 'power' sufficient to make Jacob fight and even win in a contest with an angel (Hos. 12.3–4; cf. Gen. 4.7). Similarly Jeremiah pictures it as an intoxication, as when a warhorse plunges over battlements to its death (Jer. 8.6).

In its train sin has brought suffering into the world (Gen. 3.16, 19). No child is free of this heritage, not even Noah, even though his father hoped he was (Gen. 5.29). But the greatest affliction of all which follows upon sin is the inevitability of death (Gen. 3.19). Man has indeed eaten of the tree of knowledge of good and evil, and so he must surely die (Gen. 2.17).

We have now reached in our study an aspect of the nature of God that is very difficult to apprehend.[12] We are told that Moses believed that God is 'merciful and gracious, longsuffering, and

---

[11]   Jung's Psychology has demonstrated the unity that exists between the personality of parents and their children. A child can dream about the complexes of its parents: Frieda Fordham, *Introduction to Jung's Psychology*, 1953, p. 105. Note also how Jung's 'Archetypes of the Collective Unconscious' resemble biblical thought on the question of Israel's identification of herself with her ancestors.

[12]   See W. Eichrodt, *Forschnngsglaube und Theodizee im AT*; in Festschrift Otto Proksch, 1934, pp. 45 ff.

abundant in goodness and truth', etc. (Ex. 34.6). In fact, we cannot overemphasize the point that it is God's true nature which is so described. God would know no wrath if this world which he has made were not a fallen world. The strongest oath that God can take is by himself or by his own life. 'As I live, saith the Lord God, I have no pleasure in the death of the wicked' (Ezek. 33.11). 'For a small moment have I forsaken thee; but with great mercies will I gather thee. In an outburst of wrath[13] I hid my face from thee for a moment; but with everlasting kindness, *hesedh 'olam*, will I have mercy on thee, saith the Lord thy Redeemer' (Isa. 54.7–8). The last word does not lie with the waters of the Flood, but with the Rainbow of promise (Gen. 9.12–17).

We recall that the description of God's active love towards Israel in which Moses believed occurs a number of times in the OT, in Jeremiah (33.11), in Jonah (4.2), in Joel (2.13), and so on. In all probability this recurrence of the identical words points to the use by Israel of this description of God in the form of a cultic formula, one that would be taught to the people by the local priests. If such is indeed the case, then the idea that God is merciful and gracious must have been deeply embedded in the mind of Israel. Yet the same Redactor who included those lovely words in the text of Exodus also repeated again and again that terrible description of God's hardening action. Yet now we are forced to admit that this seemingly opposite side to God's character was also sung in Israel's public worship, and must therefore also have deeply moved the people of God. If the Church has felt that the 95th Psalm ought to be recited frequently and even daily as an act of worship, then in all probability, and in default of direct evidence, it was used similarly in the days of the Second Temple. This Psalmist draws upon the Exodus 'nexus' of events as a warning to his contemporary audience: 'Today if ye will hear his voice, Harden not your heart, as in the provocation, and as in the day of temptation in the wilderness; When your fathers tempted me, and saw my work . . . unto whom I sware in my wrath, that they should not enter into my rest' (Ps. 95.7, 11).

---

[13] Cf. J. Skinner, *Isaiah*, Vol.11, *Cambridge Bible*, ad loc.

The Curse

The whole earth thus lies under the curse of the living God. When Israel was refused entrance to the Promised Land, as the quotation from Ps. 95 reminds us, even Israel's great representative leader, Moses, had to share in the effects of the curse. Moses, it was believed, was unique amongst men in that he saw God 'face to face' (Ex. 33.11). 'Moses was very meek, above all the men which were upon the face of the earth' (Num. 12.3). Moses even offered to make himself a sacrifice for his people – 'Oh, this people have sinned a great sin, and have made them gods of gold. Yet now, if thou wilt forgive their sin –; and if not, blot me, I pray thee, out of thy book which thou hast written' (Ex. 32.31–32). Yet even that Moses lay under the curse of God. It was not possible for Moses to separate himself from the humanity in which he shared, and to turn round and walk back of his own volition into the Garden of Eden.[14]

Now, if such a situation is what Israel, God's chosen people, must face, so that, in the course of time the nation as a whole must needs be destroyed from off the face of the land which God had given it, then how much more must all the heathen nations lie under the wrath of God. Most of the prophets deal with this topic. The description by Zephaniah of the *dies irae* (Zeph. 1.2 ff.) is perhaps the best known of all: 'I will utterly consume all things from off the earth, saith the Lord . . . I will cut off man from off the earth'. Yet Jeremiah presents us with the most incisive illustration of all of the reality of the wrath of God to be found in the whole OT, viz., the picture of 'the cup of unholy communion' (Jer. 25.15–33). 'For thus saith the Lord God of Israel unto me; Take the wine cup of this fury at my hand, and cause all the nations, to whom I send thee, to drink it. And they shall drink, and be moved, and be mad . . . ' There follows a list of virtually all the known kingdoms of the day, with the 'blanket' addition of the words 'and all the kingdoms of the world, which are upon the face of the

---

[14] See Eugene Arden, 'How Moses failed God', *JBL*, Vol. LXXVI, March, pp. 50–52, with reference to 20.10.

earth'. Then follows: 'Thus saith the Lord of hosts, the God of Israel; Drink ye, and be drunken, and spue, and fall, and rise no more, because of the sword which I will send among you . . . and if they refuse to take the cup . . . thus saith the Lord of hosts; Ye shall certainly drink . . . for the Lord hath a controversy with the nations. Behold, evil shall go forth from nation to nation . . . and the slain of the Lord shall be at that day from one end of the earth even unto the other end of the earth . . . '

'I am the Lord, and there is none else, there is no God beside me . . . I form the light and create darkness: I make peace and create evil: I the Lord do all these things' (Isa. 45.5, 7). In the beginning God separated the Light from the Darkness, and out of Chaos he produced order and life. But God did not destroy *tehom*, the deeps of chaos, in the beginning of his way. God's Spirit brooded *over tehom*. Chaos has remained as part of God's creation, since it is still necessary for his purposes and plan (Gen. 1.2–5).

Both man's rebellion and God's response thereto in wrath can thus be understood only on the basis of the repeated asseveration of the priestly writer that *everything* which God has made is good, even man's inner *yetser* towards rebellion. Thus it is that even the wrath of man God will make to praise him. 'The store of the infinite fullness (plural) of (man's) wrath wilt thou gird upon thee' (Ps. 76.10). How this tension between the goodness and the severity of God is resolved becomes apparent as we watch God's action unfolding in the history of his people, Israel.

Part Three

God and Israel

Thirteen

Israel and Revelation

Last century men imagined that it should be ideally possible to write objective history. To that end the great series 'The Cambridge Ancient (and Modern) History' came into being in the early decades of this century. These series represent the sincere attempt of a group of historians to set down in as straightforward and as objective a manner as possible a total picture of the events that occurred in periods and areas of the world's history, so far as they are known. But the mass of mere facts is so great that the historian must necessarily select if he is to be readable at all. He is thus constantly being compelled to make subjective judgements as to which facts he is to record and which he must leave out. Thus the weighing up of the relative importance of one event over against another is a problem which can be resolved only subjectively in the mind of the author. Such is true also in the case of the tracing of cause and effect over the years and over the centuries. Not only so, but the historian brings to his task an unconscious predilection for certain types of human character, while the decision he takes regarding the space he must allow for the activities of, say, kings, in comparison with commoners also springs from an interest already formed in his mind. Again, the modern historian cannot but regard the ancient world with modern eyes, nor can he help being conditioned in his thinking by the particular kind of society whose air he breathes, whether it be communist, democratic, or any other. While most important of all, his whole approach to the selection of his material will depend on whether he sees the world of men *sub specie aeternitatis*, or whether he leaves God and his purposes out of the story he is retelling. These observations we must keep in mind when we compare modern history writing with the biblical histories.

Within the last century many excellent histories of Israel have appeared. Especially since archaeology began to contribute an ever-increasing volume of knowledge, both about the life of the inhabitants of the Holy Land, and of the great empires that surrounded it, it has become more possible to write an 'objective' and 'factual' account of the story of the Jews before the Christian era. If we were to take the biblical text alone, however, as our source material for a history, we would find it difficult to reconstruct this 'objective' narrative of events which the modern historian holds as the ideal. On the other hand, over the last hundred years, scholarship has been able to approach much closer to the original sources of the biblical material than was previously possible. The discipline of source criticism has helped it here. With the aid of the latter, scholars have uncovered a factual basis for the majority of the historical narratives, and have laid bare the *Sitz im Leben* or historical situation, for example, of many of the utterances of the great prophets. The documentary theory of the origin of the Pentateuch, again, has bequeathed to our generation what is on the whole a good working framework, on the basis of which the modern historian has been able to set in their order the elements that comprise the very important first five books of the Bible; and the more recent analysis of the oral traditions lying behind the generally accepted documents has pushed our knowledge of the factual material incorporated in our present documents back to earlier generations still.

This search for sources in the OT, however, is an activity comparable with the search for the core of an onion. Once we have peeled off layer after layer of an onion, there is little left to show that, before we commenced to do so, it was an onion we had been handling in the first place, a vegetable which is good to eat as a whole. In other words, it is difficult to find any plain, objective narrative in the OT that could be regarded, to use our analogy, as the core of the original onion. Yet that there is a core around which the layers are wrapped, we have no doubt.

The Sinai event must have been historical. The traditions about it are older than D and P themselves. Amos (3.2) and Hosea (2.14–15) both know of them. Elijah too refers to the Covenant made at Sinai (I Kings 19.14), and the Elijah-Elisha cycle of stories was evidently in existence in the seventh century.[1]

But the problem that presents itself to us when we persist in peeling the onion is that when we finally reach its centre, it is extremely difficult to recognize the core to be the core for which we were searching. This problem arises from the fact that the core of the books of the OT deals with an account of an event in history, which, if stripped of all interpretative material, is no more striking and interesting an event than hundreds of others like it in an ancient world that has known countless migrations of peoples and tribes. The core that we come to at last, it would seem, is merely a nexus of historical incidents dealing with one more migration of an obscure near eastern people fleeing from oppression under the hand of the ancient civilization of Egypt. What we reach is a narrative core which goes on to tell of the manner in which this people fought its way in to take possession of a land already occupied by other races and peoples, just as those peoples had already done in their turn, and just as Goths, Huns, Vandals and Jutes were to do in later years in others lands.

In 1928 Kurt Galling[2] analysed the two different traditions that speak of the manner in which Yahweh 'chose' his people Israel. The one is concerned with the call of Abraham, the other with the deliverance from the bondage of Egypt. Galling showed clearly that it was the Exodus tradition alone that, generally speaking, drew the attention of the later prophetic interpreters of Israel's history. The tradition of the descent from Abraham, on the other

---

[1] G. Fohrer, *Elia*, 1957, pp. 42–47.

[2] Die Erwählungstraditionen Israels, pp. 674 and 87–92. We should note that A. Alt answered Galling's thesis the following year in Der Gott der Väter. He sought to show that the stories of Abraham, Isaac and Jacob were originally elements in the tradition held before the Israelites entered and captured Canaan; and that the memory of God's meeting with each of the Patriarchs in turn is enshrined in independent traditions each belonging to different tribal units.

hand, he showed to be referred to only occasionally in the Psalms and in pre-exilic literature (apart from the patriarchal narratives), while the theme of the Exodus was a constant and therefore a living tradition (cf. Amos 5.25; Hos. 2.15; Jer. 2.2; 7.22 ff). The traditions, that Israel as an entity stemmed from Abraham, and that Israel was born out of Egypt, would lead in any case to an acknowledgement of gratitude to God and a sense of dependence upon him; and both traditions witnessed to the fact that history unfolds according to a plan in the mind of God. The prophets sought to expound the two living traditions, and showed that God could use them both. 'For my thoughts are not your thoughts . . . saith the Lord' (Isa. 55.8). The final Redactor of the Pentateuch, as we have it now, also skilfully dovetailed the one tradition with the other. In no sense do we deviate from the centrality of this living tradition, therefore, when we speak of the Exodus as being the 'core' of the history of the people of Israel, even though the promise of that people's 'birth' had been given before the days of Moses.

Yet we know that we cannot rest satisfied even if we have been able to reach down to this mere historical core. And the reason for our not being satisfied is a scientific one. An onion, we know, is not just its core. In fact, once we have peeled off the layers in order to find the core, what we have done is to destroy the onion as a whole, so that in fact it is no longer an onion at all. Similarly, the Exodus nexus of events, if this be regarded as the core of the Pentateuchal tradition, need not be recognized as the action of God Almighty in any sense different from God's action in the movement of any nomadic tribe on the steppes of central Siberia or on the plains of the then unknown America. The point is that, whether we call the layers by names such as J E D and P, or care to subdivide them, or whether we recognize oral traditions in the form of layers earlier even than the Book of Jasher,[3] each of the layers witnesses to the fact that the far-off event recorded in the book of Exodus is an event utterly different in significance from all other and similar migrations. Even if the school of Pentateuchal 'Form Critics' is right in its claim that the letters J E D and P

---

[3] See Josh. 10.13; II Sam. 1.18.

present extensive periods of oral traditions, and were not in fact written 'documents' at all, the cruciality of Israel's conception of the significance of the Exodus event is not in the least invalidated.[4] This is because it is the intensity of the memory of the Exodus and the dominant role it played in Israel's thinking that are the significant factors. Consequently it is irrelevant whether that tradition was preserved in oral or in written form. Two recent 'Introductions' to the OT make this fact quite clear.[5] That the authors of narrative 'documents', whether written or oral, regarded the task of writing history, not simply as a factual recording of events, but primarily as an attempt to understand their significance in the light of God's purposes for Israel, has been realized by the majority of OT critics over the last twenty years. G. von Rad, for example, has greatly contributed to our understanding of this theme[6] and so has G. Ernest Wright.[7] The latter summarizes succinctly the significant arguments for this kind of approach to an understanding of the biblical traditions in his study *God Who Acts*.

According to this manner of seeing the growth and development of Israel's early traditions, then, we recognize how each of the layers, and each, moreover, in its own way, regards the Exodus-Sinai Wilderness historical nexus as a purposeful act of

---

[4] See *Oral Tradition* by E. Nielsen (S.C.M., 1954), which expounds the work of the Scandinavian school in this field; also G.W. Anderson, 'Some Aspects of the Uppsala School of OT Study', *HTR*, XLIII (1950), pp. 239–56; but in criticism of the work of the school, see C.R. North, 'The Place of Oral Tradition in the Growth of the OT', *ET*, LXI (1949–50), pp. 292–6.

[5] *Einleitung in das Alte Testament*, by Otto Eissfeldt, 1934, and *Introduction to the Old Testament*, by A. Bentzen, 1948–49, especially I, pp. 102–264 and II, pp. 80. It is also one of the themes of Johannes Hempel's *Die althebräische Literatur und ihr hellenistischjüdisches* Nachleben, 1934.

[6] *Das formgeschichtliche Problem des Hexateuths*, 1938, and Das erste Buch Mose, 1949.

[7] *God Who Acts*, 1952. See also W. Eichrodt, 'Offenbarung und Geschichte im AT', *TZ*, 4. Jahrgang, Heft 5, pp. 321 ff.

God. Each in other words recognizes not only the fact of the Exodus as the origin of the people of Israel, but it also interprets that fact in its own way. But in interpreting it, it retells the story in such a manner that it becomes virtually impossible to separate interpretation from historical events. Interpretation, in reality, becomes as much part of the divine event as the original historical occurrence itself.

If, for example, we analyse the record of the passage of the Red Sea, as we are told it in Ex. 14, and then seek to isolate the record left us by J and separate it from the much later description of the event that has been given us by the document P, this peculiar and indefinable relation of the layers to the core becomes increasingly clear. Now, it is recognized in virtually all critical commentaries that the mid portion of v. 21 in that chapter is from the hand of J. Verse 21 runs: 'And the Lord caused the sea to go back by a strong east wind all the night'. This factual description of a natural event is sometimes hailed as being nearer the 'truth' than P's imaginative description which follows in the next verse: 'And the waters were a wall unto them on their right hand and on their left'. Between the composition of the two documents J and P there lies some four hundred years of inter-pretative thought. Now amongst other OT writings, there is a Psalm which overtly sets out to expound the meaning of the Exodus as a 'mashal'. A *mashal*, amongst other things, is an interpretative story. We are able to date the composition of Psalm 78 to within a century, since the Psalmist writes confessedly after the year 722 B.C., when Ephraim fell to the Assyrians (see vv. 67–68); but he knows nothing of the Fall of Jerusalem which took place over a century later. Thus Psalm 78 was conceived between the composition of the documents J and P. In his *mashal*, or parable (see v. 2), our Psalmist expounds the mighty acts of God in the Exodus event by referring to it purely in terms of divine grace and purpose (vv. 5–8). Being an interpretative story, a *mashal* is not primarily concerned with facts as such; rather it is a story whose function is to convey truth in picture form. When Professor Delitzsch translated the NT into modern Hebrew, he very rightly chose this word to translate our Lord's word 'parable'.[8] In the case of Ps. 78, the word mashal is paralleled with the second noun *ḥidhah*, in the plural. In both the AV and the ARSV the latter is translated as 'dark sayings' (v. 2).[9]

Now, in using such a phrase as this the Psalmist must have had in mind something as follows: Men of olden time, men like J and those before him, had reported the mighty events of the past with a sense of mystery in their tones. That sense of mystery could now, at the later period in which he lived, be conveyed only in parabolic and poetic terms. And so our Psalmist invites his brethren, with a sense of awe in their hearts, to sing the words of his Psalm and regard them as a description of that mighty event of far-off times, to sing them even as they might a credal statement: 'he divided the sea, and caused them to pass through; and he made the waters to stand as an heap'. Then, generations after the Psalm had first been sung, P, knowing that the Psalmist was right in regarding the Exodus event as a *pele'*, a 'wonder', an event which is somehow mixed up with the supernatural, an event not to be understood merely in terms of this world, adopted the method of the Psalm. Thus it is that Ex. 14.22, coming from the hand of P, and written

---

[8]   Three times in Ezekiel an allegory or parable is called a *mashal*, viz. 17.2; 20.49; and 24.3. Basically the verb *m-sh-l* implies the idea of 'to be like'. So also does the verb *d-m-h*. A noun formed from the latter, viz., *demuth*, is one of the words used of man made in the 'likeness' of God in Gen. 1.26; cf. Isa. 40.18, 25. The verb itself, again, conveys the conception that the prophets could present their message by symbolic action as well as by speech (cf. Hos. 12.10). Ezek. 14.8 parallels *mashal* with *'oth* (sign): 'I will make him a sign and a proverb'. The sign was an empirical event which carried in itself its own eschatological significance. See A.R. Johnson, art. '*Mashal*', in *Wisdom in Israel and the Ancient near East*, 1955; O Eissfeldt, 'Der Mashal im Alten Testament', *BZAW*, XXIV, 1913; A.S. Herbert, 'The Parable (Mašal) in the Old Testament', *SJT*; 7, 1954, pp. 180–96; J. Paterson, *The Book that is Alive*, 1954, p. 46; cf. also Mark 3.23; 7.17, for 'dark saying'.

[9]   This is its meaning in the Greek of Prov. 1.6; but the LXX of Ezek. 17.2 translates it as διήγημα a 'tale', while Hab. 2.6 has it as πρόβλημα. J. Jeremias in *The Parables of Jesus* (English edition, translated by S.H. Hooke), 1954, 3rd ed. p. 14, note 21, gives a list of the biblical and extra-biblical translations of *mashal* and *ḥidhah*.

at least seven hundred years after the event in question, *correctly* describes the waters of the Red Sea, not as having been merely blown back by a mighty wind, but as having been held *back* by the hand of the living God. P is able to make this declaration because God had indeed been a 'wall' to his people right throughout all the years of their national life (cf. the use of the term for human aid, I Sam. 25.16, and for divine, Isa. 26.1).

To revert to the analogy we have set out to use, we might regard the latest strata of the OT as the outer layers of the onion. In them we have interpretative material of the kind that comes from the pen of the writers of Neh. 9; Josh. 24 and the Psalm embedded in Exodus 15. These passages each retell the story of God's dealings with his people in what is virtually credal form. Again then, the document J would be representative of our earliest written material and constitute an inner layer. Now, when we lay these various layers side by side, and read them regardless of the fact that often hundreds of years can separate them and their writers, we are immediately struck by the essential unity of outlook that pervades them all. In all the layers that we can isolate, in fact, we come across this identical phenomenon, that whether the Exodus is spoken of factually or lyrically, the event which took place in that ancient period of time is regarded as no other than an act of the living God. We quote Ex. 14.21 again, J's factual account of the event, as we called it, this time to make clear the emphasis of the verse: 'And *Yahweh caused* the sea to go back by a strong east wind all the night'.[10] In other words, there appears to be no *merely* factual inner core of objective narrative at all. The conclusion that we are forced to, therefore, is this. At every level throughout the story of Israel, from that of the earliest documents or from oral tradition itself, down to the latest editing of the post-exilic years, the core of the story of the Exodus from Egypt is acknowledged to have been an event of such a nature that it cannot be fully described in terms of this world's human language.

Yet still we have not exhausted the significance of the analogy of the onion. An onion is more than a core with superimposed

---

[10]   Cf. *The Fulness of Time*, by John Marsh, 1952, p. 45

yers thereupon. An onion is both the sum total of the relation between the layers and the core, and it is also a total entity in itself, different in kind and in appearance in its totality from an orange or a fig.

J and P and all the other interpreters of Israel's past are layers, then, in the tradition. But as such, these interpreters themselves stand out from the total situation which they are seeking to interpret. They are voices from within an Israel, the core of whose existence is more than a mere fortuitous concatenation of atoms. From the earliest records to the latest these interpreters believed that the core upon which they took their stand was an in-breaking of the God of the heavens into this world by means of an historical event. Not only so, it was an in-breaking, they believed, not merely within the natural order, but one performed in such a manner that their nation could see a redemptive purpose behind this mighty act of God. It is true that all the natural events that occurred at the time of the Exodus may be explained, and explained away, in terms of volcanic activity or some other uncommon sequence of odd but comprehensible phenomena. But Israel's interpreters believed that those natural phenomena represented nothing less than an in-breaking of God, not only into nature, but also into the conscious-ness of this one people out of the many other possible peoples of the earth whom God might have chosen. They believed, moreover, that this one people alone had been in the position to respond to the divine initiative that had occurred within the events with the 'yes' of faith. They saw that if Moses had not responded to the call of God in faith, then God would have had to choose another course of action (Ex. 4.18).[11] On the other hand, that series of far-off events which Israel's interpreters, one after the other, saw to be a primal act of the living God, was in fact dismissed by generations of Philistines and Moabites, when they heard of them from the lips of neighbouring Israelites, as 'just one of those things you can easily explain'. For example, we note from I Sam. 4.8 that the Philistines evidently saw no significance in the facts of the Exodus event, since they described those facts incorrectly.

---

[11] H. Rowley, *The Faith of Israel*, 1956, p. 42.

In acknowledging the fact that throughout the whole sub-sequent history of Israel each generation, or at least representative persons of each generation, made the same declaration of faith about this primal act of God, though describing their response to it in different terms, we are faced with the following interesting and vitally important corollary. We are faced with the fact that there could have been no action of God in history unless God had first secured and chosen a people to whom he could reveal his will in action, and that it was empirical Israel that made the response of faith in the OT story. Thus the purposes of God in this world of space and time are fully dependent upon the fact of empirical Israel. Nay more. As we shall hope to make clear as our argument proceeds, the whole cosmic purpose of God, when he created the heavens and the earth, hinges upon the historical fact of God's choice of empirical Israel.

Before abandoning then our analogy of the onion, let us sum up what it has to say to us. We learn from the fact of the Exodus something about God when he acted within space and time and called Israel out of Egypt to be his instrument in his plan. But that 'core'-activity is not understandable by itself as a naked act. It has been interpreted to the world by many minds. But each interpre-tation has of necessity been conditioned by the core round which it is wrapped. The interpreters were all representatives of the empirical Israel which had been born of God, and through which God's act had been made visible to the world. In other words, before us in the Pentateuch lie God's action, Israel's response, and the various interpreters' descriptions of both, each conceivable only in terms of the other. That is why the OT can never be understood merely as 'the history of the Jews', although much of the history of the Jews is to be found within its pages. Nor can we ever hope to isolate, from within the OT alone, the historical core of events round which later generations have woven their inter-pretations. And this is because, as we have seen, the so-called historical core is not, paradoxically speaking, a 'historical' core at all in the modern sense, but rather a supra-historical one.

In the same manner we are not to think of the OT as being merely the Word of God spoken through the lips of prophets and the pens of historians, and so to be understood today as embody-ing the mind of God in a neat and wholly objective and written form. The Word of God in the OT has not come to us, as it were, on a silver salver. The OT is not conceivable as the Voice of God, heard by man, and then set down in human words. Each one of the writers of the Bible, whether known to us or unknown, prophet, priest or king, was a member of this empirical Israel, the People of God. Every word that any Israelite wrote and that has come down to us from any section of the corpus of Israel's literature, was penned by a people that had already been wholly conditioned by the primal act of God that we have described.[12]

Thus the OT has come down to us, not in any straight line, so to speak, as the 'mere' Word of God, but in a form that we can envisage rather as a triangular relationship. Firstly, it is evident that in the pages of the OT 'Holy men spake as they were moved by the Holy Ghost' (II Peter 1.21). But secondly, we are to remember that these 'holy men' were all representative of the Israel that God had already chosen and redeemed. That is to say, while the Scriptures have certainly been mediated to us through the Holy Spirit, they have also been mediated to us through empirical Israel. Then thirdly, and finally, the knowledge of God that comes to us by his Spirit through Israel is a knowledge that is conditioned by the mutual relationship and interaction of the Holy Spirit and Israel, as Israel makes her interpretative response to what is, we recall, the primal act of God himself. Israel has been called by God's Name (II Chron. 7.14; Dan. 9.19). It is under-standable, then, why Israel's story should be bound up with him whose Name she bore (cf. Josh. 7.9, and see p. 43).

---

[12] Cf. Anton Jirku, *Die älteste Geschichte Israels im Rahmen lehrhafter Darstellungen*, 1917, where he discusses the significance of the 'summa-ries' of Israel's early history contained in Josh. 24, Pss. 78 and 105 and in Deut. 29.

Fourteen

The Significance of the Exodus

Our first task will be to examine certain of the interpretative 'meshalim' from the pens of OT writers, and seek to discover what they made of the fact of the empirical Israel in those pictorial terms which they used, the Israel of which they themselves were a part. We shall not forget that they used these *meshalim* under the inspiration of the Holy Spirit of the God who had chosen Israel. Incidentally, too, we shall notice that the figures of speech, the parables, the patterns of thought, call them what we will, which we shall be handling, are common to virtually the whole range of OT literature. There is a value, a real and important value, in what historical criticism has enabled us to do. It has enabled us to observe the growth of Israel's religion from the early and primitive levels that were scarcely distinguishable from the levels at which Israel's neighbours and fellow citizens in the land of Canaan practised their faith; and it has enabled us to see Israel's religion flower in a faith that was ready to approximate to and to move over into the faith of the NT writers. Yet even while we observe this growth in faith and understanding on the part of Israel, we become aware of the paradoxical truth, that the thought-patterns of Israel hardly changed at all throughout the whole length of Israel's story. For example, the wild and primitive poetry of that wild and primitive woman, Deborah, (Judg. 5) contains in *essence* the fully developed pattern of faith of the great poet-prophet, Deutero-Isaiah. Accordingly, as we examine the interpretative thought-patterns to be found within the OT itself, we notice that we are being drawn to admit an essential unity within its literature. Despite its multifarious origins, the OT presents us with a unity of thought such as no human mind could ever have impressed upon it (cf. Pss. 66.5–6; 68.7–8;77.14–20; 81.5–10; 103.7; 105.8; 106.45; Amos 2.9–10; 3.1–2; Hos. 2.14–15; 9.10; 11.5; 12.9, 13; 13.4–5; Micah 6.4–5; Isa. 1.2; 10.26; 11.11–16; etc.).

We have said that the first 'moment' in Israel's story was the great Exodus event, the calling of a rabble people out of the bondage of Egypt to become a nation in their own right. Yet at once we are aware that the Exodus event is not the first item to be dealt with by the interpreters of Israel's story. The whole contents of the book of Genesis precede the record of the Exodus.

As products of our western, secular educational institutions, we find it difficult to realize that for the OT writers the Exodus-Sinai event was really the first and primal event for them to record. They record it in two traditions to be found in the earliest narratives. One is the tradition which speaks of Israel's birth as a people when 'the mountains melted before the Lord, even that Sinai from before the Lord God of Israel' (Judg. 5.5). The poem in Hab. 3 speaks in the same way, of God coming from Teman, and of his glory covering the heavens (v. 3); but it goes on at v. 8 to include the crossing of the Red Sea. The latter we regard then as the other and dominant tradition relating to the call of Israel. Other passages, however, unite the twin ideas. Ps. 44, for example, unites and fuses the two traditions just as they are united and fused in the composite narrative of the Book of Exodus. In other words, what we observe in the mind of the writers is that conception which we have now repeatedly emphasized, viz., that God's primal action on earth was his action whereby he created and redeemed his people, Israel. In this regard see also Hos. 12.9; 13.4; Jer. 2.6–7; and Isa. 63.7–14.

However, there is a further complication in the matter of God's primal action. We recall that the might of Pharaoh at the period of the Exodus is compared with that of 'Tannin' (Ex. 7.9 RV margin). Once again, then, we realize how difficult it is to determine whether the Red Sea is really the subject of the theological inspiration of Israel's interpreters, or whether it is the primal ocean, *tehom*, the chaotic watery mass from which God formed the world. To return to Habakkuk, we now notice in 3.10 this same juxtaposition of ideas: 'The mountains saw thee and trembled: the overflowing of the water passed by: the deep (*tehom*) uttered his voice, and lifted up his hands on high'. In the same way it is with just such a *double entendre* that the two Psalms, 135.6–12 and 136, report upon the whole Exodus nexus of events. We on our part are inclined to regard the Exodus as primarily the story of God's action in the redemption of his people. But those Psalms virtually identify God's action in giving birth to Israel with his action in creating the earth. That is to say, if we take those two Psalms as representative of the thought of an ancient people that knew nothing of our scientific approach to the origins of things, we are presented with the conception that Israel is called to praise her Lord on two counts. Firstly, the Psalmists praise God for calling Israel into being as a people; but secondly, they praise him for the creation of the cosmos as a whole, for they see that at the heart of God's creative purpose is his mighty plan to redeem his creation through his people Israel. Or to put this truth in the form in which J. Hempel expressed it: 'The history of Israel and that of the Cosmos are one.'[1]

It is obvious that no one in OT times supposed that the Exodus was actually prior in time to the Creation of the world. On the other hand, Creation had come about, it was felt, just in order that there might be a platform, a setting, for that which was really prior to it, viz., the gracious loving purpose of the living God. And even as empirical Israel was essential for that gracious loving purpose to work out, so too God's redemption and adoption of that people was part of the plan that God had had in mind from before the foundation of the cosmos.

The battle between Yahweh and Leviathan that is so often spoken of in the OT was no mere mythological event thought of as taking place before the foundation of the world. It was a theological, rather than a cosmological myth which Isaiah and

---

[1] *Altes Testament und Geschichte*, 1930, p. 18.

other OT writers had in view (cf. Ps. 89.9–10; Ezek. 32.2; Isa. 51.9–10, on the basis of Isa. 27.1: 'In that day the Lord with his sore and great and strong sword shall punish leviathan the piercing serpent, even leviathan that crooked serpent; and he shall slay the dragon that is in the sea'). It was a myth that had to do with God's continual war against evil. Not only so, but it was a myth with which the meaning and purpose of empirical Israel was all bound up. Of this we are made aware in the following verse (Isa. 27.2), where Isaiah refers to Israel in connexion with the serpent myth under his favourite figure for Israel as God's vineyard: 'In that day, sing ye unto her, A vineyard of red wine. I the Lord do keep it'. In the same way, Ps. 74, which begins by reminding God that Israel is his chosen people, similarly goes on to 'scramble' what seem to us, with our insistence upon historical perspective, to be really two moments in the activity of God. The Psalm speaks of God's victory over Leviathan as taking place, not just at Creation's dawn, but also at the crossing of the Red Sea (cf. especially vv. 12–14, and see p. 113).

The significance of the Exodus, then, is very profound. It was seen to be more than the mere redemption of a people from the bondage of an alien race. For the interpreters of the OT writing from within Israel itself, the Exodus had two mighty and significant meanings. In the first place, it was an event of cosmic significance. It was an event that had total meaning both for time and for eternity. In other words, it was an eschatological event. That is why it could be sung about in an act of worship, or else recited as a cultic act, when, by faith, the worshipper found himself directly confronted by the living God (cf. Pss. 44; 78; Deut. 26.5b; Josh. 24.2b–13). Farm labourers may have had the story taught them on the occasions of the great religious festivals, and prophets, priests and kings probably each found opportunities to declaim the mighty acts of God as a means of witnessing to their faith in Yahweh's interest in his people (cf. Pss. 22.4–5; 66.1–7; 103.7 ff., etc.). 'To the Hebrew, consciousness made a unity of successive events in time, so that the past was alive in the present, and by a historical memory a people remained self-identical'.[2] In the second place, this eschatological Exodus-event was an event altogether inconceivable without the prior existence on earth of empirical Israel, and without the extraordinary interpretation which that same Israel put upon itself as it theologized in retrospect upon the meaning of its existence.

The book of Genesis, therefore, contains for us what we could with justification call the 'afterthoughts' of J E and P, or of the oral traditions lying behind them, once those writers have first of all interpreted the Exodus. Every single one of the documents or traditions of the Pentateuchal corpus originated, of course, subsequent to the Exodus event. The book of Genesis thus gives us 'merely' the necessary background to the choice and adoption of Israel as the People of God.

As the Prologue to the book of Genesis draws to an end, and the ultimate questions of God's providence are unfolded in majestic yet severely simple language, we pass from *Urgeschichte* (Primal-history) to *Heilsgeschichte* (Salvation-history) with the call of Abraham, and the dawn of the archaeological period (Gen. 12). Yet the use of the latter term must not obscure the fact that Israel was no mere passive instrument in the hands of the Holy Spirit. Once the Exodus took place we are shown an empirical people that was continually moulding and conditioning its own history, despite the fact that that history had begun as a great divine event. What we read of so often throughout the whole OT is the insistence with which Israel thwarted the divine will that sought to work itself out through Israel's story, yet which, paradoxically, was bound up with that people who sought to thwart it. Of the pre-Exodus, patriarchal period, we have little factual information, it is true. Archaeology has laid bare before our eyes conditions in Babylonia, Canaan and Egypt quite consonant with the conditions remembered by the traditions lying behind the Genesis narratives. But for the persons of Abraham, Isaac, Jacob and Joseph we have no factual evidence whatsoever. Therefore all

---

[2]   Th. Boman, *Das Hebräische Denken im Verglich mit dem Griechischen*, 1952, p. 34. See also A. Weiser, *Glaube und Geschichte im AT*, 1931, Beiträge zur Wissenschaft von A.u.N.T., 4.F. 4.H.

we can do is to accept their historicity in faith, whether we regard them as persons, or whether we regard them, as the last generation was inclined to do, as names belonging to tribes and groups. Yet we should have no real difficulty in making this act of faith, because even if we were not to possess any traditions of the activities of the Patriarchs whatsoever, we should have to invent another Abraham, Isaac and Jacob in order to understand the Genesis of a people that could come to the birth, fully developed, as it were, and having behind it all the promises that Israel did actually cherish as its own.[3] Thus 'our father Abraham' (Luke 1.73) was no mere eponymous ancestor of their race to the interpreters of Israel's story. He was the father, under God, of a people whose real Father was God himself. He was the equivalent of the Joseph of the NT story, necessary to complete the picture of a human family such as that into which Jesus himself was born. Yet Joseph was not the real father of his Son. The real Father was no human person at all, but God himself. In the same way, we may say that the people of Israel, regarded as one entity, was, for the reason we have just outlined, just as much a child of promise as was the Son of Mary (Gen. 15.4 and Matt. 1.20). Or, to put the truth in other words, and in the manner in which both the OT and the NT have expressed it, the whole people of Israel lay in promise in the loins of Abraham (Gen. 15.4; 35.10–11; Heb. 7.5)

After we pass the 12th chapter of Genesis we see this people, the sons of Abraham, growing and multiplying in fulfilment of the words of the divine promise. Yet throughout this period they are a people who have no particular importance in themselves. They can only be seen, through the eyes of J E and P, to have a *post-eventu* significance for those who know the end of the story from the beginning. That is why it is not fundamentally important to the theology of the OT if the modern historian assures us that it was not all Israel that came up out of Egypt, or that the Leah tribes reached Canaan before the Rachel tribes arrived. At the present moment the study of Israel's early period has brought us

---

[3] G.A. Danell, *Studies in the Name in the Israel in the Old Testament*, 1946, pp. 10, 19, etc.

to the point where we recognize that we cannot allow ourselves to be dogmatic about historical detail. On the other hand, the point that is really fundamental is that a representative group of Israel at least did actually come up out of Egypt. Thus it is that eventually, and again in fulfilment of the promise, we find them 'increased abundantly, and multiplied, and waxed exceeding mighty' (Ex. 1.7), on the eve of that fateful moment in God's cosmic plan when this people should come to the birth and be adopted as God's Son. This was to be the real moment, in fact, as Israel's interpreters conceived it, of the birth, not only of a nation, but also of the cosmos, which was, paradoxically speaking, already lying waiting to be redeemed through Israel, that peculiar people whom God was now about to use.

We shall now turn to see how Israel herself regarded God's developing plan and what her connexion with it actually was. To do so we shall have to examine a series of figures which Israel herself employed to enable her to understand clearly her unique relationship to God.

Fifteen

Some Interpretations of Israel by Israel

(1) The Figure of the Vine

The Vine is frequently employed in the OT as a figure for Israel as a people. The Vine was regarded in ancient times as the type of effervescent life, and as the symbol of a vitality which shows itself able to produce an immense number of individual shoots.[1] But as a supplement to the figure, the setting of the Vine was also frequently included in the picture. Thus the mind was allowed to range from the Vine to the Vineyard in which it grew.

Hosea may have been the first, chronologically speaking, to suggest the use of the figure. He employs the symbol when he refers to Israel's failure to bring forth fruit as a healthy Vine ought to do (Hos. 10.1). Then Isaiah follows, taking up the figure and developing it. In Isa. 3.14 he suggests that it is the rulers of Israel who have despoiled the Vineyard of God. But in chap. 5 he broadens what before was only a figure into his well known parable. Therein he refers to God as the Husbandman, and describes how God has carefully tended the Vine in the Vineyard which he had prepared and walled. But, just as in the case of Hosea's indictment, here too the Vine fails the Husbandman, even though the latter had loved it as he would love his 'well-beloved'.

Jeremiah, a century later than Isaiah, remembers the figure, and uses it to advantage (Jer. 2.21; 12.10). Joel too seems to know

---

[1]   J. Jeremias, *The Old Testament in the Light of the Ancient East*, 1, p. 209.

it (Joel 1.7); and there is a mystical allusion to it with reference to Judah in the so-called 'Blessings of Jacob' (Gen. 49.10–12). (This passage, however, which probably dates from just before the monarchy, may not carry the kind of 'parabolic' significance which Isaiah so clearly had in mind, but may refer only to the fact that the land of Judah was rich in vineyards.) After the Exile had begun, however, we find three references, this time in Ezekiel, to this parable or *mashal* which Hosea had first introduced (Ezek. 15.1–6; 17; 19.10–14).[2]

Of all the post-Isaianic uses of the figure, however, that of Psalm 80 is possibly the most important. This Psalm must have been composed at the earliest subsequent to the Fall of Samaria in 722 B.C. but more probably after the destruction of Jerusalem in 587 B.C. Here we are presented with every element that the figure can be developed to show (Ps. 80.8–14). The Psalm begins by referring to the Vine which God had brought out of Egypt, and for which he had prepared the ground in Palestine by driving out the heathen. It was there in Palestine that he had planted it (cf. Ex. 15.17, whence the word, or at least the idea of 'plant' may have been taken. The latter passage constitutes the 'Redemption Song' sung to commemorate the Exodus event, and which was later embodied in the Exodus narrative). The roots of the Vine filled the soil, its shoots reached the traditional frontiers of Solomon's day. But God, so ran the figure, had now allowed the wild beasts to break in and trample down the Vine, and its tender shoots had now been burnt down to the ground. The Psalm, however, ends with a prayer of faith in the power of God's saving activity. We shall have reason to revert to this Psalm on later occasions, since it incorporates other figures as well which we must also examine.

The figure of the Vine now leaves us with the following suggestions in mind. One Vine was evidently sufficient to represent the *totum corpus* of Israel. The one plant, however, subdivided into innumerable branches, twigs and shoots, called variously in Hebrew 'sons' (Ps. 80.15) and 'daughters' (Gen.

---

[2]   See Strack-Billerbeck, *KzNT*, 2, p. 563.

49.22), while below ground it took deep root in the soil which
God had prepared to receive it. This meant, of course, that it was
God who first planted it. It then grew at God's bidding, and with
God's love and care. But yet it was God who had now trampled,
burnt and destroyed the Vine, on the plea that it had failed him
as he sought to use it for his purpose. The immediate instruments
of this destruction, we are told, were the armies of invading
nations; yet it was God who had created those invading nations,
and so it was God who had therefore allowed their murderous
soldiery to wreck their lustful will upon the Vineyard which God
had loved like an only son (Isa. 5.1).

The figure of the Vine, then, seeks to express in picture
language, in the language of *mashal* or parable, the vital relation
that was meant to obtain between Israel and God; and at the
same time the destruction of the Vine proclaims the outcome of
Israel's refusal to be used as the instrument through which the
purposes of God were intended to work out.[3] This failure on
Israel's part to allow herself to be the true Vine is recognized even
before the Exile takes place in the so-called 'Song of Moses'
(Deut. 32.32–33).

(2) The Figure of the Son of God

How ancient is the 22nd verse of the 4th chapter of Exodus? 'Thus
saith the Lord, Israel is my Son, even my firstborn'. Most of the
commentaries attribute it to a redactor. Yet even if the verse is a
late interpretation and interpolation, it probably precedes in time

---

[3] In the post-biblical period this figure was greatly cherished. Thus, with
reference to Ps. 80, Gen. Rabba 88.5 says specifically: 'The Vine in this
passage refers to Israel'. Lev. Rabba 36.2, with reference to the same
Psalm, produces a lengthy exegesis on the same theme. This Rabbinical
interpretation of the figure would thus be current in NT times. Mark
12.1–12 takes this interpretation for granted. John 15.1 is a reference to
Jer. 2.21, to the ἄμπελος ἀληθινή, the true vine, which Israel ought to
have been.

the 11th chapter of Hosea with its well developed figure of Israel as the Son of God. When we examine the Hebrew text of Hos. 2, however, unfortunately we find it in a far from perfect state. The editors of the ARSV have made the best of a difficult task when they turn those verses into English. Yet what an important picture we receive from the few lines at the beginning of the chapter, expressing as they do one of the two daring figures which Hosea uses to describe empirical Israel. (We shall note the other presently.) 'When Israel was a child, then I loved him, and called my son out of Egypt'. Here we are told that God the Father had called out of Egypt this peculiar people and that thereupon he had adopted his Son (on the basis of Ex. 4.22); and that he had done so for no other reason than just that he loved the Son (Deut. 4.37). But this Son did not at the time appreciate what his Father had done for him. The more the Father called him to his arms, the more recalcitrantly he ran the other way (Hos. 11.2). The Son exhibited this self-will inherent in his nature by giving his love to other gods and idols. Yet it was Yahweh who had taught this little lad to take his very first steps (v. 3). If the boy should fall and hurt his knees, it was the Father who comforted him in his arms. But the Son did not know that it was I (said God) who was healing his childish sores. Thereafter the figure changes somewhat, but we shall continue our virtual paraphrase of it in the following words: 'I did not force my Son to draw the plough as an ox, but actually drew him instead to myself with thongs of love and compassion. As when the day's work is over the good farmer eases the yoke and removes the bit from the mouth of his beast, so did I also tenderly remove his childish bonds at nightfall, and bent down and fed him ere he fell asleep' (v. 4). And so we are presented with this tender picture of God the Father lovingly caring for and bringing up this wayward Son whom he had adopted as his own. In the same way, Psalm 80, which we quoted with reference to the 'Vine' figure, refers to all Israel as God's 'Son': 'Look down . . . upon the son whom thou hast reared for thyself' (ARSV footnote to v. 15).

In Ex. 4.22 God calls his Son his 'first born', *bechor*. The Septuagint naturally enough translates this Hebrew word by πρωτότοκος. Now, this is not the only instance where the OT refers to God as the Father of Israel (cf. Deut. 32.6, 18; Jer. 3.14, 19; 31.9; Isa. 63.16; 64.8; Mal. 1.6; 2.10; I Chron. 29.10; to use the chronological order of composition). Nor is Ex. 4.22 the only occasion when Israel is hailed as God's 'first-born' Son (cf. Jer. 31.9). Moreover, in at least eight other instances the Israelites are referred to as 'sons' of God, in the plural. However, that same chapter of Jeremiah which refers to Israel as God's first-born Son goes on to refer to him again as God's 'dear', *yaqqir*, Son (LXX ἀγαπητός, his 'darling' child. This paralleling of 'first born' with 'dear' and 'beloved' was a natural interchange of terms arising from the very precious nature of the first-born child in any family.[4] Thus, while the individual Israelite could be called God's 'beloved' just as on occasions the individual person was referred to as God's 'Son', or 'child' in the AV (Deut. 33.12; II Sam. 12.24; Isa. 1.2; Neh. 13.26; Ps. 60.5; Ps. 127.2), yet the term 'beloved Son' could and undoubtedly did apply to Israel as a *corpus* (Isa. 5.1; Jer. 11.15) just as truly as it did to individual sons of God.

Now, we have just noted that individuals within the total corpus of Israel could be regarded as sons of God. Those most likely to be so regarded were naturally the foremost individual men in Israel. They could be addressed by the title 'son' in the singular, in the same manner as was the whole nation which the individual represented in his special capacity. The text of Ps. 2.12 ('Kiss the Son', with reference to the king) is, of course, recognized to present the translators with difficulties. For example, the LXX has not understood the word *bar* to mean 'son' at all, nor have any others of the later versions, except the Syriac. But in v. 7 of the same Psalm the newly crowned king is explicitly hailed with the words: 'Thou art my Son; this day have I begotten thee'. Ps. 89.26–7, again, clearly hails the king as God's 'first-born' son. Moreover, if we follow the suggestions of the 'Myth and Ritual' school of OT exegetes, this Psalm may even have reference to a re-enthronement festival held annually on New

---

[4]   Cf. E.A. Abbott, *From Letter to Spirit*, 1903, p. 195 ff.

Year's Day.[5] There is no dubiety, however, about II Sam. 7.14, where the king is explicitly hailed as God's Son.

The choice of the epithet 'son' for a representative member of the people of Israel is not the only interesting feature in the phrase we are now examining. The adjective which describes the son is important as well as the noun. Three times over, in the story of the sacrifice of the boy Isaac, for example (Gen. 22.2, 12, 16), when God addresses Abraham about his son, he employs the adjective *yaḥidh*, 'only', 'unique' along with the word for son. Now, this adjective 'only' occurs again with reference to a son in three other passages as well, viz., Amos 8.10; Jer. 6.26; and Zech. 12.10.[6] And interestingly enough, on each occasion the adjective *yaḥidh*, 'only' is rendered by the word 'beloved', ἀγαπητός in the LXX version. Yet we have already noticed that Jeremiah equated 'first-born' with 'only' when he sought to find an adjective that meant 'beloved'. Both these adjectives then, may be rendered by the one Greek adjective ἀγαπητός. In other words, before the end of the second century B.C., by the time that the Hebrew text of the OT had been rendered into Greek, the concept covered by the word 'beloved' was felt to sum up and declare the depths of meaning rendered by both 'first-born' and 'only' son. As we have seen, the adjective *yaḥidh* is actually used (*a*) in the case of an only child, such as Isaac; (*b*) in the case of a king when he is regarded as representative of Israel as a whole; and (*c*) as a figure for that whole corpus of Israel which is so vitally important a medium of the revelation of God in the OT.

Thus we learn from the use that the OT makes of the figure of the Son that God is no less than the Father of Israel. We do well, however, to define at once the scope of the word Father as it is

---

[5]   Cf. S. Mowinckel, *Psalmenstudien II: Das Thronbesteigungsfest Jahwäs und des Ursprung der Eschatologie, 1922, pp. 112 ff., and 177 f.* Also A.R. Johnson, 'The Rôle of the King in the Jerusalem Cultus', in *The Labyrinth*, 1935, pp. 73–111, and *Sacral Kingship in Ancient Israel, 1955, p. 23 n. See pp. 301 ff.*

[6]   And to a daughter in Judg. 11.34, where in the LXX (A), 'only' is again equated with 'beloved'.

used of God in the OT. The idea of 'father of . . . ,' 'son of' has two uses in Hebrew. (*a*) It refers to the ordinary human relationship of physical descent. But (*b*) it may describe a moral relationship, such as can be observed in one who completely exhibits the spirit of another. Thus the familiar phrase 'Sons of Belial' (Judg. 19.22; I Sam. 2.12; etc.) is not used of people whose father bore that name. These 'sons' are those whose nature shows the evil tendencies of the mythical bearer of the name. In other words, the phrase just means 'bad men'. The loving, moral relationship implied in the Son of God figure, however, may be paralleled by the Mother-Son relationship (cf. Isa. 49.15; 50.1; 66.13, where, of course, a physical relationship might indeed have been expected). Yet there is never any suggestion of a physical relationship between the biblical Father and Son. Rather it is the relationship of Creator and created, as we can discover when we see how the figures of Father and Creator can be set side by side (cf. Isa. 43.15; Deut. 32.6, 18). Deut. 32.6 runs: 'Is he not thy father, thy *begetter*, he who fashioned thee and set thee up?' The verb *qanah* in Hebrew almost defies translation. It is as vague in definition as is the English verb 'to get'. It means to 'acquire', 'buy'=, and virtually almost to 'beget' (cf. Prov. 8.22 and p. 109 fn.). Yet in this case the meaning of the verb is obviously defined by the words 'he who fashioned thee'=, *'asah* (the ordinary verb for 'to make'). God had *bara'*, created, Israel therefore (Isa. 43.15), and had 'fashioned' him of old. So there is no suggestion of physical begetting, as with Israel's neighbours and their gods. The conception of Israel as God's first-born, only-begotten, or beloved Son is one that is unique in the world's thought.[7]

God adopted Israel, then, 'at birth' (cf. Ezek. 16.6). Immediately thereafter he redeemed his Son by ransoming him from the power of Pharaoh in return for Pharaoh's first-born son (Ex. 4.24). It is thus this act of God which renders Israel's sonship unique. Hosea now interprets the story of the Son for us in its next phase. He tells us how, in natural sequence, God taught his beloved Son to walk. The verb 'to walk' in Hebrew, viz. *halach*, we should note, is used elsewhere (e.g. Ex. 16.4; Lev. 26.3 (both

---

[7]   Cf. G. Dalman, *The Words of Jesus*, 1902, p. 273.

P); II Kings 10.31 (D); Micah 4.5; Jer. 9.13; Dan. 9.10) to describe the keeping of the revealed will of God.[8] In a corresponding manner also the noun *halachah*, 'way', which derives from the verb 'to walk', is one of the nouns used to describe what we today would call 'religion' (a word which does not occur in the AV of the OT, cf. Gen. 18.19; Deut. 5.33). If we can believe that the germs of later thought are to be found in the teachings of the great prophets, then the phrase 'God taught his Son to walk', will contain at least an element of what is written into the Pentateuch in Exodus and Leviticus, viz., that whatever written 'law' was in existence in their day was indeed *halachah*, the 'way' that Israel was meant to follow. God 'instructed' his Son (Deut. 32.10) so that he grew in wisdom (i.e. by the fear of the Lord, which is wisdom, Job. 28.28), in stature (by multiplying and filling the land), and in favour with God and man (cf. the flowering of Israel's kingdom during the reign of Solomon).

The figure of the Son is an advance upon the figure of the Vine. If one knows the Vineyard, one knows little about the Husbandman. But if one knows the Son, one is led at once to know the Father.[9]

(3) The Figure of the Son of Man

The battle has now raged long and loud around the exact NT significance of the term 'Son of man', as it was used by Jesus himself and as it is recorded in the Gospels. No good purpose would be served by going over that ground again.

---

[8] Later, of course, Rabbinical exegetes believed that this revealed will of God was set down in the Torah, the 'Law'. They taught all Jewry to believe in turn that the latter was the revelation as such which God had given at Sinai through the hand of Moses.

[9] G. Dalman, op. cit., pp. 268–89, etc., declares that the title 'Son of God' was not used of the Messiah in Jesus' day (cf. Vincent Taylor, *The Names of Jesus*, 1953, p. 53), though Strack-Billerbeck, op. cit., 3, 15–22, suggests that on occasions it may have been. Yet, of course, Matt. 3.17 'This is my beloved Son' clearly represents the LXX rendering of 'chosen one', or 'unique' son (See Schrenk, *TWzNT*, 2, p. 738).

We shall then accept the findings of the consensus of scholar-ship and regard the figure as meaning something like 'true, representative Adam', or 'Man in his very essence'.[10] Our imme-diate concern is to notice that the empirical Israel of the OT story is undoubtedly described by just those very words. We find them, for example, in that same 80th Psalm to which we have already referred hen discussing the figures of the Vine and of the Son.

We recall that this 'interpretative' Psalm looks back over the past history of the people of Israel to the moment when God brought them out of Egypt and planted them as a vine in their promised land. After the Psalmist has developed his parable, however, he goes on to remind God that his people have met with the wrath of an enemy. To describe this new situation our Psalmist now changes the figure (v. 17) in a highly significant manner. In the parallelism of expression normal to Hebrew verse, he now calls Israel by two names, viz., (*a*) 'the man of thy right hand' and (*b*) 'the son of man whom thou madest strong (or, "reared") for thyself'. The former expression, as a description of Israel, may actually be a pun upon the name Benjamin. But whether it is a pun or not, we should note the vital significance of the picture language that is used together with the importance and significance of the right hand of a man. Benjamin was the beloved tribe of old. As the eponymous ancestor of his tribe, he was the apple of his father's eye (Gen. 44.20). He was the only one of the twelve sons reputed to have been born in the land of promise (Gen. 35.18–19). In later times again the Messianic line was regarded as necessarily stem-ming from the tribe of Benjamin, although that little tribe had sunk its political identity in the larger unit of Judah. In Ps. 68.27 Benjamin heads the list of those tribes who are to bless God and be blessed in turn. The holy city, Jerusalem (according to some traditions), lay within the territory of Benjamin. Saul, the anointed of the Lord, was 'necessarily' a Benjaminite (I Sam. 9.21). David, too, the 'beloved' son (though the word *dodh* may be Accadian in origin, and so mean 'prince') (I Sam. 16.1) also sprang from

---

[10] It is not possible here to enter into the recent discussion on the figure that has been aroused by Professor Bultmann.

Benjamin, since he was a Bethlehemite.[11] It was in Benjamin that Samuel felt the kingdom had to be renewed (I Sam. 11.14). In other words, 'the man of thy right hand' was the chosen and beloved representative of the people of Israel.

The parallelism of Hebrew poetry demands that each idea should be repeated in different words. In this case, the expression 'Son of man' parallels the idea we have just examined and therefore must convey an idea similar to and even identical with it. Following upon the discussion we have now had, the phrase 'Son of man' in this instance may be understood to represent one of three conceptions. (1) It may speak of God's chosen and beloved one as an individual. (2) It may refer to the whole of Israel as a corporate entity, in a manner parallel to the meaning lying behind the figure of the Vine. (3) It may combine those two poles of meaning, and signify simultaneously (*a*) the whole of Israel at once, as well as (*b*) Israel represented in her 'chosen' and 'beloved' one. If this third case is what the Psalmist had in mind, then we have a form parallel to a conception we have already noted, where the king in his own person could represent the whole *corpus* of his people before God.

We are aware of the oscillation of thought that is connected with the use of the word *'adham* in the early stories of Genesis. J can pass from an account of the creation of 'humanity' and continue to tell a story in which Adam has now become one individual man (Gen. 3).

This oscillation of thought between an individual and a collective meaning of the word *'adham* is probably present here also in the mind of our Psalmist. In all probability, as we have said, he penned his Psalm at a period between the composition and compilation of the two documents, J and P. Moreover, he may well have had before him our Psalm 8. The fourth verse of the Psalm runs: 'What is *'enosh*, that thou art mindful of him? and the son of man, that thou visitest him?' The poetic parallelism of the line must equate 'son of man' with *'enosh*. This word has the

---

[11] The town is sometimes called Bethlehem-Judah (cf. Judg. 17.7), because part of Benjamin was absorbed in Judah.

same individual and yet collective reference as the commoner noun *'adham*.[12]

It is in the light of such a view of the phrase 'son of man', then, that we turn to the definitive figure of 'a Son of man' in Dan. 7.2–14. The author must undoubtedly have been acquainted with Ps. 80. So 'one hke the Son of man' (Dan. 7.13) will *prima facie* mean one who, though an individual, is a representative of Israel, one in whom the whole *corpus* of Israel is present. This *corpus* is alluded to under another name. It is the 'people of the saints of the Most High' who are to possess the kingdom which God will give them (Dan. 7.22, 27).[13]

A new moral emphasis is now made by 'Daniel' upon the phrase 'son of man'. He obviously compares and contrasts the Son of man figure with that of king Nebuchadnezzar. As a Babylonian monarch, Nebuchadnezzar would be hailed by his subjects as 'king of kings and lord of lords' (Ezek. 26.7). He was thus the apex of all humanity. He was indeed 'representative-man.' Yet Nebuchadnezzar was a gross sinner. He had to discover that there was One stronger than he, viz. the King of heaven, all of whose works 'are right, and his ways are just; and those who walk in pride he is able to abase' (Dan. 4.37 ARSV). Nebuchadnezzar therefore suffers the punishment of God and is condemned to 'eat grass as oxen . . . till his hairs were grown like eagle's feathers, and his nails like birds' claws' (4.33). What this passage points out is that, while it is natural for a beast to be a beast, yet it is 'beastly' for a man not to be a man. If the mad king, who is the apex of the triangle whose base is all mankind, is conceived

---

[12]   Cf. Gen. 4.26; for individual references, cf. Job 5.17; 13.9; Ps. 55.14; Jer. 20.10, etc. For collective references, cf. Isa. 24.6; Ps. 56.2; Job 4.17 etc. *'Enosh* and *'adham* are paralleled in Isa 13.12, and *'enosh* and *ben 'adham* in Isa. 56.2. See also P.A.H. de Boer, 'Jahu's Ordination of Heaven and Earth, An Essay on Ps. 8', *OS*, Deel 2 p. 183.

[13]   C.H. Dodd, op. cit. p. 103. cf. T.W. Mansdon, *The Teaching of Jesus*, 1931, 2nd ed. 1951, p. 212, pp. 227–8, pp. 231–2, pp. 269–70; also in *BJRL*, xxxii, 1949–50, p. 174, Manson points out that the Son does not come from heaven, but goes up to heaven, there to receive the kingdom. What else, we might add, could be said of Israel? cf. also O. Cullmann, *Peter – Disciple, Apostle, Martyr*, 1954, p. 166 and p. 189.

to be on a level with the beasts of the field, then surely the figure of the Son of man is in a different moral category. If it were not so, then it could not be said of the Son of man that to him 'there was given dominion, and glory, and a kingdom, that all the people, nations, and languages, should serve him: his dominion is an everlasting dominion, which shall not pass away' (7.14).

(4) The Figure of the Bride

Hosea's great contribution to our knowledge of the relationship between God and Israel is the figure he gives us of Israel as the Bride of Yahweh. Yet others too refer to Israel's apostasy as 'going a-whoring after other gods' (e.g. Deut. 31.16; Ps. 73.27; Ezek. 16; 23.3, etc.). Though Amos does not use the word Bride, he evidently has the same kind of figure in mind as has Hosea. This we recognize from his choice of a verb. 'You only have I *known*', says God to Israel, 'of all the families of the earth' (Amos 3.2).

The verb *yadha'* (to know) and its noun, *da'ath*, refer not only to what we call cognitive knowledge, but also to knowledge gained through the emotions as well as the intellect. E.g., both the verb and the noun may be used with the words 'good and evil', to produce the phrase 'knowing good and evil' (Deut. 1.39; Isa. 7.15). This was to possess total knowledge, knowledge 'from A to Z' (See footnote p. 25). Of course such was the prerogative of divinity alone (Gen. 3.5). Yet an aspect of knowing in this total sense is apparent when a man 'knows' his wife. Only then can conception take place (Gen. 4.1). Now, if Amos' 'You only have I known' had stood alone, we would have refrained from pressing it to this point. But it does not. Jeremiah, e.g., uses the figure of the marriage relationship quite explicitly to describe Israel's relationship to Yahweh: 'For I am married (a husband) unto you' (Jer. 3.14; also 2.2; 3.1; 31.32).[14] Lovers' language frequently occurs

---

[14]   Cf. N.W. Porteous, in *OS*, Deel VIII, 'Semantics and OT Theology', 1950, pp. ff.; S. Mowinckel, *Die Erkentnis Gottes bei den alttestamentlichen Propheten*, 1941; H.W. Wolff, in ' "Wissen um Gott" bei Hosea als Urform von Theologie', *Evangelische Theologie, Juni*, 1953, Heft 12, p. 533, would even translate 'knowledge of God' by our word Theology!

between God and Israel. The attractive phrase 'speak ye comfortably to . . . ' which in Hebrew is literally 'speak to the heart of . . .' occurs eight times in the OT.[15] In five of them the reference is to the wooing of a lover. Thus when the phrase is twice uttered by God (Isa. 40.2; Hos. 2.14) we do well to associate it with the Bride figure. The tenderness of true marriage love is well expressed in these words spoken during the Exile: 'For thy Maker is thy husband. . . . Yahweh called thee . . . a wife of youth' (Isa. 54.5–6).

It is Hosea's development of the figure, however, which is the classic one for our purpose. (His other great figure is that of Son which we have already examined.) In the little book of Hosea, without a doubt, the whole body of Israel, empirical, sinful Israel, is regarded as the Bride of Yahweh. Just exactly what the word 'Bride' connotes is another question. It is possible that it may mean only 'one who is engaged', 'espoused', as in the story of Joseph and Mary in the NT. On the other hand, it may just as reasonably be held to mean married, in the full sense of the word. Now, Hosea expounds his figure by playing upon the two contemporary meanings of the word *ba'al*. A *ba'al* in Hosea's time was a local male god of fertility, with whose worship there was associated all manner of licentious and adulterous rites. But *ba'al* could also mean 'lord', 'master', 'husband', particularly the lord and master of a harem of women. Between a *ba'al* and a pack of fluttering, sensuous harem wives there could be no experience of true love whatsoever. That is to say, declares Hosea, Israel has lowered her relationship to God down to this 'harem' level of sensuality, and so has lost the true conception of married love. In Hos. 2.16, however, God has promised to restore his erring Bride and to deal with her in such total love and with such absolute forgiveness that the husband-wife relationship will thereafter be established on a new basis altogether. Israel will no longer think of her God as merely *ba'al*, but will now regard him as *'ish*. The word *'ish*, of course, means 'man', but it may just as well mean 'husband'. Its use here however certainly implies what a Scottish woman, for example, means when she introduces her husband to a friend,

---

[15] C.R. North, *Isaiah 40–55*, Torch Commentary, 1952, p. 38.

with the words: 'Meet my man'. Her 'man' is the husband she proudly introduces, because she belongs to him, and he to her peculiarly. Hosea was undoubtedly referring in this daring figure to a monogamous marriage between Yahweh and Israel such as was consonant with the true theological insights of the best of Israel's interpreters.

Now, Hosea wrote about the middle of the eighth century B.C. The J document in Genesis contains material considerably older than the time of Hosea. The P document, on the other hand, in its final form, is probably post-exilic, though containing material that may well be as ancient as J's. We do not know then how to date the significant comment in Gen. 2.24 which the final editor has probably added to J's narrative. After referring to the creation of woman from the rib of man he declares: 'Therefore shall a man leave his father and his mother, and shall cleave unto his wife, and they shall be one flesh'. This much we can confidently say, that in the post-exilic period, when the Pentateuch had assumed the form in which we now possess it, and the 'Book of the Twelve', in which Hosea is to be found, had been virtually 'canonized' by the people of Israel, that strange people had accepted as from God himself the two dicta contained in Gen. 2.24 and Hos. 2.16. Not only so, but they now set them side by side in the one sacred Scripture. That is to say, they regarded both dicta as the Word of God to be believed, accepted and made incarnate in their community life.

We may well ask ourselves if the Israel of the post-exilic theocratic state fully realized the shattering significance and the extraordinary implications of the juxtaposition of those two passages. It is true that in the post-biblical literature the figure of Israel as the Bride is recognized and rejoiced in, as we see from the period of the discussions in the Talmud.[16] But before that, by the beginning of the second century B.C., it is clear that much

---

[16]   Cf. Strack-Billerbeck, *KzNT*, I, p. 313 ff. we find a discussion on the matter in Ex. R. 15, 30, on Ex. 12.2, and in 43a, 29 with reference to Isa. 54.5 'Thy Maker is thine Husband, the Lord of hosts is his name'. Canticles Rabbah again is dominated by the concept.

thinking was being done on the figure. We gather this from the LXX translation. E.g. the verb used in Gen. 2.24 for man and woman becoming one flesh, viz. κολλᾶσθαι, and which is quoted in the NT from this passage with reference to the union of a man with a harlot (I Cor. 6.16), becomes the translation of the less colourful Hebrew verb *dabhaq be* 'to cleave to'. And, of course, Israel was a harlot. The verb is employed in this way in Deut. 10.20 for the unique relationship between Israel and her God, and is actually added to the text in Deut. 6.13, a verse with a similar content. But for Israel in late OT times to have taken the Bride figure *seriously* and *literally* in the light of Gen. 2.24, would have constituted for her little less than blasphemy. Indeed that is the opinion of the Synagogue to this present day. It is only those who see the completion of the OT in the NT for whom the figure comes most truly alive.

'The twain become one flesh'! What an amazing figure. How indeed could post-exilic Judaism make anything of such a dictum in the connexion we have in view? In a post-exilic book we see what God's attitude to marriage is understood to be. 'Did not he make one?' asks Malachi, speaking of marriage and divorce, but only of the marriage relationship between man and woman. 'And wherefore one? That he might seek a godly seed' (Mal. 2.15); but then he adds with reference to God: 'He hateth divorce'. Now, long before Malachi's day, as we have seen, Hosea had wrestled with the significance of the unique relationship between Israel and her God in this very light.

It is to Hosea, as we are aware, that we owe the full development of the Hebrew word *ḥesedh*. *Ḥesedh*, amongst other connotations, is the 'loyal-love' which is the real essence of the marriage relationship, the true bond, the very content of the marriage tie or covenant.[17] 'How shall I give thee up, Ephraim? how shall I deliver thee, Israel?' (or, 'divorce' you and hand you over to other lovers) 'I will not execute the fierceness of mine anger . . . for I am God, and not man; the Holy One in the midst of thee', that is to say, *one flesh with thee!* (Hos. 11.8–9).

---

[17] The discussion of the word *ḥesedh* is renewed in Part Four, Chap. 18.

At this point we must admit the difficulty, to which we have only just referred before, that the content of the word Bride, as Hosea uses it, is not easy to define. The words 'bride' and 'bridegroom' are used on several occasions by Jeremiah (2.32; 7.34; 16.9; 25.10; 33.11) a century later than Hosea. There it is difficult for us to decide whether they refer to 'engaged couples' or to 'newly-weds'. The great simile in Isa. 62.5, a passage from the post-exilic period, again, leaves the modern mind in the same doubt about interpretation as it does with Jeremiah. The passage is to be set alongside Hosea's choice of language. It goes: 'For as a young man marrieth a virgin, so shall thy sons marry thee: and as the bridegroom rejoiceth over the bride, so shall thy God rejoice over thee'. Now, is Hosea's analogy from experience based upon a marriage already consummated, or is it one that has still to take place? What does he mean when he says of the woman Gomer: 'She is not my wife' (Hos. 2.2 AV) and puts her away as unclean? For the moment let us take it that the marriage has been a true marriage but that it has been disrupted by Gomer's unfaithfulness. If such be the case, then we are to remember that Hosea now goes on to argue from the analogy of his own relationship with his wife to the relationship which he declares must similarly obtain between Yahweh and his wife, Israel. By his emphasis on the word *ḥesedh*, the word he uses to describe the content of the covenant, he is therefore probably declaring that the marriage between Yahweh and his Bride had also taken place long before, when in fact they 'covenanted' together at the foot of Mount Sinai, and Israel took her 'marriage vow' in the words: 'And all the people answered together, All that the Lord hath spoken we will do' (Ex. 19.8, 24.3). This tne, is one possible interpretation of Hosea's thoughts. If it be a valid one, then we see the point of another pronouncement of his. He speaks of the time when the Bride will come back to her Husband and they will experience a new honeymoon together, just as they had once done already in the happy days of the Wilderness wanderings (Hos. 2.14).

We note in passing that this lesser-known tradition, that the Wilderness journey was indeed a happy period, and not the period of strife and murmuring that other traditions record, is also to be found in Jer. 2.1–3 and in Ezek. 20.33–38. That is to say, this other tradition, preserved in Hosea, Jeremiah and Ezekiel, regards the Wilderness as that period in her experience when Israel found her Husband to be all-sufficient, and when she felt satisfied to rest utterly in his hands.

On the other hand, there is a second and alternative interpretation of Hosea's words. Our confidence in a dogmatic assertion of the validity of the first interpretation is shaken when we note the tenses of the verbs used in Hos. 2. In that chapter it will be 'at that day', i.e., at the Day of the Lord, at the dawn of the messianic kingdom, which is spoken of by other prophets such as Isaiah and Micah in similar language, that this great event will come to pass and Israel will become one flesh with Yahweh her divine Husband. So we are faced with the following question – did the marriage between Yahweh and Israel in Hosea's opinion actually take place at Sinai? If this is indeed so (and this was our first alternative), then is the marriage to be regarded as already consummated, but broken by 'Gomer's' unfaithfulness? Is the marriage, then, merely to be renewed in the messianic future, the Day of the Lord? Or, on the other hand (and this is our second alternative), is the marriage still to be entered upon *for the first time* on the Day of the Lord? An escape from the dilemma can be made if we recognize that both aspects of the meaning of the divine marriage could have been in Hosea's mind at one and the same time. He may well have regarded the Sinai covenant of marriage as already fulfilled, and have believed that his people did at that time enter into a unique relationship with Yahweh. But at the same time Hosea may well have regarded the Sinai covenant 'eschatologically', i.e., as the 'first-fruits' of a marriage, the fulness of whose union had not yet, in Hosea's day, been experienced in all its true and deep sense and meaning.

The 'eschatological' interpretation of Hosea's figure of marriage does indeed offer an answer to the queries raised in the mind by the two conflicting theories. In the light of it his interpretation may be stated simply, as follows: Israel was truly married to Yahweh at Sinai; and yet Israel is not yet married, since the Sinai event is but the *arrabon* (to borrow a NT word), the pledge, of the total experience of marriage that is still possible for Israel, and which she will undergo some day in God's good time.[18]

It would seem that the great prophets felt no incongruity about mixing their metaphors. Their object in using picture language was to express truth from all possible angles. Thus in Jer. 3.19–20 we have the figures of the Father-Son relationship between God and Israel and that of the Husband-Wife relationship set side by side, even when different genders have to be used for 'wife' and 'son'. We have seen that Ps. 80 contains most of the figures we are examining. There no attempt is made at any logical connexion between them. Hosea, however, keeps his two figures distinct and separate, that of the Bride in chaps. 1–3, and that of the Son in chap. 2, though, as we saw, he may bring them both together (11.8).[19] It would appear that he deliberately held the two figures in tension over against each other. His figure of the Son emphasizes his belief that the care and love of Yahweh for his people are to be viewed in the light of the concept of prevenient grace. Even before the Son came forth from the womb, i.e., when he was born out of Egypt, so to speak, he had been planned and prepared for by the Father throughout what we call the patriarchal period, following upon the divine promise to Abraham (Hos. 12.3–4). The figure of the Bride, on the other hand, gives us the complementary emphasis that there is a time before her hand is asked in marriage when the woman exists in her own right as an individual; it is during that period, however, that she awakes to the mystery of the meaning of love and discovers that there is some other person who loves her, and who is offering to give her status, a home, comfort, and care. But the figure of the Bride reminds us of this other important factor as well: The Bride's response to the offer of marriage, if true love is to enter into the relationship at all, must be one of total surrender. It must involve the surrender of the body, as well as of the soul, to the Beloved.

---

[18]   This seems to be the view of certain of the later Rabbis. They declared that the Messianic Age would be the marriage of Israel to God. Cf. Strack-Billerbeck, *KzNT*, on Matt. 9.15.

[19]   Similarly, in Isa. 41.8 Israel is addressed as a man, but in v. 14 as a woman; in 51.12 in the masculine plural and feminine singular in the one verse.

(5) The Figure of the Rock

The ancient rock city of Petra or Sela, the capital of the neighbouring land of Edom (cf. Obad. 3), was a familiar feature to
generations of Israelite people. Here before their very eyes lay the
amazing phenomenon of a whole city hewn out of the living rock,
with homes, temples and fortifications all seemingly impregnable
in their rocky fastness. It is understandable therefore that the idea
of Rock should come to symbolize for the Hebrews a place of
refuge which was truly able to protect. Some six times over in the
book of Judges alone we are told of men literally taking refuge in
rocky fastnesses. Ps. 104.18 speaks of the rocks as a refuge for the
wild beasts. So we are not surprised that the Hebrew mind made
use of the figure as a description of the God in whom Israel had
learned to put her trust and who by reason of the 'faithfulness' of
his nature, would never let his people go.

There are two common Hebrew nouns for Rock in the OT,
viz., *sela'* and *tsur*, and there seems to be little vital difference in
meaning between them.[20] Thus in II Sam. 22.2–3 (= Ps. 18.2–3)
the two words are used in turn from one verse to the next:
'Yahweh is my rock (*sela'*), and my fortress, and my deliverer;
God of my rock', (*tsur*), (or, as the LXX and the Syriac have it:
'My God is my rock'). *Sela'* is in fact employed as a description
of God some nine times elsewhere, and *tsur* some twenty-nine
times in all. Many of these usages are clear and explicit. Thus Ps.
89.26 runs: '(David) shall cry unto me, Thou art my father, my
God, and the rock of my salvation'; and there are eleven similar
expressions in the Psalms. The so-called 'Song of Moses' in Deut.
32 is quite as explicit in its use of the figure as any of the Psalms.
In it God is the Rock (v. 4), the Rock of Jeshurun's (Israel's)
salvation (v. 15), while in v. 18 Israel is reminded in the words of
a poetic parallelism that 'of the Rock that begat thee thou art
unmindful, and hast forgotten God that formed thee'. In v. 30
again 'Rock' is paralleled with 'Yahweh', while in Num. 1.5 we

---

[20] S.H. Hooke, 'The Corner-Stone of Scripture', in *The Siege Perilous*,
1956, p. 236.

meet a man, Elizur, whose name means 'God is rock'.[21] Koehler quotes[22] with approval Friedrich Delitzsch's exegesis of the name Shaddai, the title for God usually translated as 'Almighty'. The latter declares that it derives from the Assyrian *shedu*, meaning 'mountain'. There is a biblical reference which might support this view. In Num. 1.10 and 12 *tsur* and *shaddai* seem to be used actually as parallel terms.

There is a third word for Rock in the MT of the OT, however, viz., *keph*. It occurs but twice (Jer. 4.29 and Job 30.6), and both times it appears in the plural. However, the Targum to Isa. 32.2 and Ps. 40.2 translates *sela'* by the singular *kepha'* in Aramaic. Thus it may be a loan-word from Aramaic. We know from the name Cephas in the Gospels that it was the usual word for 'rock' in contemporary Aramaic. The exact significance of the word, however, is disputed. The *OHL* translates it as a 'rock of refuge'. This meaning was suggested over a century ago in Gesenius' Lexicon, with the addition that it means a rock in a desolate and weary land where a fugitive may find shelter. Koehler's *Lexicon* translates it as 'isolated hill', Beaussier's *Dictionnaire* as 'pointed rock'. Dalman, however, in *ANH*, offers a secondary meaning to the word as it is used in extra-biblical literature; he translates it as the 'bank' of a river. Both aspects of the word may have been in the Psalmist's mind when he pictured God as the Rock against which the floods of the primal chaotic sea beat in vain (Ps. 29.10, where 'flood' is *mabbul*, of the Deluge story, Gen. 9.11, etc., cf. also Ps. 93).[23]

There are two instances where Isaiah calls Yahweh *tsur*, viz., 17.10 and 30.29. Although the former passage occurs in one of the 'oracles on foreign nations', some of which Isaiah cannot have written, yet, as Skinner remarks, the Isaianic authorship of this particular oracle is beyond question.[24] Of the authenticity of the

---

[21] See Wiegand, 'Der Gottesname Tsur', *ZAW*, 1890, pp. 5 ff.
[22] *Thelogie des Alten Testaments*, 3rd ed. 1953, p. 236, note 42.
[23] This double connotation may also lie behind the parable of the house built upon a rock (God?), and at the same time upon the safe rocky bank of a river, in contrast to the bed of a dry sandy wady; Matt. 7.24–27.
[24] Cambridge Bible, *Isaiah*, I, p. 141.

other verse there is no doubt either. Therefore it is interesting that Isaiah can apply to a human figure the same expression that he has already used of God: 'Behold a king shall reign in righteousness, and princes shall rule in judgment. And a man shall be . . . as the shadow of a great rock in a weary land' (Isa. 32.2). What he is saying is that in the messianic future each and every man (the noun seems to be distributive in sense) will be to the poor and needy what God is to Israel as a whole, that is, he will become a rock in whose shadow they may hide from the pitiless eastern sun in the same way as Israel 'takes refuge' in God.

Isaiah here gives us what is only, after all, an attractive figure of speech. And yet, in common with so many other OT writers, his figures of speech convey concepts of deep significance. Thus what he is seeking to say by his figure is that in the messianic future Israel will echo a particular function of her God, that of being a refuge to the weary and the worn. Isaiah could not have suggested that this would ever be possible, unless Israel had believed already in the existence of a vital relationship between God and herself, such as could be paralleled by the relationship of that between Father and Son (cf. Isa. 1.2).

Now, in Isa. 8.14 we meet still another poetic parallelism. On examining it we discover an identity of meaning between the two disparate words Rock and Stone. There Isaiah says of Yahweh: 'And he shall be for a sanctuary (N.B. the purpose of the Rock above); but for a *stone* of stumbling and for a *rock* of offence to both the houses of Israel'. In this declaration, then, the word Rock, *tsur*, employed as a figure for Yahweh, is paralleled with still another word, viz., with *'ebhen*, which means a 'stone'. What we have before us, then, is a natural development of the figure of Rock, since it is not possible to envisage a man stumbling over a rocky fortress. Not only so, but it is a very forceful figure. It reveals to us a picture of God as an outcrop of rock, or as a stone fallen from a crag, against which little man has the audacity to kick his foot. In post-exilic times the author of Zech. 12.3 read those words of Isaiah, it would seem, and did with them and with the word *'ebhen* what Isaiah in 32.2 had already done with the word *tsur*. He spoke of Jerusalem (i.e. the People of God) as being commissioned by God to be a stone of offence to the Gentiles, in the same way as God himself (in Isa. 8.14) was already an offence, in his turn, to the People of God. Such a statement is a striking paradox. The Stone had of course actually been set as a blessing in Israel's midst: 'Behold, I lay in Zion for a foundation a stone, a tried stone, a precious[25] corner stone, a sure foundation . . . ' (Isa. 28.16) upon which the edifice of a believing people could arise.[26]

The 'stone' in both parts of the book of Zechariah, then, demands a somewhat detailed discussion at this point. Soon after the Return from Exile, the prophet Zechariah had had a series of 'night-visions' dealing with Joshua, the High Priest of the newly-reconstituted state of Judah. We recall how any representative figure, be he prophet, priest or king, could sum up in his own person all that Israel as a *corpus* was meant to be. As we watch him standing before the angel of Yahweh, we realize that Joshua represents the whole people of Israel, the 'chosen Jerusalem' (Zech. 3.2), now plucked as a brand out of the burning fire of the Exile. Nothing more can be expected of Joshua (and so of Israel) if he were to act merely on his own initiative. This is because he is alienated from the advancing purposes of God's saving activity, and stands clothed in filthy garments. But now Joshua is given a clean raiment, as the symbol of God's forgiveness and renewing love. Before the Exile Jeremiah had promised that once Israel should obtain faithful shepherds, the House of David would arise again (Jer. 23.1–6). To that end, then, God himself now places a Stone before the eyes of Joshua, engraved with the seven eyes of God – a symbol of the omnipresent care of God for all the earth (Zech. 3.9). This same stone becomes the foundation of the new Temple which the governor, Zerubbabel, has begun (4.9–10); it becomes indeed the very rock on which

---

[25]   Later Judaism emphasized the precious nature of the Stone. See *KzNT*, 1, pp. 875–7.

[26]   Cf. John the Baptist's pun in the original Aramaic in Matt. 3.9 = Luke 3.8 'God is able of these stones, *'abhnaia*, to raise up sons, *benaia*, unto Abraham'.

the Temple stands (cf. II Sam. 24.24–25). On the other hand, mighty Babylon, the great enemy of Israel, had also been a mountain, a rock (Zech. 4.7); yet not a stone of that rock would be used to form a foundation of God's house: 'Behold, I am against thee, O destroying mountain, saith the Lord, which destroyest all the earth; and I will stretch out mine hand upon thee, and roll thee down from the rocks, and will make thee a burnt mountain. For they shall not take of thee a stone for a corner, nor a stone for foundations . . . ' (Jer. 51.25–26). Indeed, the mighty mountain would now become a plain before Zerubbabel. His function then would be to bring forth the true headstone with shoutings (Zech. 4.7), (or, with the LXX, 'bring it forth to the light'), thus making visible to the eyes of all that the laying of the stone was the sheer gift of God's grace alone.

From this many-sided picture we may sum up Zechariah's message in the following terms. God, who is the rock himself, is about to lay in Israel's midst by grace alone that rock which would become the foundation of Israel's renewed life. Through the representative figure (or figures) of Joshua (and Zerubbabel), all Israel was being commissioned to become the 'house' built upon that rock. That house would partake of the rock-like qualities of its divine foundation. It would be like a rock itself. 'They that are afar off shall come and build in the Temple of the Lord' (Zech. 6.15). Thus Zechariah ends his visions with a re-emphasis upon Isaiah's dictum that the tried and precious stone would be a sure foundation on which others too might build (Isa. 28.16).[27]

But the stone which God had set in the midst could be a rock of offence as well as, at the same time, a sure foundation. God 'shall be for a sanctuary; but for a stone of stumbling and a rock of offence to both the houses of Israel . . . and many among them shall stumble, and fall, and be broken, and be snared, and be taken' (Isa. 8.14–15). If God could be such to Israel *before* the

---

[27]   The Targum on this verse claims that the Stone is Messiah. Cf. also *Sanhedrin* 38a. For a discussion of the significance of this stone, see S.H. Hooke, op. cit., pp. 239 ff.

Exile, as he indeed had been, then renewed and reconstituted Israel *after* the Exile could equally become the rock on which the Gentiles in their turn could stumble. Such is the theme of the earlier section of the poem in Jer. 51 which we quoted above: 'With thee (Israel) will I break in pieces the horse and his rider . . .' (vv. 21 ff.). The People of God had now indeed partaken of the essence of the Rock whence they were hewn.

Such a picture must have been in the mind of Daniel when he interpreted Nebuchadnezzar's dream in Dan. 2. There the great image, representing the godless human institutions of the Gentiles, is to be broken by the stone cut without hands (i.e. hewn out by God and not man), and this stone, Israel, was then to become a great mountain and fill the whole earth (Dan. 2.31–35, 45). By this late period, then (*c.* 160 B.C.), the figure of the rock had evidently become completely comprehensible as a figure for Israel, the People of God. Thus, no matter what messianic interpretation the NT places on the words of Ps. 118.22: 'The stone which the builders refused is become the head stone of the corner', the Israelites had undoubtedly already learned to apply it to themselves, and they had done so because they knew that they were founded upon that Rock which, ultimately speaking, was their God.[28] Thus they looked forward to the day when they would be able to repeat with exultation the succeeding verse of the Psalm: 'This is the Lord's doing; it is marvellous in our eyes'.[29]

---

[28]   We thus understand how the NT can speak of a 'living stone' (I Peter 2.4). The Greek λίθος is the usual word for a worked stone, πέτρα for the natural rock. See E.G. Selwyn, *The First Epistle of Peter*, 1949, p. 158.

[29]   There is an interesting parallel in the Rabbinical tradition to the idea of the People or God as Rock. The tradition referred to a builder who could not at first find a firm foundation, but only swamp. At last he discovered a Rock beneath the swamp. Even so, ran the tradition, God passed over the preceding generations as unsound, till he saw Abraham, and said: 'I have found a Rock'. Therefore he called Abraham Rock, as it is said, 'Look unto the Rock whence ye are hewn' (Isa. 51.1), and he called Israel 'Rocks'. Quoted from E.A. Abbott, Diatessarica, § 3595, with reference to Yalkut I, 243b.

(6) The Figure of the Servant

The Servant is undoubtedly a key figure for an understanding of the relationship between God and the People of God in the OT. We shall be obliged to return to it in Part Four, when the question of Atonement will be before us. Meanwhile we must establish how the figure is used.

The 'servant' in the OT is really 'slave', *'ebhedh*, one who belongs to a master. In religious usage, therefore, it signifies 'the humble self-description of the pious in the presence of his God'.[30] He is necessarily humble, since he is God's 'slave'. What content then are we to give to the word 'slave'?

From earliest times the attitude of a Hebrew slave-owner to his Hebrew slave was regulated by law. In fact, one of the finest examples of humanitarian legislation which the ancient world can show is to be found in Ex. 21.2. There it is enacted that a Hebrew slave must revert automatically to full freedom after six years service of his master. Not only so, but the later and more developed Deuteronomic legislation requires the slave-owner to endow his departing slave with sufficient 'capital' to enable him to begin life again as a free man on a sound economic basis (Deut. 15.12–15). The still later priestly legislation adds to the moral content of the Exodus Code in another form. It requires that a Hebrew slave, during the years of his service, shall not be regarded as the mere chattel of his master, but be employed under conditions similar to those of any daily wage earner, *sachir*, or as a foreign worker offering himself for wages, *toshabh*: 'For they are *my* slaves, which I brought forth out of the land of Egypt: they shall not be sold as bondmen. Thou shalt not rule over him with rigour; but shalt fear thy God' (Lev. 25.42–3). These later laws evidently merely codified that which quite early in Israel's history had become the accepted attitude for a Hebrew master to take to his fellow Hebrew slave. We believe this, since it is the E code,

---

[30] W. Zimmerli and J. Jeremias, *The Servant of God*, Studies in Biblical Theology, No. 20, 1957, p. 13, being an English translation of article Παις Θεου in *TWNT*.

written after Solomon had virtually enslaved his whole people, which adds the following supplement to the above: 'But if the servant shall plainly say, I love my master, my wife, my children, I will not go out free; then his master shall bring him unto the *'elohim*, judges (AV), (or, to the judgement-seat of God, LXX), and shall bring him to the door, or (that is to say) the doorpost; and his master shall bore his ear through with an awl; and he shall serve him for ever' (Ex. 21.5–6). Deut. 15.17 suggests that the idea of the ceremony was that the willing slave should thus be permanently attached to his master's household.

Later writers spiritualized this vivid, voluntary act. 'Sacrifice and offering thou didst not desire; mine ears hast thou pierced . . . I delight to do thy will, O my God; yea, thy law is within my heart' (Ps. 40.6, 8).

Thus, when we meet with the figure of the 'servant of Yahweh' in Deutero-Isaiah, we are bound to keep in mind the above definition of the idea.

Inset within the work of Deutero-Isaiah are four 'Servant-Songs', so-called ever since they were isolated by Duhm last century, viz., (1) Isa. 42.1–4; (2) 49.1–6; (3) 50.4–9; (4) 52.13–53.12. However, there is universal agreement neither on the exact delineation of the Songs, nor on the question of their authorship. [31] Our concern is not with such questions, but with the identity of the Servant. Now, in Isa. 49.3 explicit identification of the Servant with Israel is made, in this the second 'Servant-Song': 'Thou art my Servant, O Israel, in whom I will be glorified'. [32] Two

---

[31] For a full introduction to the Songs, see C.R. North, *The Suffering Servant in Deutero-Isaiah*, 1948, supplemented by H.H. Rowley, *The Servant of the Lord in the Light of Three Decades of Criticism*, 1952.

[32] S. Mowinckel, in *He That Cometh*, 1956, Note XI, pp. 462 ff., has recently argued that manuscript evidence for the word 'Israel' at this point is poor. But he has been amply answered by H.H. Rowley in a review of his book. In 'The Servant Mission', *Interpretation*, July, 1954, pp. 259 ff. Professor Rowley points to twelve passages where 'many of the things which are predicated of the Servant inside the Songs are predicated of Israel outside the Songs'. On the other hand Israel is addressed as the Servant at least seven times outside of the Songs, viz. 41.8; 42.19; 43.10; 44.1; 44.21; 45.4; 48–20.

verses later, however, we find the following (ARSV): 'It is too light a thing that you should be my servant to raise up the tribes of Jacob and to restore the preserved (in Babylon) of Israel; I will give you as a light to the nations, that my salvation may reach to the end of the earth'. In other words, the faithful element within Israel, the believing inner core of the nation, is to be God's Servant, first to raise up the outer 'layers' of the people, those whose faith is only nominal or even non-existent; and then, second, to be the instrument of God's saving purpose to all mankind. Here 'Israel', the Servant, is closely akin to the Remnant of the people of whom Isaiah had spoken almost two centuries before (Isa. 1.9, *saridh*; 10.20, *she'ar*: 37.4, *she'erith*, etc.). They are at times to be identified with those Hebrews whom north, south, east and west are to 'give up' as the Exile draws to a close (Isa. 43.6, etc.). The speaker in the third Servant-Song seems to be the spokesman of this Remnant as it is suffering in far-off Babylonia (Isa. 50.4 ff.).

There is still a third kind of Servant, however, mentioned in the Songs. Without any doubt at all the figure sketched in the fourth Song (Isa. 52.13–53.12) is that of an individual. The question as to whether this individual could still be Israel will be before us in a later chapter (see pp. 289 ff. and 325 ff.), but only when we have pursued the question whether Israel *could* suffer vicariously for the redemption of the Gentiles. Meanwhile we take note of two final points. First, we note that the words of the Magnificat make the identification of the Servant with Israel as a whole: 'He hath holpen his servant Israel . . . ' (Luke 1.54). But second, we recall the fluidity of thought characteristic of Israel's expression of her understanding of the relationship that exists between a group and its representative. If Israel thought thus about the *ba'al* and his wives in pre-monarchical days, then Israel could similarly identify the *one* representative Servant with the Servant People as a whole.

Six figures have been sufficient for our purpose to reveal the unique relationship that obtains between God and Israel. There are other lesser figures which we might have adduced. For example, there is the Shepherd-Sheep figure (cf. Ps. 80.1, again! Ps.

23.1; Isa. 40.11; etc.); and there is the Dew figure. Thus Hos. 14.5 declares of God: 'I will be as the dew unto Israel', whereas Micah 5.7 insists that 'the remnant of Jacob shall be in the midst of many people(s) as a dew from Yahweh'. In other words, Israel was to be to the Gentiles what she had become through her peculiar relationship to God. But each of the six major figures stresses its own facet of that truth in the pictorial manner which is characteristic of Israel's conception of God. Within the framework of each picture, moreover, the individual takes his legitimate place within the total society of Israel. Our mental image of the Vine, for example, is that of a plant which is one entity in itself. Yet the Vine is portrayed in Ps. 80 as being composed of a multiplicity of shoots and roots, all sharing in the vital sap that flows in the main stem. The Son of God figure, again, is a constant reminder that each of the children of Israel is himself a son of God, within the corporate Son (Isa. 1.2; Deut. 32.5; Jer. 3.14; etc.). It is not only the whole nation that can be addressed as Son of man, a representative individual Israelite can find his métier under that address within the *corpus* of Israel (Ezek. 2.1, *et passim*). Finally, it was only when Hosea, as an individual within Israel, knew what it was to be in love with an individual woman, that he drew his profound analogy of a like relationship existing between Israel and her God.[33]

---

[33]   The call of Israel, the unique relationship between Israel and God, and the story of God's dealings with Israel within the range of a historical period available for our study, are all given factors for the theologian to handle. The story of Israel can be assessed within the realm of fact. Systematic theologians should therefore take the fact of Israel into account more than many do. A systematic theology that begins by adducing arguments for the existence of God without first recognizing the fact of Israel, with whom God is indissolubly bound up, is obviously travelling in a direction counter to biblical thinking.

Part Four

The Zeal of the Lord

Sixteen

God's Purpose for Fallen Man

This Part Four of our study must now be in the nature of a synthesis. In Part One we examined what the OT has to say about the Person of the living God. We saw in Part Two that God's attitude to the universe, including man, which he himself has created, must needs be one of wrath, since both fallen angels and men are in a state of rebellion against God's purposes for them. Part Three comprised a series of pictures, each complementary to the other, portraying the unique relationship which has obtained in history between God and one nation of men. So unique and so strange is that relationship that we are compelled to ask the question what God intended to do through it. The answer to that question will be the subject of this Part Four.

The purpose of God in creating man, then, has been opposed by the will of man and of certain angelic powers. God loves freedom. He has given all living elements in creation freedom to oppose his will – so greatly does he prize freedom. He left the very 'sons of God', or angelic beings, free to lust after the daughters of men (Gen. 6.1–4); and he left man on earth, before the Fall, equally free either to control the serpent or to submit to its wiles (Gen. 3). God's premundane plan depended upon the willing co-operation of his free creatures. That co-operation was not forthcoming. Yet God would not force his creatures to obedience if they were not willing to obey. So we read: 'It repented the Lord that he had made man on the earth' (Gen. 6.6). The verb *niham*, meaning 'comforted himself', implies that God had sorrowfully to determine on a new course of action, since man's sin and self-will had checked his initial plan of grace.

We are not to read the book of Genesis, however, as if it were a systematic theology presented in the 'Greek' manner. We are to remember that its final editor lived after the great prophets had already interpreted the redemptive activity of God as they had seen it working out over many hundreds of years of Israel's life and experience. What the final editor of Genesis thus set out to do was to summarize in a series of theological pictures, and not in systematic language, the faith which Israel had reached, under the influence of the teaching of her great prophets, by the end of the period of the Exile.

There is a passage in Genesis which many theologians regard as an indication that man is not without a rudimentary moral awareness despite his fallen state. The so-called Noahic Code (Gen. 9.1–7) lays down in the form of divine revelation a bare minimum of moral behaviour necessary for the preservation of any kind of communal life.[1] On the other hand, Chaos and Darkness rule both 'heaven' and 'earth', both spirit and matter. God sees that 'every imagination of the thoughts of his (man's) heart was only evil continually' (Gen. 6.5). On the one hand, and in a sense parallel to the Noahic Code as it relates to man, wild nature knows and obeys the divine ordinances: 'Even the stork in the heavens knows her times, and the turtledove, swallow, and crane keep the time of their coming' (Jer. 8.7, ARSV) – even when 'my people know not the ordinance of the Lord'. The dilemma which faces God, then, is the following – God is faithful, that is, reliable and trustworthy, steadfast and true to himself. He cannot go back upon the Covenant which he has made with all mankind. Thus God promises never to allow the watery chaos to overwhelm the life of the world (Gen. 9.8–17). He cannot go back; he can only go forward. But man will not go forward with him. What is God then to do?

---

[1] 'It is from the Hebrew Bible that the idea of natural revelation permeates literature. The idea is scarcely Greek, because the latter tends to identify Nature with Will, which the Hebrews avoided. To the Hebrew it is the Good that is manifest, not the Arbitrary', I. Abrahams, op. cit., p. 30. See Gen. Rabbah 16.9; 34.8.

The new plan with which God comforts himself is indicated for the first time in the quasi-historical twelfth chapter of Genesis. The first eleven chapters of that book, as we have seen, are not historical, although they contain memories of historical material. Rather they declare the relevance and significance of the historical action to follow. They are the Prologue to the coming Drama of salvation. They make clear in picture form that God's original purpose cannot now be implemented; sin has frustrated that plan. But God's new plan, in which he 'overrules' the power of sin, is now made plain within the area which we know as history, even though sin rules therein. Sin is not an abstract idea. Sin is the attitude of rebellion against God that is displayed by living historical man. God's new plan then is to enfold within his purpose certain men and women who are sinners, and to use their limited allegiance to himself, of all things, as the means whereby he can complete his original plan of love. Through this small yet responsive group God's purpose will reach to all mankind, even to the heavenly places. Such is the faith of Trito-Isaiah in the post-exilic period, as we shall hope to demonstrate in the last chapter of Part Four. This group is responsive because it shows faith. Yet even that faith God has first to implant in their hearts. Thus the coming action of God is one of grace alone. Through involvement with this group God will achieve a grander purpose than he would if the world had remained 'good' as at the first (Gen. 1.31), and sin had never entered in. The time for showing grace to Zion has come, *in order that* the nations might fear Yahweh (Ps. 102.13–15; cf. Mal. 1.11). Moreover, the new plan now takes history absolutely seriously. We know this, because the plan takes evil rulers in history absolutely seriously. Nebuchadnezzar, for example (Dan. 4.32), who overran and destroyed God's Holy City, is called by God 'my servant' (Jer. 27.6); and God puts the whole *oikumene*, the inhabited earth, into Nebuchadnezzar's power (v. 5), including that people who are to be his instrument of salvation. Heathen kings do not know that they are God's servants. 'Ah, Assyria, the rod of my anger, the staff of my fury' (Isa. 10.3–7 ARSV), ' . . . against the people of my wrath I command him . . . but he does not so intend'. So God 'overrules' the devices of the heathen, as we see also in the case of that other conqueror, Cyrus (Isa. 44.28; 45.1). Cyrus is quite unaware that Israel's God is using him when he sends home the displaced persons within his conquered territory. It is not the device of Cyrus, but the zeal of the Lord of Hosts which performs this (Isa. 46.11; cf. II Kings = 19.31 Isa. 37.32; 9.7). Out of evil God plans now to produce good; out of death, life.

To reach this mighty end, God, whose Spirit could clothe itself with Gideon, now determines to 'clothe himself' (cf. Judg. 6.34 Heb.) with an empirical, historical, factual but also perverse people. The significance of this extraordinary verb is exemplified in rather equally daring language by Deutero-Isaiah when he declares that Israel is to be the garment of God's glory (Isa. 44.23). God actually humbles himself to become as closely identified with Israel, whom he even calls his 'angel' (Isa. 42.19), as he is with the angels in heaven (Part One, chap. 6). Through God's intimate relationship with Israel all the nations of the earth will be redeemed from the power of sin. Then Israel will actually be God's reward! (Isa. 40.10). But in order to be the garment of the living God, Israel must first cease to serve, *'abhadh*, Pharaoh, and turn instead to serve Yahweh (Ex. 5.3).[2] Such total service will lead her into strange paths indeed.

Central to God's choice of action, then, we observe once again the ultimate paradox of omnipotent humility. God who is *shaddai*, Almighty, and *bore'*, Creator, who declares the end from the beginning (Isa. 46.10), and who could recreate his universe with the same ease with which he first created it, chooses to go another road. What he chooses to do, for no understandable reason except that of love (Deut. 4.37), is to humble himself, nay, to empty himself, to become one flesh with the empirical people of Israel, his own creation, a people that lay under the curse of God himself! It is through his union, then, with this accursed people dwelling upon this accursed earth that God is revealed to us in the OT to

---

[2]   J. Pedersen, op. cit., I–II, pp. 476 ff., etc. Note that this verb also means 'to work'. Man has to 'work' for his living (Gen. 3.23) and also 'serve' God.

be working out his plan for the redemption, not only of the Israel whom he loves, not even only of all mankind, but also of his whole fallen and rebellious universe. God's choice of Israel exemplifies the mystery of love. When a young man chooses as his bride one of two sisters, he 'loves' one, and then, to use the semitic idiom of the OT, he 'hates' the other. Thus: 'I have loved Jacob, and I hated Esau' God says in connexion with the election of Israel (cf. Mal. 1.2–3). This does not mean that when God 'loved' Israel, he 'damned' Esau. It just means that God did not choose Esau to be his Bride. The reason for God's choice is as inscrutable as that of the young man.

We must now watch for certain essentially Hebraic conceptions of what is involved in the divine plan. Firstly, the plan moves forward in a series of 'times', '*eth* or 'moments', as we might say, each of which is a crisis when God 'visits', *paqadh*, his people in a special manner cf. Ps. 102.13; Isa. 30.18; 40.2; 49.13; Jer. 29.10; 30.18; 31.20; Hab. 2.3). Secondly, each visitation by God is shown to be a compound of both judgement and mercy, not, as is sometimes supposed, the one isolated from the other (cf. Isa. 10.3–4; Micah 7.4, 7; Ps. 8.4; 80.14). Then, thirdly, God's action at each 'moment' is of ultimate significance, it is 'eschatological', in the sense that each moment has relevance for the End of the total plan. This conception, like so much else in Hebraic thought, is presented to us in the form of pictures.

'The plan' is to go forward under Joshua. Moses is about to die. 'I am a hundred and twenty years old this day . . . also the Lord hath said unto me, Thou shalt not go over this Jordan. The Lord thy God, *he will go over before thee*, and he will destroy these nations from before thee, and thou shalt possess them; and Joshua, *he shall go over before thee*, as the Lord hath said' (Deut. 31.2–3). We note the identity of language, and how what God 'says' in 'heaven' becomes actual on 'earth'. Conversely, once Joshua has crossed the Jordan, he is confronted by 'a man'. The latter informs Joshua that he is the captain of the host of Yahweh. But Joshua is the captain of the host of Yahweh 'on earth'. 'Loose thy shoe from off thy foot; for the place whereon thou standest is holy' (Josh. 5.13–15). So it is that Joshua learns that what he is doing on earth is valid in the realm of the spirit; (see p. 68); and that everywhere he sets his foot is holy, because every action of his, every footstep that he takes, has significance not only for the immediate future, but for all eternity.

Seventeen

The Five 'Moments' in Israel's Experience

There are normally three significant 'moments' in the life of men and women on this earth. These three moments we speak of under the names of birth, marriage and death. It is with these three events that the human span is associated and bounded on this earth. Now, since such is true of an individual man's experience of existence, we ought to expect to find three similar 'moments' in the experience of God's corporate Son, the empirical People of Israel.

Of the first two we have already spoken in Part Three, chap. 15 (4). We have noted, for example, how the interpreters of Israel, from within the Body of Israel itself, are aware of the mystery of Israel's birth; how at one moment and at one point of history they were 'no people' (Deut. 26.5), but how God then called them into being as his Son and gave them life. We have noted again the second 'moment' in Israel's experience. That 'moment' happened at the foot of Sinai, when Israel was wedded to her God.[1]

The third 'moment' in Israel's story is nowhere better described than in the book of Lamentations, that little collection of poems dealing with the mystery of the 'death' of Israel, and written almost at once after the event recorded. In the year 587 B.C.[2] the

---

[1] See Appendix at end of chapter.

[2] Latest archaeological research suggests this date; cf. G.E. Wright, *Biblical Archaeology*, 1957, p. 177. But 586 is the familiar landmark to most people.

long and glorious story of Israel had come, as it seemed, to a terrible end. The promise made by God to Abraham so long before, that in him all nations would 'bless themselves' – that promise was now null and void. It was God who had given Israel birth. Of that there was no doubt at all. It was God who had proposed the unequal alliance and who had offered himself in marriage to Israel at Sinai. Of that also there was no doubt again. And now it was God once more who had brought about the third 'moment' which overtakes every soul to whom he gives the gift of life; it was God who had put his people to death when he permitted the Babylonian power not only to lay the Holy City in ruins, but also to take into Exile the Body itself which once had been actually wed to God its beloved Husband (Lam. 1.13–15; 2.1–8, etc.). 'Is it nothing to you, all ye that pass by? behold, and see if there be any sorrow like unto my sorrow, which is done unto me, where-with the Lord hath afflicted me in the day of his fierce anger' (Lam. 1.12).

On the basis of a scientifically exact historical analysis of what took place in 587 B.C. we should not be led astray from the *interpretation* of the Fall of Jerusalem which the OT itself gives us from within its pages. In actual fact, it was not the whole of Israel that was destroyed by the conquering power. Many peasants were left to work upon the land (cf. II Kings 25.22). Disconsolate groups were still living amongst the ruins in 582 B.C., sufficient in numbers and strength to enable a third deportation by the Babylonians to take place. Considerable numbers of Israelites, moreover, were left behind in the Negebh, Bethel, etc., untouched, as it seems, by the destruction of the capital city.[3] A contrary report is that recorded by Baruch (Jer. 43.6–7). He affirmed that *all* survivors of the siege went off, voluntarily or involuntarily, to Egypt. This may be in the nature of an exaggeration. Yet Jeremiah foretold that all who went to Egypt would perish (Jer. 44.11, 12, 14). It is the *theological* interpretation of the End of Israel as a political and religious entity, however, with which we are here concerned, the theory which Israel herself held

---

[3]   W.F. Albright, *The Biblical Period*, 1952, p. 48.

later of that devastating event. Objectively speaking, we know *post eventu* that those Israelites who remained on Palestinian soil, just as truly as those who fled to Egypt, were no longer of significance for the sacred historian. They were Jeremiah's 'bad figs' (Jer. 24.8); and from Jeremiah's point of view what actually happed to those bad figs was that they simply fell out of the advancing purpose of the God of Israel. Thus, those people who later on became known as Samaritans not only turned out to be historically insignificant, but theologically speaking were actually no longer considered by Israel to share in the divine election. As we shall see later, our interpreters regard this as self-evident. The Samaritans were not chosen of God, simply because they never had to suffer the pains and death of the Exile in Babylon even though they believed themselves in 432 B.C.. to be legitimate members of Israel.[4] This kind of argument holds good also for the biblical interpretation of the birth of Israel at the Exodus. It is possible, on the basis of the evidence available, to accept the proposition that certain of the Twelve Tribes were never in Egypt at all, and consequently never emerged from Egypt under the hand of Moses.[5] But the later OT writers would not have been interested in historical discussions such as these. What they were primarily interested in was the theological significance of the 'birth' of their people.

We noted earlier in this study the dominant place which the Exodus nexus of events holds both in the literature and in the thinking of the people who call themselves by the name of Israel. The Exodus is the touch-stone by which all else is judged. The Exodus is the *raison d'être* of everything that Israel is and hopes to be. But now we must note as well the equally vital influence of the crushing experience of the Fall of Jerusalem and of the Exile in a foreign land both on the contemporary thinking of Israel and on the latter's interpretation of its past, including that of the

---

[4]   A. Lods, *The Prophets and the Rise of Judaism* (1937), p. 318.
[5]   Cf. *From Joseph to Joshua*, by H.H. Rowley, 1950, p. 105 f. T.J. Meek in *Hebrew Origins*, rev. ed. 1950, advances the theory that only a small group came out, chiefly the tribe of Levi. See p. 165.

Exodus event itself. It is in the book of Lamentations that we see most clearly reflected the anguish and the surprised despair of that Israel who was utterly assured, on the basis both of the Exodus and of the marriage covenant made at Sinai, that God would never let his people go. They believed this on the ground that he was the kind of God who kept his promises. He had revealed himself already in Israel's history as the faithful God. Therefore he was bound to remain loyal to the Covenant which he had made with Israel at Sinai. The Word of God stands for ever (Lam. 5.19–20).

The Fall of Jerusalem as the Act of God

Yet there is another aspect of Israel's thought prominent in the book of Lamentations, to which we must now refer. The book is infused with the realization that God's strange act in destroying his people was an act of well-merited punishment (Lam. 1.8; 1.18; 4.13, etc.). The book shows a consciousness of the complete justice of God in punishing Israel as severely as he had done (Lam. 2.17; 3.39; 3.42; 4.11, etc.). The prophets had spent their strength in seeking to declare to Israel its sin, but with little avail at the time. As a result of the preaching of Amos, Hosea, Micah and Isaiah there had been a temporary and superficial reformation under king Hezekiah. A century later Jeremiah saw another superficial and still less permanent reformation in the days of king Josiah. But a reformation of public morals and of the cult is not the same as a true and heartfelt repentance. It was the heart of Israel that was like a grub in an apple (Hos. 5.12), that was deceitful above all things and desperately wicked (Jer. 17.9). Israel had lived in a constant state of rebellion against God (Amos 2.4, 6). 'Israel doth not know, my people doth not consider . . . a seed of evildoers . . . they have forsaken the Lord, they have despised the Holy One of Israel, they are gone away backward' (Isa. 1.3–4). 'Sons have I reared and brought up, but they have rebelled against me' (Isa. 1.2). 'They knew not that it was I who healed them' (Hos. 11.3). 'From the sole of the foot unto the head there is no soundness in it' (Isa. 1.6). In what? In the Body of the Son, in the

Body of the Bride of that God, who is the utterly pure, utterly righteous, utterly holy, utterly transcendent God, the Maker of the heavens and the earth! Nowhere in the world's literature is such a striking and awe-inspiring paradox expressed as in the eleventh chapter of Hosea. The nature of the paradox resides in the statement that the utterly Holy God and the utterly putrid Body of Israel had become *one flesh* by the predestined foreknowledge and sheer unmerited grace of the God who had become Yahweh's Husband.

'When Israel offended (became guilty) in Baal, he died' (Hos. 13.1). It is not only the NT which is conscious that the wages of sin is death. What we see interpreted for us in the OT book of Lamentations is the punishment of death as the only possible outcome of Israel's apostasy from God, of Israel's adultery with other gods and so of Israel's breach of the covenant of marriage. Israel had been granted opportunity after opportunity of returning in love to her Husband. 'Rising up early and speaking, but ye heard not; I called you but ye answered not' (Isa. 30.15). In Part Two, chap 12, we read of Jeremiah's vision of the wine cup of God's fury (Jer. 25.15 ff.). Whoso drank of that cup would go 'reeling' down to a terrible death. Now Israel had indeed drunk of it, declared Deutero-Isaiah in far-off Babylon (Isa. 51.17). Prophet after prophet had not only spoken but had acted the message of love and warning; e.g. Jeremiah, in chap. 28, made use of the acted parable of 'The wooden and the iron yokes'. But without avail. And so in 587 B.C. the blow had fallen at last and Jerusalem was now no more. The promise given to Abraham was now evidently null and void. The purpose displayed in the choice of Israel of old, the glorious Exodus, the Sinai covenant, the giving to Israel of its promised land – all was now in vain. And it had been frustrated because there was in reality one power upon earth that was stronger than the love of God, and that power was sin. It seemed that God had been wrong again in making his second plan. Thus Israel died a real death, the death that is the punishment for the sin of apostasy (Jer. 15.9), and in the Exile was really dead and buried (Ezek. 37.12). Jeremiah had already called the professional mourning women to come and weep over the corpse (Jer. 9.17). Israel did not just seem to be dead. Her national life was at an end. Her theological *raison d'être* was reduced to vanity. God had failed, and this was now the end of all things. It was the end of *all* things in a terrible and awe-inspiring sense, and not just the end of Israel. This was because God's planned purpose for the redemption of the cosmos, which had been bound up with the empirical people of Israel,[6] had now obviously been destroyed for good and all. That People had failed God's confidence in them at that point in the history of the world where God needed them and them alone.

As we cast our eye over the whole range of the literature of the OT it is caught and held by that 'strange' (Isa. 28.21) event of 587 B.C. when the chosen city of the chosen People was destroyed by the fires of God. Indeed, the shock of that event was so severe, that the school of P writers can even read back its significance into the Mosaic period. Moreover, the fall of Jerusalem becomes the great interpretative factor in the explanation of events in the centuries that followed upon it as well, as we see from the writings of Ezekiel, Deutero-Isaiah, of the Chronicler, of the author of Job, and from Daniel and the Fourth Esdras. Meanwhile we should note that in four separate references Lamentations makes clear that it recognizes that the Day of the Lord, the Day of destruction and death, the Day of the Lord's judgement, had *come* in the Fall of Jerusalem in 587 B.C. (Lam. 1.13; 2.1; 2.21, 22).[7] That is to say, Lamentations recognizes 'The decisive and epochal nature of the fall of the city'.[8] In total contrast to this belief, however, the Poems which comprise the book speak of the Day of the Lord as an event that is also still to come (Lam. 1.21), a sentiment which is echoed by later writers who lived and wrote long after the Exile was over (cf. Mal. 3.17, etc.).

How can we resolve that paradox? The answer must be that the epochal or *sui generis*[9] nature of that historical Day the OT

---

6   O. Cullmann, *Christ and Time*, 1950, p. 189.
7   Norman K. Gottwald, *Studies in the Book of Lamentations*, 1954, p. 83.
8   Ibid., p. 84.
9   Ibid., p. 84.

writers regarded in an eschatological light. What Israel learned of God and of God's purposes for her in the 'fires' of 587 B.C. (see Isa. 48.10 and Zech. 3.2) was nothing less than *revelation* of what God's purposes eternally are. In other words, the revelation made in 587 B.C. is a revelation of the ways of God that is valid for all time, nay, for 'beyond time', as well as for the life of man within the bounds of history.

God Brings Life out of Death

We have now reviewed the three 'moments' common to every man in the cycle of life, as they appear in the prophetic interpretation of the OT people of Israel, viz., birth, marriage and death. To the natural man, of course, these three moments are all that cover the whole span of human activity. At death the cycle is complete. That third and last moment is the end. But not so did the prophetic interpreters of Israel think their thoughts. Their faith in God was unshakable, despite the mystery of Israel's death with which they were faced (cf. Lam. 3.22–26, 31, 37–40). If Israel was in some sense one flesh with the living God, then Israel must continue to live in him. He had promised to 'become with' Israel throughout history; would he not continue to do so at that moment when they needed him most?

At a period which would appear to us, as we look back upon it from our safe *post eventu* vantage point, to have been the very trough of the wave in the devastating experience of the Exile, the veritable 'Easter Saturday of the soul of Israel',[10] the prophet Ezekiel is given the unexampled vision of the *fourth* moment still to come in the experience of his people Israel. Ezek. 37 presents us with a vision of the *Body of Israel*, no less, arising from the death of the Exile. The fact that God granted Ezekiel this vision at all made clear to that very human prophet the astounding reality that the continuing grace of God was a truer and more potent reality than the physical death of his people Israel.

---

[10] This is the popular word of today. To call it 'Holy Saturday' in this context would be out of place.

We read of the first step in the re-formation of the physical body of Israel that had 'died' in 587 B.C., and note how the Body was still at that time in continuity with the pre-exilic Body of Israel. 'The bones came together bone to his bone' (Ezek. 37.7). The Body is recognizable as such because it comprises the old bones and sinews that had lain scattered on the valley, *biq'ah*, of Babylonia. At this point in Israel's resurrection experience, however, there is still no breath in those bones. But there had been no breath in those other bones, when, as J puts it, God had first formed the physical shape of the body of Man (Gen. 2.7). There we read that it was only after he had done so that God then breathed into his creature the breath of life, so that Man became a living *nephesh*. That first moment was now being repeated. The fourth moment was none other than a repetition of the first. Creation, as we saw in Part Two, is only to be understood in terms of recreation or redemption. God was now breathing into the flesh and bones which he had brought up out of the dust of the Euphrates valley (Ezek. 37.12) and they were beginning to live, and to stand upon their feet, an exceeding great army. 'Then said he unto me, Son of man, these bones are the whole house of Israel'. So the whole house of Israel (i.e. both Judah and Israel, cf. Jer. 3.18), now standing upon its feet, alive and erect, was incontrovertible evidence in itself that the promise given to Abraham and repeated to Jacob, that 'in thee shall all the families of the earth be blessed' (Gen. 28.4) could never finally be set aside. The Return from Exile is a fact of history. Isa. 64.1–8, for example, refers to a believing group now back in the land of Judah that was aware that God had indeed acted in history and restored his people to newness of life. This group, however, is full of dismay. The people whom God has raised, they see, are just as erring and sinful as they had ever been. Malachi, probably a near-contemporary of Trito-Isaiah, has to expound the ways of God as they are working out in the new, post-exilic situation. He speaks to a people that has almost lost its hope. In answer to their despondency, he now points forward to the final outcome and resolution of God's great act of renewal that had taken place in 538 B.C. (Mal. 3.1–4, 6) the date soon after which we can place the return. He knew that the 'End' was not yet, even though the

'Resurrection' of his people had by now become a fact of history in the past. He recognized that he was living in the *Zwischenzeit*, 'between the times', so that he had to discover a balance between the 'realized eschatology' of the fulfilment of the hopes of Deutero-Isaiah (cf. Isa. 40), in that Israel had now come home indeed from the Exile in Babylon, and the expectation of an End not yet reached. The task he set himself, therefore, as he sought to expound God's ways, was similar to that which lay before the early Church in the period after the Resurrection of Christ. Living thus 'between the times', the post-exilic prophets bore the tension in their bones of which the Reformers spoke when they described the Christian man as both *justus et peccator* (Isa. 66.5–24; Mal. 3.2–3). The 'Resurrection' of Israel, they knew, could never be fully appropriated on this earth, since it was but the first-fruits of the new birth of the cosmos (*hak-kol*[11] Jer. 10.16) that was still to come. The eschatological society, in other words, they knew, is not born in a day. The final outcome of what God has instituted, however, must surely come to pass. God does not bring to the birth, and then not cause to bring forth (Isa. 66.7–13). Professor C.H. Dodd must be right, then, when he says: 'The resurrection of Christ *is* the resurrection of Israel of which the prophet (Hos. 6.1–3) spoke.[12]

The End of God's Purpose

Ezekiel's vision proceeds. God now gives the promise to Israel through Ezekiel of a fifth 'moment' still to come. God proclaims 'I will open your graves, and cause you to come up out of your graves, and bring you into the land of Israel' (Ezek. 37.12). Now, the land of Israel was, of course, always considered the land of promise.[13] In fact, the prophetic *post eventu* interpretation of the

---

[11] This Hebrew word, meaning 'the totality', is not to be understood in the 'Greek' sense of 'cosmos'. The latter is not found in OT Hebrew. Its nearest representation is the phrase 'heaven and earth', as in Gen. 1.1; Isa. 37.16; 66.1 etc.

[12] *According to the Scriptures*, 1952, p. 103.

[13] Note how the LXX uses the word κληρονομία to describe it (Ps. 78(79).1).

significance of the land into which God had led his People was that it was 'a land flowing with milk and honey' (cf. Deut. 5, etc.). This kind of thing was said of it, we should note, by interpreters of Israel's relationship to God while they were living in it at a date long subsequent to the period of the Wilderness journey. Such writers knew full well that Palestine, while it was a moderately productive country indeed, in comparison with the deserts to its south and east, yet had many barren areas and much unproductive wilderness within its bounds. In other words, they were all well aware that the terms 'Canaan', the 'Holy Land', the 'land of Israel', a 'land flowing with milk and honey', signified more than the mere physical, geographical area in which the descendants of Abraham were then dwelling. These names, they knew, had an eschatological significance beyond their immediate connotation. A. Jeremias points out that 'A land of milk and honey' is one of the typical expressions used by several ancient peoples for a picture of the recapitulation of the complete cosmos.[14] Of this we are made still further aware when we recall that 'milk and honey' were the traditional food of the gods in near eastern mythological language.[15] The Holy Land was thus the land where Israel was to partake of divine food, food such as God alone could provide; and the land of Canaan was to point to the ultimate 'Holy Land' which the whole creation would one day inherit when the divine plan finally reached its consummation (cf. Isa. 35; Zech. 14.8–11; etc.).

We have just said that the continuity of identity between the preexilic and the post-exilic Israel was described by Ezekiel in terms of a resurrection which he saw in the light of the first creation of Man. Now once more, this time in connexion with the *land* of Israel, we have the same eschatological hope displayed as was displayed of the People itself, viz., that beyond the fourth 'moment' of resurrection God would bring Israel into her land indeed, but yet her land of Canaan now raised to a new and heavenly stature. Ezekiel speaks of what is indeed an historical

---

[14]   *The Old Testament in the Light of the Ancient East*, 1911, p. 170.
[15]   Ibid.

Return to come; but he does so in such a manner that that Return is indistinguishable from an entry into a land that bears a new significance. In this manner of thinking Ezekiel was obviously one with his great contemporary and successor, the author of Isaiah chapters 40–55. Only a few years later than Ezekiel's vision, the latter envisaged the Return from Exile to the land of Israel as a repetition of the Exodus experience, when Israel had first been brought, in Moses' time, into the land that had been promised to her (Isa. 43.1–7, 14–17, 18–21). Consequently, Trito-Isaiah, in the next generation again, living not long after the Return, can exultantly announce that the latter will assume its ultimate validity only when God shall have married the *land* as well as Israel herself. In doing so, God will have raised his Bride Israel from death to newness of life. The passage in Isa. 62.1–4 (cf. Hos. 2.18–23) which deals with this conception, comes from a period when Israel could look back upon the Return from Exile as an accomplished fact of history, and could recognize that the fourth 'moment' foreseen by Ezekiel had indeed now taken place at a point of time in the nation's past. Accordingly it is possible for this writer, in his turn, to look forward to the fifth and final 'moment' in God's plan, a moment in which he speaks (he can no other) in eschatological terms alone. What he points to in his pictorial terms is the final and ultimate End of all things, that moment when God will have brought his mighty purposes to their final conclusion, and will have brought home all creation to the Promised Land.

The above thus represents the manner in which Israel's life and *raison d'être* were interpreted by the OT writers themselves, using, as they did, a system which allotted to God's plan for Israel five mighty and significant 'moments'. We have noted the promise of Israel's birth, a promise that was understood by Israel in the mystical sense that all Israel had once existed in the loins of Abraham (Gen. 35.11). In illustration of this view of Israel's birth we might adduce Isa. 49.1,where occur words referring specifically to the Servant Israel: 'The Lord hath called me from the womb; from the bowels of my mother hath he made mention of my name'. We next noted the first 'moment' of Israel's birth from out of the pain of Egypt (Ex. 20.2; Deut. 7.6; Hos. 11.1), and immediate subsequent baptism (cf. I Cor. 10.2); we then noted the second 'moment' when Israel was married to Yahweh at Sinai; and as St Paul adds, her subsequent education through Revelation (Torah) (cf. Gal. 3.24) and the spoken Word of the Prophets (e.g. Jer. 7.25). Then we have watched the terrible third 'moment' take place when Israel not only died as a result of her sins, but was buried (Ezek. 37.12), and 'descended into hell' (Lam. 1.12–13; 2.3; Jonah 2.2).[16]

We have seen how Ezekiel was led to expect in faith a fourth 'moment' in the story of his people, Israel, and how Deutero-Isaiah too felt that he was at the very dawn of that day of cosmic significance (Isa. 40.1–5, 9–11). And finally we have noted the expectation of the fifth and final 'moment' in the story of redemption when even the ruins and the waste places (Ezek. 36.36) would be built, when the desert would rejoice and blossom as the rose (Isa. 35.1), and when, after the resurrection of the Bride and her reconciliation with her divine Lover, even the land that was under a curse consequent upon the sin of Adam (Gen. 3.17) would be married to God and share in the total reconciliation of the cosmos (Isa. 62.1–4).

Some Corollaries

We would do well to pause at this point to allude to several corollaries connected with biblical theology which follow from the above interpretation of God's dealings with his people, Israel.

---

[16] If we had been repeating the Apostles' Creed together we would now have arrived at the clause 'On the third day . . . ' So we pause to examine this phrase. Its usage in the OT is an interesting one. There the phrase 'three days' is employed to mark any period of time during which there is tension and the darkness which cannot see the dawn. The phrase is used, for example, of the period of nervous waiting for the Revelation at Mount Sinai (Ex. 19.16). It was only on the third day thereafter that new life began for Israel. It was at the end of a similar period again that king Hezekiah began his time of new life (II Kings 20.5). Hosea lays it down almost as a principle, moreover (Hos. 6.2), that God uses a period such as two or three days before raising up his people again to 'live in his sight'.

Firstly, the above interpretation seems to solve for us the problem of the Apocrypha. It could now reasonably be said that the total knowledge of God's saving purpose for the cosmos is revealed to us in the two Testaments which comprise the Bible as the Protestant Churches receive it, following St Jerome. The five 'moments' in the life of Israel, which the Hebrew Old Testament Canon is sufficient to give us, correspond exactly with a like five 'moments' in the work of Christ.[17] Therefore, any doctrine which we may discover in the Apocrypha that is nowhere paralleled by a similar doctrine in the full 'five-moment' period in the story of Christ as it is revealed in the NT,[18] is not likely to be an authentic element in the total biblical revelation. On the contrary, the intertestamental literature as a whole, inclusive of the Apocrypha, can mislead us as we look for the fulfilment of the OT in the NT. The Apocalyptic literature characteristic of the intertestamental period (sc. the book of Enoch) tends to lose faith in God's purpose and ability to use Israel as his instrument of redemption, and to lose sight of the prophetic conception of the fundamental significance and relevance of this earth in God's scheme and plan.[19] That is to say, it tends to lose the eschatological sense of the *relevance* of this life here and now which is characteristic of the prophets and looks for an End to the whole confusion of the immediate pre-Christian period by an *ex machina* act of a God who has despaired of his world.

Secondly, our 'five-moment' scheme provides us with a new content to the much debated and much-handled word in our time,

---

[17] The Fourth Gospel regards Christ as the true Bridegroom at the marriage in Cana of Galilee (John 2.1–11). Before the feast is ended, his ὥρα arrives. The wine of the New Covenant then begins to flow. See also Matt. 9.15 = Mark 2.19 = Luke 5.34; John 3.29; Rev. 18.23.

[18] Birth, 'marriage' (including the giving of the new Torah, Matt. 5; see W.D. Davies, *Paul and Rabbinic Judaism*, 1948, p. 73), death, resurrection and exaltation.

[19] Cf. R.H. Charles, *Eschatology*, 1913, but first delivered as lectures in 1898–99, pp. 211–297, where he argues that the transference of the hopes of the faithful from the material world to heaven took place about 100 B.C.

viz., Eschatology. Half a century ago R.H. Charles could subtitle his monumental study of Eschatology: 'A Critical History of the Doctrine of a Future Life'. That is to say, he conceived of the idea of the *eschaton*, the End, as the life that lies beyond what we know as death. Today we give the word Eschatology a different and wider connotation. This is because much study of the OT has taken place between the days of Charles and ourselves. The word still includes for us all that Charles understood by the term. But it also reminds us that the total experience of God's grace known to Israel was an experience that was meaningful actually while it was being experienced. It reminds us that this life which we live here on this earth is itself significant for eternity, and that eternity is actually shaped and moulded by the purpose of God as that purpose works out in *this* life that we know here and now. Just as the two faces of a coin are inseparable from each other, and each represents but one aspect of the whole coin, so the realms of 'matter' and 'spirit', of this earth and its meaning, are inseparable from each other.[20] The OT writers were well aware that each and every 'now' in the sequence of time in human life is an eternally significant 'now' (Ps. 95.7–8; cf. Isa. 49.8; II Cor. 6.2). The word Eschatology, then, as we use it today, seeks to express the biblical conception of the other dimension that is integrated with and conditioned by the response of men and women to the call of God in each of God's 'to-days'.[21]

Thirdly, the story of the OT people of Israel now takes on a new significance. The pattern of God's dealings firstly with the first Israel, then with Christ, the second Israel, and finally with the Church, the third Israel, is seen to be identical. Since this is so, we recognize that the books of the Hebrew OT contain 'vertical' revelation, parallel with the 'vertical' revelation found in the NT. The NT is thus not primarily the horizontal fulfilment of the OT; the OT is not a mere finger-post pointing forward in time to the NT. Since the OT is the Word of God and contains in its pages

---

[20] See 'Eschatology in the Old Testament', by G.A.F. Knight, *SJT*, Vol. 4, No. 4, Dec. 1951.

[21] Cf. the post-biblical conception that Paradise is contemporary but hidden. *TWNT*, V, p. 765.

revelation itself, then it reveals the same God as does the NT, and shows that he works in the same way, and towards the same ends, at all periods in the history of man. Thus the very concept covered by the word 'Israel' points to a 'continuum' of revelation in the one Body spoken of from Genesis to Revelation. In the Scriptures Israel is not the subject of revelation. Israel is the continuing framework through which, by grace, revelation constantly expresses itself. Paradoxically, the line drawn through that continuum is broken at two distinct moments in its length, viz., between Israel and Christ, and between Christ and his Church. Christ the sinless one is wholly distinct both from the Israel of the sinful twelve tribes before him, and from the new Israel of the sinful twelve apostles after him (Matt. 19.28= Luke 22.30). He is 'from above' (John 8.23) and man is not. Yet the continuum is indeed a reality, both because the Israel of old was raised 'from above' (Ezek. 37), and the Israel of the book of Acts was also born 'from above' (Acts 2) on the day of Pentecost.

Nowhere in the NT do we find it suggested that our Lord 'founded' a Church on earth. This is because he did not need to do so. Consequently the NT writers are firmly of the opinion that the Christian Church is continuous, in some manner, with the Israel of old (Acts 7.38; 15.14; Rom. 9.25–26; 11.16 ff.; Gal. 3.7, 29; 6.16; Phil. 3.3; Heb. 4.9; I Peter 2; Rev. 7.9). Israel, the People of God, may split asunder because of the sin of man (I Kings 12.16), but the purposes of God continue to work out through the schism (I Kings 12.24). On the other hand her prophets come to see that it is the will of God that the People of God should be one. Both parties to the schism are to be reunited in such a manner that the one will not be absorbed in or submit to the other (Ezek. 37.15–22). Israel may go through violent transformations and reformations and radically alter her form of priesthood (II Kings 23.8–9); individuals within Israel may set themselves up as priests under the leading of the Spirit although they are not in the 'succession' (Judg. 6.17 ff.; 13.19); Israel may even seemingly be destroyed as a corporate 'body', as happened in 587 B.C. Yet because God has covenanted to 'become with' Israel, not even that people's apostasy can alter God's fixed purpose of love (Hos.

11.8–9). The People of God is clearly a 'continuum', not of nature, but of grace alone, throughout all the centuries till the present day.

Fourthly, the 'five-moment' interpretation of the story of Israel renders the OT the divinely given commentary upon the NT which aids the believer to understand more profoundly how God deals with his own individual soul. The adopted Son, Israel, is described in the OT as a sinner redeemed by God's grace. The story of Israel is thus the story of 'me' writ large, and painted on an extensive canvas, covering a period not just of three-score years and ten, but of a thousand years. With such a large canvas, he who runs may read. Each facet of the truth of God can now be more nearly observed. And since the individual most surely knows in the secret of his heart the reality of the first three 'moments' which Israel knew, he is now presented with a significant hope as well. This is because the story of this other sinful and adopted Son did not end with death. The Christian believer has already discovered that in his baptism he has passed beyond the moment of death and has entered into eternal life. This is true for him, because he is already 'in Christ', the second Israel. The first Israel, too, however, is 'in Christ', since 'before Abraham was, I am' (John 8.58). Moreover we now know that the first Israel waited in confident hope for the fifth 'moment' to dawn. The Christian believer today, then, assured by the witness of the Holy Spirit himself, can also look forward with joy to that fifth 'moment' when he too will enter into the glory which is laid up for those who love their Lord.

Appendix

St Paul undoubtedly regarded God's dealings with his corporate Son, Israel, in terms of such an exegesis. Exegesis remains exegesis, only so long as we cling faithfully to history. St Paul's discussion of the meaning of Israel's first two 'moments' is called by some 'eisegesis' rather than 'exegesis'. He says: 'Moreover, brethren, I would not that ye should be ignorant, how that all our fathers were under the cloud, and all passed through the sea;

and were baptized unto Moses in the cloud and in the sea; and did all eat the same spiritual meat; and did all drink the same spiritual drink: for they drank of the spiritual Rock that followed them: and that Rock was Christ' (I Cor. 10.1–4). This typological eisegesis is in the Rabbinical manner.[22] Yet both here and in Rom. 9–11 it is the fact of Israel as a historical people which compels Paul to seek to interpret their *raison d'être*. In order to do this, Paul makes use of events that happened to, and concepts connected with, the life of Jesus.

Now, it so happens that in the OT there exists a complete analogy to the method of interpretation which St Paul uses in the NT. The author of the P documents lived and wrote long after the first Temple was destroyed in 587 B.C. Yet he uses his knowledge of that Temple, such as it was, to interpret the significance of the Tabernacle of the Wilderness period, though the latter was a structure which existed long before the period of the Temple of Solomon. As we also know, if it had not been for P, we would never have been given the theology of the Tabernacle which has been preserved for us in the Pentateuch. Yet that theological interpretation P has created by reading back the significance of the Temple into the far distant period of the Tabernacle. It is a theology created by one who already knew the end of the process of theological growth and development and who could thus see the significance of the beginning from the end.

P is not alone in the development of such typological exegesis. The D school had already employed it in earlier years. The final author of the book of Joshua, again, lived at a time when the conquest of Canaan had long been complete. That therefore is why he regards the conquest under Joshua as a complete and final one. Yet from our point of view we know that his 'interpretative' historical writing does not agree with the early chapters of Judges, which suggest that Joshua's conquest was by no means complete. (For another view, see G. Ernest Wright, 'The Present State of

---

[22] See *Paul's Use of the Old Testament*, E. Earle Ellis, 1957, pp. 88 ff.; In *KzNT*, 3, p. 408 we read that the Rabbis applied the Rock figure to God.

Biblical Archaeology', in *The Study of the Bible Today and Tomorrow*, 1947.)

Now, if this theological approach to the interpretation of the ways of God with Israel is considered to be typology, then typology is a legitimate method of interpretation. St Paul's is merely a copy of that employed by D and P. He too knows the end of the story. This time the end is in Christ; and so he is in the position to read back significance into the beginning. What he does is to interpret God's action in the life of Israel in the light of what he knows God's action to have been so recently, from his point of view, in Christ. So he parallels the life of Israel with the life of Christ. No sooner had God brought his Son to the birth, he declares, than God baptized him 'in the cloud and in the sea'. He did so before Israel was able to take the promise of loyalty to him. God's action in baptizing his 'infant' Son was thus an act of prevenient grace. No suggestion is ever made in the Exodus story that Israel first repented of her sins, and was only then considered worthy of this baptism.

Thereafter came the marriage covenant, when Israel said 'We will' (Ex. 19.8), in answer to the offer made by Israel's God. Israel was still a 'wife of youth' (Mal. 2.14). Such a marriage is consonant with what was customary at the time. In Gen. 24.59 we read that Rebecca was brought to her wedding by her nurse; on the other hand she was no child (v. 16), and could speak for herself (v. 57).

It is obviously not a stumbling block to the Semitic mind to swing from the picture of 'son' in the masculine, to that of 'bride' in the feminine. We have seen already how the mind could swing from 'vine' to 'vineyard', yet retain a continuity of teaching.

There follows what we have already noticed, the education of the Son by the imparting of Torah, the Law. But now St Paul adds in a new element to the story to complement Hosea's double figure, that of Son and Bride. Yahweh, he says, now fed his people with spiritual food and drink, providing them with their viaticum for the way. They needed the strength obtainable from the second biblical sacrament now that they had received the first in order that they might grow in grace and be empowered to withstand the temptations of the Wilderness.

If we, travelling by another road than St Paul, discover in the story of the People of God five 'moments' which can be paralleled by five similar moments in the story of Christ, we are not thereby necessarily indulging in typology at all. So long as we remain true to a historical exegesis, we are then taking the OT seriously as revelation; in that case we are not surprised to find that it tells us the same things about the eternal God as does the NT.

Eighteen

The Covenant

The idea of the Covenant dominates the whole OT. The original meaning of the noun *berith* has been much discussed. It may derive from the rarely used verb *barah*, 'to eat'. In that case the primary emphasis in the making of the covenant is upon the cultic meal that may accompany an act of worship. Thus Isaac ate a meal of this nature as a mark of his covenant with Abimelech (Gen. 26.30). The fact that the verb most often used for 'to make' a covenant is *karath*, 'to cut', lends credence to this derivation of its meaning.[1] On the other hand, Abraham 'cut' his animals into pieces, not in order to eat them, but to sacrifice with them, on the occasion when God made a covenant with him (Gen. 15.1–18), to the end that his seed should inherit the land on which he stood. But again, the root of the noun *berith* may be Assyrian in origin; and if so, its original meaning may be 'fetter' or 'bond'.[2] The word seems to bear this meaning in Ezek. 20.37.

What the original meaning of the word was is not so important to us as the meaning which the Hebrews put into it in OT times. Of course there was the kind of covenant that obtained between man and man, or between nation and nation (e.g. Ex. 23.32), that

[1] See Kautzsch in *HDB*, vol. V, p. 630b.
[2] *TWNT*, 11, article διαθήκη i, pp. 106–9; also 3, p. 108; Henry S. Gehman, *Theology Today*, April, 1950, p. 27; G.E. Mendenhall, in *Law and Covenant in Israel and the Ancient Near East*, 1955, shows interesting parallels between Israel's Covenant and those between contemporary nations.

is, between two equal parties who agree to give each other mutual help in time of need. Thus when David and Jonathan swore eternal loyalty to each other on equal terms, in order to mark the equality of their covenant, they exchanged every piece of clothing and every weapon that they possessed. Again, a covenant could be imposed from above, and therefore could only be accepted by those to whom it was offered. It was that type of covenant which king Ahab, for example, imposed on vanquished Ben-hadad of Syria (I Kings 20.34).[3]

The Covenant made at Sinai, however, was of another nature altogether. It was an imposed covenant,[4] indeed, but it was imposed upon a willing people. As Jeremiah understood it, when he looked back from the seventh century upon the giving of the Covenant at a point in history six hundred years before, its essence lay in these words of God: 'Obey my voice, and I will be your God and ye shall be my people' (Jer. 7.23). As to how much of J's and E's narrative in the book of Exodus incorporates a factual memory of the events that took place at Sinai, it is now impossible to say. We have looked at this problem already in Part Three, chap. 13. Certainly the whole story, as it has been written up for us by P and the still later redactors, presents us not merely with facts, but also with a theological interpretation of those facts. Approaching it thus theologically, the covenant made at Sinai is seen to have been more clearly interpreted to the Hebrew mind under the figure of a covenant of marriage than under any other form.

Firstly, then, in OT times the bridegroom had to pay a *mohar*, or purchase-money for his bride (Ex. 22.16; Deut. 22.29). He was then betrothed to the girl (Gen. 24.49 ff.; Judg. 14.7 ff.). Thus marriage was primarily a legal bond. Normally the girl had no choice in the matter of her husband. Nor did she bring a 'dowry' to the marriage according to ancient Hebrew custom. Once married, moreover, the woman became her husband's property,

---

[3] For a full discussion of the various types of biblical covenant see John Pedersen, op. cit., I–II, pp. 263–310.

[4] R. Kraetszchmar, *Die Bundtsvorstellung im A.T.*, 1896; in Deut., pp. 123 ff.; in Jer., Ezek., and Deut.–Isa, p. 147.

to do with as he pleased. He was her *ba'al*, lord and master; so that the woman's word for marriage in Hebrew was 'to be ba'al-ed' by a man (Prov. 30.23). He could divorce her (Deut. 24.1 f.), but she could not divorce him; in fact the latter idea occurs nowhere at all in the OT. The husband's right to divorce his wife, however, was withdrawn by D in two cases. One was if he had falsely accused his wife of not having been a virgin when he married her (Deut. 22.19); the other was in the case where he had wronged a virgin and was consequently compelled to marry her (Deut. 22.28). On the other hand, by the end of the OT period divorce was regarded as contrary to the will of God in all respects. By then, the wife was held to be the mother of the 'seed of God', and as such was to be loved and cherished even when she grew to be old (Mal. 2.14–16). Now, as we have seen already in Part Three, chap. 15 (4), since Israel's understanding of the marriage covenant throws great light upon her understanding of God's covenant with her at the foot of Sinai, we should pay attention to some of the analogies involved *seriatim*.

The sixth chapter of Exodus contains an exposition of the Sinai covenant largely from the pen of P. The exposition is in the form of a 'pre-view' given to Moses of the significance of the events about to take place after the crossing of the Red Sea. It begins with the words: 'And I have also established my covenant with them, to give them the land of Canaan, the land of their pilgrimage wherein they were strangers' (Ex. 6.4). We recall that it is not the woman who brings the dowry, but the man who bestows his property upon his bride. Israel had already lived in Canaan in the patriarchal period in the persons of her eponymous ancestors. But at that time she had been a stranger (*ger*) in what was still to her a strange land. The ger was a resident alien, one who therefore lived without rights or privileges. Accordingly he could be at the mercy of any unscrupulous ruler or landlord. It was for this reason that the *ger* was given protection under the 'book of the Covenant' like that offered to the widow and the orphan (Ex. 22.21, 22); 'for ye were strangers' yourselves before the Sinai covenant was given.

The word 'stranger' reminds us of the effect of the curse laid upon Cain in punishment for murdering his brother Abel

(Gen. 4.11, 14). He was condemned to be a 'fugitive' and a 'vagabond', *na'wa-nadh*, in the earth. And he was to dwell (what a paradox!) in the land of Nod (Gen. 4.16). The paradox resides in the fact that the word *nodh* itself means 'wandering'. So then mankind 'dwelt' in the land of 'wandering' and had even tried to build a 'permanent' city in Nod (Gen. 4.17). But once God offered marriage to this one branch of all the descendants of Adam, then the whole situation of this people that was to become the Bride of God was altered. She was now no longer a wanderer (the word 'Hebrew', *ibhri*, may also possibly be so understood) or a stranger on the earth; now she had found the security of a husband and home, and the permanent possession of a land of her own.

At a later point in the Exodus narrative we read of the following incident. We learn that after the ratification of the Covenant at Sinai, 'the people sat down to eat and drink' (Ex. 24.11; 32.6). This is just what we would expect to occur at the happy event that a marriage is. Thereafter, moreover, at least one school of interpreters of Israel's story saw the Wilderness wanderings as a period of happy fellowship between the Bride and the divine Bridegroom, a honeymoon period where Israel rested thankfully in the strength of her mighty Lover (Part Three, chap. 15 (4)).

That the covenant should have been a costly experience for the divine Husband is not surprising when we remember that the Bride was wholly the receiver. 'Gather my saints together unto me: those that have made a covenant with me by sacrifice' (Ps. 50.5; cf. Zech. 9.11). God had had to redeem his people, Israel, at the 'cost' of the sacrifice of Pharaoh's son (Ex. 4.23), who, after all, was God's own son as well; and now again the costliness of the covenant is signified by the shedding of blood. 'And Moses took the blood, and sprinkled it on the people, and said, Behold the blood of the covenant, which the Lord hath made with you' (Ex. 24.8).

The 'costliness' of God's redemptive action all throughout his dealings with Israel is set forth by the frequent use of the verb *padhah* to ransom. While the verb as originally used implied a financial transaction, or the substitution of one object of value for another, we must not press such a literal meaning upon it when it is used of God. The first-born of both man and beast had to be ransomed *from* God at the cost of the spilling of the blood of animals which God himself had created (Ex. 13.12–13). God *padhah-ed* Israel from Egypt (Deut. 7.8), evidently at the cost of Pharaoh's son (Ex. 4.23). Later he was to *hoshia'* (a verb whose use we shall examine in chap. 20) Israel, this time from the hand of Cyrus, who conquered Babylonia. Thereupon he gave Cyrus in exchange (*kopher* 'ransomprice') an empire in Africa, comprising Egypt, Ethiopia and Seba (Isa. 43.3; cf. Job 33.24).[5]

The AV frequently confuses *padhah* with another verb, *ga'al*, to redeem. The action which this second verb describes was originally that performed by the kinsman of a man who had lost his property and who had fallen into slavery (Lev. 25.25, 47 ff.; 27.13; Num. 35.19; Deut. 19.6) it was also that of Boaz who both married Ruth and paid money to 'redeem' her property (Ruth 3.12–13; 4.1–12).[6] When applied to God, therefore, the emphasis is now upon the graciousness of the act rather than upon its cost, even although the latter is still present. 'Fear not, for I have redeemed thee, I have called thee by thy name; thou art mine' (Isa. 43.1). 'Ye have sold yourselves for nought; and ye shall be redeemed without money' (Isa. 52.3).[7]

As part of the divine Husband's offer to make a marriage covenant with Israel, then, we are given to hear words of tender love and pity. We return to Ex. 6.5: 'I have heard the groaning of the children of Israel . . . I will bring you out from under the burdens of the Egyptians, and I will rid you of their bondage, and I will redeem (*ga'al*) you' (cf. Ps. 74.2).

Then just as in the case of the human lover who reveals his inner soul to his beloved, so Yahweh adds the great word of self-revelation. 'I am Yahweh'. This self-revelation we are to understand, of course, in terms of Ex. 3, that passage which

---

[5]   See S.H. Hooke, 'The Theory and Practice of Substitution', in *The Siege Perilous*, 1956, pp. 204–21.

[6]   See G.A.F. Knight, *Ruth and Jonah*, Torch Commentary, 2nd ed., 1956, pp. 36–37. Also S.R. Driver, *Deuteronomy*, ICC., 1895, p. 100.

[7]   See *TWB*, pp. 185 ff.

contains the earlier narrative written by J (see Part One, chap. 3). Thereafter Yahweh 'takes' his 'bride': 'I will take you to me for a people, and I will be to you a God'; 'and ye shall know that I am Yahweh your God' (Ex. 6.7), and you will thus experience the assurance which any bride comes to know as she rests in utter confidence in her lover. Yahweh now adds that he will provide the whole dowry, by giving Israel the land which he had promised to Abraham, Isaac and Jacob (v. 8). Finally the passage ends with an oath. Just as a human marriage includes the solemn vow, so here God swears by that which only he can swear, viz., by himself: 'I am Yahweh' (v. 8).

It is Israel's privilege throughout her subsequent history, in consequence, to 'give thanks' *hodhah*, not merely, be it said, as an act of gratitude, though that aspect of her worship is there, but as the voluntary acknowledgement of her divine Husband's legitimate claim upon her (cf. Ps. 105.1; 106.1; 107.1). Yet here again we witness the unspeakable humility of the divine Lover. The movement in Israel's praise may take two directions, one subjective, and one objective. In the one, Israel gives thanks by recording as an act of worship the mighty acts of God done on her behalf (cf. p. 163), a form of 'counting her many blessings'; but her praise may also take the form of blessing God (cf. Ps. 103.1; 104.1). We recall how the action of blessing was the conveying of an element of the will of the blesser to the one blessed (Part One, chap. 5). In other words, the all sufficient God was willing to accept a blessing from Israel as part of Israel's worship. [8]

The Content of the Covenant

Such then is P's interpretation of the inner significance of the Covenant which God offered to Israel at Sinai. Any human marriage comprises two aspects of the union. In the first place, marriage is a legal contract, to which both parties assent before

---

[8] Cf. G.A.F. Knight, *A Biblical Approach to the Doctrine of the Trinity*, 1953, p. 74; also Th. Robinson, *The Poetry of the OT*, 1947, p. 162.

witnesses; but secondly it is also that moment when both parties, having plighted their troth, promise to be faithful and loyal to each other till their life's end. The Sinai Covenant is to be understood to contain both these aspects of the union at once. Firstly, it was a *berith*.[9] 'Now therefore, if ye will obey my voice indeed, and keep my covenant, then ye shall be a peculiar treasure unto me above all people' (Ex.19.5).

Israel is not normally known in the OT as a *goi*, a 'nation', like any other nation. Israel is normally[10] known as the *'am yahweh*, the 'people of Yahweh'. Moreover, this *'am* is regularly seen by the priestly writers in the light of its peculiar relationship to God. The People of God is frequently described as a *qahal*, a word whose meaning is best understood when we recognize that it probably derives from the word for 'voice', *qol*.[11] Israel is the People 'called out' by God's voice from amongst other peoples. This is because God has 'chosen', *bahar*, Israel as a 'peculiar possession', *segullah* (Ex. 19.5, etc.) a king's private treasure (I Chron. 29.3). The hearing of God's voice at Sinai was looked upon as *yom qahal*, the Day of being called into being. Israel was thus to be holy, even as God himself is holy (cf. the 'Holiness Code', Lev. 17 ff.). The LXX translation of *qahal* is most usually the word ἐκκλησία ι. This means that by the second century B.C. the Covenant People was recognized to be the Community of the Called. To express the total relationship that therefore obtained between Yahweh and this people whom he had called, the noun *hesedh* is normally employed.

The *berith*, then, was the outer husk of the nut. But secondly, the Covenant contained an inner kernel. All its moral content, apart from its legal aspect, is summed up in the word *hesedh*. We must now look more closely at this word.

---

[9]   N. Glueck, 'Das Wort *hesed* im alttestamentlichen Sprachgebrauch', *ZAW*, Supplement No. 47, 1927. Cf. R. Kraetszchmar, op. cit., pp. 244 ff.

[10]   Ex. 19.6 is an exception. There Israel is actually called a *goi qadhosh*.

[11]   *TWNT*; 2, article ἐκκλησία; also to be found in English translation in *Bible Key Words*, 'Church', 1950, pp. 51–56.

The Signficance of the Nouns *Ḥesedh* and *Ḥen*

No one word in English can cover all that the word *ḥesedh* implies. We recall that the eastern marriage, unlike the western marriage of today, was an 'imposed' marriage. The bride had no say in the choice of her husband. But if he were obviously a good man, ready and willing to offer her status, a home, a future, along with his promise to love and to cherish her, then she would naturally give a willing 'yes' to the offer that he made. Thus the word *ḥesedh* meant different things for Yahweh and for Israel. On God's side it implied in the first place his unswerving loyalty to Israel. Thus *ḥesedh* may approach in content that great term *'aman*, a root which represents the faithfulness of the unchanging God. The root *'aman* could be used of pillars which stand firmly (II Kings 18.16), or it represented the idea of firm, sure and lasting – a 'sure place' (Isa. 22.23), 'sure waters' (Isa. 33.16), that is, waters which can be relied on, and so on. But it bore a like significance in the moral sphere as well. A priest might be described as 'reliable' or 'trustworthy' (I Sam. 2.35) if he were a good man who faithfully executed his office. The noun *'emunah*, then, means 'steadfastness', 'trustworthiness', 'faithfulness'. In II Kings 22.5–7 we read that 'the doers of the work (in repairing the Temple) . . . dealt faithfully' (i.e. with *'emunah*) in their building project.

This 'reliability', this 'trustworthiness' of God was thus an aspect of the *ḥesedh* he ever showed towards Israel. Consequently a Psalmist can declare: 'I will sing of the *ḥasdhe* of Yahweh (the various aspects or activities of Yahweh's *ḥesedh*) for ever' (Ps. 89.1). Then in poetic parallelism he continues: 'With my mouth will I make known thy *'emunah* to all generations'. That God's *ḥesedh* remains for ever is the subject of the refrain of Ps. 138 (cf. Jer. 33.11). Thus, then, Yahweh's *ḥesedh* was an attitude of self-consistent trustworthiness both towards Israel, and towards individuals within Israel (e.g. Job. 10.12).

But out of that self-consistent trustworthiness on God's part sprang all that was implied when one who was of such a nature made a covenant with another. God's *ḥesedh* to Israel included within it both goodness and kindness (I Sam. 20.14); and since the divine Husband was infinitely strong, and the Bride was very weak, God's hesedh also included the conception of pity and mercy: 'The Lord is longsuffering and of great mercy' (Num. 14.18); in fact the word 'mercy' is one of the commonest means of translating the term hesedh that the AV employs. We gather that hesedh is rightly translated thus, when, as sometimes happens it is paralleled by the noun rahamaim, which means 'compassion' (cf. Jer. 16.5). The latter noun actually derives from the word for 'womb', so that its emphasis is on the conception of God's 'mother love'. It is therefore close also to the noun 'ahabhah,[12] when the latter is used of God: 'The Lord did not set his love, hashaq be, upon you nor choose you because ye were more in number than any people; for ye were the fewest of all people, but because the Lord loved you, 'ahabhah, and because he would keep the oath which he had sworn unto your fathers' (Deut. 7.7 f., etc.). We see then that the great redemptive words describing God's loving choice and care of Israel tend to merge into one another and even overlap one another.[13]

There is another Hebrew word that is used to expound God's constant attitude of faithfulness to Israel, and that is hen, grace. We recall how throughout the whole of Israel's story the prophets declare the word of God against her, on the ground that she is in continual rebellion against her divine Lover. Never at any point in her history, then, did Israel in any sense deserve God's hesedh.[14] All that God did for her he did of grace alone. The Hebrew noun hen does not possess the content of the NT word χάρις i. Seldom does the LXX translate hen by χάρις i since the latter word, before NT times, carried the thought of a semi-physical gracefulness or charm. Hen is rather hesedh in its sovereign form, favour to the indifferent, and to the disloyal.[15] The Hebrew

[12]   D. Winton Thomas, 'The Root 'ahabh, "love", in Hebrew', ZAW, 16. Band, 1939, Heft 1/2, pp. 57 ff.
[13]   T.F. Torrance, 'The Doctrine of Grace in the OT', SJT; 1948, Vol. 1, No. 1, p. 63.
[14]   H.H. Rowley, The Re-discovery of the Old Testament, 1945, p. 84.
[15]   D.R. Ap-Thomas, 'Some Aspects of the Root HNN in the OT', JSS, April, 1957, pp. 128 ff.

who set his slave free after six years of service was to send him away *ḥinnom*, freely, gratis (Ex. 21.2). 'The wicked borroweth, and payeth not again: but the righteous dealeth graciously, and giveth' (Ps. 37.21). So does God deal with Israel (Isa. 30.18, 19; Amos 5.15; Zech. 4.7). 'The people that were left of the sword found grace in the wilderness' (Jer. 31.2). The two words *ḥen* and *ḥesedh* occur together in that great sentence of God's self-revelation which we have quoted before, and which seems to belong to the oldest stratum in the Pentateuch: 'And the Lord passed by before him (Moses) and proclaimed, The Lord, the Lord God, merciful and *gracious*, *ḥannun*, longsuffering and abundant in *ḥesedh* and *'emeth* (from the root *'aman*), keeping mercy for thousands . . . ' (Ex. 34.6–7).

The word *ḥesedh* must bear another content, however, when it is used of Israel's response to God's imposition of his covenant upon her. In Israel's case, the word must necessarily convey primarily the conception of loyalty. Israel must not sur, turn aside, or apostatize (Ex. 32.8), or *'azabh*, forsake (Prov. 2.17; Deut. 28.20) Yahweh, but, on the other hand, she must *dabhaq be*, cleave to him (Deut. 11.22). She must not go after her own thoughts (Isa. 65.2), but rather walk in God's way (Deut. 11.22), and swear by his name (Neh. 9.5). To do these things is Israel's very great privilege (Ps. 135). A representative Israelite, such as a prophet, accordingly wore a mark on the brow to show that he belonged to Yahweh (I Kings 20.38, 41). The idea is expressed in parabolic form also in Ezek. 9.4, where we are told that Ezekiel was to set a mark on the brow of all those who regretted and bemoaned the idol worship that was going on in Jerusalem; the idea occurs also in Isa. 44.5, where individuals amongst the Gentiles are pictured as desirous of entering the Covenant People.[16] In his own characteristic manner the Deuteronomist makes clear the attitude which Israel is bound to take towards Yahweh. On the one hand God is 'the faithful God, which keepeth covenant, *berith*, and mercy, *ḥesedh*' (Deut. 7.9) on his part. But the passage goes on: 'Thou shalt therefore keep the command-

---

[16] C. Lindhagen, *The Servant Motif in the Old Testament*, 1950, pp. 91 ff.

ment, and the statutes, and the judgements, which I command thee this day to do them' (v. 11). God has the *jus domini* over his wife in the manner, not of the modern, but of the ancient husband. Israel's 'loyalty' must therefore show itself primarily in obedience. And since it must be obedience to a revealed 'commandment, statutes and judgements', then obedience for Israel must take the form, at least, of a pious devotion to the cult (Isa. 57.1). But Israel's response to God's *hesedh* should possess more content than just that. It should contain within it the personal affection of the bride for her husband (Jer. 2.2). Israel's loyal-love to Yahweh might even entail the exclusion of devotion to the cult! (Hos. 6.6).

The correlative of the *hen* which God bestowed upon Israel was thus Israel's consciousness of her need for it. A common phrase is 'to find favour in the eyes of', a phrase which is used in the first place of ordinary human relationships (e.g. Gen. 30.27; Num. 32.5). Therefore it occurs when a word is needed to describe Israel's response to God, whether in the words of individuals or in utterances made by the nation as a whole. Moses begs of God: 'If I have found grace in thy sight show me now thy way' (Ex. 33.13). Other individual Israelites who know that they belong within the covenant love, *hesedh*, of God, call themselves *hasidh* (a word which is sometimes written in English as Chassid). This emphasis is made particularly in the post-exilic period. The *hasidh* was the pious man, the man who sought to be loyal to God's initial act of grace at Sinai. The whole nation as one unit could be disloyal to God's *hesedh*, and thus could be more a *goi* than an '*am*, a *goi lo' hasidh* (Ps. 43.1), yet the individual pious Israelite believed that if he 'waited upon' God (Ps. 33.20), 'hoped in' God (Ps. 130.7), and other such terms, God's grace, *hen*, and loyalty, *hesedh*, were such that God would always hear his voice. In the OT God's forgiveness always comes before human repentance (cf. Isa. 44.22). Thus the word *hasidh* came to describe God's individual beloved child, if he sought wholly to respond in a reflected loyalty and devotion to the love which he had first and already received from God within the covenant relationship. 'Neither wilt thou suffer thine holy one (AV, goodly one ARSV) to see corruption' (Ps. 16.10).[17] The *'ish ḥesedh* remained, of course, a sinful man, though he sought indeed to be a merciful man (Prov. 11.17). But this he learned to be only because God had already been merciful to him.

The important 'summary' of OT religion which is to be found in the book of Micah employs our word in this derived sense: 'What doth the Lord require of thee, but to do justly, to love *ḥesedh*, and to walk humbly with thy God?' (Micah 6.8). Thus, in a word, we see that the OT does not seek primarily to teach morality. This is because it regards all morality as derived from the state of *ḥesedh* which the believing individual within Israel must feel in response to Gods' offer of his *ḥesedh*; yet, paradoxically, no literature in all the world has so much to say as the OT upon moral values and upon rules and regulations for a healthy community life. The keeping of these is thus the ethical response expected of Israel. Amongst Israel's neighbours, ritual concerned itself with the unseen, ethics with the seen.[18] But in Israel's case the two were, ideally, one. To that end the prophets taught Israel not to 'spiritualize' religion; Israel was to remember that her religion embodied a marriage of matter and spirit. Thus both sacrifice and ethics were to be expressions of a heart set on fire with love in response to the initial act of a God of *ḥen* and *ḥesedh*.

---

[17] See H.H. Rowley, *The Faith of Israel*, 1956, p. 130, note 1, for a discussion of the relationship of the word *ḥasidh* to *ḥesedh*.

[18] H. Wheeler Robinson, *Inspiration and Revelation in the Old Testament*, 1946, p. 79.

Nineteen

The Book of the Covenant

The *berith* imposed by God upon Israel might soon have been forgotten, had it not been that the 'commandment, and the statutes, and the judgements which I command thee this day to do them' (*v. supra*) demanded a practical expression by Israel of her loyalty and devotion to her God.

How much of the so-called 'Law of Moses' is as old as Moses himself is a subject upon which it would be foolish to dogmatize. It is quite obvious, however, that the greater part of D's and P's legislative material comprises the compendium of law that grew up in Israel over the years, as law grows, snowball-like, in any land. All of it was thus the 'Law of Moses' because it was all deduced from the original material which the latter gave to Israel.

In the form in which it crystallized in the post-exilic period, the Torah contains several Codes of Law.[1] We shall draw attention only to a few aspects of this 'legal' material. The Torah contains ancient 'ritual' commands (e.g. Ex. 34.10–26) as well as the more 'ethicized' Decalogue of common use (Ex. 20.1–17 and Deut. 5.6–21). It contains *mishpatim*, or case law (e.g. Num. 31.25–30, incorporated in the Torah as a result of David's judicial decision recorded in I Sam. 30.24–25); and it contains *ḥuqqim*, or statutes 'inscribed' *ḥqq*, probably originally on stone (e.g. Ex. 30.21). Upon such as these much of the later paradeictic legislation was

---

[1] R.H. Pfeiffer, *Introduction to the Old Testament*, 1952, p. 210, enumerates seven.

evidently built, until in the period immediately after the Exile the priestly editors incorporated in the written Torah the works of all their predecessors.[2]

All this legislation, seen as the outflow of the work of Moses at Mount Sinai, was regarded in the post-exilic period as the 'Book of the Covenant' that was made at Sinai between God and Israel. The Torah contained, it was believed by the late post-exilic period, the whole rule of life that God required of his people. This rule covered every aspect both of communal and of private life. If God was indeed a jealous God, or as we would say today a God with 'totalitarian' claims upon his Covenant People, then those claims must inevitably affect every facet of Israel's life (Deut. 18.13). The 'zeal of the Lord' was in fact his jealous love for Israel. We may perhaps bridge the difference aroused in our minds between the ideas of 'zeal' and 'jealousy' when we realize that the one Hebrew word, *qin'ah* may translate either English noun. We must remember that God's purpose in offering his people the 'Law' was part of that 'zeal of the Lord' for the return of his fallen world to himself of which we have already spoken. God had chosen his Son Israel to be his instrument to that end. Israel had therefore to be trained and taught to understand his task. Israel had still been a little boy when God entrusted him with the Law (Hos. 11.1). Israel had therefore to learn the meaning of obedience to God in every department of his life. The sermonic material in the first eleven chapters of Deuteronomy makes the meaning of Israel's relationship to God clear to the people of the seventh century B.C. at a time when men like Jeremiah and Habakkuk were seeking to expound, under God, what really was the purpose of Israel's calling.

The sacrificial laws kept Israel in touch with Yahweh at those points in her life where she was tempted to follow her Canaanite neighbours in their worship of the fertility gods.[3] Thus Israel's

---

[2] See A. Alt. *Die Urspr ünge des israelitischen Rechts*, 1934, in *Kleine Schriften*, 1953, pp. 279 ff.

[3] J. Pedersen, op. cit., 3–4, pp. 334–75. We need to use both the masculine and the feminine genders if we would be faithful to the many figures which the OT employs to describe Israel.

legislators did wisely in incorporating into the cult of Yahweh the festivals which marked the seasons of the agricultural year.

The Passover festival, as we read of it in Ex. 12, is obviously a festival older than the Exodus from Egypt itself It was originally a spring festival (possibly connected with moon worship), marking the opening of the agricultural year (Ex. 12.2–3). It is evidence of the genius of Moses that he seized upon the festival and adapted it so that it became the first festival in his people's cult. Not only was it a spring festival, and therefore highly meaningful to a peasant people, but it also developed into the festival that commemorated Yahweh's mighty act in setting Israel free from the domination of Pharaoh.[4] And then, in the process of time, it became that festival in which the members of each Israelite household relived those mighty events, and through the observance of which they personalized God's action with their forefathers within the realm of their own experience. The Israelite family came, in fact, to know the truth of the Exodus for itself. 'And when thy son asketh thee in time to come, saying, What mean the testimonies, and the statutes, and the judgments, which the Lord our God hath commanded you? Then thou shalt say unto thy son, *We* were Pharaoh's bondmen in Egypt; and the Lord brought *us* out of Egypt with a mighty hand' (Deut. 6.20–1).

At the present day we recognize that it is notoriously difficult to define who is a Jew and who is not. But in OT times no such difficulty presented itself. The Israelite was he who could join with his brethren in the confession that we have just quoted.[5] Moreover, it is for this reason, too, that the Passover became a combination of a private feast and a temple or national festival by the end of the OT period; people both went to Jerusalem on pilgrimage, and celebrated the Paschal night in private homes.[6]

Again, virtually all peasant peoples hold harvest festivals, and in all probability Israel did so from earliest times. Under the guidance of generations of priestly educators of the people such

---

[4]   J. Pedersen, op. cit., 1940, p. 445.

[5]   Ibid., p. 409.

[6]   Ibid., p. 413

a festival derived from pagan sources was also incorporated into the cult (Ex. 23.16; 34.22). But what the priests most strangely and wonderfully managed to do was to channel the spontaneous rejoicing of a people whose very life depended upon the ingathering of their poor little crop, so that their wheat harvest festival was also linked with a rejoicing for this very same deliverance from the bondage of Egypt (Deut. 16.9–12).

The last of the three pilgrimage feasts which is mentioned in the laws was associated with the fruit or grape harvest. Its ancient nature is attested by such a story as we have recorded for us in Judges 21. But it becomes a 'law of Moses' in Lev. 23.33–36, 39–40. By the late period of the priestly code the festival was now a religious convocation lasting over a week. It had in fact developed into what we call 'the feast of booths', and served to personalize for each successive generation of Israelites the experience of their forefathers when they too lived in booths (or at least not in permanent stone houses) during the forty years journey in the Wilderness. In other words, the festival of the grape harvest was also made to serve as an action performed annually within the cultic year, so that it too could link the present experience of rejoicing at the harvest with the long past Exodus nexus of events when Yahweh redeemed his people from the power of Egypt or the monster Rahab.

The Comprehensive Nature of Israelite Law

Surely it is an aspect of the mystery of the self-revelation of God within the life of Israel that he should have so moved the hearts of those who both legislated on the basis of the original Mosaic law and who expounded to the people the implications of that law for their daily lives, that they should have taught the common people to regard the keeping of the Law of Moses as a mark of their common *hesedh* towards Yahweh who had given them the Law. Thus it was not only Israel's festivals which were thus orientated towards an exposition of the original *berith*. Many of the individual items of legislation carried as their peroration a 'sanction' which placed them in a similar category. The Israelites were taught the meaning of every aspect of *ḥesedh* as it must needs be worked out between man and man.[7] They were invited to do so, often with such an expression as the following: 'Love ye therefore the stranger (the resident-alien): for ye were strangers in the land of Egypt' (Deut. 10.19); or again, they were reminded to set their fellow Hebrew slaves free after six years of service, furnishing them liberally with gifts to set them up again in life – and this for the same reason as before, because they too had been slaves released by God from bondage in Egypt (Deut. 15.12–15). In Egypt Israel had known no law: she had lived in a land of 'chaos'. Now, however, Israel possessed a law given her by God, in the service of which she could find perfect freedom. Such is the theme of the long 119th Psalm: 'Thy word is a lamp unto my feet, and a light unto my path' (v. 105); 'I love thy commandments above gold' (v. 127); 'Order my steps in thy word, and let not any iniquity have dominion over me' (v. 133).

The unique effect of such a love for the Law was that Israel, from being a fissiparous amphictyony of tribes, was slowly but surely welded into one brotherhood under God. Hammurabi's Code in Babylonia, the Assyrian Code, and the Hittite Codes[8] all employed what we know as 'class legislation', i.e., one law for the aristocrat and one for the peasant. But the 'Law of Moses' is wholly new in this regard, even though many of its laws are rooted in the common law of the ancient Near East. Rich and poor, free man and slave, all receive a like punishment for a similar misdeed. Some have imagined that the Mosaic code introduced a retrograde step in the advance of civilization when the so-called 'lex talionis' was included in 'the Book of the

---

[7]   The emphasis upon *individual* responsibility is in contrast to the requirements of the other eastern codes. See W. Eichrodt, *Man in the Old Testament*, 1951, pp. 9–13.

[8]   *The Babylonian Laws*, 2 vols., G.R. Driver and J.C. Miles, 1952. *The Assyrian Laws*, G.R. Driver and J.C. Miles, 1935. *The Hittite Laws*, E. Neufeld, 1951. We know only a very little about Sumerian law; cf. S.N. Kramer, *From the Tablets of Sumer*, 1956, 'The First Moses', pp. 47–51.

Covenant' (Ex. 21.23–25). However, we should remember the following two points: (*a*) this law applied to *all* men, not just to the rich; the poor now had the *right* to equal treatment; (*b*) this law was so far ahead of its time that men even today sometimes disregard it. In the Second World War it often happened that in reprisal for the destruction of one individual of the enemy, ten or a hundred hostages were put to death.

The Mosaic Law thus brought into the world a new respect for human life.[9] None of the Codes ever suggest punishing a man by putting him behind prison bars, far less by the mutilation practised to this day in many lands. Instead the guilty party had to repay the damage he had caused by hard work over the years (e.g. Ex. 21.22, 32). Even the slave who had no rights at all amongst all other nations, even amongst the Greeks, found in the Code an article of law which protected him against the whim of the master whom he served (Ex. 21.26–27).

In any ancient society three classes in the community normally found themselves at a disadvantage, viz. widows, orphans, and foreigners living as resident aliens. The Mosaic Law, in contradistinction to all others, therefore provided a *go'el* for the widow. He was the next-of-kin male and it was incumbent upon him to marry any such destitute widow (Deut. 25.1–10).[10] The alien, again, residing temporarily within the bounds of Israel, had no rights at law, no redress from his neighbour if he found himself in trouble – just as Israel had had no redress when she lay under the lash of her Egyptian taskmasters. These three classes are therefore cared for by the law and mentioned repeatedly, the salutary reminder being added in each instance: 'and thou shalt remember that thou wast a bondman in Egypt' (Lev. 19.34; Deut. 16.12).

Again, since the whole land belonged to Yahweh, no individual Israelite was to imagine that he possessed any land in his own

---

[9] G.E. Wright, *The Biblical Doctrine of Man in Society*, 1954, p. 94 and p. 101.

[10] In the little book of Ruth, Boaz acts in this capacity to the young widow, after a nearer relative has refused to do so. See G.A.F. Knight, Torch Commentary, *Ruth and Jonah*, sec. ed. 1956, p. 40.

right. 'The land is mine, saith the Lord' (Lev. 25.23). Yet Yahweh gave it to Israel as a whole (Deut. 1.8, etc.). Certain families within Israel thereupon used the land allotted to them (by God!) (Josh. 13 ff.), but only on condition that all members of the tribe or family might share in the income derived from the land. Family property could not be alienated in perpetuity. In the year of Jubilee, all land reverted to its original lessee from God, no matter whether he were a fool or a good husbandman (Lev. 25.8–17). All those who were dependent upon the land were bound to help each other over bad harvests by loans for which no interest might be demanded (Lev. 25.35–38). That is to say, human relationships were esteemed more important than the making of money, especially out of human distress.

That all the codes of law within the Pentateuch were intended to provide a structure within which true brotherhood amongst the People of God could take form and shape, might be demonstrated by citing a few more laws.

'No man shall take the nether or the upper millstone to pledge: for he taketh a man's life to pledge' (Deut. 24.6). The peasant in Israel lived from day to day. The millstone was the one essential possession of any family, for on it the evening meal was ground. In other words, family life, the law points out, is more important in the eyes of God than the value of a stone. In the same vein is Lev. 19.13: 'The wages of him that is hired shall not abide with thee until the morning'. The good of the day-labourer's family must be in the forefront of an employer's mind.

To curse the deaf was to take mean advantage of a brother man (Lev. 19.14); to cheat with weights and balances (Deut. 25.13, 15) was to put self interest before true fellowship. To ensure the safety of one's neighbour's life and limb (Deut. 22.8) was surely a basic essential of community life if men were to look upon one another as precious in the sight of God. Such specific injunctions had of course to be modified and altered with the passing of the years, and with the fundamental reordering of human society; but the spirit of them was such, that Israel was taught to know God's true will for her life in community in all details.

To that end, the priestly writers employ a most important 'sanction'. Israel was ever to be aware that, since Yahweh is the holy God, then his people must be holy too. His people *are* his people, for the reason that Yahweh has chosen them for a specific purpose. If Yahweh is ever to use them, and he proposes indeed to use them by means of a relationship with them so extraordinary and profound that it is virtually beyond the thought of man, then this 'peculiar possession' of God must needs be holy too even as Yahweh himself is holy (e.g. Lev. 20.26). The typical Israelite is actually to walk before God with a perfect heart (Ps. 101.2).

The Comprehensive Nature of Torah

It is interesting to observe the manner in which Israel adapted practices and beliefs common to the life of the whole ancient Near East, and developed them to subserve both her theology and her cult. There are thus virtually no 'dead-ends' in the theology of the OT. This is because even borrowed practices and beliefs fit into the general developing pattern of Israel's faith.

In the early period, for example, it was believed that Yahweh manifested his will to his people by means of dreams (cf. Gen. 28.10 f.; 37.5; 40.5 f.), by a divining cup (Gen. 44.2), by the sacred dice, Urim and Thummim (I Sam. 28.6), and so on. But in later years the faith of Israel sublimated such primitive ideas; thus a Psalmist could be aware of the touch and guidance of God's Spirit upon his own spirit without the need of any such intermedia (cf. Ps. 5.11). The genius of the Hebrew thinker was such that when he borrowed ideas and practices from his neighbours, he so transformed them in the borrowing that they became vehicles for a new and deeper knowledge of the will of Yahweh. The earliest codes of law within the Torah often closely resemble the other ancient codes, especially that of Hammurabi of Babylon, who lived probably about 1800 B.C.[11] But the highly ethicized and

---

[11] There is a valuable comparison between the two codes in an Appendix to G.W. Wade's *Old Testament History*, 1934 (12th edition), p. 489.

moralized legislation of the Deuteronomic code, and its embody-
ing of individual items within the cultus commemorating God's
moral and *saving* action at the Exodus are now as different from
the original Hammurabic parallels as are the fruits of a tree from
its roots. There is no doubt that the practice of holding a weekly
Sabbath rest was not original to Israel. Yet we see how the Sabbath
was not only incorporated into the cult (Ex. 20.8–11), but was
also given eschatological significance for Israel and a place even
in the experience of God (Gen. 2.2–3).

Moreover, the word 'Torah' is the name given latterly to the
whole first five books of the OT. What we today regard as 'law'
is thus only a part of the book's contents. The word 'Torah' must
therefore have meant to the Hebrews after the period of Ezra not
only a collection of laws, but at the same time those laws as they
took shape in the developing life of Israel, the chosen instrument
of God's redemptive purpose, following upon the actuation of
God's plan in the call of Abraham. The noun *torah* is built from
the Hiphil, transitive, form of the verb *yarah*. *Yarah* means 'to
shoot', but the Hiphil, while also meaning such, means as well 'to
teach'. When one man teaches another, he shoots ideas from his
own into the other's mind (Prov. 3.1; Ps. 78.1; etc.). But in so
doing he 'reveals' what is in his own. Thus Torah means both
'teaching' and 'revelation' seen as one. The Hebrews thus moved
a long way from the primitive conception of revelation as the use
of sacred dice, and such like.

The early stories in Genesis are part of Israel's total Torah.
They are rooted in a mythological series of explanations of the
origins of the universe common to the whole Near Eastern world.
But Gen. 1 (the Creation), or Gen. 3 (the Fall), for example, are
no longer mythology. These chapters, as we have seen, present us
with theology written in the form of pictures. The genius of such
a method of presenting truth lies in the fact that, while the
interpretation of the picture may change from age to age, the
picture itself remains constant for all men in every age. The picture
in the Genesis story has become, in fact, not mythology, but the
Word of God itself, now speaking decisively and dynamically to

all manner of people in all places according to the capacity of each to understand it.

To point to the comprehensive nature and abiding value of Torah we might adduce what has been called the 'vestigial trace' to be found within it in regard to the practice of circumcision. The practice was by no means confined to Israel, since we know that many of Israel's semitic neighbours practised this 'initiatory' rite (cf. Jer. 9.26). Israel's historians are not in fact unanimous as to when and how the practice began in Israel. There is, for example, a story in connexion with circumcision in the very odd 'erratic block' of material that occurs in Ex. 4.24–26.[12] The author of Josh. 5.2 f. imagines that it must have been Joshua himself who introduced the practice. Elsewhere it is just taken for granted that the Israelites who came out of Egypt were already circumcised (Ex. 12.48), probably on the ground, as the priestly school narrates, that the patriarchs before them were circumcised at the command of God (Gen. 17.9–14).

Consequently, just as the observance of the spring festival was 'adopted' into the frameword of the Covenant, so too was this practice of circumcision. The story of God's command to Abraham to circumcise both himself and his son and all the male children of his company (Gen. 17.9–14) is therefore retrospectively made part of the Covenant, of the *berith* between Yahweh and his special people, and loyalty to the carrying out of God's command in this regard becomes another aspect of Israel's *hesedh*. On the other hand, there takes place with regard to the practice of circumcision as remarkable a transformation of its significance as the change in depth that took place between the Babylonian myth of creation and the first chapter of Genesis. We saw in Part Three how Israel was taught of God by degrees to understand the

---

[12] For a discussion of this difficult passage, see Joh. de Groot, *OS*, Deel 11, 'The Story of the Bloody Husband', pp. 10 ff.; also J. Hehn, *ZAW*, 1932, pp. 1 ff.; and J. Coppens, *Eph. Theol. Lov.*, 1941, pp. 68 ff. These agree that here we have no aetiological legend. No Israelite would ever have suggested of Yahweh the idea of a *jus primae noctis*.

profound mystery that her body, as the Bride of Yahweh, was intended to be one flesh with that of her divine Husband. Her interpretation of the primitive and even barbaric rite of circumcision was thus later wholly transfigured in significance. Circumcision is performed upon that male organ which actually unites man and wife as one flesh. Women are not circumcised in the OT, on the ground that they adhere to the fellowship of the People of God through physical union with men who are circumcised. We see then how the rite grew latterly to assume the symbol of the perfect moral union between Yahweh and his Bride Israel such as is both the will and the command of Israel's God (Deut. 30.6; cf. Col. 2.11). So it is that the prophets emphasize as Israel's primary need that she should 'know' God, a word whose frequent sexual significance we noted on p. 25. That is why, to 'know' God, a man requires a 'circumcised heart' (Deut. 10.16; 30.6). Such intimate knowledge is the medium of all true understanding of God's will (Hos. 4.1, 6; 5.4; 6.3; 8.2; Jer. 2.8; 4.22; 9.3, 6, 24; 22.15–16; 24.7; 31.34, etc.).

Yet there is another word which shows even more clearly how deep the relationship may be between Yahweh and his people, indeed, between Yahweh and individuals from amongst his people. We have seen that Yahweh chose Israel, for no other reason than that he loved her (p. 225). Consequently, Israel is summoned to love Yahweh in return for the love he has first shown her (Deut. 6.5). It is instructive to take account of the period of Israel's history when this particular understanding of what God was asking of his people was formulated. It was formulated, it would seem, during the first half of the seventh century, during the long dark night of the reign of king Manasseh. The latter introduced to Jerusalem every kind of heathen abomination and 'did that which was evil in the sight of the Lord's beyond what any king had ever done (II Kings 21.2). True religion, as we would say today, went underground 'for the duration'. The people of Judah were encouraged to approach the many newly introduced deities in the same manner as any ancient nation approached its gods. The servants of any deity of that period were united to their god in bonds primarily of fear or flattery. But in the Preamble to the

Deuteronomic Code, in contrast to the then prevailing view, the Israelite was actually commanded to *love* his deity (what an extraordinary conception for the ancient world!), to love Yahweh with all his heart (i.e., with his intelligence), with all his soul (i.e., with his total personality, his whole *nephesh*), and with all his might (i.e., with all the forcefulness at his command). We can understand, then, how the outstanding sentiments expressed in this passage could be singled out in later centuries and recognized to be the most important element in the whole OT Law (cf. Matt. 22.37 = Mark 12.30 = Luke 10.27).

No one would care to suggest that the Prophets were a vestigial remnant within the OT, even though as a class they died out actually within the OT period! (Zech. 13.4). No more then is the Law. The Zeal of the Lord required it for the furtherance of his plan. The Law, understood as it should be in terms of the Hebrew word Torah, thus assumes its necessary place in God's education of his people. Including within it the early chapters of Genesis as well as the sermons of Deuteronomy, it reveals itself in its final, post-exilic form, not as a set of legislations which Israel will later necessarily outgrow, but as one harmonious whole of revelation such as is necessary for an understanding of the *hesedh* which God showed to Israel in the first place, and which Israel is to show to God in return. It is true that no Israelite was ever able wholly to 'keep the Law', although the injunction was laid upon him that he must, 'that Yahweh might preserve us alive' (Deut. 6.24). In fact, it was because of Israel's sinful nature and consequent inability to keep the Law which sprang from, the Sinai Covenant that Jeremiah looked to the day when God would make a new coven ant with Israel (Jer. 31.31–34). Yet the Israel with whom he would make the new covenant would then be a renewed and transformed people. They would no longer need to be taught the 'Law', because 'in that day' they would keep it spontaneously. They would, of course, always be glad to have before them a 'framework' of the oral life such as the articles of the law provided, through which their now spontaneous *hesedh* could show itself in action. But their *hesedh* would now be such that Israel would no longer need the old 'Law'. Israel would then be standing in a new relationship to God, one that would show itself as *'emunah* (see p. 224). This *'emunah* on Israel's part would be her answer to the God who had shown himself to be a God of *'emunah* (Deut. 32.4) towards Israel in all his works and ways (Ps. 33.4; 36.5; etc.).

Twenty

God's Action within Israel

That Yahweh had a cosmic plan, which he was actively pursuing through his people, Israel, Isaiah was perhaps the first to see with clarity.[1] This plan he called God's *'etsah* (the noun deriving from the verb *ya'ats*): 'This also cometh forth from the Lord of hosts, which is wonderful in counsel, and excellent in working' (Isa. 28.29); 'For the Lord of hosts hath purposed, and who shall disannul it?' (14.26–27; cf. also 5.19; 19.3, 12, 17; 23.9; 29.15; 30.1. Deutero-Isaiah uses the same term; cf. Isa. 46.10).

At his inaugural vision (Isa. 6) Isaiah beheld no less than the End to which all history is moving, since his vision was of what is beyond history. Beyond the pain, turmoil and chaos of this world he beheld the Glory of God. The plan of God must therefore be such that out of the present chaos 'the whole earth (will be) full of his glory' (v. 3). A century later Jeremiah has only one word to add to this conception. It is as if he were to say 'not only the whole earth, but *hak-kol*, 'the totality' of all things (Jer. 10.16) will be filled with God's glory'.

God's action within history is primarily to use the historical people of Israel to this end. The redemption from Egypt, the giving of the Law and the setting of his covenant-love upon Israel, are thus the first steps in God's *'etsah*. The fact that those books which we call the 'historical books', viz., Joshua, Judges, I and II Samuel, and I and II Kings, are known in the Hebrew Bible as 'the former

---

[1] Joh. Fichtner, 'Jahwes Plan in der Botschaft des Jesaja', *ZAW*, 1951, Heft 1/2, pp. 17 ff.

Prophets' shows how we in our turn are to regard them. They are primarily an *interpretation* of Israel's history. They show how the plan of God works out over the period from the days of Joshua till the beginning of the Exile, the climax of God's ways with Israel.

The Theology of the Prescence

'Within' her is virtually what Israel did believe. 'But will God indeed dwell on the earth? behold, the heaven and heaven of heavens cannot contain thee: how much less this house that I have builded?' (I Kings 8.27). These words, attributed to Solomon by the Deuteronomic editor, represent the developed theology of the 'Presence' of God in Israel's midst, an immanential conception which perfectly balances the transcendental view of God which is often regarded as normative in OT thought. This immanential emphasis is represented pictorially in the next phrase used by Solomon: 'Yet have thou respect unto the prayer of thy servant . . . that thine eyes may be open . . . toward the place of which thou hast said, My name shall be there' (vv. 28–29). That is to say, while the 'Person' of God dwells 'in heaven' (v. 45), his *alter ego* (see the argument in Part One, chap. 5), in the shape of his Name, dwells in Israel's midst, actually within the sanctuary on Zion hill (Ps. 74.2, etc.).

In accordance with this view of the Deuteronomist, a view which is expressed in a forthright manner in Deut. 12, *passim*, and II Kings 21.4, 7, the prophet Amos can declare that Yahweh 'will roar from Zion, and utter his voice from Jerusalem' (Amos 1.2), rather than 'from heaven'. Isaiah expresses the paradox that the Lord of hosts dwells (*sic!*) in mount Zion (Isa. 8.18; cf. Ps. 76.2). Jeremiah accepts the paradox without question (cf. Jer. 7.12–15; 15.1–2; 16.11–13; 23.33, 39). Ezekiel envisages the Glory of God coming back to the Temple after the Exile, so that the name of the city will then be 'Yahweh is there' (Ezek. 48.35). Isa. 60.13 calls the post-exilic sanctuary 'the place of my feet'. And Daniel, far-off in captivity, was expected in the second century B.C., when the book was written, to face towards Jerusalem when saying his prayers (Dan. 6.10).

The priestly writers read back this 'theology of the Presence' into the Wilderness period. They use the imagery of Ezekiel, and can describe the in-dwelling Presence of God in the Tabernacle of the Wilderness in such a phrase as: 'Then the cloud covered the tent of meeting, and the glory of the Lord filled the tabernacle'. The conception is made explicit again in other language in Lev. 26.11–12: 'And I will set my tabernacle, *mishkan* (a noun from the verbal root meaning "to dwell") among you, and my *nephesh* will not abhor you. And I will walk (Hithpael, in the sense of "walking about", as in Gen. 3.8, where God "walked about" in the Garden) among you, and will be your God, and ye shall be my people'.[2]

Another name for the Tabernacle is *'ohel mo'edh* (Ex. 27.21), the Tent of Meeting, that spot on earth where God condescends to meet with man. But since the Tabernacle contained, engraved on stone, the moral purpose of God for Israel, the testimony of the solemn divine charge to Israel, it could also bear the name of *'ohel ha-'edhuth* (Num. 9.15; 18.2, etc.), the Tent of Testimony. God could be present in Israel's midst, not as mere naked power, not even just as a moral Being, but actually as the Forgiver of Israel. God's Presence then rested on the *kapporeth* (Num. 7.89), a word which, since Luther first translated it into German as Gnadenstuhl, has been rendered in English as 'mercy-seat'. This noun derives from the root kipper, a verb whose significance we discuss on pp. 284 ff.

God's *mishpaṭ*

Another aspect of God's creative activity within Israel is summed up in the Hebrew noun *mishpaṭ* (see also p. 230). In its simple usage this word means a 'judgement' enunciated by a *shophet*, a judge. Consequently the Torah contains, amongst much else, the

---

[2] The above is the theme of W.J. Phythian-Adams' *The People and the Presence*, 1942. See also B.D. Erdmans, *OS*, Del I, 1942, 'Sojourn in the Tent of Jahu', p. 7. On the other hand, God's 'name' did not necessarily reside in Jerusalem alone (Isa. 30.27).

'judgements' of the great divine Judge (e.g. Ex. 24.3). In the case of the divine mishpaṭ, however, God gives his judgements only to the Covenant People, and within the realm where his *ḥesedh*, his covenant-love, is operative. Now, God's spoken judgements make clear the way of life which he demands of his Covenant People. Strangers could not be expected to know the *mishpaṭ* of Israel's God (II Kings 17.26). That was why Samuel wrote the '*mishpaṭ* of the kingdom' in a book (I Sam. 10.25) and 'laid it up before Yahweh'. Yahweh's *mishpaṭ*, however, is a 'righteous' *mishpaṭ* (Gen. 18.25; Isa. 40.27–28; etc.). Thus Yahweh's *mishpaṭ* must necessarily be justice itself, since his *mishpaṭ* will naturally be true to his very Self. It was Amos' great plea that, within the life of the Covenant People, *mishpaṭ* should run down as waters, and *tsedheq*, righteousness, as a perennial stream (Amos 5.24).[3] Only then would God's *mishpaṭ* for Israel be fully expressed in her private and public life.

The essence of God's *mishpaṭ* is contained in the Ten Commandments. It was the genius of Israel to make clear to the Covenant People, by means of an acted parable, the moral rule of God amongst them. Traditionally, the Decalogue, the summary of the whole Law, had been inscribed by the finger of Yahweh himself on two tablets of stone (Ex. 31.18; Deut. 4.13). These tablets were then placed within the Ark inside the *mishkan* (see above), that place on earth where God could be present in the midst of his people's life (Deut. 10.5). The connexion between ethics and religion was thus made limpidly clear.

God's indwelling Presence in Israel is always creative. Just as a potter can make something new out of a spoiled lump of clay, so can God do with Israel (Jer. 18.1–10). 'Behold, I will make thee a *new* threshing instrument having teeth', says God to the Israel whose national life has newly been destroyed (Isa. 41.15). Out of evil God produces good, out of death, life. This central motif of the OT we shall observe from many angles. Now, God does so, because he is 'righteous'.

---

[3] The noun *tsedheq* is most frequently used of the righteousness of God; the feminine *tsedhaqah* is its effect in man. The former is the divine 'right' which establishes salvation, the latter the human order which is an element of it. Cf. J. Skinner, *Isaiah*, p. 67.

God's righteousness

Righteousness, *tsedheq*, is no more an attribute of God than is his holiness; for it is as much an aspect of God's saving activity as is his *hesedh*. Isaiah thus expounds the term in the words: 'The Holy God shows himself holy in righteousness' (Isa. 5.16, ARSV). The holiness of God becomes visible to our eyes, so to speak, in the form of righteousness.

The concept of righteousness in the OT is not limited to the idea of 'being good'. The root *ts-d-q* means 'to be right', in the sense of 'to be normal'. But man is neither normal nor right. Man is a sinner. Man lives in a state of rebellion against his Creator, and cannot *shubh*, return, of his own volition (Part Two, chap. 11). It is God alone who can make man normal, or put him right. Now, the Hiphil verbal form, *hitsdiq*, bears exactly this meaning, so that the noun 'righteousness' consequently embraces the idea of 'putting right', or of 'putting in the right' one who in the first place is in the wrong, or else who is suffering, who is in need, or who in any other respect requires to be 'saved' and helped (cf. Isa. 45.8, where 'salvation' and 'righteousness' (AV) are equated). All this is clearly stated in the following verse: 'Fear thou not; for I am with thee: be not dismayed; for I am thy God: I will strengthen thee; yea, I will uphold thee with the right hand of my righteousness, *bimin tsidhqi*' (Isa. 41.10). Here the element of deliverance from evil *into* a state of being in the right is clearly evidenced.

The LXX and the Targum seem to read into the Hebrew text at times, even where the Hebrew does not explicitly declare it, the conception that in all that God does to Israel he is 'prospering' Israel's way. Thus where Barak says to Deborah (Judg. 4.8): 'If thou wilt not go with me, I will not go', the LXX adds 'for I know not the day on which the Lord prospers his angel'. Or again, in Judg. 4.14, where we find: 'Up; for this is the day in which Yahweh hath delivered Sisera into thine hand: is not Yahweh gone out before thee?' the Targum interprets 'Hath not the Angel of Yahweh gone forth to make progress before thee?'[4] In other

---

[4] L.H. Brockington, 'Septuagint and Targum', *ZAW*, 66. Band, 1954, Heft 1/2, pp. 80 ff.

words, both those later versions seek to express the 'feel' of the Hebrew text, when the latter refers to God's righteous acts within the life of Israel.

The noun 'righteousness' can therefore on occasions be paralleled with the noun 'salvation', as actually occurs in Isa. 45.8; 51.5, *et al*. This fact leads us to the examination of two more nouns, viz., *yesha'* and *shalom*.

God's Action in Israel's History

The verbal root *y-sh-'* occurs normally in the Hiphil, the transitive form of the verb. Its Qal form must have borne originally the conception of being wide or spacious. The Hiphil then means to bring into a wide space, to give width and breadth to, and so to liberate from what is narrow and oppressive. That is how it comes to mean 'to save'. The Hiphil participle of the verb, *moshia'*, is a common noun for 'saviour'. Thus the Hiphil form of the verb may speak of deliverance from an enemy in battle (Judg. 3.31; 6.15; I Sam. 10.27); and the *moshia'*, saviour, was he who performed the task (Judg. 3.9; II Kings 13.5).

Throughout the whole pre-exilic period 'the Canaanite was then in the land' (Gen. 12.6). The religion of the Canaanites has become much better known to us since the uncovering of the library at Ras Shamra in 1928. We can now fully appreciate the prophetic denunciations of the worship carried on at the 'high places', much of which evidently took place alongside that of the worship of Yahweh. Fundamental to the worship of the local baals by Israel's neighbours was the furthering of the fertility cults (see p. 178). The Sodomites of the OT (I Kings 14.24; 15.12; 22.46; II Kings 23.7) were male and female cultic prostitutes. Their function was understood in terms of the ancient view of sympathetic magic. By inducing human life themselves they believed they were ensuring the resurrection from the death of the dry, parched, late-summer season of the forces of nature, personalized as the local gods of fertility.[5] Unless such gods were to rise again, then there would be neither crops in the spring nor young calves in the stalls. This 'cyclic' view of nature was most attractive even to the Hebrew peasant. He found that he could actually share in an act which assured that next year his barns would be full. Moreover, he had the pleasure thereby of 'controlling' his god. On the other hand, Yahweh insisted on controlling him. It was not so easy for him to understand that it was Yahweh who gave him his corn (Hos. 2.8), since the local priest had taught him rather that Yahweh was he who had brought up his ancestors from Egypt, and who was maker of the heavens and the earth (Deut. 26.1–11). Perhaps such a great God was not fully conversant with his local situation (Amos 4.9). Moreover, Yahweh was an invisible God. The Golden Calves set up by Jeroboam at Bethel and Dan in the Northern Kingdom (I Kings 12.28) must certainly have helped the simple countryman to understand what his divinity looked like, but those calves must also have been dangerously like the bull which epitomized the baal worship of the Canaanites, the bull being the symbol of virility and fertility. Yet the action of Jeroboam in setting up his golden calves may possibly be excused. It is possible he believed that the bull 'held up' Yahweh (who remained invisible) just as the cherubim held him up in the darkness of the Sanctuary of the Jerusalem Temple.[6]

On the other hand, human nature being what it is, the originally non-moral activities of the cult naturally developed into licentiousness. The story of how Aaron gave Israel a molten calf to worship in the Wilderness (Ex. 32), and of how the worship ended up in a licentious riot, is not likely to be a contemporary piece of history. More probably it epitomizes the tension between

---

[5] For a description of the cult with its accompanying myth, see S. Mowinckel, *He That Cometh*, 1956, p. 53 f.

[6] The Storm-god, Hadad, is depicted, as any Baal might be, on the back of a bull in a recent archaeological discovery. See photograph in G.E. Wright, *Biblical Archaeology*, 1956, p. 148. See also W.F. Albright, 'What were the Cherubim?', *The Biblical Archaeologist*, I. 1, 1938, pp. 1–3.

loyalty to Yahweh and loyalty to Baal, of which we read so much in the two books of Kings. Baal worship was evidently *attractive* even to the people known as the Bride of Yahweh. In the heart of men at all times the sexual urge is strong, and even those who belong to the People of God know how Yahweh is doing battle to woo their hearts to the proper use of sex from allegiance to recurring miasmas of sexual desire.

If we remove the emphasis from the conception of rescuing from, to that of saving for or into some new state, then we obtain a much wider view of the meaning of the verb *hoshia'*. For example in the AV rendering of II Sam. 8.14 we read: 'The Lord *preserved* David whithersoever he went'. Here the verb *hoshia'* lays stress particularly on the effect of God's action in 'saving' David, and gives us to understand that David had entered into a wider sphere, had entered indeed a new dimension of being. According to the intertestamental Jewish tradition, the book of Judges, as we have seen, was not regarded as one of Israel's books of 'history'. It belonged rather to the 'former prophets', in contra-distinction to such 'latter prophets' as Isaiah and Jeremiah. In calling the historical books of the OT by such a name, the rabbis evidently supposed that the book of Judges not only recounted the facts of the pre-monarchical period, but at the same time interpreted those facts as the great prophets viewed them, since they lived and taught during the period when 'Judges' was being compiled. The Deuteronomists who drew it up did so, in other words, after the great eighth century prophets had taught Israel to regard history as the sphere of God's saving activity. Amongst other topics, then, the book of Judges recounts the exploits of twelve (or perhaps thirteen) 'judges', who act as 'saviours' to Israel in the sense we have examined above. But in six examples out of the dozen or so recorded, an interesting pattern of activity is described. The following is the cycle of events that occurs on six successive occasions: (1) the children of Israel did evil in the sight of the Lord; (2) the anger of the Lord was hot against Israel; (3) he sold them into the hand of . . . ; (4) the children of Israel cried unto the Lord; (5) the Lord raised up a *moshia'* for the children of Israel, who delivered them; (6) and the land had rest for forty years (cf. Judg. 3.7–11, 12–30, etc.). The book of Deuteronomy, compiled about the same period as the book of 'Judges', gives us rules for conducting Yahweh's wars (Deut. 20; 21.1–14; 23.10–14; 24.5; 25.17–19). These rules evidently arose from the experience gained as early as the period of the Judges. The compiler is equally sure that if Israel but keeps the 'rules', God will lead his people to victory.[7]

It is obvious from the above example of the writers' philosophy of history that these deliverers did not act in their own strength alone. They were charismatic leaders, impelled by the Spirit of God. Each was raised up by God to meet a specific situation; thereafter he might even sink back into obscurity and not be heard of again. But in each case these saviours did more than just save their people, or a section of their people, *from* trouble; they 'saved' them into 'rest', a rest which lasted in each case for forty years, that is to say, for a whole generation in the life of man. We need not be detained by the six times repeated stylized account of God's saving activity through a human instrument or by the equally stylized figure of forty years. What we are to recognize is that the modern English word 'peace' is not sufficient to translate the concept of 'rest' into which each *moshia'* brought his people under God. The English word 'peace' in such a context as the warlike stories in the book of Judges would infer a mere cessation of hostilities. But to the Hebrew prophets who precede or are contemporary with the Deuteronomist, the noun *shalom* bears an infinitely profounder meaning than does the modern English word 'peace'.[8]

To Isaiah, for example, *shalom* could mean tranquillity or contentment, confidence or assurance (Isa. 32.17), and thus refer to the inner state of soul of an individual. To a Psalmist again, it

[7] G. von Rad, *Studies in Deuteronomy*, Studies in Biblical Theology, 9, 1953, pp. 45–59, *Der Heilige Krieg im alten Israel*, 1951.

[8] This is another instance of the new content that Israel could put into a word or an idea common to its Semitic neighbours. *Shulman* or *Shalim* was originally the Canaanite god responsible for health and well-being. His name is apparent as the third and fourth syllables of the word Jerusalem. See also C.F. Evans, *TWB*, article 'Peace', pp. 165–6.

could mean the material security known to a group of people living in community (Ps. 69.32); while for Jeremiah it included the warmth and fulness of joy that one finds in true friendship (Jer. 20.10). In that case the word *shalom* covered the right relations which can ideally obtain amongst men living together in harmony. The noun *shalom* can even refer to physical health (Gen. 43.27), or to general welfare (II Kings 10.13). The verbal root from which it derives conveys the conception of being whole or being complete or sound; consequently the transitive form of the verb means to make whole, to restore, to complete. What is true then as an experience possible to man, and between man and man, must be true also of that obtaining between God and man. In Isa. 54.10 God's *ḥesedh* towards Israel is paralleled with the 'covenant of *shalom*' which God promises will abide with Israel for ever.

A Modern Illustration of the Meaning of *Shalom*

Before seeking to discuss the further ramifications of this comprehensive word, I would illustrate the total conception borne by this Hebrew noun by describing the activities of a gipsy orchestra as it performs in eastern Europe. A gipsy orchestra is composed of men who have played the violin from the moment they were old enough to stand on their own feet and hold a violin in their hands. Thus in the first place each member of the orchestra has thoroughly mastered his own private instrument. But secondly, each individual player has learned to play in harmony with all the other members of the orchestra. The third and distinctive feature of a gipsy orchestra, however, is seen in the relationship that obtains between the members of the orchestra and its conductor, that individual whom Hungarians call its *primás*. While the latter may call upon his orchestra to play a piece that they already know, he may also improvise a tune even while he is conducting his band. Thus the members of the gipsy orchestra must constantly keep their eyes fixed upon the *primás*. Not only must they know how to play their instrument; not only must they know how to play in harmony with each other as a group; they must also be able to produce harmonies, in harmony with each other, that will also agree with the tune which the primás is improvising before them from the melody which is resounding in his head.[9]

Now let us seek to apply this parable or analogy to the purpose of God in the life of Israel, as that purpose was understood and interpreted by the great prophets, and reflected by the writers of the Psalms. 'Peace be within thy walls', sang the Psalmist about Jerusalem (Ps. 122.7) 'and prosperity (or quietness, ease, security) within thy palaces.' Such is the ideal for Jerusalem, (*yerush-sha-lom*) possession of peace, the holy city, holy because of its special relationship to the holy God. But since it is children of Adam who dwell within the holy city, *shalom* is not yet to be found within its walls. To reach this great ideal three things are therefore necessary. Firstly, each individual Israelite must learn to know *shalom* within his own heart and soul: 'I will both lay me down in peace, and sleep: for thou, Lord, only makest me dwell in safety' (Ps. 4.8). In other words, he must learn to play his own instrument harmomously. The individualizing of the faith enunciated by the prophets, as we see it being done in sections of the book of Proverbs and in certain of the Psalms, demonstrates how in the latter half of the OT period the individual Israelite sought to know *shalom* in his own being, and to carry there an inner peace of soul. But secondly, he had to learn to live in harmony with his neighbours. No prophet is more emphatic on this point than Amos. Selfish indulgence in luxuries, when the mass of the people are yet impoverished (Amos 6.4–6) is sufficient to bring the judgement of God upon Israel. Selling wheat underweight and overcharging the poor (Amos 8.5–6) disrupts the essentially brotherly community life which is the object of Israel's laws. The village streets of ancient Palestine were narrow. But they might boast one or more

---

[9] I am aware that Dr. Karl Barth points to the parable of the gipsy orchestra without developing it in a lecture delivered in Hungary in 1948. The lecture is translated into English in *Against the Stream*, 1954, p. 70. But the striking significance of the three-way relationship and interdependence in a gipsy orchestra came home to me in the years when I lived in Hungary before the war – and before I heard Dr. Barth lecturing in that land in 1936!

open square or *rehobh*. Down the middle of this main street or *rehobh*, on both sides of which the merchants had erected their stalls, ran a gutter to carry off the dirt and rubbish. Present-day Nazareth, known to countless tourists, possesses just such a gutter with a sludge of dirty water trickling down its length. As Amos gazed at dirty water such as that passing by the stalls where selfishness and greed separated man from man, and where there was no harmonious fellowship and unity in society, he made the famous utterance to which we referred above: 'Let justice, *mishpat*, run down as waters, and righteousness, *tsedhaqah*, as a mighty (perennial) stream' (Amos 5.24).

Finally, neither the individuals who comprise the community, nor the community in its turn can ever know true *shalom* or harmony, unless, keeping their eye upon the conductor, they learn from him what harmonies they must all play together. It is the conductor alone who knows the tune. The tune is in his head, not theirs. It is their duty to follow obediently as he leads them to the final harmony. 'Look unto me, and be ye saved (Niphal, passive, of *yasha*'), all the ends of the earth: for I am God, and there is none else' (Isa. 45.22). The command comes in many forms to 'Seek the Lord', and not another 'primas'. Amos, for example, employs the verb *darash*, which is used of a suppliant treading the courts of a shrine in search of guidance from his god (Amos 5.4–6). Some of the Psalmists, however, 'sublimate' this verb to make it speak of the personal touch with the spirit of God that a man may experience in private prayer (Ps. 24.6; Deut. 4.29, etc.).

The Place of the Individual within the Community

Israel's God is thus ceaselessly striving to make Israel righteous, or, put her right, or, make her 'normal', *hitsdiq*, by working in her midst as her *moshia*' or saviour, and thus bring in a state of *shalom*, fulness of life, harmony, satisfaction, completion, integrity – all these English words together are required to express the Hebrew noun – both in her communal life and in the life of individual men and women. Israelite man was aware (*a*) that he was one, in a lineal, vertical capacity, with his fathers. Thus Ezek. 16.45–46: 'Your mother was a Hittite, and your father an Amorite, and thine elder sister is Samaria'; or Deut. 26.5: 'A Syrian ready to perish was my father'. He was one even with Adam, the father of the race, since each individual person is a son of Adam (Ps. 8.4). He was aware (*b*) of a lateral relationship, so that his *nephesh* was bound up in the bundle of life with all his brethren contemporary with himself (I Sam. 25.29). Yet he knew full well (*c*) that each individual *nephesh* within this bundle of life was individually and directly in touch with the spirit of the living God. It was within this nexus of human relationships, then, stretching backwards and forwards in time, and right and left throughout all living and contemporary Israelites that the Spirit of God was creating one *corpus* in the spirit of *shalom*.

Surprisingly enough, within this living *corpus* the individual as such is never lost. The OT contains the stories of many outstanding personalities, all of whom were individuals in the sense that we understand individuality, such as Deborah, Samson, David, Naboth Nabotli and Jeremiah. Yet each and all of these individuals is obviously what he is because he is a tendril on the Vine which God brought up out of Egypt. One of the marks of the Wisdom literature of the OT is that it individualizes the teaching of the great prophets. The latter expounded primarily the ways of God with Israel as Son, Servant, Bride, as a whole united *corpus*. But the wisdom writers showed what was asked of an individual Israelite, living as a member of the Covenant People, and how in the post-exilic period he was meant to personalize the moral teachings of the pre-exilic prophets in his everyday life and work. The great dramatic poem of Job, for example, does not deal with the problem of suffering as such as it affects mankind. Its concern is why one particular man, whose name happens to be Job, should suffer – and not just why he should *suffer*, but why *God* should send him suffering. Thus the wisdom literature is concerned to show why any one individual Israelite should seek God's Wisdom and pursue it.

We saw that for God to be righteous meant that he brought about a new condition for Israel. That must then be true also for the individual Israelite. If the individual Israelite were indeed a righteous man, then it meant that it was God who had put him right (Job 9.15, 20, etc.).[10] On this ground, the individual Israelite dare not glory in his righteousness, believing that he is 'good' because he keeps the statutes and judgements of God. In the OT goodness is not 'being good' in the modern sense of the phrase. It is not the keeping of the Ten Commandments, or the fulfilling of the Law. Actually, it is only the religious man in the OT who can speak of righteousness and of sin; righteousness is rather the response in gratitude of the man who has been 'put right'. OT righteousness is thus very close to the otherworldly type of righteousness of the NT, the turning of the other cheek, the going of the second mile, since it involves the individual Israelite in the *producing of shalom* through coming into right relationships with others. What we today call 'being good' is thus only a secondary by-product for OT man of the *new* state of *shalom* which God alone is bringing about (Isa. 2.1–5) as he works within the hearts of individuals who themselves are tendrils on the Vine that has been redeemed already.

This reference to Isaiah reminds us that it was the great prophets through whom God primarily expressed his Word. Just as God has messengers (*mal'achim*, or 'angels') in the realm of the spirit, so the prophets are his *mal'achim* within Israel (Isa. 42.19; Hag. 1.13; II Chron. 36.15–16; and cf. the very name Malachi). The prophet could be known as a 'man of God' (I Kings 17.18); but then so too could an angel (Judg. 13.6). Thus it is obvious that the Word of God used similar messengers both on earth and in the realm of the spirit. This is made clear when we remember that the prophet never speaks *a* Word of God, but always *the* Word of God. The prophets, however, did not always rejoice to be the bearers of God's Word. Jeremiah, for example, knew himself to be in the *sodh*, the inner counsel, of God (Jer. 23.18, 22); yet the message he learned therefrom he felt to be a burning fire shut up in his bones (Jer. 20.9). Like Jonah, Jeremiah would dearly have loved to run away from the pain of the message that he bore within his heart (Jer. 4.19). It was obvious to the prophets as a whole, as

---

[10]   See *BDB*, ad loc., p. 842.

we shall see as we proceed, that the *shalom* which it was God's good purpose to give to Israel could be attained only through sorrow and even the pains of death.

The Remnant

All Israel as such, however, never responded to the call of Yahweh to be his faithful people. In other words, Israel after the flesh was never at any time identical with Israel after the spirit.[11] The people who came up out of Egypt were not Hebrews only – 'a mixed multitude went up also with them' (Ex. 12.38). When Paul declares, in I Cor. 10.1 ' . . . all our fathers were under the cloud . . . ' he must have been aware that many Gentile peoples shared the experience of Sinai with the Hebrews.[12] Then we read in Judg. 3.1–5: 'Now these are the nations which the Lord left, to prove Israel by them . . . Philistines . . . Canaanites, Sidonians, Hivites . . . Hittites, Amorites, Perizzites and Jebusites'. In the time of Solomon this non-Israelite 'underworld' was virtually enslaved (I Kings 9.21). Yet this 'proletariat' was undoubtedly part of the body politic of Israel, sharing in her fate, and looking to her future. The proportion of 'strangers' within the body politic of Israel must have been even greater after the Exile. Trito-Isaiah mentions them (Isa. 56.3 ff.) and insists that they are to share in all the privileges and responsibilities of the people of God. Throughout the so-called historical books, which reflect the teaching of the great prophets, we are shown how the '*am yahweh* as a whole, the People of God, might become, through disobedience, a mere *goi*, a Gentile nation. But it was not with a *goi* that God had made his covenant in the first place (Isa. 1.9–10). The centre and soul of a *goi* is not Jerusalem, but Sodom. The OT clearly shows, therefore, that the People of God would not necessarily comprise merely Israel after the flesh in

---

[11] See Th. C. Vriezen, *Die Erwählung Israels nach dem Alten Testament*, 1953, passim. Also A.R. Hulst, *Der Name 'Israel' im Deuteronomium*, *OS*, Deal IX, p. 163.

[12] *KzNT*, III, pp. 406–8.

the future, since it had never done so in the past, and since its 'centre' might possibly cease to be in Jerusalem (Deut. 8.19–20).[13] Who, then, were the heirs of the divine election?[14]

It was in the spacious days of David and Solomon that the Israelites held the greatest area of territory in their history (I Kings 8.65). Later it was believed that this was the outcome of the promises of God made to Abraham and Jacob (Gen. 12.2; 28.13–14). Solomon even called his son Rehoboam, meaning 'the people has become wide-spread'. The word '*am* occurs as the last syllable in that name, and is significant there since it was rarely used in Hebrew names. Yet the rival king Jeroboam similarly bears a name meaning 'the people of Yahweh have multiplied'. But from this point on we read of the royal declension from the pure worship of Yahweh which so greatly disturbed the contemporary prophets. Having married many foreign wives, including (a great prize!) an Egyptian princess, Solomon found many troubles coming his way as part of the dowry they brought. His legendary thousand wives and concubines brought with them into the life of the People of God the worship of many heathen gods and the temptation to adopt licentious practices (I Kings 11.1–8). The Deuteronomist, again, makes special mention of an ominous incident. Solomon actually sold a piece of the 'holy land', he reports, to the pagan king Hiram of Tyre (I Kings 9.11). Then, more than half a century later, in 878 B.C., Ben-Hadad of Damascus took away all Israel's territory, along with its inhabitants, that lay to the east of the Jordan; moreover, he did so at the invitation of Asa king of Jerusalem, who had entered upon a fratricidal quarrel with Baasha king of Israel, the northern kingdom. Later still, king Ahaz's faithlessness brought the loss, in Isaiah's day (cf. Isa. 9.12) of a number of border towns to the Philistine cities (II Chron. 28.17–18). The 'heritage of the Lord' (Josh. 1.2–4) was thus shrinking visibly.[15] The split between the kingdoms had been

---

[13] See Th. C. Vriezen, op. cit.
[14] Phrase used by H.H. Rowley, *The Biblical Doctrine of Election*, 1950, p. 139.
[15] Cf. W. Vischer, *Les Premiers Prophètes*, 1951, pp. 385–400, 533–549.

actuated indeed by the folly of Rehoboam, and aggravated by the sin of Jeroboam (I Kings 13.34), as the Deuteronomic author believed; yet the split in the heritage of Israel that occurred in 933 B.C. (a date recently brought down as much as a decade) had been ultimately Yahweh's doing – 'for this thing is from me' Yahweh had said through the mouth of Shemaiah the prophet (I Kings 12.24). It was evidently not the will of Yahweh, however, that Israel should cease to be conceived as comprising other than her traditional twelve tribes. Thus, even after the loss of the trans-Jordanian tribes,[16] Elijah, the northern prophet, could take twelve stones to represent both north and south together (I Kings 18.31; cf. Isa. 11.11–13; Jer. 33.7; Ezek. 37.15–28). Even after the Exile, and later in the NT literature, moreover, Israel was still envisaged under the form of God's chosen Twelve Tribes (Matt. 19.28; James 1.1; Rev. 7.4–8). Yet the real *'am yahweh* was never identified with the historical twelve. Although Judah (and Benjamin – see the LXX of I Kings 12.20) had now become the sphere of the divine promise so far as the line of David was concerned, yet there were still many believers in Yahweh in the northern kingdom, 'all the knees which have not bowed to Baal' (I Kings 19.18). Similarly, in the South, the *'am yahweh* was not necessarily synonymous with political Judah (and Benjamin). After the areas north of Samaria had been lost to the Syrians in 732 B.C., and the northern kingdom as a political entity had fallen in a welter of blood and anguish in 721 B.C., Judah continued to display the divided mind of which Jeremiah has so much to tell us. It is true that till 587 B.C. the 'lamp of David' never went out in Judah, yet after the first destruction of Jerusalem in 598 B.C. Jeremiah could declare that those who were carried into Exile at that juncture were Yahweh's 'good figs', while the bad figs lying in the next basket were those whom God could no longer use (Jer. 24.5–7).[17] Ezekiel, however, could find some of the 'Remnant'

---

[16] Lost under Joahaz, and evidently temporarily recovered under Joash. Amos 6.13 mentions Lo-debhar and Qarnaim (Heb.), places in Trans-Jordan, as if they again belonged to the northern kingdom.

[17] Sargon's inscription gives the figure as 27.290. See S.L. Caiger, *Bible and Spade*, 1936, p. 148.

still living in Jerusalem at the period between the two sieges of the city. The latter were those 'that sigh and that cry for all the abominations that be done' in the city of Jerusalem (Ezek. 9.4).

As the doom which the prophets recognized to be the necessary effect of God's wrath upon sin approached ever nearer the stiffnecked people of Israel, the conception that God would permit a Remnant to survive came to the fore in their thoughts. Yet not all the prophets possessed a clear doctrine of a Remnant. Those that do (e.g. Amos, Micah, Isaiah, Jeremiah, Ezekiel, Joel, Trito Isaiah (Isa. 65.8–10). Obadiah and Zephaniah (3.12–13) employ a number of nominal roots to convey their thoughts. Thus Joel (2.32) uses the root *palat*, deliver, from which he takes his noun, for those who will be saved 'on that day', while the root *sha'ar* was Isaiah's commonest choice of a word in this connexion.

Amos was sure that the coming 'Day of the Lord+' would be darkness and not light (Amos 5.18). When it came, then the Remnant that would survive the coming holocaust would be no more than two legs which a shepherd had rescued from the mouth of a lion, or worse still, just a piece of an ear (Amos 3.12). Isaiah, on the contrary, seems to have regarded his own disciples as the nucleus of the Remnant (Isa. 8.15–18), almost, in fact, as what we would call an *ecclesiola in ecclesia*. Anyway, he was utterly convinced that there would be a Remnant, and clearly declares his mind on a number of occasions (Isa. 1.9; 7.3; 10.20; 11.16; 28.5, etc.). Ezekiel's doctrine of the Remnant is strikingly different from that of the earlier prophets. In Ezek. 12.16 the Remnant comprises 'a few men' whom God will 'leave from the sword, from the famine, and from the pestilence'. This thought is repeated and amplified later in 14.22–23. That is to say, the Remnant has not, as Jeremiah had declared, been carried away already, in 598 B.C., to Babylon, but would be selected from those who were about to go through the siege that took place in 588–7 B.C. The fact that the prophets disagreed about the constitution of the Remnant is not important. After all, it is not man, but God, who alone knows who are the true believers (cf. II Kings 19.18). What is important is that the fact of a Remnant is central to the thoughts of so many of them.

Then again, the historians of the period could look back over their history in the faith that God had been active in like manner from earliest times. They told of Abraham praying to God to spare the city of Sodom, and of how God agreed to do so on account of a mere handful of 'righteous' inhabitants (Gen. 18.23–33). And they told of how the People of God had once all turned as a body to worship the Golden Calf, and of how God in his wrath had threatened to use the line of Moses alone to make of them the great nation that Israel was meant to be (Ex. 32.1–10).

Judah and Jerusalem did, of course, finally fall in 587 B.C., and the 'Remnant' house of Judah, bearing the 'lamp of David', was thus finally and totally destroyed as a political entity (Part Four, chap. 17). The paradox that a Remnant would actually survive out of this total destruction is stated by the editor of the chapter which contains Isaiah's inaugural vision. He recognized that it was not sufficient to expect that even a tenth part of Israel would be the coming Remnant (Isa. 6.13). His last words (not to be found in the LXX, yet extant in the St Mark Scroll A) are: 'the holy seed is the stump of it'. Our editor had the insight to realize, whether before or after the Exile we cannot be sure, (*a*) that the seed must fall into the ground and die before it can grow to be the stem of a new tree, so that Israel as a *continuum* is not a *continuum* after the flesh, but a *continuum* of grace alone; and (*b*) that a resurrection in some form or other must follow upon the act of God in destroying the people of his choice (cf. Deut. 30.12; 68.18; Isa. 26.17–19; 43.2; 53.11; 54.1; 66.9; Jer; 1.10 = 45.4; Jer. 6.24; Micah 4.9–10; Hos. 2.15; 13.13–14; Jonah 2.10).

The reason why the phrase in question has been placed at the end of chapter 6 is not far to seek. When Isaiah was confronted with the unspeakable glory of God and recognized that he was a sinner indeed, we read that he exclaimed: 'Woe is me, for *nidhmethi*. This passive verb means 'to be made to cease', 'to be undone' in the sense of being taken to pieces, so that one is no longer an integrated creature. In other words we see that Isaiah felt himself at this point to be slipping into 'chaos'. It is thereupon only through the terrifying experience of being touched by fire that the angel of Yahweh reintegrates him as a responsible child of God.

The final point that we would make about this incident, then, is the connexion between the spoken word of God and Isaiah's experience of descending to the depths and of being rescued thence by the angel. God says to him 'Lo, this hath touched thy lips, and thine iniquity is taken away, and thy sin purged' (v. 7). The renewal which God grants to Israel after the latter has descended into the fires of the destruction of Jerusalem and the 'death' of the Exile, is thus the renewal of the forgiveness of her sins. After the Exile is past, the forgiveness of God is explicitly identified with the resurrection he gives to this 'brand plucked from the burning' (Zech. 3.1–7).

The Individualization of the Remnant Concept

Once the little state of Judah had been reconstituted after the Return from Exile, we note that the thoughts of Israel in this regard continued to run on similar lines. In the post-exilic period the stricter or more self-consciously believing amongst the Jews came to regard their more careless and thoughtless brethren as having forfeited the right to remain God's true instrument. The book of Proverbs, for example, classifies under various names those groups within the (Israelite) community who thus no longer belong to the true Remnant of Israel. The group farthest removed from the true Israelite is the *lets*, the scorner. The latter takes a fiendish delight in his folly (Prov. 1.22) and even refuses to listen (13.1). Then there is the *nabhal*, the churl (17.7); the *'ewil*, who is both incorrigible (17.10) and licentious (7.6–23); the *kesil*, who is obstinately stupid (1.22); and finally, the *pethi*, whom we today would call the merely 'silly ass' (22.3).

Per contra, it is now the 'wise' man, the *hacham*, who seems to be the true Israelite in the eyes of the post-exilic Sages. 'Be not wise in thine own eyes: fear the Lord, and depart from evil' (3.7). It is natural that God is to be feared. 'Who may stand in thy sight when once thou art angry?' (Ps. 76.7). The following psalm provides a wonderful description of a thunderstorm (Ps. 77.16–19). No wonder God is to be feared as he manifests himself in nature.[18] But the wisdom writers are concerned also that man should be aware of God's wrath against sin. The wisdom of which they speak will 'deliver thee from the way of the wicked man' (Prov. 2.12), and make thee rejoice in a merchandise that is 'better than the merchandise of silver' (3.13). This is because wisdom is of God himself, for 'the Lord by wisdom hath founded the earth; by understanding hath he established the heavens' (3.19). The wise man, therefore, knows the way of God more truly than does the fool: 'The fear of the Lord is the beginning of knowledge: but fools despise wisdom and instruction' (1.7). Indeed, the Sages see no hope for the fool at all. 'The heart of fools proclaimeth foolishness' (12.23). 'Speak not in the ears of a fool: for he will despise the wisdom of thy words' (23.9). In fact, you can do nothing at all with the fool. He is really incorrigible. He has actually cut himself off from the knowledge of God (1.30–32).

This rather intellectual judgement upon those not so mentally alert as were the Sages is paralleled by a moral division between man and man apparent within the Psalms. There the humble, believing man, the '*ani*,[19] perhaps even he who is poor in this world's goods, begins to consider that he is the true *hasidh*.[20] This word, often translated 'saint' (Ps. 30.4; 31.23; 79.2, etc.), and sometimes 'holy one' (Ps. 16.10), has now seemingly developed to mean 'true believer' over against the mass of nominally conforming Israelites. The *hasidh* is the true believer, not because of

---

[18] H.A. Brongers, 'The Fear of the Lord', *OS*, Deel V, pp. 151 ff.

[19] There are two Hebrew words which are very alike, viz., '*anau* and '*ani*, the one meaning 'meek' and the other 'poor'. In the transmission of the text those two words were often confused; even in the NT we are aware of the confusion in the original Semitic tongue behind the Greek; cf. Matt. 5.3 with Luke 6.20. See article 'Remnant' by G. Henton Davies in *TWB*, 1950, pp. 188–91.

[20] E.g. Ps. 74.19; 76.9. In the historical books 'the poor of the land' are regarded almost as a righteous remnant over against the more sophisticated educated classes who became caught up with the syncretism of faiths that was characteristic of the courts of the nations (II Kings 25.12; cf. also Jer. 39.10; 52.16, and Micah 3).

any innate righteousness to which he can point as his own, but because God has delivered him 'to live'.[21] Joseph, for example, is described as a *miḥyah* (from the root *ḥayah*, 'to live': 'Now therefore be not grieved, nor angry with yourselves, that ye sold me hither: for God did send me before you to "preserve life", as a *miḥyah*' (Gen. 45.5). So too in Isa. 4.3, the Remnant consists of all those 'who are written "for life" in Jerusalem'.[22] The *ḥasidh* is 'thy (individual) holy one' (Ps. 16.10), because the living and holy God has imputed to him his own righteousness. 'In that day shall the Lord of hosts be for a crown of glory, and for a diadem of beauty, unto the residue of his people' (Isa. 28.5). The Sages, and some of the post-exilic Psalmists, had thus successfully individualized the pre-exilic prophetic doctrine of the Remnant, and thus regarded various minority groups within Israel as the rightful heirs of the divine election.

In the period after the Sages had performed this task, we have the book of Daniel. Its author could assure his hard-pressed contemporaries, as they lived through the Maccabean wars, that 'many shall be purified, and made white, and tried' (12.10), so that 'blessed is he that waiteth' (12.12). The name Chassidim, again, is that given to the followers of Mattathias and his sons following upon the wars (I Macc. 2.42). Soon thereafter the Covenanting group who lived in community in Qumran seem to have regarded themselves (*a*) as a priestly group, yet (*b*) as the true Judah. When the great war against the Sons of Darkness should commence, the Covenanters would represent all Israel in it, and would carry into battle the ensigns of all the twelve tribes of Israel.[23] The very word Pharisee, too, *may* (for this interpretation has been questioned), mean in Aramaic 'separated one'. We read in the NT, for example, of certain Pharisees at least who despised the uneducated common folk who were not learned in the Law (John 7.49). Finally, at the point where the NT story begins, we

---

[21]   G.H. Davies, ibid. See also p. 228.

[22]   G.H. Davies, ibid.

[23]   T.H. Gaster, *The Scriptures of the Dead Sea Sect*, 1957, 'The Zadokite Document' p. 77; 'The War of the Sons of Light and the Sons of Darkness', p. 266.

meet a group of pious, humble folk who are 'waiting for the consolation of Israel' (Luke 2.25), viz., Zacharias, Elizabeth, Simeon, Anna and others, and of whom the blessed Virgin Mary was undoubtedly one.

The Action of God Observable within one Individual

The fascinatingly interesting interplay of the divine election, as seen in the choice of one individual Israelite, and of the parallel divine judgement upon that same Israelite as a sinful man, is nowhere better set forth than in the story of the hero, David. This is true even though David lived in the early 'collective' period in Israel's history, before the individualizing process to which we referred above had gathered momentum, and though many of the stories about him have obviously come down to us in the form of saga.

We may dismiss much of the interpretation in the idealized account of David's life given us by the Chronicler, and seek for information about him primarily from the very human document of the books of Samuel. That record does not moralize upon his character; it offers no 'religious' talk. The whole saga reads like secular history. Yet this same narrative is saturated with the belief that God controls all events, that history is here and now the arena of the judgement of God, that this life matters, matters to such a degree that even eternity is being moulded by the incidence of seemingly insignificant events (cf. Jer. 12.4).

In the book of Samuel we are presented with the biography of an attractive and thoughtful young man, who turns out to be the architect of the kingdom of both Judah and Israel. Before his first appearance, at a time when there was 'no king in Israel, every man did that which was right in his own. eyes' (Judg. 21.25). David's genius in capturing and making the 'neutral' stronghold of Jerusalem (a city within whose name the word *shalom* occurs – see Part Four, chap. 25 (6)) into the capital for the two sections of the people, Judah and Israel, was a mark of that genius for which he was noted. He followed this action of his by calling the captured city 'the city of David' (II Sam. 5.7), thus giving even its name a neutral expression. Within one generation David transformed an amphictyony of tribes into a united nation; raised the standard of living beyond all possible expectation; enlarged the borders of the kingdom to an extent it never exceeded; centralized and developed the worship of Israel's God in his neutral capital city, and gave the people peace and security such as they had never known before in their history. Moreover, if the traditions used by the historians are accurate, David developed the cult and instituted bands of singers even before the Temple was built by his son, Solomon. And then, of course, according to tradition again, it was David who initiated within Israel the practice (possibly copying the still earlier Canaanite practice) of composing *tehillim*, praises or psalms to God.

In the single figure of David, that individual whose story occupies more space in the OT than that of any other character, we are given to see *in parvo* the whole drama of the struggle between Light and Darkness, Order and Chaos, Good and Evil, which takes place, as we have seen, even *within* the overruling plan and purpose of almighty God. So the story of David is not 'mere' history, any more than is the story of Israel, even though it is told as secular history and the name of God hardly occurs in it. It is history so meaningful that we can describe it by no other adjective than that of eschatological (see Part Four, chap. 17 for this use of the term). The reality of this was recognized by later editors of the Psalms. They sought to associate a number of the Psalms with incidents in the life of David (e.g. Pss. 3; 7; 18; etc.). In all probability they knew quite well that they had no historical justification for so doing. Yet in the final analysis these editors acted well. They knew that the incidents to which they attached those Psalms were meaningful incidents. This meant that these incidents were meaningful, not just for 1,000 B.C., but for all time and beyond time. The delivery of Jerusalem from the hand of Sennacherib in 701 B.C. may actually have been the *Sitz im Leben* of a number of Psalms of Thanksgiving for a national deliverance (e.g. Pss. 75 and 76). But the deliverance which God had wrought for Israel was a deliverance of the same nature as that which he had wrought for David when the latter was hard-pressed by Saul (see the heading of Ps. 18). God's saving activity is therefore something which any and all generations can hymn, whether the singer has been saved from Sennacherib, or from Napoleon, or from any other power.

Now, even while David continues to be the architect under God of the People of God, he becomes the perpetrator of two outstanding sins, either of which was sufficient to put him right outside the covenant relationship instituted by God at Sinai (Lev. 20.10; Num. 31.19), the sphere within which God's grace is operative. David instigated a murder (II Sam. 11.14–17), and David committed adultery (II Sam. 11.2–5). Thereafter, as the story proceeds, we behold two operations in progress. We watch the slow but steady disintegration of David's character, and the consequent judgement of God upon him; but we watch the still profounder saving action of the Holy Spirit of God despite that disintegration.

David becomes unable to control his physical appetites; so he has the mortification of seeing his son Amnon inheriting his sexual weakness (II Sam. 13). David uses murder to advance his private aims, so he has the mortification of seeing his beloved son Absalom inheriting that trait in his character (II Sam. 13). As David's story advances, we watch him losing control, not only of himself, but also of his family; and finally the great kingdom which David had built up slips from his grasp as well. David, the 'beloved' (though the name may actually mean 'chieftain') of Yahweh, the 'sweet singer of Israel', and, as we shall examine later, the only individual Israelite in historic times with whom God enters into a special covenant (II Sam. 7) – that same individual son of Adam gives way bit by bit to the insidious pressure of *tohu* within his own soul. If we were to dare translate the Hebrew term *shalom* by the very modern concept of 'integration', then what we see unfolding in the story of David is the slow 'disintegration' of his character, as the 'wholeness' and 'integrity' of a man whose life had once been rooted in Yahweh breaks up and crumbles into chaos.[24]

---

[24] Two contrasting studies of the character of David are to be found in A.C. Welch's *Kings and Prophets of Israel*, 1952, pp. 80–106; and in W. Vischer's *Les Premiers Prophètes, 1951*, pp. 256–314.

In total contrast to the disintegration of David's character we now observe the gracious action of a saving God. Out of weakness God creates strength. Later ages look back upon David as the ideal king, so that the era of *shalom* still to come will be recognizable in the light of the historical Davidic kingdom of the past; and the one whom God will use to bring about his reign of 'peace' will be a 'son' of David, that is, according to the Semitic idiom, one who will totally represent the spirit and purpose of his famous ancestor. Out of the defeat which David's character suffered, God 'saved' *hoshia*', or 'preserved' him (II Sam. 8.6) 'whithersoever he went'. Since David did not know *shalom* in his own soul, but rather its reverse, for what we are given to see is a weak and vacillating character, then the *shalom* into which he did indeed enter must have been a 'peace that is not of this world', one that was the gift of God alone.

And so it is that later Psalmists, reflecting on the story of grace as they see it in the life of David and of others like him, are able to interpret their own experience in the light of his. They are aware of the *tohu* in their own subconscious mind, but at the same time of the grace of God which, like the 'everlasting arms' which are underneath (Deut. 33.27), reaches even lower than 'the waters under the earth' (Ex. 20.4), and thus lower than the lowest depth of their own mysterious and self-centred being. When one Psalmist writes (Ps. 139.15): 'My substance was not hid from thee, when I was made in secret, and curiously wrought in the lowest parts of the earth', he is not expressing the curious belief that God created his *nephesh* somewhere under the soil. What he is doing is to express in typical Semitic picture language his faith that, in the mystery of God's providence, his little *nephesh* is one with the world of which his body is a part. Just as in the depths of the earth there lies a watery chaos, yet God rules and is in control over that chaos, so also deep inside himself there are disintegrating factors which could, but for the grace of God, lead him to nothing less than a 'descent into hell'.[25] But God who knows him to the depths

---

[25] The title of a religious allegory dealing with this topic by Charles Williams, 1949. See also Part Two, chap. 11.

of his being (Ps. 139.1–12), and who has power over Darkness as well as over Light (vv. 11–12), has already 'saved' him, even when he was still but an embryo in his mother's womb (v. 13), and has led him *through tohu* into a *shalom* (vv. 17–18) which can be described quite simply only as communion with God.

God's righteousness, then, is nothing less than his saving activity, as he brings men, through *tohu*, into his promised shalom. And what is true for the individual Israelite must be true also in respect of God's total plan for the world that he has made. The use God makes of his Son-Servant-Bride Israel to that end is the ultimate expression of his whole saving activity as he seeks to bring back the whole of his creation into the *shalom* which he planned for it in the beginning.

What we shall have to establish next, then, is how the God of the OT effects his saving purpose in face of the resistance of a world that does not know or desire his *shalom*.

Twenty-One

The Potency of Old Testament Images

We have now handled a number of OT images – Son, Bride, Rock, Glory, and so on. We ought therefore, before proceeding any further, to face resolutely the question which Rudolf Bultmann and others have raised at the present day. The question is this – is it possible to demythologize the OT?

The question would, of course, have been inconceivable to OT man himself. Since he was aware that it is not possible for man the creature to know the essence of God his Maker, he was obliged to pictorialize what otherwise would have remained beyond his ken. And so he gave himself and us the anthropomorphic pictures of God which we have now examined from many angles. Again, since the *kind* of God he envisaged, who confronted him directly in the 'I-thou' relationship of spirit upon spirit, was a God who made himself known only in righteous acts, then it was wholly natural for OT man to seek to understand his God in descriptive terms, and by recounting to himself or others word-pictures of what he actually conceived God to be like as God revealed himself in action.

It is highly important for us to recall the potency of the word, as all Semitic peoples conceived it, and to remember how a word spoken with intent could not return unto the speaker void (see Part One, chap. 5). It was because of this manner of thought that the Hebrew mind was able to objectify the spoken word, especially the Word of God, and, as we have said, to envisage God's Word in action in the form of angels.

Now, what is true for the spoken word is true also for the mental concept. We recall that the Hebrews drew no line between thinking, dreaming, and speaking (Jer. 23.25). If a Hebrew sought to envisage the concept, say, of Grace, he was not able to do so any more than we; and this was because he, just as we, found it impossible to draw any kind of picture of Grace as such. All he (and we!) was able to conceive was a picture of God acting towards him in grace. In other words, he envisaged Grace clothed in a mental picture. Now, the mental picture of Grace which he entertained cannot be identified with the concept of Grace in its essence. We recall that it was not God who led his people through the Wilderness; it was an angel of God, acting on his behalf (Ex. 23.20); yet, as we would say, it was indeed God himself, but now God pictorialized by this highly imaginative people.

We can therefore well understand how the mental image which Hebrew man entertained in his mind became for him the actual complement of the spiritual truth which the image pictorialized. The image of the particular eternal truth which occupied his mind at any one moment came not merely to be a material or a psychological *illustration* of that truth in terms of the world in which the thinker lived; it came to be the channel of that truth itself. Moreover, two factors helped to assure OT man that such was a valid way of thinking. Firstly, it is amazing to what extent virtually *identical* mental pictures of a theological concept are held by thinkers and writers at all levels and stages through the whole literature of the OT from its earliest to its latest documents. Such is not the case outside the Bible. For example, a very different picture springs to the mind of twentieth century man when the word 'charity' is uttered than sprang to the mind of medieval man only five hundred years ago. On the other hand, the significant value of OT man's mental picture of Fire, for example, in relation to the world of the spirit beyond, was virtually constant over a period of a thousand years of OT history – and on into the literature of the NT writers as well.

Secondly, the OT thinkers were assured of the validity of the images which they entertained because they believed that those images, constant throughout their history, were given to their believing minds by none other than God himself. Thus the Hebrew prophet seems to have accepted as axiomatic a real unity between the essence of truth and the expression of that truth in divinely inspired human thought patterns. Jeremiah, for example, has only to look at an almond tree to have in his mind's eye a mental image of the three Hebrew consonants which can be understood to read either 'almond tree' or 'watching over' (Jer. 1.11–12, RV). The absolute faith that God was watching over his people then became an objective reality to his mind.

The God-given OT figures of Husband, Vine, Servant, Rock, Son, Fire, Light and so on, are thus not to be dismissed on the ground that they are merely figures of speech, merely 'parables' of that which they seek to represent. These images were considered by their writers to be potent in their own right, and to convey to the mind of the observer the essential truth which lay behind them in the realm of the Spirit, in the realm of the Word, in the realm of the unknowable God.

It is for this reason, for example, that we no longer call certain of the odd actions of the great prophets merely acted parables.[1] For example, we have Jeremiah hiding his girdle in a rock (Jer. 13.1–11 or Ezekiel digging through the wall of his house (Ezek. 12.1–11). We have learned from Wheeler Robinson, Georg Fohrer, Th. Boman, A. Guilleaume, and others to regard these actions as actions potent in themselves, actions which, under the hand of God, initiate a new movement of the divine Spirit in the affairs of men. Wheeler Robinson has called this activity of theirs 'Prophetic Symbolism'. This potent activity of the prophet took the form of action just because the prophet had at some point become aware that he must be obedient to a mental pattern that had formed itself, not of his own volition, but from God, within

---

[1] Cf. H. Wheeler Robinson, Old Testament Essays, 1927, p. 2 f.; and *Two Hebrew Prophets*, 1948, p. 85. G. Ch. Aalders, *De Profeten des Ouden Verbonds*, 1918, p. 95, p. 103. A. van den Born, *De symbolische handelingen der Oud- Testamentische profeten*, 1935, p. 25, 33. G. Hoelscher, *Die Profeten*, 1914, p. 155. A Guilleaume, *Prophecy and Divination among the Hebrews and other Semites*, 1938, p. 192. George Fohrer, *Die symbolischen Handlungen der Propheten*, 1953, pp. 98–107.

his own human mind. Then it was only by expressing in action the content of his mental picture that he was enabled to declare objectively to his fellows the reality of the intent of the otherwise inscrutable God.

This so-called Prophetic Symbolism, then, leads us to understand still another facet of the OT view of the interrelatedness of word and deed. Every act that takes place on this earth, every 'thing', *dabhar*, according to OT thought, must necessarily have significance. Its *raison d'être* is to represent in terms of things, of matter, *dabhar*, the final and ultimate purpose (still *dabhar*) which lies behind the 'thing' and towards which all 'things' are moving till they reach their climax. That climax will be reached only when the disintegrating factor which at present separates thing, *dabhar*, from its meaning, *dabhar*, viz. sin, will be finally destroyed. When the End is reached at last, then both aspects of *dabhar* will have been finally integrated, and God will have brought in his transcendent heaven, *dabhar*, and new transcendent earth, *dabhar*, (dare we now translate these two English words by this same Hebrew word?) by a fusion of the two in one.

Again, there would have been no revelation at all had it not been for the fact of empirical Israel. The knowledge of God granted us in the OT takes the form of God's gracious activity within the life of Israel, along with the response of Israel to the flow of that grace in one historical situation after another. Thus we realize that if there had been no Israel, there would have been no revelation.

The interpretation of Israel's *raison d'être* is thus of the utmost importance. The interpretation which Israel made is obviously governed by images, rather than by concepts or even historical facts. It was the image which constrained the Hebrew mind to interpret the historical fact, and not vice versa. This is manifest when we recognize that the biblical images are both persistent and consistent. It is natural that the image persisted, since the Hebrew believed implicitly that the image which he saw with his mind's eye had its source in the mind of God himself.

We recognize then that it is quite out of the question to seek to 'demythologize' the OT. Throughout the whole OT period the

Word is becoming more and more integrated with Thing. The result is (*a*) it is impossible to conceive, for example, of the concept of Glory without picturing Glory as the prophets do in terms of Light and Fire. And (*b*) it is impossible to conceive of the self-emptying of God at the feet of man in total humility without taking full cognizance of the factuality of that stiff-necked, perverse, rebellious people with whom God entered into relations deeper and more wondrous than anything that the human mind could ever have conceived.

Twenty-Two

'Our God is a Consuming Fire'

The potency of OT images is nowhere more clearly evident than in the case of the image of Fire. We saw in Part One, chap. 8 how the Glory of God, an image indeed, was regarded by the Hebrews in a semi-metaphysical light, as if God's Glory were an objective reality in the realm of the Spirit. Moreover, we recall how the Glory of God was envisaged also in terms of the figure of Fire. We shall therefore co-ordinate the various ways in which the figure of Fire is used in the OT.

A. *Fire as a Natural Phenomenon.* A large number of biblical references may be found pointing to the fact that the Glory of God in early times was conceived through the image of the natural phenomenon of Fire. A fiery pillar was thus an aspect of the theophany at Sinai (Ex. 13.21; 24.17, etc.), a phenomenon moreover that was to be repeated, Isaiah believed, at the new Exodus that God would eventually accomplish (Isa. 4.5). Moreover Fire, as representative of God's invading Glory, could draw close to man and perform a specific act of burning (cf. Lev. 9.23–24, where 'glory' and 'fire' are equated; Num. 16.19–21, 35; Ps. 18.8, etc.), just as an individual flame can leap forth from the fire that is its source, and scorch a man's hand or arm. Such then is the natural and primary use of the figure of Fire.

B. *Fire as a Figure for War.* The figure, however, became greatly developed with time. It was used, for example, for various aspects of the horrors of war. Thus: 'For there is a fire gone out of

Heshbon, a flame from the city of Sihon' (Num. 21.28; cf. Amos 1.4); or 'They have cast fire into thy sanctuary' (Ps. 74.7); or again, 'Our holy and our beautiful house . . . is burned up with fire' (Isa. 64.11). As we see from this last reference, the figure was used specifically to describe the destruction of Solomon's Temple and the city of Jerusalem in 587 B.C.

C. *Fire as Emanating from God.* Other passages in the OT therefore put the emphasis upon the source of the fire and declare that the fire of war is caused by Yahweh himself. The fact that it was Israel's God himself who destroyed the Holy City is thus again and again expressed in this kind of language. The figure occurs in our important Ps. 80: (The vineyard) 'is burned with fire, it is cut down' (Ps. 80.16). The idea is found very particularly in the book of Lamentations: 'From above hath he sent fire into my bones' (Lam. 1.13), and so also Lam. 2.3–4; 4.11, etc. There are similar references in I Chron. 21.26; Ezek. 10.2; 39.6; etc. (cf. the DSS 1QH iii, 28ff.).

D. *Fire as a Representation of God in Action.* Just as that physical entity which we know as Fire is never static, in fact cannot be static, but must continually be active in order to be Fire at all, so the fiery purposes of God are known to us in space and time only by such activity as we can see. It was a God of Fire who made a covenant with Abraham (Gen. 15.17). Again, God shows himself in action in such phrases as: 'The voice of the Lord divideth the flames of fire' (Ps. 29.7); or, 'Our God shall come, a fire shall devour before him' (Ps. 50.3); or again, 'Is not my word like a fire? saith the Lord' (Jer. 23.29; cf. also Isa. 30.30; Jer. 5.14; Ps. 83.14–15, etc.). In the light of such conceptions, Jeremiah could look back upon the sojourn in Egypt as in an 'iron furnace' (Jer. 11.4).

E. *Fire as a Representation of the Wrath of God.* As we have seen, nowhere in the OT does man conceive of God without the element of wrath in his nature. Fichtner collates the cases where the concept of God's wrath is envisaged under the form of Fire.[1]

---

[1]   *TWNT*, V, p. 292 and p. 399.

Certain instances show that the figures are employed because Wrath is something that produces heat. Fichtner brings together those nouns and verbs which the anthropomorphic language of the OT frequently employs in this regard. Thus we have such phrases as 'God's nose grew hot', 'His anger was hot', 'The heat of his anger', etc. Accordingly it was only a short step, when one used anthropomorphic language, to speak of God's 'lips', 'breath' or 'tongue' as instruments of his Fire (cf. Isa. 30.27, 33; Jer. 15.14 – where 'aph may be read either as 'nose' or 'anger' – Jer. 17.4; Ezek. 21.31; 22.31; I Chron. 13.10, etc.). So the last step of all in this particular chain of figurative language is to speak of God himself as a consuming Fire (Deut. 4.24; cf Isa. 42.25; Ps. 78.21).

F.   *Fire as the Outward Representation of God.* Thus the emphasis upon the fact that it is God who sends Fire upon the earth could only have been made by men who believed that Fire is representative of the nature of the God of heaven himself.[2] Thus we have: 'Who maketh his angels spirits, his ministers a flaming fire' (Ps. 104.4; cf. Ex. 24.17). This verse takes it for granted that God, who is Spirit, is to be conceived as Fire, because the angels are here shooting flames which perform the will of the Fire from which they issue. Nor can we dismiss the figure because it occurs in poetry. It is common to both poetry and prose. In Isa. 30.27, e.g., God's Fire is equated with his Name. The whole realm of God's Glory, that is to say, the outer manifestation of his essential Being, is thus patently conceivable in terms of Fire (cf. Joel 2.30). It was a fiery chariot that came down from the realm of the Spirit and which received Elijah up to heaven (II Kings 2.11). Again, it was fiery horses and chariots which Elisha and his servant in their turn saw when the heavens opened to their eyes (II Kings 6.17). The precious stones of Ezekiel's myth of the Garden of Eden were stones of fire, because they lay on the holy mountain of God (Ezek. 28.13–14). The OT can state this truth in straightforward as well as poetical language. Deut. 4.24 declares in as categorical language that God is Fire as the NT declares that he is Love. The passage reads: 'For the Lord thy God is a consuming Fire, even a

------

2   Cf. 'My Glory and my very Self', Num. Rabbah, 4, 6.

jealous God'. Moreover, this plain statement is repeated by both Isaiah of Jerusalem and by TritoIsaiah in the following words: 'And the light of Israel shall be for a fire, and his Holy One for a flame, and it shall burn and devour his thorns and his briers in one day'; and 'For behold, the Lord will come with fire . . . and his rebuke with flames of fire, for by fire and by his sword will the Lord plead with all flesh' (Isa. 10.17; 66.15–16). The loving, creative activity of God, when confronted with sin and evil, is therefore constantly and normally envisaged under the figure of Fire. Thus: 'Thou shalt make them as a fiery oven in the time of thine anger; the Lord shall swallow them up in his wrath, and fire shall devour them' (Ps. 21.9; also Ps. 68.2; 78.21; 79.5). As a final and striking example of this prophetic understanding of the manifestation of the Wrath of God we may quote the utterance of Isaiah of Jerusalem in Isa. 33.12: 'The people shall be as the burnings of lime, as thorns cut up shall they be burned in the fire'.

G.   *God as Fire within Israel.* The great prophets constantly emphasize the truth that the God whom the heaven of heavens cannot contain is yet present in the midst of Israel. But the corollary of such a truth impels those same prophets to declare what is otherwise expressible only in terms of extreme paradox. Since Israel is specially chosen, then she is specially responsible (Amos 3.2). The Wrath of God must lie heavier upon her than upon any other nation (Joel 2.1–11; II Chron. 36.16; Isa. 1.2–4). Consequently, the unspeakably Holy God can be present in the midst of Israel only in the form of Fire or Furnace. The prophets do not reject this conception as insupportable. They use it freely. 'Saith the Lord, whose Fire is in Zion, and his Furnace is in Jerusalem' (Isa. 31.9). So vivid and so appalling in its consequences for Israel is the idea contained in the latter phrase in this oracle of Isaiah that the Septuagint translators refused to render it literally. And yet the wording of Isaiah's oracle is consistent with the earliest revelation of himself which God granted to the youthful prophet at the moment of his call years before, at that moment when Isaiah had found that at the very heart of God there is that which can only be conceived and understood by mortal man in terms of a flame of Fire (Isa. 6.6). Consequently, all throughout his prophetic activity Isaiah is conscious of the presence of the living God in the midst of his people as a kind of terrible and devouring Fire. Yet we have already suggested that Isaiah was not the first to make use of this particular figure. The figure of Fire is common to the thinking of the whole range of biblical literature, so that Isaiah owed the image to none other than the Holy Spirit himself. How else, we might well ask, could the juxtaposition of God's unspeakable Glory and unutterable Holiness with the putrid (cf Hos. 5.12; Isa. 1.6) Body of Israel be expressed in pictorial categories? Surely language such as this brings out in a total and absolute manner the central mystery of the presence of God in the midst of sinful Israel: 'The sinners in Zion are afraid; fearfulness hath surprised the hypocrites. Who among us shall dwell with the devouring fire? Who among us shall dwell with everlasting burnings?' (Isa. 33.14)

H. *The Ethical Significance of the Concept.* The Fires of God, however, cannot be merely capricious flames. They must represent, as we have said, the loving, saving, activity of a God of purpose, such as the God of the OT has revealed himself to be. There must be moral content to the action of the Fire. Thus it is that when sinful man comes into contact with the flames of the Fires of God, what he is really coming into contact with is the immediate presence of a God who is ever dealing with man for moral ends (cf. Ps. 57.4; 66.12; Amos 4.11). If we examine with care all the usages by the great prophets of this vital image, several other aspects of the significance of the image appear. For example, we find that the prophets say three things about Fire. There are passages which show that they recognized that (*a*) fire burns, (*b*) fire refines, and (*c*) fire destroys. Thus, for example, (*a*) 'I will make thee to pass with mine enemies into a land which thou knowest not, for a fire is kindled in mine anger, which shall burn upon you' (Jer. 15.14). Then again, (*b*) 'But who may abide the day of his coming? and who shall stand when he appeareth? for he is like a refiner's fire' (Mal. 3.2; cf. Isa. 48.10).[3] Finally (c), 'As wax melteth before the fire, so let the wicked perish at the presence of God' (Ps. 68.2).

Fire is essentially destructive. 'Central to the whole matter of the interrelation of suffering, sin and wrath is the direct activity of Yahweh in the city's destruction . . . Lest the reader (of Lamentations) overlook the true nature of the disaster, the poet ceaselessly reiterates the theme of Yahweh as the relentless, destroying God'.[4] The figure of the Fires of God thus expresses clearly and absolutely the heinousness of human sin, as well as the stark, relentless, insatiable Wrath of God against it. But the use of the figure is also the first step towards our understanding of the biblical consciousness that the 'new thing' which God has in mind to bring to pass can only happen through and beyond the death and resurrection of all his own stupid self-reliance and self-glorification in which poor man insists on putting value (cf. Zech. 3.2, where Joshua, the High Priest, representative of all Israel, is regarded as a brand plucked out of the fire).

We must now seek to discover how these three aspects of the 'fiery' purposes of God, understood so clearly as they were by the prophets, became visible to the inner eye of the Hebrew people through the experiences to which they were subjected by God.

I.   *The Casting of Fire as Historical Event.* The Exile was a great interpretative experience for the thinkers of Israel. Falling back upon the language of Isaiah who had died over a century before, the exilic and then the post-exilic prophetic voices sought to understand the meaning of the Exile not only as a historical event, but also as an act of God. Jeremiah had already learned to think of events contemporary with himself in terms of Fire, even before

---

[3]   This conception persists even in the extra-biblical Dead Sea Scrolls. See *A Hymn from the Scrolls*, where M. Wallenstein translates lines 39–42 thus: 'And thou has brought him (the humble one) in a refining pot for gold, (yea) into the works of fire. And (Thou hast made him as pure as) silver purified in the smith's furnace, so as to refine it sevenfold'.
[4]   N.K. Gottwald, *Studies in the Book of Lamentations*, 1954, p. 73.

the second captivity had taken place (Jer. 29.20–23). Later, however, from within the experience of the Exile itself, Ezekiel could speak of the Vine of Israel as having been destroyed by fire (Ezek. 15.7; 19.10–14), a Fire which God himself had undoubtedly caused. Now, it is clear to us, as we look back on the Exile from our vantage point of today, that when the exiles employed this interpretative figure to expound the event through which they had lived, they were learning by the aid of the Holy Spirit to see the whole sequence of events in a new light. They had watched the city they loved being destroyed by fire. They had seen *God*, no less, cast fire into *their* Sanctuary and *his*. It was *his*, because it was that place in which his very Name had dwelt (Deut. 12.5, etc; I Kings 8.29; Ps. 74.2). So they proceeded to describe the terrible experience of exile that followed the fall of Jerusalem, and which their people had now undergone, by declaring that they had but moved from one Fire (the fall of Jerusalem) to another Fire. For the horrors of the Exile were no less than just such an experience (cf. Ps. 89.46; Ezek. 21.32, etc.). A much later expositor, again, viz., the writer of the book of Daniel, from his vantage point of the second century B.C., was able to correlate the events through which his forefathers had passed, and to set the seal of a profound interpretation upon them. He recognized that the Exile could best be described as a Burning Fiery Furnace, a furnace of pain, horror and devastation of soul. He explained what he believed about that Furnace by means of highly revealing *midrash* upon the Exile experience. The story in Dan. 3 of the three representative Israelites who walked in the Furnace of the Exile in Babylon in the time of Nebuchadnezzar thus gives us the essential interpretation of that terrible event. The Israelites had watched the Fire of God destroying their beloved city. Now that Fire had pursued them into the horrors of the Exile. But fire does not only destroy: fire also refines and purifies. The author of Daniel, in conformity with the thought of the great prophets, obviously sees the figure of Fire in this light too. He sees it as a conceptual representation of God's saving love in action. Yet God acts in a manner different from the goldsmith, when the latter seeks to separate the gold from the dross. The goldsmith has to stand back from the heat and pain of the fire. He has to blow upon and feed the flames of the furnace from a safe distance outside the furnace walls. On the other hand, what the Israelites had come to discover 'existentially', so to speak, about God's saving action, as a result of their terrible experience in Babylon, was that when they found themselves in the furnace with all its scorching flames, they found themselves at the same time in the very Fires of God. They found that the Fires of the Exile were no less than the consuming love of the God of Israel himself, the significance and purpose of whose Being they were now being privileged to probe for the first time in the world's history. This is because it was while the three representative Israelites were in the Burning Fiery Furnace that they discovered they were sharing in its pain with a fourth, one like a Son of God (or, of the gods), i.e. a divine being, a manifestation in space and time of the divine Being himself (Dan. 3.25). Deutero-Isaiah, while still in Babylon himself, had undoubtedly already recognized the truth which this figure of the meaning of the Exile conveyed, and which the author of Daniel made explicit from his later vantage point. When thou walkedst through the Fires of God, he had come to understand, that is, when thou goest through the pain and the horror of the Exile, 'thou shalt not be burned; neither shall the flame kindle upon thee; fear not, thou art mine, *I will be with thee*' (Isa. 43.2, and note the quotation from Ex. 3.12).

We have reminded ourselves of the consistency of biblical thought in its use of identical pictorial images over many generations. Here we have leaped from prophet to historian, from pre-exilic to postexilic interpreter; and nowhere have we ever found any inconsistency of thought. So real is this consistency that four hundred years before Deutero-Isaiah thus sought to explain the essentially loving and saving activity of God in the terms we have just quoted, the document J had similarly interpreted another far-off event. According to the J narrative, Moses discovered through the vision he had received of God in the Burning Bush, that God was not remote and unconcerned at the pain and suffering of Moses' fellow Israelites in Egypt; he discovered, in fact, that God was *in* the pain and horror and sorrow of that veritable hell on earth, that actualization of the chaos of *tehom*, suffering *with* his people, though unconsumed, just because he is God and cannot die (cf. Hab. 1.12, whose original text read 'Thou diest not').

Finally then, before we pass on to apply the evidence we have collected to the subject we have in hand, let us once more realize what a motley of concepts are virtually fused as one in this extraordinary biblical figure. The figure declares that God manifests himself to human consciousness; but it comprehends within that manifestation God's 'strange work', as Isaiah called it (Isa. 28.21), with the children of men. There is wrath figured in the concept, there is pain, sorrow and war. But there is also redemptive purpose as well. Thus it is natural that even the figure of the messianic king in Isa. 9.5 should emerge into the range of our vision from out of a welter of 'burning and fuel of fire'. That picture concludes with the words: 'The zeal of the Lord of hosts will perform this' (Isa. 9.7). Following Isaiah, the Deuteronomist actually expounds the idea of the zeal of the Lord by declaring: 'For the Lord thy God is a consuming fire, (that is) a jealous God' (Deut. 4.24). And all these strange word pictures, all these many facets of the work and significance of Fire, these all represent what that strange biblical word Glory has to say to us of the outward manifestation of the inner essence of the God of the OT, who is otherwise unknowable; and of the same God, as the NT believes, as he who is the Father of our Lord Jesus Christ!

Appendix

Kaj Munk's own Introduction to his play *He sits at the Melting-Pot; translated from the Danish by R.P. Keigwin, George Allen & Unwin, Ltd., London, 1953.*

The earth is on fire. There have been times in the history of mankind when it was possible to forget this; but our own time is not one of these. On at least seven days in every week we are reminded that we have been flung into a spluttering, seething bonfire.

Are these flames that beset us the flames of destruction? We do not know. Often our hearts grow sick with far at the sight of them. But the Christian faith says that the faith about us is the fire of the furnace. The Christian faith cannot prove this, and, indeed, makes no attempt to. It says so simply because that is what was foretold it. The earth is in the melting-pot.

The Christian God is a great God. He is so great that he cannot do with less than a god as stoker at his foundry. It is the god in hell who shovels in the coal under God's melting-pot. That is why the heat is so terrific. And it has to be, in order that the dross may be cleansed away.

Will it be cleansed away? What does mankind know? An explosion might scatter everything to the winds. Or the world might be reduced to cinders. Christianity robs life of none of its thrills. It is the religion of drama.

But for that reason it claims that there is a meaning in the apparently meaningless horror of this world-conflagration. And it builds a hopeful dream of a way-out to 'a new heaven and a new earth, in which justice dwells'.

He sits at the melting-pot, does the Master's own Son. Alike at the individual's and at all mankind's.

Twenty-Three

Sacrifice and Atonement

The sacrificial cult in Israel developed greatly throughout the centuries. In its earlier forms, at least three motifs are visible to the eye.[1] (i) Certain sacrifices were made with the end in view of obtaining communion between God and man. Thus the *zebhah* was a sacrifice where part of the animal was eaten by the worshipper, and part by God.[2] God's share 'went up' to him in smoke (cf. Lev. 17.5; I Sam. 2.15). (ii) Certain sacrifices were in the nature of gifts to God to make him propitious towards the worshipper. In this category are to be found freewill-offerings, thank-offerings, and votive-offerings (cf. Lev. 22.18 ff.) (iii) Others again were offered in the belief that by the slaying of the animal, vital power was released, and man could then continue to live in the presence of the living God and not be destroyed (cf. Lev. 1.4).[3] After the principle which we examined earlier, however, where we saw how one man could represent a group, and sum that group up in himself, it was only the head of the enlarged

---

[1] As suggested by W.O.E. Oesterley, *Sacrifices in Ancient Israel*, 1938, pp. 11 ff.

[2] N.H. Snaith, 'Sacrifices in the OT', *VT*, 1957, pp. 308 ff., does not agree that the god ate part of the sacrifice in the ancient Semitic cults.

[3] See Johs. Pedersen, op. cit. III–IV, pp. 315 ff.; S.R. Driver, *Introduction to the Literature of the Old Testament*, 1891, pp. 39 ff.; F.C.N. Hicks, *The Fullness of Sacrifice*, 3rd ed., 1946, pp. 11 ff.; H.H. Rowley, 'The Meaning of Sacrifice', *BJRL*, Vol. 33, No. 1; G.B. Gray, *Sacrifice in the Old Testament*, 1925, *passim*.

family group who thus offered sacrifice (Lev. 1.4), and who thus effected the release of that power for the benefit of the whole dependent family. Moreover, since the life of the animal resided actually in its blood (Lev. 17.11, 14), the pouring out of the blood signified the actual offering of life, indeed, of life through death.[4]

Our knowledge of the early sacrificial worship of Israel comes to us from the pens of various writers, all of whose works have fused various oral traditions, and which have been edited by still later hands again. A study of what is early in them, then, and of what is late, is a complex task and probably impossible of fulfilment. But by post-exilic times, that is to say, in the period after the figure of the Suffering Servant had been set before the eyes of the People of God, the essential elements in all the early ritual had evidently been drawn together in the Temple worship. In the days before the Exile, the great prophets had protested that ritual alone without a right intention was anathema to the God who, through Moses, had given the cult to Israel (Amos 4.4–5; 5.21–24; Isa. 1.10–15; Jer. 7.21–26). The *opus operatum*, in other words, was foreign to the prophetic understanding of sacrificial worship. If Israel really sought (i) to find communion with her God, (ii) to give him gifts that came truly from the heart, and (iii) to set free God's full and free forgiveness in their lives; if, in other words, she hoped her sacrifices would be effective, then she dare not separate between matter and spirit, or, as we see those terms in this particular context, she must be sure that her actions were integrated with her intentions.

As the centuries went by, it evidently came home to the minds of the most aware of Israel's thinkers that such an ideal state of unity between act and intention could never be. It was a nation of sinners who performed the cult, nay, it was not the *'am yahweh*, the People of God at all, but 'the rulers of Sodom' and 'the people of Gomorrah' (Isa. 1.10). Thus the whole sacrificial cult, they saw, was evidently pointless and a misconception of the will of God. Amos, for example, had sarcastically suggested that Israel should put the whole emphasis of her worship upon mere activity divorced

---

[4] See G. Pidoux, *L'Homme dans l'Ancient Testament*, Cah. Theol. 32, 1953, p. 49; also *TWB*, art. 'Sacrifice', by C.R. North, pp. 206–14.

from its true meaning and purpose; so he went on to make suggestions as to how Israel could be even more punctilious in the performance of her sacrifices! (Amos 4.4–5). This was because Amos fully realized that it could only be a people whose heart was wholly pure, and whose intention was unswervingly loyal, who could effectively offer sacrifice in any of its many forms.

Thus it was that Israel came to learn that an *effective* sacrificial act could be offered only by God himself. If sinful man should by any chance succeed in constraining God to do his will, then man's act was no longer sacrifice, but magic.[5] A religious act entails surrender to the will of the Creator God, but magic is the constraint of God by man.

In despair of ever being able to meet the requirements of true sacrificial worship, and thus to obtain the forgiveness of God for the sins of the whole people, the comprehensive, or 'blanket' annual ceremony known as the Day of Atonement was instituted in the period after the return from Exile. Perhaps the cessation of all sacrifices with the destruction of the Temple had cast doubts for the first time on the ancient practice of sacrifice as such. The complicated ritual of the Day of Atonement may be found in Lev. 16, and more fully in the Mishna Tractate *Yoma*. The so-called 'sin', or 'trespass', or 'guilt' offering, *'asham*, likewise came into its own after the Exile, though it seems to have been developing before that period (Lev. 5.14–6.7; 7.1–7; Num. 5.5–8). Its main purpose was to make expiation for what a man owed as a debt, a deliberate debt, the owing of which was a sin such as could put him right outside the community of the Covenant People, beyond the place where the grace of God was operative through the normal sacrifices. In this regard, it was parallel in its purpose with that of the ritual in the Day of Atonement (cf. Lev. 6.7). Now, in order to render this particular sacrifice effective the sacrificer had to offer a ram without blemish. The ram represented an important principle.

The verb 'to atone', *kipper*, in Hebrew, means 'to cover over', or, as it means in Akkadian, 'to wash away'. It was the great hope of Israel that, although she could never expect to make a pure and a perfect act of sacrifice, yet she might persuade her God to put

---

[5] H.H. Rowley, op. cit., p. 94.

his hand over her sins, and thus to cover them, so that he could no longer see them with his eyes (Ps. 32.1; Jer. 18.23). The expressions 'to wash away', 'to wipe away' sins were also used of God's action (like the Akkadian meaning of *kipper*) (cf. Ps. 51.2; Prov. 6.33). In private, and possibly also in public prayer, the true Israelite was heard pleading with God in such terms, evidently in the consciousness that his sins separated him from God even as the disease of leprosy could separate him from the Covenant People (Lev. 14.1–3). But the OT saint had no *assurance* that his prayer would ever be answered. He could not possibly imagine that God would forgive in the realm of the spirit without simultaneously (for this is a unified world) forgiving in the realm of things or action. That is why the great 'penitential' Psalm (Ps. 51), where the worshipper pleads with God to wash him and purge him thoroughly, yet ends with what, to one who has not learned to think as the Hebrews thought, seems like an anti-climax: 'Then shalt thou be pleased with the sacrifices of righteousness . . . then shall they offer bullocks upon thine altar'.

There had been one man, however, whose heart had been pure in the sight of God, viz., Moses. Moses had seen God 'face to face' (Ex. 33.11), and had thus learned to know his will. Moses had truly loved his people, nay, he had been prepared so to identify himself with them, after the revolting episode of the Golden Calf, that he was enabled to address them thus: 'Ye have sinned a great sin: and now I will go up unto the Lord; peradventure I shall make an atonement, *kipper*, for your sin'. And then, turning to God, he continued: 'Yet now, if thou wilt forgive their sin –; and if not, blot me, I pray thee, out of thy book which thou hast written' (Ex. 32.30,32; cf. Deut. 1.37; Hos. 12.13). Moses did no less than offer his own body to be the sacrifice which would render effective in the realm of action what he knew was true of the purpose of God in the realm of spirit. But God did not accept Moses' offer (Ex. 32.33). The body of Moses could not be the perfect sacrifice, since Moses, though meek (Num. 12.3), and obedient (Ex. 4.19–20), was still a recalcitrant sinner (Ex. 2.12; 4.13–14). The *'asham*, the trespass-offering of the priestly legislation (Lev. 5.14–6.7) must needs be a ram *without blemish*.

No heavenly, or spiritual, or angelic, intercessor either could hope to make an *effective* atonement in the realm of matter by the very nature of things (Job 33.22–24; Dan. 12.1; Tobit 12.15; Test. of Dan. 6.1–2: Enoch, *passim*). It could only be one of flesh and blood who could *effectively* be the atoning factor for the flesh and blood sins of the stiff-necked People of God. Only he could validate the three sacrificial principles which we have enunciated – (1) Be the means of full communion between God and man; (2) Be in himself the all-sufficient thank-offering due from man to God; (3) Be the instrument through whom man dare approach the living God of Fire without being burned. He would thus mediate a total forgiveness for man, and enable man to continue to live in the divine presence. The honour of becoming this medium, whereby the whole world might gain *shalom*, God offered to his own Servant and Bride, Israel, even though, paradoxically, that same nation needed to be saved into *shalom* herself.

Twenty-Four

The 'Crucifixion' of Israel

The great pre-exilic prophets had expounded the relationship between God and Israel under the figures, amongst others, of Son of God, Bride of God, and Servant of God. DeuteroIsaiah now brings all three together. His message in this regard is summed up in two momentous declarations: (1) 'Thou art my servant, O Israel, in whom I will be glorified' (Isa. 49.3), and (2) 'The Lord hath redeemed Jacob, and glorified himself in Israel' (Isa. 44.23).

The term 'Servant of Yahweh', or 'my Servant', occurs frequently in Deutero-Isaiah, e.g. in Isa. 41.8 ff., 42.18–22; 44.1, 2, 21, 26; 45.4; 50.10. In Isa. 41.8. ff.; 44.1, 2, 21; 45.4, and in Jer. 30.10 and Ezek. 28.25, the term Servant is definitely identified with or explained by the word 'Israel'. In Isa. 42.1–5 the LXX version inserts 'Jacob' before 'my Servant' and 'Israel' before 'my chosen', showing that the identification with the nation goes back before pre-Christian times. (See p. 191.)

We have spoken in Part One, chap. 8 of the Glory of God, using as our example the noun *kabhodh*. But other nouns occur with the same meaning, and are used in the same way, e.g. *hadhar*, *hodh*, and *tiph'arah*[1] (cf. Isa. 35.2; Ps. 8.5; 78.61, etc.). The verb from which the last of these nouns derives, viz. *pa'ar*, is that which occurs in both quotations from Deutero-Isaiah; moreover, this verb is used in a manner parallel to the verb *k-b-d* which has been before us already (cf Isa. 63.12; Ps. 71.8).

---

[1] Johs. Pedersen, op. cit., 1–2, p. 237, identifies these words in meaning.

Now, the first three portraits of the Servant (Isa. 42.1–4; 49.1–6; 50.4–9) reveal to us an Israel that is very human indeed. She knows that she has been called from the womb for her task (49.1), that she has been trained and lovingly educated and led to this end (49.2). She knows that her task is to comfort the weary, and bind up the broken in heart (50.4, and cf. 61.1–3), not only within the ranks of Israel herself, but even to the ends of the earth, so that through her body the salvation of God may reach all men everywhere. She knows that such a calling will bring upon her only calumny and suffering (50.6), yet that if she were but to offer herself wholly, her God would be with her in the Fire (50.7). Nevertheless she holds back from the demand of total submission to her divine Husband.

Israel, like Moses in earlier times, cannot offer her own body for the redemption of the world. Her sin is too great; she is alienated from her Lover. In fact, she does not even realize what her calling is. 'Who is blind but my servant?' (42.19). On the other hand, God who hates divorce (Mal. 2.16) cannot go back on his word to Israel, on the troth which he plighted at Sinai. 'How shall I give thee up, Ephraim? how shall I deliver thee, Israel? . . . I will not execute the fierceness of mine anger . . . for I am God, and not man; the Holy One *in the midst* of thee' (Hos. 11.8–9). God must be true to the absolute consistency of his love and of the divine election; but he must also be true to the absolute consistency of that judgement upon sin which stems from his wrath against it. 'That was part of the deepest agony of Jeremiah. The astonishing thing here is that the more God gave himself to this people, the more he forced this people to be what it was in its sin and self-will, to be in truth what it actually was, a rebel. The very self-emptying of God in holy love not only revealed Israel's sin, but intensified it'.[2]

So now we meet with the supreme contradiction that results from the juxtaposition of the OT's potent images. In the first place, according to Deutero-Isaiah (see Part Three, chap. 15, (6)),

---

[2] T.F. Torrance, 'The Israel of God', *Interpretation*, July, 1956, p. 309. Cf. also Isa. 6.9–10.

God is now about to marry the Bride to whom he was espoused at Sinai; when he does so, then she will indeed be one flesh with her divine Husband. But in the second place, the 'flesh' of God, as we have seen, is regarded as his Glory, and his Glory is envisaged under the form of Fire. God is about to be glorified in Israel. Therefore his Glory will be made manifest in her very flesh. 'Only in thee (Israel) is God, and not another' (Isa. 45.14); 'My glory will I not give to another' (Isa. 42.8), i.e., to another people, *not* to another god; and certainly not to a 'graven' image; God will give his Glory to that nation alone, which, made in the image of God, has been called to be his Bride (cf. Deut. 29.29).

As the outcome of the fact that the biblical figure of Fire has so many facets, and thus conveys truth from many angles, three vital conceptions now become clear, yet all of these are inextricably woven together. Firstly, the Wrath of God in righteous judgement must burn in the Fire the sinful Bride who has become the incarnation of evil. As a Son, Israel had become perverted (Ezek. 16.1–5); as a Bride, she had turned into a harlot (Ezek. 16.6 ff.). Secondly, at the same time as undergoing in the Fire the penalty for her apostasy, Israel's body is called to be the *'asham*, by the offering of which, as a sacrifice that is burned in the Fire, the redemption of the Gentiles is to be won. Thirdly, God, who is Fire himself, now takes Israel to himself. By his act of union with Israel, the Fire which he himself is, now renders effective in and through the flesh of Israel, the sacrifice which sinful Israel is unable to offer.

There can be little doubt that, since Deutero-Isaiah wrote in the Exile himself, the events of the year 587 B.C. were for him the climax and the symbol of all God's dealings with his people, that they were, in fact, the 'crucifixion' by God himself of his own beloved Son. Israel had been 'past praying for', as Jeremiah had known in his heart (Jer. 7.16; 11.14). 'And when this people, or a priest, shall ask thee saying, What is the burden of the Lord? then thou shalt say unto them, Ye are the burden! (LXX and Vulgate). I will cast you off, saith the Lord' (Jer. 23.33; 25.8–9; 30.12–15).

Yet, the action of God in crucifying Israel must necessarily be effective. God has spoken, and his Word cannot return unto him void. That is the mark of God's faithfulness. Let us realize, then, that such is the tenor of the last of the four Servant-Songs (Isa. 52.13–53.12), and that puts it in a different category from the first three. The effectiveness of God's uttered Word, such is the theme of the poem, is now about to be seen in action. Yet we have already been brought to understand that it speaks not just of the offering of the body of Israel. The body she offers here has now become, ideally, 'one flesh' with the Glory of the holy God; or conversely, by his voluntary union with Israel, God himself unites himself with a body which, when it is sacrificed, will at last render effective on earth that which is the will of God in heaven. This sacrifice must be truly the perfect sacrifice, because in it God Almighty will empty out his *nephesh* as an *'asham* (Isa. 53.10, 12), or guilt-offering; the zeal of the Lord will *hiskil*, will produce an effective action (52.13), so that he will *hitsdiq*, justify, many, i.e., set many in the right (53.11) Moreover, since *tohu* is in the very heart of those whom God will finally put right, God's ultimate victory will be over the powers of Chaos and Darkness just as much as it will be over human sin.

This image presented to us in Isa. 53 remains, however, nothing more than an image. Yet it is a fact of history that God did indeed first crucify his people and then raise them up to newness of life and restore them to their land. But that mighty act had now been accomplished, and still Israel had thereby in no sense become the Saviour of the world, even although the pattern of God's saving activity had now been made visible at this the fourth of the five 'moments' of her experience. But, as we have said, the pattern had indeed been set. This meant that, if the moment should ever come when God, in his total humility, were indeed to identify himself by means of his Glory with the sinful body of Israel, and the twain should indeed become one flesh, then we would be enabled to see with blinding clarity the body of the Servant-Son-Bride being subsumed into the very life of God. We would be made to see, too, that the Resurrection of the Servant would be bound to follow upon his self-offering, once he had 'borne our griefs and carried our sorrows' (Isa. 53.4). In the case of historical Israel, it was only when she had shattered herself upon the Covenant of her God, and when she had paid the ultimate penalty for her rebelliousness and pride, that God raised her up and renewed her, and out of 'crucifixion' and death there came joy and newness of life (Isa. 40.1–11; Ezek. 37). But in the case of the ideal still to come, such would no longer be the case.

The fourth Servant-Song (Isa. 52.13–53.12) thus presents us with a very different picture of the Servant from that of diffident Israel which is portrayed in the other three Songs; and yet it is still the same Servant who is described. For one thing, this time the whole meaning of Israel's existence is summed up in the person of one Servant, and this Servant is declared to be one who is now wholly obedient, even unto death. Consequently, we may claim with awe that the picture set before us now is the image, no longer of sinful and diffident Israel, but of an Israel which at last has become one flesh with, and therefore shares one will with, her divine Lover. Here Israel is become the representation of God to the world. Here Israel is that entity employed by God to show forth his relationship to the world. Here Israel is shown to exist in the miracle of the Real Presence and the Present Grace of God (Ex. 29.42 ff.; I Kings 8.12 ff.).[3] Here Israel is shown to exist merely for the purpose of giving her body to be burned that the world might be saved.

But more; although the Servant is still pictured as smitten *by* God (Isa. 53.4), and although it is Yahweh who 'laid on him the iniquity of us all' (v. 6), yet we are to realize the majesty of the conception that it is now Yahweh himself who, because he is become one flesh with Israel, has become the Suffering Servant which Israel could not be. It is Yahweh himself who now bears the sin of Israel (what a paradox!) as well as the sin of the world. We should note that Deutero-Isaiah had already expressed this very conception in a passage which is independent of the 'Songs'. The passage runs: 'I did not impose the office of the servant upon *thee* (demanding expiatory offering and incense)', says God . . . 'but thou didst make *me* the servant (who dealt) with thy sins, and made

---

[3] G. von Rad, 'Typologische Auslegung des Alten Testaments,' Evangelische Theologie, 1952, Juli/Aug., Heft 1/2, p. 19. Luke 2.32.

me toil over thine iniquities' (Isa. 43.23–24).[4]

So this then is how Almighty God finally 'glorifies himself' in Israel (Isa. 44.23; 49.3). He does so by identifying himself with the empirical entity and historical reality that we know as Israel after the flesh. Thus God's utter self-emptying and absolute humility are now evidenced to mortal eyes in action in the realm of matter, of human life, at that moment when God, no less, presents his body, in Israel, as a living sacrifice.

Now, must this saving activity of God remain merely in the realm of the ideal? Is the self-offering of God in the figure in Isa. 53 to remain only a picture of what God might do if he were to become one flesh with Israel in more than mere 'image' form? In answer to that question we must adduce three elements in Hebrew thought, one of which we have not as yet examined.

(i)   The Hebrew language possesses only two verbal 'tenses', one showing completed, and the other incomplete action. Hebrew 'tenses' do not mark the past or the future of an action as modern English verbs can do. Grammarians have called a usage which employs the Hebrew perfect tense to express a future action by the title of 'The Hebrew Prophetic Perfect'. If a prophet sought to declare that since God had spoken, then that which God had said was bound to come to pass, he could use the perfect form of the verb, the 'completed' tense in Hebrew. Thus, for example, Isaiah can declare in the *past* or completed tense about the future messianic king: 'Unto us a child *has been* born!' (Isa. 9.6). It is in this manner, then, that Deutero-Isaiah paints the supremely important picture contained in Isa. 53 with the use of perfects of the verb. God has spoken this image to his heart. The Word of God cannot return unto God void. Therefore this image will indeed some day become reality.

(ii) Isa. 53 is the nadir in OT thought and practice of the device which we saw H. Wheeler Robinson has called 'Prophetic

---

[4]   Cf. W. Vischer, *Das Kerygma des Alten Testaments*, 1955, p. 21. Note also how Isa. 51.4–5 assigns to Yahweh the function in redemption which 42.1–4 has already assigned to the Servant.

Symbolism'. When Jeremiah smashed his water-pot (Jer. 19), he was erecting a bridge over which the Word of God must pass till it issued in the destruction of Jerusalem. In doing what he did, he was not constraining God as if by magic to do his, Jeremiah's, will. He smashed the pot in obedience to the mental image which he knew God had put within his mind to form the necessary bridge. It was in this tradition, then, that our Poet-Prophet conjured up the mental image which he bore within his mind. The image possibly originated for him when he mused upon the offer of Moses to God of old to be the substitute for the sins of his people; or again, possibly, as the result of his witnessing the symbolic smiting of the king by the high priest at the annual enthronement festival in Babylon;[5] yet most probably of all from his own true insight into the meaning of the Exile.[6] Therefore, by recording on 'paper' this image which he knew that God had given him, he was creating just that bridge over which the Word was one day bound to pass. In other words, he was creating, under the impulsion of the Spirit of God, a *fait accompli* in the realm of God's creative and redemptive activity.

(iii) In featuring the Servant in the fourth Song, not as Israel regarded as one *corpus*, but as one individual *nephesh*, who was evidently to suffer *for* Israel as well as *with* Israel, our author was demonstrating that fluidity of thought which we saw throughout Part One and in Part Three, chap. 15 (6) to be characteristic of the manner in which the Hebrews expressed themselves. One man could represent the group of which he was the 'ba'al'. The whole group could claim to be

---

[5] See J.M.P. Smith, *The Prophets and their Times*, rev. ed. by W.A. Irwin, 1946, pp. 234 ff.

[6] For all the possibilities before him, see C.R. North, *The Suffering Servant in Deutero-Isaiah*, 1948, pp. 20–42; 47–57; 72–103. I myself cannot imagine that the Servant concept owes anything at all to the Babylonian royal 'death-and-resurrection' motif, any more than the death and resurrection of Christ owe anything to the mystery religions of a later period.

in the personage who stood at the apex of any particular triangle of human society. The people could be in their king, the branches could be *in* the vine. So in the same way, all Israel could most certainly be *in* one representative Israelite, who would sum up in his own person as Servant all that Israel was meant to be.[7]

---

[7]   The student of Christian theology will realize that a Christian doctrine of the Atonement must take the above issues into account. The work of Christ is indeed substitutionary, since he alone is the sinless one. But Christ must also have acted as our Representative when he gave himself as the Servant. Those who would lay the whole stress upon the substitutionary nature of Christ's Atonement are selecting from the OT only those elements from the sacrificial cult which lead to such a view. But thereby they ignore the involvement of Israel with its own Godgiven cult. The cult and the sacrifices might have developed *sua sponte* in Syria or in Greece. But as a fact of history they did not. The cult developed within the life of that people with whom God had once entered into a unique relationship. Therefore that people, in some manner or other, must have become involved in the substitutionary, *eph-hapax* nature of the self-offering of the Servant.

Twenty-Five

'At That Day . . .'

We have held constantly before us that important belief on Israel's part that in the past God had performed great things for her. Now we must examine an equally potent belief that was also held by Israel, at least from the period of the monarchy, and one which becomes ever more patent as the story of Israel unfolds. It is that in the future also God will act. This day of God's coming action was spoken of by Amos (5.18) as 'The Day of the Lord'. We shall use that title now as the generic name for a variety of biblical beliefs about the future.

It is interesting to note this dual vision of Israel's writers, in that they looked both forward and back. Other ancient nations looked back alone. They recalled with pride their great and glorious origin. Such was the case with the Greeks, the Romans, the Babylonians, and others. The Hebrews alone looked both ways. Yet it was natural for them to do so, because they alone believed in the 'living' God. Before Israel was, God is. Thus after Israel is, God will be. Again, since Israel as a people was created by God for his own ends, and Israel's history has a purpose running through it, then Israel's history must have an End to which it is moving, as well as a point from which it began. Moreover, since God had set Israel within a universe which he had created in the beginning, then that universe too must have an End. On the other hand, the End to which the whole OT is looking forward, emphasis upon which is such a dominant note within it, is not merely and only the historical last moment in a series of historical moments; it is also and primarily the *meaning* of the whole series of moments. In other words, the Day of the Lord to which the whole OT looks forward is, teleologically speaking, the object of an eschatological hope, rather than a calendar date that is to be the last of all calendar dates in time.

Set within the total eschatological expectation of Israel is what may be called Israel's messianic hope. At this point we must pause to ensure that we understand the meaning of this latter phrase and see it in its true perspective.

There has always been an element within the Church, as we are well aware, that has approached the OT with the primary preconception that the main topic of its pages is the delineation of a figure known as the Messiah; and that the characterization of that figure is, as it were, a 'pre-view' of the Jesus of the NT. However, the great majority of the OT writings has nothing to say whatsoever about any such figure. Yet the latter writings are surely as truly the 'Holy Writ' of the Christian Church as are those few passages which do undoubtedly speak in this narrowly 'messianic' manner. On the other hand, it is the OT as a whole which is 'messianic', as this present work seeks to show, and not merely a few elements in its composition. So far as the AV is concerned, the word 'messiah' occurs in the book of Daniel alone (9.25–26). As Professor T.W. Manson has pointed out, however, so unlike is he to the Prince Messiah of the Isaianic passages (see below) that the idea of Messiah does not occur in the book of Daniel at all.[1] The word *mashiah* primarily means 'anointed'. As such, the word was applied to many of God's servants. A priest could be 'messiah' in this sense (I Sam. 12.3), and so could an Israelite king (Saul, I Sam. 16.6; David, II Sam. 22.51; or any king in the line of David, Ps. 2.2; Lam. 4.20, etc.). Yet even pagan king Cyrus of Persia is hailed as the Lord's messiah or anointed one (Isa. 45.1); and any ordinary, humble, believing 'son of man' seems to have called himself by the title when addressing God in prayer (cf. Ps. 28.8; 84.9; 89.38).

---

[1] *The Servant-Messiah*, 1953, p. 72.

On the other hand, the title was more specifically used of the Davidic line, and it is with this element in the thought of the OT that we begin to define Israel's messianic hope. I say advisedly 'begin', since the eschatological End, to which the whole OT moves forward, is very much more comprehensive than the conception that a 'messiah' will one day appear within Israel. The End to which several of the prophets, both before and after the Exile, look forward, the coming Day of the Lord, is nothing less than the accomplishment of God's total purpose for his world, through the instrumentality of Israel. That the conception of the End is thus portrayed on a vast canvas should occasion us no surprise. The OT is here dealing with what is too great for the mind of man to grasp. Therefore it can give no clear cut vision of the End. What it does do is to employ the language of imagery to convey the theological conceptions involved in the idea of the End. And just as in the case of the NT, where the vision of the celestial city granted to St John the Divine is conveyed to our human consciousness by means of images whose source is in this known world of ours, with its gold and precious stones, so also is it with the case of the OT End. The latter is defined in picture language all of which is understandable in terms of this world of space and time.

At this point we might make use of a figure of our own. We might liken the whole eschatological hope of Israel to a many-stranded rope. Each of the strands of the rope is an important element in its own right in the portraying of the End. Yet we do not possess a rope unless all the strands are properly interwoven. Again, when we hold the *middle* of a rope in our hands, it is not easy to perceive the separateness of each of its many strands, or to see how each strand ministers to the function of the rope as a whole. So it is with Israel's eschatological hope. It happens that we who are confronted with that hope find ourselves standing at 'the middle of the rope'. Therefore we are called on to remember that each of the strands of Israel's hope is inseparable from its fellows, and that it can be understood only in the light of the whole function of the rope. With this figure in mind, we shall now briefly review the more important strands of the rope.

(1) *Son of David*.[2] The author of II Sam. 7.12–16 records that
the prophet Nathan, as the mouthpiece of God, makes two
promises to King David: (*a*) that his son will hold a unique
relationship to God: 'I will be his father, and he shall be my son';
and (*b*) that the line of David will be 'established for ever'.[3] The
king, however, is never exclusively the choice of Yahweh. Yahweh
is faithful to the dynasty. The king is also the choice of Israel, who
is ever fickle (II Sam. 16.18).[4] Abigail had previously expressed
to David, even before his enthronement, the confidence that 'the
Lord will certainly make my lord a sure, *ne'eman*, house' (I Sam.
25.28). Yahweh himself, of course, was a 'sure' or 'faithful',
ne'eman, God. He does not change. Therefore if God should
adopt a line of kings to be his son, then God will certainly continue
to be faithful to that line even though Israel, or part of Israel,
should not. The faithfulness of God to the dynasty of his choice
is manifest in the case of the very first of the line after David, viz.,
Solomon. Such a belief is put into the mouth of Benaiah ben
Jehoiada: 'Amen', he said (using the root of the noun *ne'eman*);
'as Yahweh has been *with* my lord the king, even *will he be*, (or,
become with, the Qere reading) Solomon' (I Kings 1.36–37; cf. II
Sam. 7.9; Ps. 89.21, 24). These words are, of course, identical
with the promise given to Moses (Ex. 3.12), and parallel with the
significance of the name Immanuel (see below, p. 321). The
conception is echoed in II Sam. 23.5, in a psalm that expounds
the significance of the promise made to David: 'Although my
house be not so with God (i.e., not wholly faithful to its calling),
yet he hath made with me an everlasting covenant ordered in all
things, and sure, *ne'eman*'. One of the main themes of the books
of Chronicles, written as they were in the post-exilic period, is just

---

[2] See A.G. Herbert, *The Throne of David*, 1941, chap. 2, for certain of
the following categories.

[3] The language used is very similar to what have been called the Egyptian
'royal novels'. It is interesting to note once again how Israel steps out of
her eastern environment and gives this ancient literary type an eschatological significance that is unique. See L. Rost, *Die Überlieferung der
Thronnachfolge Davids*, 1926, pp. 47 ff.

[4] L. Koehler, *Die Theologie des Alten Testament*, 1953, p. 66.

the exaltation of the royal line of David. Before David arose, 'naturally' the life of Israel was chaotic (Judg. 21.25). David changed all that. Even II Sam. 22.44, certainly much earlier in origin than Chronicles, can present the following mighty claim for him: 'Thou has kept me to be the head of the Gentiles'.[5]

The unfortunate truth that the line of David was not wholly faithful to its calling is evident from the historians' account of the behaviour of David's successors. David had been an adulterer (II Sam. 11; see pp. 265 ff.), so he had to suffer the chagrin of seeing his line through his eldest son, Amnon, set aside as a result of that son's inherited lust (II Sam. 3.2; 13). 'No such thing (as fornication) ought to be done in Israel' (II Sam. 13.12). David had also been a murderer (II Sam. 11.14–17). Accordingly, he had to suffer the humiliation of seeing his favourite son, Absalom,[6] die. He too had inherited from his father this time a readiness to commit murder (II Sam. 13.28–29; 18.14). Chileab, the second son, had already died young (II Sam. 3.3); and so the story makes clear that the line of David was to be one, not necessarily of the direct descent of blood, but of grace on the part of God.

Although Solomon, who is the son who eventually comes to the throne, is also known as 'the beloved of the Lord' (such is the meaning of his other name, Jedidiah, II Sam. 12.25), he too has feet of clay. He it is who introduces polytheism along with his polygamy (I Kings 11.1–8); thereafter the 'folly' of the 'wise' father becomes actual in the behaviour of the son. Rehoboam, we remember, was instrumental in splitting the kingdom in two, even though, ultimately speaking, it had been Yahweh who brought about the split (I Kings 12.24). It is God alone who is 'wise'; the 'wise' Solomon ought never to have claimed to be such. It had been of grace alone that Israel had been chosen of old (Deut. 4.37), so that each member of the line of David was chosen of God in the same manner (I Sam. 10.24; II Sam. 6.21).

---

[5] See S. Mowinckel, op. cit., pp. 63–64, for an interesting account of the enthronement and anointing of the king in Jerusalem.

[6] On the significance of his name, see C.F. Evans, art. 'Peace', in *TWB*, 1950, pp. 165–6.

Such is the wisdom of God. In the beginning it had surely been odd of God to choose the great king David at all, since he was the great-grandson of a foreign woman (Ruth 4.18–22). Ruth the Moabitess had not even been a member of the People of God. But more extraordinary still was it that this line of David, which was to have been established for ever, should finally come to an ignoble end at the fall of Jerusalem in 587 B.C. The king who was on the throne when that event took place actually bore the name of Zedekiah, meaning 'Yahweh is victorious'. This name is closely akin to the words *yahweh tsidheqenu*, the name which Jeremiah gave to the messianic scion of David (Jer. 23.6). How paradoxical that fact must have seemed to his contemporary subjects.

Yet the great prophets would have understood with more conviction the mystery of such a paradox. They knew that Yahweh is a God who keeps his covenant and does not break his word. Thus even after Jehoiachin had been carried off to servitude and prison in 598 B.C., a prophet could exclaim that 'on that day' the yoke would be broken off Jacob's neck. 'Strangers', he was sure, will 'no more serve themselves of him; but they shall serve the Lord their God, and David their king, whom I will raise up unto them' (Jer. 30.8–9, a post-exilic passage). And Ezekiel, writing from within the Exile itself, is equally convinced that the purpose of God for the line of David must needs continue to stand (34.24; 37.24–25).

The very last words which a redactor has added to the books of Kings while he was in Exile himself is a note to the effect that the last remaining scion of the line had at last received pity and mercy from king Evil-merodach (II Kings 25.27–30), showing that the line of David was still then in existence. His great contemporary, Deutero-Isaiah, consequently could declare with assurance that 'the sure mercies of David' would always stand (Isa. 55.3). This latter phrase comprises another adjective from *'aman*, actually the word *ne'eman*, 'faithful', in the plural, along with the plural form of the word *hesedh*. The phrase therefore embodies the faith that the evidences (plural) of God's faithfulness to the covenant which he had made with the line of David were still valid and sure despite the seeming destruction of the royal line (cf. Ps. 89.1–4).[7]

(2) *The Branch*. The fall of Jerusalem, and the seeming end to the dynasty, occasioned the use by more than one prophet of a pictorial representation of the indestructibility of the Davidic line owing to the faithfulness of Yahweh. The pictorial epithet to which we now refer is that of Branch. However, that translation of the word does not convey the correct image to the mind. If we can envisage the stump of a mighty tree (in this case the stump of a spreading Vine) that has been felled and dragged away, we shall better understand the imagery contained in the various Hebrew words used by the prophets. The stump that is left looks dead and useless, and may remain so for several seasons. But one succeeding spring the seemingly dead stump sends up from its very base below the soil a little shoot or sucker (*tsemah*, Jer. 23.5; 33.15; *hoter* and *netser*, Isa. 11.1; *yoneq*, Isa. 53.2) reaching up to the air out of the dry ground now watered by the winter and spring rains of Palestine. When once it appears, the hope based upon the tree is renewed, and all the virtue in the roots pours afresh into that slender shoot. In terms of this picture, then, Isa. 11.1 speaks of a sucker issuing once again from the stump and roots of Jesse (the father of David). Jer. 23.5; 33.15 and Zech. 3.8 provide us with the same picture though they use a different word, viz. *tsemah*. In fact, the very name of Zerubbabel ('shoot from Babylon') provides Zechariah with grounds for a hope of the resurrection of the line of David (Zech. 3.8; 6.12) now that the Return has taken place.

Here we point to two motifs evident from the use of this figure.

(i)   The sucker emerges, not from David, but from the roots from which David himself springs (Isa. 11.1). In other words, the promise is independent of the line of David κατά σάρκα, after the flesh, just as it is independent of the People of God κατά σάρκα (pp. 255 ff.).

(ii)   The death-and-resurrection motif is as apparent in this the messianic theme of the line of David (cf. Ps. 20.6–8) as it is in the case of God's dealings with Israel as a whole.

---

[7]   Cf. W. Vischer, *Die Immanuel-Botshaft im Rahmen des koeniglichen Zionsfistes*, TS, No. 45, 1955.

(3) *The Royal Psalms*. It would appear (though this is only an inference) that each member of the line of David, when he ascended the throne, was hailed with a messianic enthusiasm. Thus Ps. 2 speaks of the king as God's *mashiah*, and calls him God's adopted son. In that Psalm he is God's king *par excellence* (v. 6), so that the whole world will become his possession (vv. 8–9).[8] Ps. 110 begins in a like strain: 'The Lord said unto my lord, Sit thou at my right hand, until I make thine enemies thy footstool'. Unbelievable blessings are bestowed upon the king in Ps. 21.4: 'He asked life of thee, and thou gavest it him, even length of days for ever and ever'. Ps. 45 actually goes the length of addressing the king, not merely as God's adopted son, but as God himself (v. 6).[9]

There can be no doubt about the background of thought displayed by these psalms. Such phrases do not express mere flattery, such as has surely been accorded to kings in all ages. They display the faith that, sinner though he undoubtedly was, the king as he sat upon the throne was a promise of something much greater than himself still to come. The king is the symbol of what the messianic line may be in the sight of God. The king may be just, even as God is just (Ps. 72.1), and righteous, even as God himself is righteous (Ps. 11.7). It would seem that Isaiah saw his beloved king Hezekiah in just such a 'messianic' light,[10] although he must have been well aware that Hezekiah was a weak and vacillating monarch (cf. Isa. 39); and a century later Jeremiah seems to have thought the same of the attractive young king Josiah, under whose reign he was living. After the return from Exile, the prophet Haggai (2.23) seems to have regarded Zerubbabel, who was of the Davidic line, but who was an ordinary, despondent human creature all the same, in the same messianic light; and the prophet Zechariah also seems to have

---

[8] See Ringgren, *The Messiah in the Old Testament*, 1956, pp. 11–24.

[9] The Targum of this Psalm and Midrash Rabba 41.5 (Soncino Edition, 1951, III, pp. 474–5), also on this Psalm, both works, of course, originating from the Christian period, regard the king in the light of the idea of bridegroom. Cf. pp. 323 ff.

[10] See S. Mowinckel, op. cit., p. 155.

favoured him (6.12) in this extraordinary way.[11] None of those very human kings, surely, was really conceived by contemporaries as Messiah himself. Of no human king could it be said that he would reign for ever (Ps. 72.5). But each pointed, it would seem, beyond himself to the meaning and purpose of his office. In fact, he pointed to the day when *yahweh malach*, when Yahweh would become king indeed over the people of his choice (Ezek. 20.33).

(4)   *The Enthronement Festival*. A number of scholars regard the so-called 'Royal Psalms' in an additional light. Pss. 24, 47, 72, 96, 99 and others, as this group points out, may have been composed originally for what may be called Israel's 'Covenant Festival'. That festival possibly coincided with the feast of Booths, which fell in the autumn of the year (I Kings 8; 12.32–33). Other scholars, arguing from the fact that other ancient nations practised an 'enthronement festival' which they held on their New Year's Day, have made the suggestion that it was rather Israel's New Year's Day that certain of the royal psalms (e.g. 132), along with other cultic material which has not survived the ages, were sung annually in the king's honour. As part of the ritual performed on this annual occasion by some of Israel's neighbours, the king was symbolically struck on the face by the High Priest of the cult. He was meant to die from the blow, so that he acted the part of the vegetation god of the Near East, who died each year. Then he was symbolically raised to life again, as part of the same sympathetic magical rite. By means of this second action, the god of vegetation too came alive again. Thus the king ensured the nation's livelihood once again. Few scholars, however, would suggest that this ritual actually took place in the case of Israel's king. But a number have suggested that the topic of some of the psalms to which we have alluded is the hailing of the king's victory over the powers of evil, a victory such as only God can win; in fact that these psalms form

---

[11]   The problem of whether it was Joshua or Zerubbabel, or both, whom Zechariah hailed in messianic terms is beyond the scope of our present inquiry. The Commentaries deal with the problem.

part of a re-enactment at Israel's New Year's Day ceremony of the events of primal time. These psalms, they suggest, speak of the judgement of God's and of Israel's enemies, and link up this judgement with the meaning of the creation of the world, and with the covenant that God had made with Israel at Sinai. If it is indeed true that all such ideas can be read into these psalms, then the latter are 'messianic' indeed. This is because in them it is really Yahweh who is hailed as king and conqueror over the powers of evil (Ps. 97.1; 98.1, etc.), even though it is the human king who is once more set upon the throne. That is to say, they express in terms of an acted mythology the whole cosmic purpose that God intended to bring to fruition through Israel and through Israel's kings.[12]

(5) *Some Messianic Passages.* There are certain so-called 'messianic' passages, only upon two of which we shall elaborate. These speak of one who will act for God in a manner such as God alone can act.

---

[12] Of the several possible studies of the subject in English, the two following are the most significant: (a) A.R. Johnson, *Sacral Kingship in Ancient Israel*, 1955. Johnson rejects the theory of Israelite divine kingship. While seeing no evidence that Yahweh was regarded as a dying-and-rising God, yet he believes that many of the psalms reflect a ritual combat re-presented at certain of the Israelite festivals. He does not, however, find the king to take the *rôle* of victorious God, but rather believes that the king was delivered by God in the course of a ritual which is designed, not to exalt the king, but to exalt the power of God. (b) S. Mowinckel, op. cit. Mowinckel also, against the prevailing 'Scandinavian' school, denies that Yahweh was thought of as a dying-and-rising God, or that there is any cogent evidence of the cultic or mythological identification of the king and the fertility god. Rather he sees the content of a future hope in those psalms which declare the kingly reign of Yahweh, as the human king assumes his place at 'Yahweh's right hand' Ps. 110.1). He understands 140 psalms as 'cult-Psalms'. Thus 'cultic actuality' describes what he means when others speak of 'prophetic symbolism'. But see also A. Bentzen, *King and Messiah*, 1955; H. Ringgren, op. cit., 1956; and W. Vischer, *Die Immanuel-Botschaft im Rahmen des koeniglichen Zionsfestes, TS, No. 45, 1955.*

(i) Isa. 9.2–7. In this passage the significance of the coming one is seen to be in line with God's cosmic purpose as God continues to bring light out of darkness. His coming will be a true breaking of the yoke; it will be the emergence of joy out of sorrow, it will signify victory out of defeat, and life for those who dwell in the shadow of death. This coming one will emerge from the very fires of God himself (9.5). The 'death-and-resurrection' motif, visible throughout the whole OT, is quite explicit at this point. A child will be born, the travail of whose birth will be exceedingly costly. But out of that pain will arise one of the line of David. He will thus, on the one hand, be a human being, but on the other hand, he will bear rule in a manner that is not possible for a human being to do. The increase of his government and the bringing in of what must be God's *shalom* (since man's conception of it is so limited) will never cease. This perfect rule will bring with it perfect 'justice', or 'true religion', *mishpat*, as well as 'righteousness', or even 'victory', *tsedhaqah*. This coming ruler's name is one of significance. We recall how a man's name is ideally – and surely it is the ideal that is referred to here – a description of its owner. His title is in four parts. This is possibly in contrast to the four-worded description of the powers of evil let loose, and mentioned by Isaiah in 8.1, viz., *maher-shalal-hash-baz*, 'haste-spoil-speed-booty'. He is to be a (*a*) *Wonderful Counsellor*. The root *pele*', 'wonder', is the nearest that Hebrew can offer to our idea of 'supernatural'. But since to the Hebrew mind the natural is at the same time the supernatural, because this is a sacramental universe, then our English word is not a true translation of the Hebrew. But the word *pele*' definitely connotes that which impinges on the consciousness of man from the 'other world'. Consequently Isaiah uses the root to describe the 'otherworldly' greatness of God himself. In Isa. 28.29 Yahweh is said to *hiphli*' '*etsah*, 'show marvellous, otherworldly, counsel'. (*b*) The coming figure is to be Hero-God, i.e., one who is human, yet divine. The paradox becomes clear when we remember that Isaiah uses here the phrase, *'el gibbor*, a description which, in 10.21, is applied to Yahweh himself; whereas in Ps. 89.19–20 the line of David becomes gibbor because God, 'el, sets his own strength in it. (c) He is to be *Father for ever*, i.e., a king whose reign will know no end (cf. Ps. 21.4). Such an epithet could, of course, be applied to Yahweh alone. In II Sam. 7.14–16 God had promised to be a Father for ever to the line of David (cf. also Ps. 89.26; 132.11–12). (d) He is to be *Prince of shalom*. This latter word covers, of course, the wide sweep of meaning which we have examined. It refers no less than to the fulfilment of God's cosmic plan. The significance of the word becomes clear to us when we read that the commission given to this king is to expand his kingdom in such a manner that he will bring order out of chaos. Yet it will not be he who does it. 'The zeal of the Lord of hosts will perform this' (Isa. 9.7).

(ii) *Isa. 11.1–5*. This passage is allied to the one above, and complements it. It probably originates from a later period in Isaiah's career.[13] Once again we note that it is the line of David to which reference is made. And once again it is envisaged that supra-human attributes will be seen in one who yet is a human person. It will be the spirit of Yahweh which will 'rest' quietly upon him. It had been 'an evil spirit from Yahweh', we recall, which had 'leaped upon Saul' of old (I Sam. 18.10; cf. Judg. 6.34; I Sam. 11.7; II Sam. 23.2). But now the spirit will rather rest, nuah, upon him, as it had once before upon Noah, *noah*, at the time when the waters of Chaos subsided at the Word of the Lord and the Ark 'rested' on mount Ararat (Gen. 8.4). This individual will possess what seem to be the 'seven eyes of God' (Zech. 4.10; cf. Rev. 5.6), although of course we are not in the position to make the identification. Moreover, it is later generations, particularly the LXX, which find here the 'sevenfold' Spirit of God (cf. Rev. 10.4). However that may be, the latter is to equip him to effect his task as ruler intellectually, practically, and religiously. The Law will no longer be necessary, since

---

[13] See discussion of this point by G. Fohrer, 'Zu Jes 7.14 im Zusammen-hang von Jes 7.10–22', *ZAW*, 1956, pp. 54 ff.

social justice will follow immediately from his authority. He will be the champion of the weak and humble, and will find himself in deadly combat with the godless and the tyrant. Our picture displays a solidarity between leader and those who are his people that is in conformity with the Hebrew view of society which we examined in Part One, chap. 2.[14] He will need only to speak, and his word will at once be effective, and will not return unto him void.[15] We have noted, of course, that this is a feature of the power of the Word of Yahweh himself. Again, righteousness, or victory, and faithfulness, or steadfastness, both of which belong to the saving activity of Yahweh, are to be as true to his nature as a man's girdle is close to his body.

The other passages that are usually placed in the same category as the above two are Micah 5.2–7; Jer. 23.5–8, along with a later version of the same oracle, Jer. 33.15–16; also Isa. 61.1–3; and Zech. 9.9–10[16] These passages together declare that the Spirit of Yahweh will rest upon this coming figure; that he will exhibit in himself the motif of victory out of defeat, of new life out of sorrow and death; that his concern will be with the poor, the sick and the outcast; and that his message will be the coming of the kingdom of *shalom.*

(6) *The Holy City.* It was the genius of David to choose Jerusalem to be the capital city of his united kingdom. Jerusalem lay between Judah and Ephraim, like a Canberra between New South Wales and Victoria. No old loyalties clung around it; but David instituted a new loyalty centred on himself as he dwelt within the 'City of David' (II Sam. 5.9). Again, he made Jerusalem the centre

---

[14]   Cf. Mark 8.38 (the reading of *W* and *k*) and Matt. 18.20; 25.40–45: 'Whosoever is ashamed of me and mine, etc'; and, 'Saul, Saul, why persecutest thou *me?*' See A.M. Hunter, *Interpreting Paul's Gospel,* 1954, p. 39 and p. 43.

[15]   See V. Herntrich, *Der Prophet Jesaja, Kap.* 1–12, *Das Alte Testament Deutsch,* 17, 1950, ad loc.

[16]   For a discussion of these passages, see H. Ringgren, op. cit., pp. 25–38.

of the cult, and the wandering Ark now found a permanent home. Moreover, it found a home where a tradition many centuries old was firmly rooted. The tradition was that Melchizedek had been priest there long before (Gen. 14.18). So great a priest-king had he been that he alone, in the name of the Most High God, had been in the position to bless Abraham; one would have expected rather that the father of the People of God would have blessed Melchizedek. Moreover, as a still later tradition saw the encounter (Heb. 7.1–4), this priest's name was King of Righteousness (i.e. Victory), and also King of Peace, *shalom* (or Salem);[17] so 'unearthly' was he in fact that he had neither father nor mother, having gained his authority directly from God. Such then was the divinely ordained origin, so the tradition ran, of the choice of yerush-shalom as the City of David. (See p. 251.)

The OT speaks of God's choice of David *and of Jerusalem*,[18] as well as of David's choice of the city as his own. This is true especially of the Deuteronomist. It was in Jerusalem that David was ever to have a *nir*, viz. Yahweh himself (II Sam. 22.29). As Noth points out,[19] this is probably the same word as *ner*, a 'lamp'. The Hebrew home had a light over its door, as a sign that the family was in existence, that is, had not died out. But *nir* also means 'newly broken ground', and so was a metaphor for 'a new beginning' (Jer. 4.3; Hos. 10.12). Noth therefore suggests that the true meaning of the words in I Kings 11.36: 'That David my servant may have a lamp always before me in Jerusalem' (cf. the 'perpetual lamp', Ex. 27.20; Lev. 24.2), is actually 'that David my servant may have a new beginning always before me in Jerusalem'. Perhaps, too, the word nir, he suggests, stood originally for the ner of the MT of Ps. 132.17: 'I have ordained a new beginning for mine anointed'. If so, it forms a good parallel to the word

---

[17] The biblical writers were not concerned to remember that the name came originally from that of a Canaanite god. See p. 250 n.

[18] M. Noth, 'Jerusalem und die israelitische Tradition', *OS*, Deel VIII, pp. 28 ff. See I Kings 8.16 LXX = II Chron. 6.6; I Kings 11.13, 32; Ps. 132, where Jerusalem is connected with the Davidic promise in II Sam. 7. Cf. also Isa. 31.5.

[19] Ibid.

'atsmiaḥ in the first half of the verse: 'There I will make the horn of David to *bud*', or, 'send up a sucker', *tsemah*.

As the divinely ordained city, then, and containing as it did the Temple built by Solomon, Jerusalem was recognized to be no less than the 'mountain of God's inheritance' (Ex. 15.17, and many pss.). Accordingly, it was hailed as God's footstool on earth (Lam. 2.1), or as 'the place of God's feet' (Ezek. 43.7; Zech. 14.4). It was, of course, 'the place which God chose to cause his name to dwell there' (Deut. 12.11, etc.); it was the place of the Holy of Holies, that spot where God 'dwelt' between the cherubim. The same verb *yasadh* is used of God's 'founding' the earth (Ps. 24.2; 104.5) as of the founding of the Temple (I Kings 5.17; Isa. 44.28; Ezra 3.10). The Temple on Zion hill was regarded latterly as the epitome of the cosmos,[20] just as the Tabernacle in the Wilderness had been built after a pattern existing in the heavens (Ex. 25.9, 40; Num. 8.4). The Altar of burnt offering within the Temple, too, had cosmic significance of its own. Its base was called 'the navel of the earth' (Ezek. 38.12), and its upper stage 'the mount of God' (Ezek. 43.12.[21] From it too, 'in that day', the river of life would flow to give life to the dead (Ezek 47.1–12; Joel 3.18; Zech. 13.1; 14.8), issuing probably out of the Rock or Stone which Yahweh would lay in Zion.[22] We can thus understand why the significance of Jerusalem later forms one of the great themes of the Chronicler.[23]

In I Kings 6.23, again, we read that Solomon constructed the cherubim 'within the oracle', the *debhir*, the place from which God spoke, *dabhar* (or the usual form of the verb, *dibber*). We saw in Part Four, chap. 20, that the phrase was frequently used of God's indwelling presence in the Temple (cf. II Kings 19.15; I Chron. 13.6; Ps. 80.1; 99.1; Isa. 37.16; etc.). No wonder then that men called Jerusalem 'the Holy City'. Pss. 120–30 are known, in the AV, as 'Songs of degrees'. These psalms, and others even more probably, were sung by pilgrims as they mounted the 'degrees' or

---

[20] P.A.H. de Boer, *OS*, Deel II, pp. 171 ff.

[21] W.F. Albright, *Archaeology and the Religion of Israel*, 1942, pp. 148 ff.

[22] Thus S.H. Hooke, op. cit., p. 246.

[23] See W. Rudolph, 'Problems of the Books of Chronicles', *VT*; IV, No. 4.

steps up to the Holy City from the Kidron valley, in praise of Yahweh who 'dwelt' within his Holy Temple. They prayed 'Shalom be within thy walls, O *yerush-shalom*' (Ps. 122.7), and they did so even in those periods when they knew that corruption and idolatry were rife even amongst the priestly circles (cf. II Kings 23). No more revealing picture of the atrocities and evils perpetrated *within* the very Temple of Yahweh has been penned than that to be found in Ezek. 8, a state of things that obtained evidently between the two sieges of the city (598 and 587 B.C.), a time when one would have thought that the priests would have taken the seriousness of events to heart.

Jerusalem, then, always meant more to its lovers than what the mere earthly city revealed. Even when it lay in utter ruins, God himself saw it 'graven on the palms of my hands'. In Babylon men were in the habit of tattooing the name of their god upon the palm of their hand (Isa. 44.5). This was in order to direct their loyalty to the god whose name lay before their eyes. Deutero-Isaiah now actually suggests (Isa. 49.16) that God has changed places with the pious human worshipper. In his fascinating little cameo, he declares that it is God who has tattooed forsaken Jerusalem upon the palms of his hands. But what God sees is not a mere heap of rubble. What God sees is the true Jerusalem, now complete and whole, its (rebuilt) 'walls are continually before me'. The Jerusalem which God sees is of course the Jerusalem that shall eventually be.[24] Therefore it is that 'in that day' Jerusalem will be the Holy City indeed. The Ark of the covenant will be there no longer (see p. 224), because God's presence will be known with a fulness beyond that symbolized by the *'ohel mo'edh*, the Tent of Meeting, of the Wilderness period (Jer. 3.16–19). 'In that day' it will be unique amongst all cities (Isa. 2.2; Micah 4.1), 'and all nations shall flow into it'. It is not that every human being in the world will go, but *'many* peoples' shall invite one another to go, since it is in Jerusalem that God teaches men of his ways (Isa. 2.3); 'for out of Zion shall go forth the law' (not the Law already given at Sinai, since *torah* has a much wider connotation in the prophets than that – see pp. 236 ff.), but 'the word of the Lord from Jerusalem'. Thereupon

---

[24]   See G.A. Smith, *The Book of Isaiah*, XL–LXVI, 1890, p. 385.

God himself will bring to reality the significance of the City's name, since he will have put his own *shalom* therein. It is not men who will create this peace. All that men will be left to do will be to beat their swords into plough-shares, and their spears into pruning hooks; and they will do so because God will have put a new spirit within their hearts. 'And they shall call thee, the city of the Lord, the Zion of the Holy One of Israel' (Isa. 60.14; cf. Zech. 14.21).

This, then, is why, in OT times, men could sing with joy and pride about the Holy City. The city they sang about was not the empirical city with all its sin and impurity, but the city as it was in God's eyes, and as it therefore would one day become (Ps. 48.1–5; Ps. 50.2; Lam. 2.15). Thus 'in that day' the whole world would speed to the Holy City (Zech. 8.21; Ps. 86.9). Yahweh would then be its wall (Zech. 2.4–5). Out of it would flow living waters (Zech. 14.8). Living waters produce life, not chaos. The barren hills of Judah would once more be productive when those waters flowed, and even the Dead Sea would once more be 'alive' and give fish as food for man (Ezek. 47.1–12).

What we observe in the thought of the Hebrews about their capital city, then, is a conception which is fully in accord with their unified view of all creation. The Holy City, at whose battlements they gazed in awe and love, was not only the earthly city of Jerusalem. It was, in a real sense, the centre of the universe. This was because it was a city with significance, a significance which could be understood only in terms of the divine purpose for all mankind.

(7) *The Holy Land*. As we are well aware, we can make few dogmatic statements about the historicity of the period in Israel's story before the occupation of Canaan in the days of Joshua.[25] Consequently we are not in the position to know what the Israelites really thought of its hills and valleys before the conquest. Yet in the 'sermon' passages of Deuteronomy (see particularly Deut. 8), we are given, *post eventu*, a glowing picture of the land of 'brooks of water, of fountains and depths that spring out of

---

[25]   For an extreme exposition of this view, see M. Noth, *Geschichte Israels*, 1950; and for a critique of Noth's presuppositions, see J. Bright, *Early Israel in Recent History Writing*, 1956.

valleys and hills; a land of wheat, and barley and vines, and fig-trees . . .' (Deut. 8.7–8). In comparison with the Sinai peninsula and the *negebh* region, and the 'impossible' wilderness in the physically depressed area known as El Ghor lying to the south of the Dead Sea, through which Israel supposedly marched, Canaan must have appeared to her conquerors as a paradise indeed. Yet within its bounds lie many barren hills, and dry terraced slopes, down which water rushes for a few days in the year, only to leave them thirsty and brown for the other eleven months ahead; there is the awesome desert of Judah, a stone's throw from the Holy City itself, the area which Moses would see first as he gazed from the slopes of mount Nebo; and at every peasant's back-door there ever lay the wilderness, the *midhbar*, against which he had ceaselessly to fight as he sought to preserve his *sadheh* or cultivated patch of soil from reverting to the desert.[26] Throughout the whole monarchical period the Philistines held the only good and fertile plain in Canaan, so that the Israelites themselves were relegated to the barren hills. Yet this desiccated plateau, this semi-arid ridge of hills, was known as a 'land flowing with milk and honey', as 'the most glorious of all lands' (Ezek. 20.6, ARSV), or even as a 'heritage most beauteous of all nations' (Jer. 3.19 ARSV).

The eschatological significance of the land of Canaan is thus highly apparent.[27] That barren area of the earth's surface was naturally beloved by those who were born upon it, and by those who were exiled from it (Ps. 137; Dan. 8.9; 11.16, where it is called 'that glorious land'). But since 'milk and honey' was the food of the gods (see pp. 210 f.) in the ancient world, Israel must certainly have applied the phrase to their own land in an ideal manner. They would look back upon the Wilderness journey and see how Yahweh had invited his people to 'sup' with him in *his*

---

[26]   See the vivid chapter in L. Koehler's *Hebrew Man*, English translation 1956, pp. 101 ff., where he describes the ordinary peasant's constant battle with starvation.

[27]   See Hugo Gressmann, *Der Ursprung der israelitisch jüdischen Eschatologie, 1905, p. 210. Gressmann also quotes H. Usener, Religionsgeschichtliche Untersuchungen*, III, 1899, p. 177 and p. 192, in this connexion.

land (cf. Deut. 32.13–14). In Israel's early period, Canaan was Yahweh's land in the primitive sense that each god had his own land, who could not be worshipped in the territory of another god (cf. II Kings 5.17). But the great prophets knew that Yahweh was Lord of the whole earth – and yet, Canaan was his land, *the* land. The Hebrew word *ha-arets* in many occurrences is difficult to translate. It may mean 'the earth', or it may, and often does, mean '*the* land' *par excellence*.

The Holy Land, then, like the Holy City, was not merely the rather barren land of Canaan. Since Canaan was the special land of the holy God, it too was holy, and so had a significance beyond itself. 'In that day . . .', when the coming redemption would be complete, it was not only Israel who would be truly married to God, Israel's Holy Land too would be married to him (Isa. 62.4). What this extraordinary image really implies we shall see presently, once we have discussed a few more of the 'strands' of Israel's eschatological hope.

(8) *The Ideal Priest*. The office of the priest is, of course, both universal and ancient. David established a regular priesthood in connexion with the cult. It was not long before the leading priest became known as *the* priest; and after the Exile he was entitled the High (Great) Priest. But the king originally could act as priest. We read of David's offering sacrifice (II Sam. 6.17), and of Solomon's doing likewise after he had dedicated the Temple (I Kings 8.62). In later years Jeremiah saw no inconsistency in such an action by a king (Jer. 30.21). Ezekiel therefore looked to the day when the 'prince' would once more offer sacrifice after the Exile was past (Ezek. 45.22). The Chronicler thereafter looks upon his hero, David, as the perfect priest-king. Immediately upon the return from Exile, the messianic significance attached to the pre-exilic king seems actually to have been divided between the secular governor and the new High Priest (Zech. 6.9–15). But later, when there was no secular governor, and the High Priest was both 'king' and priest, it was natural that his office should take on a very deep significance. He lived in the City of David. It was there that Melchizedek, the 'unearthly' priest-king (see p. 306) had ruled in days of old. The messianic priest-king of later

years could therefore be hailed in the following terms: 'The Lord hath sworn, and will not repent, Thou art a priest for ever after the order of Melchizedek' (Ps. 110.4). But since all Israel would one day be 'the priests of the Lord' (Isa. 61.6), the High Priest, contemporary and ideal at once, must then have been the representative of the whole People of God. On some occasions he was representative only of the priests as a class. Yet even then he and they together were regarded by Zechariah as 'men of a portent' (Zech. 3.8; cf. Isa. 8.18); that is, by the fact of their very existence, Zechariah regarded the priesthood as a promise of 'my servant the Branch' still to come. The priesthood was itself an *ecce homo*, 'Behold the man whose name is the Branch' (Zech. 6.12). Thus he made it clear that the one who was to come would not be a mere individual, but, as it were, the head of a corporate body.[28]

At this point we might connect the significance of the High Priest with the theme of 'life-through-death' which we have now done with other strands. A. de Buck points out[29] that the High Priest wore a golden flower on his turban or mitre (Ex. 28.36; 39.30; Lev. 8.9). The Temple, too, was decorated with flowers (I Kings 6.18, 29, 32, 35), and more particularly the two frontal pillars were crowned with lily, or lotus, flowers (I Kings 7.19, 22). The Hebrew understood the flower as the symbol of fragility and mortality (Isa. 40.6–8; Ps.103.15–16; Job 14.1–2; Ps.90.5–6). Yet here it is set in a place of honour. Did Israel in this connexion borrow from Egypt and other nations the additional conception that the lotus is the symbol of vital life? Thus when the High Priest stood within the Temple, did the flowers on his headdress and on the building of the Temple together symbolize man's frailty and at the same time God's purpose to renew his life like the eagle's? Both Isa. 40.31 and Ps. 103.5 show a belief in just such a juxtaposition of the renewing of life with the frailty of the flower.

(9) *The Return of the Time of Moses.*[30] Moses had been the great figure in the past. Under the hand of God he had led his people

[28] J. Herntrich, *TWNT*, IV, art. λῖεμμα, pp. 198 ff.
[29] *OS*, Deel IX, pp. 18 ff., 'La Fleur au Front du Grand-Prêtre'.
[30] This phrase comes from H. *Gressmann, Der Messias*, 1929.

in the Exodus from Egypt to the new and promised land. It would seem that the conception slowly grew that what God had done before he could and would do again. Even as early as the eighth century B.C. Isaiah was beginning to use the figure: 'O my people that dwellest in Zion, be not afraid of the Assyrian: he shall smite thee with a rod, and shall lift up his staff against thee, after the manner of Egypt . . . and as his rod was upon the sea, so shall he lift it up after the manner of Egypt' (Isa. 10.24–26). Micah, Isaiah's contemporary (if this passage is in fact from his pen), uses language that employs the same picture: 'According to the days of thy coming out of the land of Egypt will I show unto him marvellous things' (Micah 7.15; cf. Hos. 2.16–19; 12.9; Jer. 3.18; Zech. 10.11).

But it is Deutero-Isaiah who develops the conception to the full; in fact, the new Exodus is one of his main themes. His comforting words begin at once with the announcement that God is about to rescue his people from Babylon (Isa. 40.3–5); and just as the glory of the Lord had already been revealed at Sinai, so it would be revealed again. He returns to the theme in 51.9–12, pointing out that God had once before made a way for his people through the Red Sea; and in 52.12 he refers to the haste of the Passover festival in Egypt. Other passages, difficult to date, keep referring to this hopeful theme. Thus Isa. 19.23–25 speaks of the equating of Babylon with Egypt in God's plan of redemption; the lyrical passage, Isa. 35, sings of the coming Return by a highway through the desert; and the theme is echoed and taken up in Isa. 62.10. Who then was to lead the new Exodus?

When the first Return did actually take place, presumably about 537 B.C., it seems to have been led by Sheshbazzar (Ezra 1). But the eschatological hopes of the people failed to materialize on that occasion. It is of a very ordinary, human community that we read in the books of Haggai and Zechariah, both of whose utterances are dated for us at about 520 B.C., and we know virtually nothing about the personality of Sheshbazzar himself. Fifty years or so later again, Malachi once more lifts the curtain upon a despondent and disillusioned people. How was it then that Israel never abandoned wholly her eschatological hope? The answer would seem to lie in her unshakable faith in the significance of her election. We have seen (Part Four, chap 25 (3)) that, following upon Isaiah's lead, the '*am yahweh* learned to look back upon the age of Hezekiah as an intimation, a first instalment, a pledge, '*erabhon* (Gen. 38.17–18), or ἀρραβων as it is written in NT Greek (II Cor. 1.22; 5.5; Eph. 1.14) of the final messianic age. The latter, by the very nature of Israel's faith, was bound to follow the granting of the first instalment. King Josiah's age, with the discovery of the Code of Deuteronomy, and the attempt to put its precepts into practice, may also, even to his contemporary, the prophet Jeremiah, have seemed to be just such an ἀρραβων of the future. Haggai and Zechariah, once again, believed the same of their contemporary leaders. But the story does not end with them. The Dead Sea Scrolls are no more part of the OT than is the Apocrypha, and therefore do not contribute to our knowledge of its theology. Yet we are interested to observe how a like belief in the eschatological significance of a contemporary leader is still apparent in the second and first centuries B.C.. The so-called Teacher of Righteousness of the Qumran Community is sketched, not as a divine, but as an ordinary human figure; yet the covenanting community to which he belonged, so far as we can judge from those texts which are now available to us, was evidently looking to the day, still to come, when the Sons of Light would win the final war against the Sons of Darkness.[31] Would their Teacher of Righteousness still be alive when that 'new Exodus' began, or was he but a 'type' of the final Messiah still to come? Probably the Covenanters could not, or would not say. Yet obviously they believed sincerely that they were living in the 'last days' as an eschatological community. The same outlook has been true of many waiting groups within Jewry right down through the Christian centuries.[32]

---

[31] *The War of the Sons of Light and the Sons of Darkness*, translated by T.H. Gaster, in *The Scriptures of the Dead Sea Sect*, 1957, pp. 257 ff. Also M. Burrows, *The Dead Sea Scrolls*, 1956, pp. 390 ff. Gaster (p. 15) prefers to translate the title as 'right-teacher'.

[32] See J. Klausner, *The Messianic Idea in Israel*, 1955. In the NT, it is interesting to note the words spoken at the Transfiguration by Moses himself, who 'spake of his (Jesus') exodus which he should accomplish at Jerusalem' (Luke 9.31).

It is with the return of the *time* of Moses that we are here concerned. The Hebrews conceived of time quite differently from us. To the Hebrews time was identical with its substance (see p. 102). Time was identical with the development of the very events that occurred in it. For example, the OT offers us such phrases as: 'Time is rain' (Ezra. 10.13): 'This is the law . . . to teach the *day* of being unclean' (Lev. 14.57); 'I will certainly return unto thee when this time comes alive again' (Gen. 18.10; cf. II Kings 4.16).[33] The 'Day of the Lord' was thus a term full of 'substance', and was not just a mere calendar date. Nor did it suggest to the ancient Hebrews a mere philosophical idea. It referred to a fulness of time when God would act once again within history, with a great plenitude of purpose comparable with that which he had already revealed 'at that time' in the past (Deut. 1.9, 16, 18; 2.34; 3.4; etc.).[34]

(10)   *That Prophet.* No nation in all history has ever possessed a succession of guides and interpreters such as Israel knew. Hosea, Isaiah, Jeremiah and others are great figures by any reckoning. Yet it was the figure of Moses that evidently dominated the thought of Israel when the word 'prophet' fell from the lips of her people (Ex. 4.10–12). Moses was that prophet, under God, who had brought the people of Israel into being as a nation in the beginning. And so he could be set over against and contrasted with even the mighty figures of the eighth century prophets. In the NT, for example, one finds the phrase 'And beginning at Moses, and all the prophets . . .' (Luke 24.27). This was because, in the Deuteronomic material compiled during the period of the great prophets, a prophet 'like unto me' (Moses) was mentioned, whom God would one day raise up (Deut. 18.15). In the post-OT period, men speculated greatly on the identity of this prophet, but until a prophet arose who would act in a manner similar to Moses, and, under God, effect a like redemption, no individual could be given the significant title.

---

[33]   As translated by Johs. Pedersen, op. cit., I–II, p. 48.
[34]   See John Marsh, op. cit., p. 47.

On the other hand, Deut. 18.15 may equally well be translated 'The Lord thy God will raise up unto thee prophet after prophet . . .' While Moses dominated the origins of Israel's story, others too, such as Samuel, were held in the highest regard. Jeremiah even places Samuel alongside of Moses: 'Then said the Lord unto me, Though Moses and Samuel stood before me . . .' (Jer. 15.1; cf. Ps. 99.6). The NT regards the work and person of Elijah to be as important as that of Moses (Matt. 17.3=4 = Mark 9.4–5 = Luke 9.30–33), and Elijah at that time was evidently expected to return to earth again (Matt. 11.14; 16.14 = Mark 6.15; Luke 1.17, etc.; cf. Mal. 4.5). How then are we to reconcile the two traditions, (a) that Moses was the all-important prophet, whose *alter ego* would lead Israel in a second Exodus (cf. Luke 9.31), and (b) that all the prophets in succession and not just Moses, had an eschatological significance? The answer is to be found in the prophetic view of Israel's history as Heilsgeschichte, as indeed 'sacred history', the arena on which God's purposes were working out for the redemption of the whole world. We have already referred to this conception in chapters 13 and 20.

The story of the People of God is full of crises, καιροί, 'decisive moments'. At each of these crises God raised up for Israel an interpreter, a prophet, who expounded the ways of God to his contemporary generation.[35] Moses was that great prophet to whom the Lord spake 'face to face, as a man speaketh unto his friend' (Ex. 33.11). We remember that a Semitic people is not afraid to present truth in daringly pictorial language. A few verses further down we read: 'Thou canst not see my face: for there shall no man see me, and live' (Ex. 33.20. V. 11 is probably from the hand of E, and v. 20 from the final editor). Consequently we are not to take Moses' 'seeing God face to face' in any literal sense. Later prophets had the advantage of being able to look back upon the Exodus nexus of events and realize, *post eventu*, how God had indeed been active in those far-off days to redeem his people. But Moses was in a different category. Not only did he live through those events, but he was in a sense partly responsible for them. It

---

[35] See J.R.Coates, *The Saving History*, 1951.

was his faith on which God had been able to build when virtually all Israel fell into despair and apostasy (Ex. 32). Moreover, no events preceded the Exodus with which Moses could compare his own experience of the leading of God. Moses had to interpret contemporary occurrences *ab initio*. (What traditions about the patriarchs Moses possessed it is now impossible for us to know.) That is why Moses' faith is in a different category from that of all those who came after him. All who came after him could build upon him, upon the interpretation of God's mighty acts which Moses had now made once and for all (cf. Ps. 78.2–8; 105.5; 106.7–8). As one of the great eighth century prophets himself declares, it was Moses who interpreted the whole 'crisis' from Egypt even to Gilgal, that is, right until the moment of entry into the Promised Land (Micah 6.4–5).

The second great crisis arose with the loss of the Ark of the Covenant in battle with the Philistines (I Sam. 4.11). With the capturing of the outward symbol of the indwelling Presence of Yahweh with his people, the end might have come to the religion clustering round this box. Till that period Israel had been but an amphictyony of tribes, that is, an association of clans whose only link was a common faith. Samuel was the important figure, however, who guided Israel through that crisis and interpreted it for her life and future. If there had been no Elijah, again, the difference between Baal worship and Yahweh worship might not have been understood by Israel. The shattering blow of the loss of the northern kingdom, too, was expounded by the great eighth century prophets, both before and after the events; and Jeremiah was the one raised up by God to interpret the mighty 'crisis' of the fall of Jerusalem in 587 B.C. Ezekiel expounded God's purposes in and through the Exile, and Deutero-Isaiah was the interpreter of that significant 'moment' which we call the Return from Exile. Haggai, Zechariah, and Malachi, each in their own way, taught Israel God's purposes for them in the period which succeeded the fourth 'moment' (see Part Four, chap. 17) of the Return, as Israel sought to adjust herself to live 'between the times'. And finally, Trito-Isaiah and Deutero-Zechariah, and the later 'insets' within the prophets, such as the apocalyptic chapters we know as Isa.

24–27, give all the exposition necessary for the coming great fifth
'moment' in God's plan. From now on, therefore, prophets are no
longer necessary (Zech. 13.2); in fact, they are now a meaningless
anachronism. The whole five-moment cycle of revelation has been
fully interpreted, and nothing can now be added to that revelation
(see p. 213). It is Apocalyptic that now takes up the tale and which
is the successor of the Prophets. This is because Apocalyptic is
concerned with the nature and the significance of the fifth 'moment' which is not yet here, and which can only be described in
symbolic language. In the same way, once the apostolic witness
to the 'five-moment' cycle of revelation in Christ was concluded
by the death of those who had actually seen and known Christ in
the flesh, the Church closed the Canon of its new sacred literature.
Yet before doing so, it permitted within the Canon certain Apocalyptic descriptions of the ultimate end and purpose of God
through the Christian revelation. But thereafter any subsequent
tradition about Christ was considered secondary to the once-for-
all first-hand apostolic witness. The expectation of a coming
prophet, then, which is evident at the beginning of the first
Christian century (John 1.21; 7.40), *despite* the declaration of
Zech. 13.2–6, gives evidence that a prophet was expected who
would not merely add to the succession of OT prophets, but who
would sum up in himself the whole 'five-moment' prophetic
interpretation of the history of Israel.

(11) *The Sabbath*. The origins of the Sabbath are obscure, and
do not concern us here.[36] Amongst the Hebrews, however, the
Sabbath became a unique institution. By the era of the Maccabees,
it was the observance of the Sabbath which marked off the Jews
from all other peoples (I Macc. 8.27; 15.1 ff.). The day was a day
of shabhath, of 'cessation' from work (Ex. 23.12; Amos 8.4–6).
Therefore on it one 'took breath', *yinnaphesh*, and relaxed in joy
(Ex.31.17). It was a day of worship (Isa. 1.13), the day when one
could learn the will of God (II Kings 4.22 f.). This precious
possession of Israel was written into her statute book (Ex. 20.10),

---

[36] See *EB*, art. 'Sabbath', column 4179.

and men were taught to 'hallow' it for its own intrinsic value (Jer. 17.22, 27). The profanation of the day was later on regulated against both by example (Num. 15.32 ff.), and by command (Lev. 16.31; 19.3, etc.).

But being the precious gift it was, it therefore stood for more than a mere weekly day of rest. Israel learned to associate the origin of the Sabbath with the Covenant given at Sinai. God's *hesedh*, his loving bond with Israel, must surely have included in it this precious gift (sc. 'Yahweh hath *given* you the Sabbath – Ex. 16.29). So the Sabbath command became part of the Covenant (Ex. 20.10). In fact, it came to be regarded as a 'sign', *'oth*, of that Covenant (Ex. 31.17, P). On the other hand, the Sabbath is to be found preceding the giving of the Law at Sinai! (Ex. 16. The Sabbath must therefore embody an eternally valid conception, so the argument must have run, valid even apart from its incorporation in the Sinai Covenant. And since it is 'eternally valid', then its validity must pervade both 'heaven' and 'earth'. In fact, God himself must know what it means to keep the Sabbath. How can such a belief on Israel's part be substantiated?

The 'Fourth Commandment' (as it is numbered by the Reformed Churches) embodies in full the theology of the Priestly Code in this connexion. Its final clause, in the form of a sanction, runs thus: 'For in six days the Lord made heaven and earth, the sea, and all that in them is, and rested the seventh day; wherefore the Lord blessed the Sabbath day, and hallowed it' (Ex. 20.11). On the other hand, the Sabbath is not mentioned in P's narrative of the Creation (Gen. 1.1–2.4a). There we read: 'And on the seventh day God ended his work which he had made; and he rested on the seventh day, . . . and sanctified it: because that in it he had rested from all his work which God created and made' (Gen. 2.2–3). What we are told is that God 'finished' his work, and 'ceased' *shabhath*, from working. In the Fourth Commandment, however, the priestly writers definitely associate the verb *shabhath* used of *man's* cessation from work, with the noun 'Sabbath'. But then they proceed to give content to the cessation from work by commanding Israel to 'rest', *nuah*, as *God himself had rested on the seventh day* and had even *yinnaphesh* (see above), had 'taken breath' (Ex. 31.17,

P) as men are accustomed to do (Ex. 23.12, E). That is to say, they unify the concept of the Sabbath with the day of rest.

We recall that, in his significant inaugural vision, Isaiah beheld God in his holiness as he is beyond and outside of space and time. We have seen too that in the OT 'creation' and 'redemption' are mutually understandable terms (Part Three, chap. 14). Thus the Rest into which God has entered in his eternal Sabbath must be one which he is even now enjoying, since he has already entered into the End of his purpose of redemption. Obviously this truth must be held in tension over against that other with which we have occupied ourselves so much, viz., that God shares even now in the pain and suffering of his people, Israel. The eschatological significance of the OT Sabbath, then, rests in this, that the Sabbath is obviously still another pledge of the future, this time of the Rest of God himself. The Sabbath God has given to Israel to enjoy here and now. On the other hand, it is to be regarded as a pledge of the completion of the *gift* to come at the time of the End. Long after the entry into Canaan, a Psalmist could write, speaking of disobedient and backsliding Israel: 'I sware in my wrath, they shall not enter into my rest' (Ps. 95.11). The very fact, however, that 'the Psalm was written long after the entry into Canaan shows that the promised Rest is not the settlement in Palestine under Joshua mentioned in Josh. 21.44; but that "There remaineth therefore a Sabbath-rest for the People of God" (Heb. 4.9, with reference to Ps. 95.6–9).'[37]

(12) *The Virgin.* It seems that the inhabitants of a city in OT times could be considered as one unit in the feminine gender, possibly because the word for city, *'ir*, is feminine. Thus the inhabitants of Babylon are known as 'daughter of Babylon' (Ps. 137.8; Zech. 2.7), and those of Sidon by a like expression (Isa. 23.12). Again, the citizens of a whole land (*'erets* also is feminine in Hebrew) could be similarly addressed. Thus we find such phrases as 'daughter of Egypt' (Jer. 46.24), 'daughter of the Chaldeans' (Isa. 47.5), and 'daughter of Edom' (Lam. 4.21–22).

---

[37] A.G. Hebert, op. cit., p. 157.

Now, these two usages occur in the OT with reference also to the city of Jerusalem, and to the People of God.

Thus, firstly, 'daughter of Zion' is a common appellation of the people of Jerusalem as a whole.[38] In Micah it occurs four times, in Isaiah five times, in Jeremiah three times, in Lamentations three times, and so on. 'Daughter of Jerusalem' is a variant of the above (e.g. Zeph. 3.14; Zech. 9.9). Then, secondly, 'daughter of Judah', or 'daughter of my people' is found once in Isaiah, eight times in Jeremiah, and four times in Lamentations.

Now, in a manner exactly parallel to the above, the phrase 'virgin daughter of . . .' is employed both of foreign peoples (Isa. 23.12; 47.1; Jer. 46.11) and of Israel as the People of God. The LXX actually increases the number of usages, showing that by the end of the OT period the phrase had gripped the imagination of Israel's scholars. Of Israel, the phrase in its various forms occurs in Amos 5.2; Isa. 37.22; Jer. 18.13; 31.4; 31.21; Lam. 1.15; 2.13. Thus, in a word, several of the great prophets of Israel conceived of the chosen People of God in terms, amongst others, of a 'Virgin' daughter.

Now, as we have seen when discussing the figure of 'Bride' (Part Three, chap. 15 (4)), it is seldom possible to discern from the Hebrew context whether the reference is to a 'newly-wed' or only to one who has been espoused, and therefore still a virgin. Isa. 7.14, 'Behold, a virgin shall be with child . . .' is notoriously difficult to translate. The Hebrew word used is *'almah* meaning 'a young woman of marriageable age, whether married or not'. The strict word for virgin, viz., *bethulah*, is not that which occurs, although the LXX translation of *'almah* at this point is παρθένος a 'virgin'. On the other hand, in Joel 1.8 we find the phrase: 'Lament like a virgin, *bethulah*, girded with sackcloth for the husband of her youth'. However, in this case the command is directed to *all Israel*, so that all Israel is no other than the Virgin Daughter of God at the same time as being his Bride. The Isa. 7.14 passage, on the contrary, is best understood to refer to Isaiah's

---

[38] For a fuller discussion, see 'The Virgin and the Old Testament', *RTR*, Vol. XII, No. 1, Feb. 1953, pp. 1 ff.

own young wife. The birth of the latter's child within the next few months would then be a sign that the Covenant God had not forsaken his people, but was undoubtedly in their midst. It is thus rather the name Immanuel, 'immanu-el, which is the theologically important word in this context. Since the name means 'God is with us', the utterance of it makes the same kind of declaration about the God of Israel and his living purpose as does the name 'I will become with . . .' that occurs in Ex. 3.12. Then, of course, since God 'becomes with . . .' the generation of Isaiah, he continues to become with Israel until the moment when this Word too becomes flesh.

We bring to our aid at this point an important element in Israel's thinking. We recall how the 'one' could represent the 'many', and how one individual could thus represent and even sum up in himself the whole People of God. Now, nowhere in the OT is it explicitly claimed that Israel as the Virgin Daughter falls into just such a category of thought, and that the Virgin People of God would one day be represented by one particular Virgin Daughter still to come. On the other hand, the LXX, at the close of the OT period, is not alone in enlarging upon the figure of the Virgin in this typically Hebraic light, since the Dead Sea Scrolls do so as well.[39]

One of the Thanksgiving Psalms of the Community (1 QH iii), echoing various passages in the other Scrolls, and using language reminiscent of the early Hymns in Luke's Gospel,[40] employs more than one of the images which we have handled in our study. The psalm declares that this flourishing tree (*sc.* 'Vine'), the true Remnant (obviously the Qumran Community itself), is about to produce out of its roots a shoot, *netser* (or Branch), the very word used in

---

[39]   Many scholars now believe that the divergencies of the LXX text with which the Scrolls often agree, including the more frequent use of the Virgin figure, may not be mistranslations of the MT after all. They see them rather as representative of a variant Hebrew reading. This suggestion, however, must not be pressed without further prolonged study of the Scrolls.

[40]   Charles T. Fritsch, *The Qumran Commnunity'*, 1956, p. 35.

the OT by Isaiah and Jeremiah of the coming Messiah. This Branch will be born of the Virgin, who is none other than Israel herself (see Joel 1.8, referred to above), or at least Israel as she is represented by the true Remnant. He will be born, as are all babies, through the pain and suffering of the mother. The pains of travail evidently represented the persecution which the Community was then undergoing at the hands of the Roman (or Seleucid?) Empire. Israel was then pregnant, the Virgin was about to bring forth a child. Then there follows a passage about which there has been much discussion, but which seems to run: 'From the womb of her who is pregnant burst forth a wonderful counsellor with his might'.[41]

While a Theology of the OT cannot make use of post-OT literature of any sort, yet we would do well to recall that the OT canon was not yet closed when the Qumran Community was in being. It is therefore interesting to us to recognize that members of the Community at the end of the OT period were bringing together in their thoughts several of those OT images which we have already found to be vitally important for an understanding of God's purpose with Israel, viz., Branch, Remnant, Vine, Virgin, Isaiah's 'Wonderful Counsellor', and Bride; and as well, the profound conception of the death-and-resurrection motif as it is exemplified in the figure of the pains of childbirth.

(13) *The Bride of God.* At this point the 'Virgin' figure overlaps that of the eschatological 'Bride' of God. It was to be 'at that day' (Hos. 2.16; see Part Four, chap. 18) that Israel was to call her divine Lover *'ishi* my – monogamous – and therefore true husband), and no longer *ba'ali* (my lord or master). Then only would it be that the Virgin Daughter of Israel would be revealed in all her beauty. The sinful Bride is portrayed as truly beautiful only when she is radiant with the knowledge of sins forgiven, and of the possession of a righteousness which is not her own, but that of her heavenly Lover. 'For Zion's sake will I not hold my peace, and for Jerusalem's sake I will not rest, until her righteousness,

---

[41] J.V. Chamberlain, *JNES*, Vol. XIV, 1955, pp. 32 ff. See also R. Gordis, 'The "Begotten" Messiah in the Qumran Scrolls', *VT*, 1957, April, pp. 191 ff; Cf. Jer. 31.22.

tsedheq,[42] go forth as radiancy, *nogah*, and the salvation, *yosha'ah* (which she has been granted) thereof as a lamp that burneth. And the Gentiles shall see thy glory (cf. Part One, chap. 8); and thou shalt be called by a new name (i.e. she will receive her Husband's name, or nature, at marriage), which the mouth of the Lord shall name . . . and as the bridegroom rejoiceth over the bride, so shall thy God rejoice over thee' (Isa. 62.1, 2, 5). The identification of the Virgin Daughter with the Bride as the Remnant of Israel is apparent in a number of passages. 'In that day, says the Lord, I will assemble the lame . . . and those whom I have afflicted; and the lame I will make the remnant; and those who were cast off, a strong nation; . . . and you . . . hill of the daughter of Zion, to you . . . the former dominion shall come . . . Writhe and groan, O daughter of Zion, like a woman in travail . . .' (Micah 4.6–8, 10 ARSV). 'For I heard a cry as of a woman in travail, anguish as of one bringing forth her first child, the cry of the daughter of Zion gasping for breath, stretching out her hands, "Woe is me! I am fainting before murderers".' (Jer. 4.31 ARSV; cf. also Jer. 6.24; Isa. 26.17; 66.7–9.)

As we have seen, Israel must have accepted the fact that the rule of God over all his creation included his lordship over death. It was natural then that along with such a faith went the corollary that God could just as easily 'make alive' as he could destroy. Two out of the several declarations of faith which the OT offers us contain this view. The 'Song of Hannah' includes the words: 'Yahweh killeth and maketh alive: he bringeth down to Sheol, and bringeth up' (I Sam. 2.6). The longer poem, the so-called 'Song of Moses', is even more explicit. In language reminiscent of Deutero-Isaiah it begins: 'See now that I, even I, am he, and there is no god beside me; I kill and I make alive; I wound and I heal; and there is none that can deliver out of my hand. For I lift up my hand to heaven, and swear, As I live for ever . . .' (Deut. 32.39–40). Here it is not merely from sickness that Yahweh is able to save. He does not just 'make alive again' a man who had drawn near to death.

---

[42] We recall that *tsedheq* is God's righteousness; *tsedheqah* is man's. See p. 245 n.

We are left rather with the implication in our minds that, since God is the living God, it is not beyond his power to give life even to the dead. The biblical emphasis is that it is sin which brings the death of man (Ezek. 33.10). Should the day come that God might overcome the power of sin, then with sin would go the power of death. It was the tree of life which God put in the Garden of Eden in the first place (Gen. 2.9) according to the J narrative, representing God's initial purpose for man. 'As I live, saith the Lord God, I have no pleasure in the death of the wicked; but that the wicked turn from his way and live: turn ye, turn ye from your evil ways; for why will ye die, O house of Israel?' (Ezek. 33.11). A similar emphasis was made by Hosea two hundred years before the time of Ezekiel. He was faced, not with the Exile under the hand of Nebuchadnezzar but of the Assyrian power that overran his northern Ephraim in 734 and 722 B.C.. 'I will ransom them', says God, in Hos. 13.14, 'from the power of the grave; I will redeem them from death'. We omit the following two lines of the Hebrew from our discussion, since the text is not easy to decipher, and any translation we could reach would be controversial. It is the principle rather that we are to grasp here, that God is as able to bring alive again as he is able to bring to the birth.

(14) *The Suffering Servant*. We concluded our study of the Suffering Servant in Part Four, chap. 24, by recognizing that the Servant could be understood at the same time both in a corporate and in an individual capacity. The translators of the LXX evidently had such a concept in mind when they gave us the Servant passages in Greek. In all probability they were but incorporating into their translation of Deutero-Isaiah the results of theological discussions upon the Servant passages that had been carried on within Israel since the return from Exile, and since Deutero-Isaiah's writings had become available.

The English of Isa. 53.2 runs: 'He shall grow up before him as a *tender plant*', the two latter words rendering the Hebrew *yoneq*. The LXX, however, unexpectedly renders this Hebrew word by the Greek παοιδιον, 'little boy', or 'child'. Thereafter that verse parallels the concept of 'child' with the idea of 'root', that is to say, of the root which springs forth from the thirsty ground. Now, it is revealing to us to discover that the LXX translators of the passages Isa. 7.16 and 9.6 (which speak of the messianic child), have rendered the Hebrew words which they find in those passages, viz. *na'ar* and *yeledh*, both of which mean 'child', by this same Greek word παοιδιον. Thus the Greek παοιδιον is equated on the one hand in the LXX with the idea of Root, or, as we saw, rather with the word 'sucker', and on the other hand, is used as a translation of the Hebrew words that describe the messianic child. Thus the LXX virtually identifies the messianic child with the Root (or Branch, or Sucker), such as we have referred to in the phrase 'the root of Jesse', remembering that in Hebrew poetic parallelism 'tender plant' and 'root' are two words used to describe the same idea. Yet now, in Isa. 53.2, we find that the Root is also equated with the Suffering Servant!

We must now set this particular equation alongside another to be found within the same poem, viz. in Isa. 52.13. There we read in the LXX the words: 'Behold my παῖς shall understand . . .' where in Hebrew we have *'abhdi*, 'my Servant'. Now παῖς has more meanings than one. Firstly, it is virtually identical with the word παοιδιον though the latter by rights is the diminutive form of παῖς. But secondly, παῖς may convey the idea both of 'child' (or 'son') and of 'servant'. Thus, in translating the Hebrew *'ebhedh*, servant, by the word παῖς the LXX has deliberately equated the subject of the verse Isa. 52.13 with the 'tender plant' of Isa. 53.2, and so, as we have seen, with the 'root' which is none other than the root of Jesse. The Servant has now become, for the LXX, the Servant-Son, and the Servant-Son is implicitly declared to be none other than the messianic king to come, representative, in his turn, of the whole corporate Body of the People of God.

The Qumran Community, once again, seems to have been thinking along the same lines as the translators of the LXX. The Community calls itself, amongst other titles, by the name of the maskilim,[43] a title given to the righteous Remnant of Israel in the virtually contemporary, biblical book of Daniel (Dan. 12.3, 'they that be wise'). Earlier in the book of Daniel, a valuable *midrash*,

---

[43] *DSD*, IX, 12.

or interpretative story, had shown how, back in the days of the Exile, the Remnant of Israel, focused in three representative Israelites, had come through the fires of God unscathed, because God himself, in the person of 'a son of God', or of 'a son of the gods', had been with them in the furnace (Dan. 3.13 ff.). Yet this community was now about to sum up the Remnant, the *maskilim*, in the person of one man.

The word *maskilim* comes from the root *s-k-l* in its Hiphil form; the latter may be translated to mean 'to act wisely in such a manner that one's actions are effective', i.e. have practical results. Now, Isa. 52.13 has 'Behold, my servant *yaskil*, will act wisely, with effect'. I.Engnell suggests that it is no coincidence that this word is used of the Servant who is to be the instrument of God's purpose. We recall that just to eat of the fruit of the tree of the knowledge of good and evil was sufficient to make one wise as *'elohim*, divinity (Gen. 3.5–6); again, he suggests that it is not surprising to find the word repeated here and in the title of Ps. 45, the most typical of the 'royal Psalms'. This, he says, is because in each case we are supplied with a suggestion of victory of life over death – the death-and-resurrection motif once again.[44] So it would seem that the Covenanting Community identified itself with the Remnant of which the OT speaks, the Remnant which, in its turn, was summed up in the single figure of the Suffering Servant.

Again, the text of Isaiah in the St Mark's (A) Scroll, which comes from the library of the Qumran Community, has a variant reading of interest. Where the MT of Isa. 52.14 reads in the AV: 'His visage was so marred more than any man', that of St Mark's (A) Isaiah reads: 'I have anointed his visage more than any man'. The Hebrew consonants are *m-sh-h-t*. The MT vowels them as mishhath, seemingly a construct form, even before the following *min* (an unusual grammatical form). But the consonants might equally well have been vowelled as *moshhath*, as some have suggested they should be, i.e. as a Hophal, passive participle, yet in the end producing much the same meaning as the vowelling found in the

---

[44] ' "Knowledge" and "Life" in the Creation Story', in *Wisdom in Israel and in the Ancient Near East*, 1955, p. 117.

MT. But the Community has read the word as *mashaḥti*, merely adding a final *yodh* to the verb. They would thus have understood the word to mean: 'I have made him Messiah' beyond all men. Now, it is not suggested that the St. Mark's MS has preserved a better text than the MT. All that we can say at the moment is that this is the text which the Community did in fact use, wherever they found it, or even that this *yodh* they deliberately added for dogmatic reasons. But the result was that they were thus identifying themselves, as the Remnant, with the person of the Messiah himself. Incidentally, NT scholars have been largely of the opinion till recent years that the first identification of the messianic king with the Suffering Servant was made in the mind of Christ himself. In the case of the Qumran Community, therefore, we have evidence of at least one group within the OT heritage which had made this particular identification before the birth of Christ at all.

(15)   *God's Coming Intervention.* 'At that day', not only will a human king of the line of David rule; the 'Day of the Lord' will be primarily the Day of the LORD. There is a number of sub-strands of this essential and central aspect of Israel's thought.

(*a*)   *The divine Judge is coming.* At present he is in a continual state of controversy with his people (Micah 6.1–3); but that will not last for ever. 'For he cometh to judge the earth' (Ps. 96.13). Then his *mishpat* will finally prevail (see p. 244). But 'to judge' and 'to help' or 'to save' are parallel ideas in the *OT*!(cf. Isa. 1.17; Ps. 7.8; 26.1; 35.24; 43.1)

(*b*)   *The Good Shepherd.* When the shepherd lad, David, was anointed king over the people of Judah, he became the shepherd of men instead of sheep (Ps. 78.70–72). It may well have been David, the traditional writer of some of our Psalms, who introduced to Israel the image of God as the Shepherd of his people (cf. Ps. 100.3). Thus God is hailed, in our comprehensive Ps. 80, with the words, 'O Shepherd of Israel'. In Ezekiel's day, however, the human shepherds of Israel had wholly failed their flock (Ezek. 34.1–10). Therefore it was God alone who could be the good Shepherd (Ezek. 34.11–19), as Deutero-Zechariah also realized in the later postexilic period (Zech. 11.15–17; 13.7). Ezekiel, however, united as one action the coming of God as Shepherd with the appearance of the Davidic king (Ezek. 37.24).

(c) *God is coming as Saviour, moshia'.* God has already saved in the past. But 'at that day', still in the future, 'he will come and save you' (Isa. 35.4). Even should we assume that Isa. 35 is from the pen of Deutero-Isaiah (about which there is a difference of opinion), the hope expressed in this lyrical chapter was not fulfilled with the Return from Exile: 'sorrow and sighing' did not 'flee away' when Israel returned to the ruins of Zion (v. 10). Yet the Return was a true 'pledge' of God's ultimate act of salvation still to come (see § 10 of this chapter). The verb *yasha'*, as we saw in Part Four, chap. 20, has as its root the conception of 'to be wide'. The Israelites, confined to their narrow hills and valleys, always felt danger lurking behind their back. From over the crest of a hill an arrow could fly from a bow sped by an enemy hid from all sight. The Hebrew used to believe that it would be good to live on a flat, open plain, where he could see an enemy from afar. Then he would be able to lie down without fear of molestation. The Psalmists spiritualized this longing: 'He brought me forth also into a broad place' (Ps. 18.19; 31.8; 118.5) they sang, in the knowledge that God, the *moshia'* (the Hiphil participle of the verb with a transitive sense), had given them peace from their enemies. Thus they could be absolutely sure that 'at that day' God would finally give his people real *shalom*: 'For the Lord is our judge . . .' (cf. (a) above), 'the Lord is our king; he will save us' (Isa. 33.22); 'I will save my people from the east country, and from the west country; and I will bring them, and they shall dwell in the midst of Jerusalem: and they shall be my people, and I will be their God, in truth (i.e. in faithfulness) and in righteousness' (i.e. with a victorious outcome, Zech. 8.7–8). Moreover, that such is a hope of much more than salvation merely out of trials and troubles, many a Psalmist could testify, since he already possessed in his own heart a 'pledge' of the coming salvation. 'The Lord is nigh unto them that are of a broken heart; he saveth such as be of a contrite spirit' (Ps. 34.18).

In connexion with this particular 'strand' of the messianic hope, we may again notice two 'motifs' emerging. (i) Israel seems to have been aware of the significance of the name of her great hero of old, Joshua. In Hebrew the name is *yehoshua*ʻ, and means 'Yahweh saves'. Her appreciation of the relationship of Joshua to God is visible in the curious wording of Deut. 31.3, where, as we have already noted (see p. 201), both Joshua and God perform an identical action. Joshua thereupon 'saves' Israel *into* her new life in Canaan. The saving activity of Joshua in this regard is virtually that of the Word of God become flesh, as we see from the last phrase of the verse, 'Joshua, *he shall go over before thee*, as the Lord hath said'. The entry into Canaan is thus the pledge of God's final action as Saviour that is bound to follow from that which he has already performed through Joshua.[45]

(ii)   The second motif emerges from the individualizing of the experience of *shalom* to which we drew attention above. Individuals within Israel, in God's final action of salvation, are to be saved from the chaos that is to be found within the human soul, that chaos which is the counterpart of the *tohu* in the cosmos at large: 'Behold, I have taken out of thine hand the cup of reeling, even the dregs of the cup of my fury; thou shalt no more drink it again' (Isa. 51.22), so that the individual believer may now cry: 'I will take the cup of salvation . . .' (Ps. 116.13; cf. Micah 4.10; 5.3; and Part Two, chap. 12).[46]

On that day, then, the individual is to be healed by God so as to know that 'wholeness', both of body and of mind, which is

---

[45]   We recall that the Hebrew behind the name Jesus is almost identical with the Hebrew name for Joshua. Deut. 31.3 thus incidentally enlightens the significance of the words which Joseph heard in his dream (Matt. 1.21): 'And thou shalt call his name JESUS, for "he" shall save "his" people from their sins'. We see therefore that we are to place this verse alongside the great declaration of St Paul: 'God was in Christ, reconciling the world unto himself' (II Cor. 5.19).

[46]   On the basis of these passages we see how this motif continues into the NT. This cup was the cup referred to in Matt. 20.22–23 = Mark 10.38; Matt. 26.39 = Mark 14.36 = Luke 22.42 = John 18.11, which, when it was drunk, rendered possible the offering of the new cup of the New Covenant (Matt. 26.27–28 = Mark 14.23–24 = Luke 22.20; I Cor. 10.16; 11.25).

implicit in the term *shalom*; the brokenhearted will be bound up (Isa. 61.1), but the blind also will see, and the lame will walk, and even leap as an hart (Isa. 35.5–6).

(16) *The New Covenant.* Although the old Covenant, imposed upon Israel by Yahweh at Sinai, is central to the thought of the whole OT, yet that Covenant is not the foundation upon which all OT theology is built. That foundation is the fact of Israel, coupled with God's choice of that people to serve him in a unique manner. The Covenant made at Sinai was but the means whereby God bound Israel to himself so that she might become his instrument. Since it is God's gracious grasp upon Israel that is the *continuum*, upon that people which is God's abiding instrument both of revelation and of redemption, then the Covenant itself could conceivably outlive its usefulness.

Jeremiah understood this at as early a moment in Israel's story as that when Judah was in imminent danger of collapse. The period of Covenant relationship he then saw to be drawing to a close. But since God's faithfulness was greater than the terms of any covenant, he realized that the Covenant made at Sinai would not necessarily stand for ever. Since the mighty purposes of God were about to enter upon a new phase, once the lesson of the 'death-and-resurrection' of Israel had been demonstrated and learned, then it was obvious to one of his depth of insight into the purposes of almighty God (Jer. 23.18) that God would one day impose a new covenant upon Israel to fit the new situation that he was about to inaugurate. Deutero-Isaiah was aware that, although Israel had broken the first covenant, God was stronger than Israel's apostasy. If God were but to become one flesh with the Bride of his choice, then he would accomplish for that Bride what she could not do for herself. God, in Israel, might then produce a fitting instrument to be a light to lighten the Gentiles, and to be his salvation unto the ends of the earth. The new people, although continuous with the old, would then be bound to God in a new covenant to cover the facts of the new situation. 'Behold, the days come, saith the Lord, that I will make a new covenant with the house of Israel, and with the house of Judah: not according to the covenant that I made with their fathers in the day that I took them by the hand (cf. Hos. 11.1) to bring them out of the land of Egypt; which my covenant they brake, although I was an husband unto them (cf. Hos. 1–3), saith the Lord' (Jer. 31.31–32). Rather it will be a covenant of a new nature, because it will be made with a people possessing a new nature. 'But this shall be the covenant that I will make with the house of Israel; after those days, saith the Lord, I will put my law in their inward parts, and write it in their hearts; and will be their God (cf. Ex. 3.12), and they shall be my people' (Jer. 31.33; cf. Ex. 19.6).

Not many years later Ezekiel was impelled to say much the same thing in his own words: 'Then will I sprinkle clean water upon you, and ye shall be clean: from all your filthiness, and from all your idols, will I cleanse you. A new heart also will I give you, and a new spirit will I put within you: and I will take away the stony heart out of your flesh, and I will give you an heart of flesh' (Ezek. 36.25–26).

Here again the individual takes his rightful place in the new Covenant People. Deutero-Isaiah expresses this truth by passing on God's invitation to individual men and women (and his invitation must have included his Babylonian bystanders), sinners and backsliders all, nations known and unknown, 'everyone that thirsteth', to come and eat and drink without money and without price, and receive the blessedness of God's mercy and abundant pardon. Just as God's ḥesedh, his loyal-love to David, had never failed and never would fail, so men and women all would find an equal ḥesedh on God's part as the content of the covenant which he was about to offer to the whole world of men (Isa. 55.1–7).

(17) *The Outpouring of the Spirit.*[47] Ezekiel had declared (see above) that 'a new spirit will I put within you'. He continues: 'And I will put my spirit within you, and (thereby) cause you to walk in my statutes' (Ezek. 36.27). The giving of the Spirit is thus linked (*a*) with the giving of the New Covenant. The Psalmist who wrote the words 'Wash me thoroughly from mine iniquity, and cleanse me from my sin . . . *then* shalt thou be pleased with the sacrifices of righteousness . . . *then* shall they offer bullocks upon thine altar'

---

[47] Cf. p. 86.

(Ps. 51.2, 19) was already beginning to understand what the Prophets believed God would yet do for all Israel. It is natural then that the Psalmist should add to his prayer the words: 'Take not thy holy spirit from me' (v. 11). The nature of the Spirit is described primarily in Isa. 11.2–3 (cf. Part One, chap. 7), where, in its six or sevenfold character, it is shown to be symbolic of the total and comprehensive nature of the presence of God in the coming Kingdom. But the giving of the spirit is thus (*b*) also linked with the coming one of the line of David. (*c*) In the third place, Isa. 61.1–3 outlines the activities of the spirit-endowed Servant who is to come. As Servant, he is to do the kind of things that the coming King is to do. Isa. 42.1 declares that the Servant is the Servant on the very ground that God *will have put* (the Hebrew prophetic perfect) his Spirit upon him. While in Joel 2.28–29 the outpouring of the Spirit will be upon all God's 'servants', both male and female. The word *'ebhedh* is the masculine word for servant. The feminine is expressed by two other nouns, *'amah* and *shiphhah*. *This is so, for example, in the Fourth Commandment, where 'manservant' and 'maidservant' are 'ebhedh* and shiphhah respectively (Ex. 20.10). Since all Israel is called to be God's Servant (Isa. 43.1), the meaning of the passage in Joel is that all members of Israel, both male and female, will, 'at that day', representatively and distributively, become the Servant of God.

Since it is the Spirit of God himself which will come upon the Servant in that day, therefore it is natural that the Servant will do what God does. Right from the beginning, God had shown himself to do and to be what he had declared unto Moses: 'I am the Lord that healeth thee' (Ex. 15.26). Isa. 61.1 makes the connexion clear. 'The Spirit of the Lord is upon me; *because* the Lord hath anointed me (made me messiah) to preach good tidings unto the meek; he hath sent me to bind up the brokenhearted . . .'

Twenty-Six

New Heavens and a New Earth

Life after Death

With a return to the authority of the Scriptures at the Reformation, some Reformers felt that the virtual silence of the OT on the question of life beyond death was a great drawback to accepting it as Christian Scripture. Their fears, however, were groundless. It is natural that they should have approached the OT at that time from the background of philosophical thought which they had inherited with all Europe, and that emerged from the renewed study of the Greek philosophers that was one cause of the Renaissance. Amongst other conceptions that were 'in the air' at that period was the universally accepted doctrine of the immorality of the individual soul. It has been the modern study of the OT itself, however, which has offered the Christian Church a wholly different basis for the Christian hope of a life beyond death, and one that is fully in accord with the hope which the NT proclaims.

A point to which we have now frequently referred in our study is that for the OT writers this life that we live upon this earth is meaningful in itself. It is true that aspects of this life are not always understandable when abstracted from their context in this total faith. Thus the seeming prosperity of the wicked was a subject of much concern to thoughtful Israelites (cf. the books of Job and Habakkuk, Ps. 73, etc.). But it was a subject of concern only until the believer found the answer on returning to the whole view of life that was bound up with his faith in God (cf. Ps. 73.17; Hab. 2.4). The thoughtful Israelite held firmly to the view that the life granted to the individual man or child is a precious gift from God, and that a man's life is filled with intimations of God's grace and love. Even Ps. 73, which we have just quoted, begins with an acknowledgement of such goodness by God to Israel. We wonder today at the zest for life displayed by the great figures of the OT, such as Samson, and David, and Josiah, despite the meagre view they entertained of what lay beyond death. When OT man had lived his life, and was now 'full of days', he seems to have accepted the inevitable with grace. He believed that a good thing was about to happen to him, in that he was about to be 'gathered to his fathers', or 'to his people' (Gen. 15.15; 47.30; 49.33, etc.). The vital significance of this frequently recurring statement we shall see as we proceed. The OT saint consoled himself in regard to his approaching end with the belief that when he died, not all of him would die. Firstly, his 'memory', or his 'name' (these words are equated, e.g. in Ex. 3.15), would live on after him (Ps. 112.6; Isa. 56.3–5), and he knew that in some sense his 'name' was representative of his very personality (Ps. 109.15; Prov. 10.7. See p. 61). This meant that the life of even an obscure Israelite was *meaningful*, and would remain meaningful in days to come. Secondly, he would live on in his children. Just as physical characteristics are certainly transmitted from one generation to another, so too can a child inherit the character of an ancestor dead many years before he was born. This two-fold meaningfulness of the life of an individual Israelite was thus an important factor in inducing him to leave to succeeding generations the best possible heritage of 'name' and character that he was able. In other words, this belief was a potent sanction for the integrating of morality with life. This means that he was less preoccupied with the unknown world beyond death than with a concern for the future of the People of God.

The reason why life, to OT man, was 'good', and not in any sense a vale of tears, was because, while he passed through it, he possessed a personal fellowship with God. The whole book of Psalms testifies to the validity of such a statement. 'Truly God is good to Israel, even to such as are of a clean heart' (Ps. 73.1). 'The Lord is my light and my salvation, whom shall I fear?' (Ps. 27.1). And even though the psalms were sung corporately at public worship in the Temple, yet each individual Israelite, on the principle which we brought forward in the previous chapter, could personalize and individualize the words, and regard himself as God's individual 'holy one' (Ps. 16.10).

We have now to remind ourselves who this 'holy one' was who knew the reality of the fellowship of God here and now. We recall that the Hebrew language has no word to represent our modern idea of the 'self'. We saw that Hebrew man knew himself to be an individual only because he first realized his identity as a member of a group, and that he stood or fell with the whole group of which he was a part (Part One, chap. 2). He thus believed that his *nephesh* could not be isolated from the corporate *nephesh* of his people.

Two considerations now call for comment. Firstly, in this view of life we have an adequate reason why the OT saint found it impossible to imagine any life after death that was not lived along with his 'fathers' once he had been 'gathered to his people'. A life beyond death that was not corporate, as life on earth is corporate, just as much as it is an individual experience, was thus naturally beyond the imagination of OT man. The modern view, which is sometimes presented in the name of biblical religion, that, for example, a husband may be invited by God to enter 'heaven', and yet be willing to separate himself from the wife whom he loved on earth, and with whom he has there been one flesh, and let her go to 'hell' because of her unbelief, would be wholly inconceivable according to OT thought. That is to say, the fundamentally selfish conception that an individual man could cut himself off from his brethren and seek salvation for himself in an after life was quite foreign to Israel's understanding of her relationship to God.[1]

---

[1] Cf. Matt. 16.25; Mark 8.35; 15.30–31 = Luke 23.35–39; Luke 9.24; 17.33, etc. Matt. 24.40 = Luke 17.34 obviously draw a line between those who are in the new Israel and those who are not. But in the OT all Israelites are 'in Israel', unless they bring excommunication (cf. Lev. 17.10, etc.) upon themselves.

The second consideration is this. The *nephesh* of an individual person, regarded as an entity in itself, included within it that person's physical organs, in the same way as the individual human *nephesh* was included in the 'body' of his people. This fact presented OT man with a difficulty when he considered the possibility of a life after death. The Psalmist who sang: 'My *nephesh* (soul?) thirsteth for thee, my *basar*, flesh, longeth for thee' (Ps. 63.1), must have seen this difficulty clearly, since he immediately declares thereupon that he is in the position to bless God only so long as he lives in this world: 'Examine me, O Lord, and prove me; try my kidneys and my heart' (Ps. 26.2). The Psalmist knew well that the day would come when his *basar*, the fleshly element in him, which included the kidneys which God was asked to examine, and the flesh that had longed for God, would lie rotting in the ground. He knew from the experience of what it meant to be a man, that when God spoke to his *nephesh*, God was addressing the whole man that he knew himself to be, and that this whole man included his fleshly element. The 'Greek' notion that God addresses merely the human soul, as if the latter were an entity separable from the body, is therefore an idea alien to the Bible. The only verse in the whole OT which even suggests such a possibility occurs in Eccl. 12.7: 'Then shall the dust return unto the earth as it was: and the spirit shall return unto God who gave it'. (See p. 87.) But this writer has been strongly influenced by the philosophy of Greece, and his contribution to OT thought and theology is consequently proffered from outside of the main stream of the Hebraic experience of God.[2]

The logical outcome of this axiom of faith necessarily entailed the conception that when the physical organs perished in death, then the *nephesh* would no longer be a complete entity. Therefore the *nephesh* would not be able to praise God beyond the grave. The psalm which Hezekiah sang when he recovered from a sickness which he had imagined was to be his last, makes crystal clear the logic of Hebrew thought in this regard: 'I said in the

---

[2] H. Ranston, *Ecclesiastes and the Early Greek Wisdom Literature*, 1925; O.S. Rankin, *Israel's Wisdom Literature* 1936, pp. 124 ff.

cutting off of my days, I shall go to the gates of Sheol . . . I said, I shall not see Yahweh, even Yahweh, in the land of the living . . . for Sheol cannot praise thee, death cannot celebrate thee: they that go down into the pit, *bor*, cannot hope for thy truth. The living, the living, he shall praise thee, as I do this day . . . ' (Isa. 38.10, 11, 18, 19).

Such logic, then, arose to plague the 'holy one' who knew the love of God and the wonder of his fellowship in this life.

The Hebrews had, of course, inherited the general ancient near eastern conception of an underworld where the departed might be expected to linger. The word *she'ol*, the name of the abode of the departed, may come from a root meaning 'hollow',[3] since it represented a great cavern in the centre of the earth. At its lowest point, according to the mental imagery of some writers, lay a pit, *shaḥath* (e.g. Job 33.18; Ps. 30.9) or *bor*, the ordinary word for a water-hole (Ps. 28.1; 40.2; Isa. 14.15). The whole was guarded by gates with iron bars (Job 17.16; Ps. 107.16; Jonah 2.6). In some of the earlier passages of the OT we notice that at that time the Hebrews were no farther advanced in their thinking on Sheol than were their pagan neighbours. The departed wore the clothes which they had been accustomed to wear on earth. The prophet Samuel emerges at the behest of Saul wearing his prophet's mantle (I Sam. 28.14); and kings still wear their crowns in the caverns underground (Isa. 14.18, cf. Ezek. 32.25, though Ezekiel is here describing the burials he must have witnessed in Babylon, and which archaeology has revealed to us today). The dead still show some modicum of intelligence, however, and so they are dubbed 'the knowing ones', *yid'onim* (Lev. 19.31; 20.6; Isa. 19.3), even by such a late document as the Priestly Code. The earlier document or tradition lying behind I Sam. 28.13–20 took for granted that the dead could even forecast the future. Because all ghosts

---

[3]   As does the Anglo-Saxon word 'hell'. Another suggestion is that *she'ol* derives from *sh-'-l*, to 'ask', because it was the place of inquiry by means of necromancy. Yet Sheol does not appear to mean such in the OT. L. Koehler suggests that it derives from *sho'ah*, 'waste', 'chaos' (Isa. 6.11), so that Sheol is really the 'unworld'. See his Dictionary, ad loc. See also Part One, chap. 9, p. 117.

belong to the realm of the numinous, the mysterious, the divine, they are even called, in Isaiah's day, *'elohim* (Isa. 8.19; 29.4). On the other hand, some writers envisage the departed as existing, not as knowledgeable creatures, but as merely shadows without bodies, or as continuing a kind of shadowy existence in a profound sleep (Job 3.14–19; Isa. 14.10). The word used here by Isaiah (*repha'im*) may come either from the root 'to be weak' (*raphah*) or else be connected with the *rephaim* or giants who allegedly occupied the earth in olden days (Deut. 2.20; 3.11, 13; Josh. 17.15, etc.). On the other hand, it has been suggested that it comes from the verb *rapha'*, to heal, and so may even have a beneficent connotation.

It is obvious that those who gave us our psalms could not rest content with such primitive views of Sheol. Sheol must be more than a land of shades, of shadows, shadows of the *whole nephesh* (not half of the whole man, not a land of 'souls' as the Homeric poems depict the early Grecian underworld). The shadow of the whole *nephesh* obviously cannot adequately praise its Maker. On the other hand, it was the very logic of the Hebrews in this matter which finally led certain of the Psalmists and the author of Job to approach nearer to the hope of a life beyond death more satisfying than the current doctrine of Sheol with its pit. This logic of theirs was paradoxically no less than the logic of faith. 'Whither shall I go from thy spirit?' sang one Psalmist (139.7), 'or whither shall I flee from thy presence? If I ascend up into heaven, thou art there: if I make my bed in Sheol, behold, thou art there . . . if I say, Surely the darkness shall cover me; even the light shall be light about me'. Had not the God of Israel made the whole earth? Then had he not created Sheol as well? Did his power not stretch down to the realm of the departed? (Num. 16.30). Had not Enoch, who had 'walked with God' in this life, been 'taken', and was he not therefore still walking with God? (Gen. 5.22). 'But God will redeem my *nephesh* from the power of Sheol: for he shall receive me' (Ps. 49.15) is therefore one answer of faith to the problem of Sheol. 'Whom have I in heaven but thee? and there is none upon earth that I desire beside thee. My flesh and my heart will fail: but God is the strength of my heart, and my portion for ever, *le-'olam*'

(Ps. 73.25–26). (See p. 102.) 'Therefore my heart is glad, and my glory (or, perhaps, 'liver' – the consonants are the same) rejoiceth: my flesh also shall rest in hope. For thou wilt not leave my *nephesh* in Sheol; neither wilt thou suffer thine holy one to see the pit' (Ps. 16.9–10) 'O that thou wouldest hide me in Sheol, that thou wouldest keep me secret, until thy wrath be past, that thou wouldest appoint me a set time, and remember me! If a man die, shall he live again? all the days of my *tsabha*, "military service" or "forced labour" (in Sheol) will I wait, till my change (or release) come. (Then) thou shalt call, and I will answer thee' (Job 14.13–15). Finally, we quote without comment upon the text the notoriously difficult passage, Job 19.25–27: 'For I know that my redeemer liveth, and that he shall stand at the latter day upon the earth: and though after my skin worms destroy this body, yet in my flesh shall I see God: whom I shall see for myself, and mine eyes shall behold, and not another; though my kidneys be consumed within me'. Such then are some of the statements of faith that the OT has to give us, of a faith that refuses to accept separation beyond death from the God whom the 'holy one' has known and loved in this life. But of a doctrine of a life after death the OT knows nothing.

The Resurrection of All Things

The logic of her faith, however, led Israel to raise her eyes to very far horizons, and to look for a coming action of God far wider in its embrace than anything which the individual saint alone could ever hope to comprehend. In the first place, the logic of Israel's faith led her 'holy ones' to believe, not in the immortality of a 'soul' which they did not know they 'possessed', but in the resurrection of the whole *nephesh* which they knew themselves to be. The last chapter of Daniel looks to the day when 'many of them that sleep in the dust shall awake, some to everlasting life, and some to shame and everlasting contempt' (Dan. 12.2). Yet Israel's future hope was for much more than even the resurrection of the 'many'. The hope which Israel entertained was the hope of a resurrection, not merely of some in Israel, or even of all mankind, but the hope of a final consummation, of a resurrection, if we may say so, of all creation.

The late apocalyptic insertion in Isaiah (chaps. 24–27) speaks of God's final coming to visit both 'heaven' and 'earth' in judgement and in glory (Isa. 24.16–23). Then, since death itself is part of God's creation, 'at that time' it too will be swallowed up in the final victory (Isa. 25.8; 26.19). This victory will be fully apparent to all eyes, since God will destroy 'the face of the covering cast over all nations'. His action will thereupon be celebrated by a great feast 'on this mountain', that is, on the hill of Zion (Isa. 25.6).

In the preceding chapter we reviewed various 'strands' of the messianic hope. As we did so, we became increasingly aware of what the OT is ultimately looking for. Post-exilic Israel had learned the truth of God's mighty plan for the redemption of his creation 'existentially', so to speak, because Israel had experienced in her own life the faithfulness of God and the transforming power of his union with her. This people was now living restored to its native Judah, yet restored, as it knew well, by the grace of God alone (Isa. 40.3, 10). It was God who had saved, *hoshia'*, Israel, and who had granted her a pledge or a foretaste of that shalom in which he himself dwells eternally (Isa. 66.12). The Restoration after the Exile was therefore but an ἀρραβων of what God must necessarily eventually accomplish, viz., the ἀποκ τάστ σις πάντων, the restitution of all things, to use a NT phrase (Acts 3.21). Again, since Chaos was a state known not only to man, but also both to the inanimate universe and to certain even of the heavenly beings (see Part Two, chap. 12), then the final victory of God must be a victory over sin and 'chaos' in both 'earth' and 'heaven' (Isa. 24.21). Naturally the OT saint could not envisage any such final victory except in pictorial terms, and in terms of the kind of life which he lived here and now upon this earth. But he fully understood, as a result of his own experience of the ways of God with his people, why the 'death-and-resurrection' motif must represent a reality, not only for Israel herself, but for the whole cosmos of God's creation, before the final End could come. 'And I will show wonders in the heavens and in the earth, blood, and fire, and pillars of smoke. The sun shall be turned into darkness, and the moon into blood, before the great and terrible day of the Lord come' (Joel 2.30–31). 'The earth shall quake before them; the heavens shall tremble, the sun and moon shall be dark, and the stars shall withdraw their shining' (Joel 2.10; cf. Joel 3.15; Isa. 9.5; 13.10; Mal. 4.5; cf. Matt. 27.45, 51–53; etc.). 'And all the host of heaven shall be dissolved, and the heavens shall be rolled together as a scroll' (Isa. 34.4; cf. Ezek. 31.16). 'They shall perish, but thou shalt endure; yea, all of them shall wax old like a garment; as a vesture shalt thou change them, and they shall be changed' (Ps. 102.26). This change will only come about through the death of the old creation: 'And nation shall fight against nation till their carcases fill the earth' (Ezek. 38–39); 'I will utterly consume all things from off the earth' (Zeph. 1.2).

One aspect of the change that will take place through this cataclysmic transformation is that 'on that day' the 'curse' imposed at the Fall of man will be removed from nature, and God's condemnation upon all his creation, infused as the latter is with sin, will be at an end (Gen. 3.14–19; Isa. 24.6, 19–23; 25.7). We recall that God's covenant with Noah was to be between himself and the animal creation as well as man. This truth is expressed in poetry, in pictures which portray a new kind of universe altogether: 'The wolf also shall dwell with the lamb, and the leopard shall lie down with the kid; and the calf and the young lion and the fatling together; and a little child shall lead them . . . and the lion shall eat straw like the ox . . . they shall not hurt nor destroy in all my holy mountain' (Isa. 11.6–9 = 65.25). The 'thorns and thistles' (Gen. 3.18), too, will no longer curse the life and work of man. 'The desert (see Part Two, chap. 12) shall rejoice, and blossom as the rose. It shall blossom abundantly, and rejoice even with joy and singing: the glory of Lebanon shall be given unto it, the excellency of Carmel and Sharon, they shall see the glory of the Lord, the excellency of our God' (Isa. 35.1–2). In fact, along with the desert, the Dead Sea itself will come alive and be productive, when the Wilderness of Judah and this the Salt Sea at its feet receive the living waters that will flow from underneath the altar of the living God (Ezek. 47.1–12).

'In the sweat of thy face thou shalt eat bread' (Gen. 3.19). In those words the early theologian of Israel had coupled the curse that rested upon man with the curse that also rested upon the ground. But now God's victory is to bring about a new relationship between man and the soil, and between man and the city which he has built and in which he dwells: 'Instead of the thorn shall come up the fir tree, and instead of the brier shall come up the myrtle tree' (Isa. 55.13). 'There shall yet old men and old women dwell in the streets of Jerusalem, and every man with his staff in his hand for very age. And the streets of the city shall be full of boys and girls playing in the streets thereof' (Zech. 8.4–5). 'In that day, says the Lord of hosts, every one of you will invite his neighbour under his vine and under his fig tree' (Zech. 3.10, ARSV) and the babe will live to see a hundred years (Isa. 65.20). 'But they shall sit every man under his vine and under his fig tree; and none shall make them afraid: for the mouth of the Lord of hosts hath spoken it' (Micah 4.4).

A very 'earthly' hope? Of course. We must ever bear in mind the view of the OT writers over the period of a thousand years that it is this world of space and time which matters. This is because it is here and now that God is working out his mighty plan. Yet, paradoxically, God's plan embraces in its scope, not just this earth, but the whole realm of both heaven and earth. So the OT applies to the realm of 'heaven' what it knows God is doing here and now upon 'earth'. Of course OT man was quite unable to visualize the significance for 'heaven' (as well as for earth!) if man were to beat his swords into ploughshares, if roses were to come up instead of thistles, and if the lion were to eat straw like the ox. Wisely, then, the OT does not attempt to present us with anything like a doctrine of what the new situation will be like once God has brought in his Kingdom of *shalom* under the hand of his Davidic king, apart from the use of terms with which we are familiar here and now. On the other hand, since God has already brought Israel up out of Egypt, and has repeated the action by bringing Israel up from the death of the Exile, then all things are possible to God, whether we can picture them or not.

The Place of Israel in the Final Consummation

'Thus saith the Lord of hosts, If it be marvellous in the eyes of the remnant of this people in those days, should it also be marvellous in mine eyes? saith the Lord of hosts' (Zech. 8.6, RV). We recall that the concept of 'marvel', *pele*', or the plural noun from that root, *niphla'oth*, 'marvellous acts', referred to that which man cannot understand, and is not equivalent to our modern conception of the idea of the 'supernatural'. The ultimate *pele*', then, is to be visualized (not understood intellectually) under two heads.

(1)   God will take home to himself not only the Bride whom he espoused at Sinai, he will also marry the land! 'For thou shalt no more be termed Forsaken: neither shall thy land any more be Desolate: but thou shalt be called Hephzibah (my delight is in her), and thy land Beulah (i.e. *ba'al*-ed): for the Lord delighteth in thee, and thy land shall be married' (Isa. 62.4). (See p. 211 and pp. 309–11.) Just as the marriage of a man with a woman results in the creation of that which is a new thing, viz., a child, so too in the case of the marriage of God and the land of Israel. Deutero-Isaiah had looked to the day when God would both declare and do 'new things' (Isa. 42.9; 43.19; 48.6). Israel had certainly received the pledge of those new things in the restoration of her land of Judah. But now the outcome of the marriage of God to the land of Israel was that there would be a new creation, a new heaven and a new earth (Isa. 65.17; 66.22). In this new creation there would be no room for Darkness, Chaos, or *tohu*.[4] Yahweh would be its Light, and he would be its Glory (Isa. 60.19). The change which God was going to bring to pass must necessarily

---

[4]   We note that, after her own genius, Israel has moved very far in her thinking about the relationship between the male god of the heavens and the female goddess of earth which was characteristic of the Canaanite religions. Baal and his female consort, Asherah or Astarte, were virtually the apotheosis of heaven and earth. See also Rev. 21.1: 'And I saw a new heaven and a new earth: for the first heaven and the first earth were passed away, and there was no more *tehom*'.

affect both heaven and earth *pari passa*. Trito-Isaiah, to whom we owe the very phrase 'new heaven and a new earth', was fully of the opinion that the victory of God would transform the two at once. 'The heaven is my throne, the earth is my footstool' (Isa. 66.1–2). Such a picture demonstrates the view that heaven and earth are equally God's creation, that both are aspects of that one great totality which Jeremiah called *hak-kol* (Jer. 10.16; 51.19; cf. Ps. 103.19; I Chron. 29.12). The city of Jerusalem is more than once described as the actual 'footstool' of God upon earth (Lam. 2.1; I Chron. 28.2; cf. pp. 305 ff.). Jerusalem, as the 'centre' of the Holy Land, is thus only one aspect of the totality, so that the earthly Jerusalem points to a heavenly Jerusalem in a heavenly Holy Land. 'But be glad, and rejoice for ever in that which I create: for behold, I create Jerusalem a rejoicing, and her people a joy' (Isa. 65.18).

Since Trito-Isaiah presents us with truth in picture form, we would do well ever to keep in mind that the coming action of God, in creating new heavens and a new earth, can only be described in such language. The pictures are not to be taken literally. Symbolically they express the *meaning* of the purpose that God is bringing forth out of the present order of creation. The present order ranges in time *me-ʿolam* and continues till *ʾadh-ʿolam* (i.e. from the beginning of God's creative purpose within space and time till the end, the fruition, of that purpose within space and time).[5] What the OT means when it speaks of a new creation in which the Garden of Eden will be restored, not even the OT writers themselves could have declared. But it is evident that, since the pictures of the future embrace within them a redeemed world such as we now know, then the Garden of Eden to come is not just a repetition of the original Garden. Between the Fall and the restoration of all things the history of this world has taken place, and history has been riddled by sin, and by the apostasy and backsliding of the chosen People of God.

---

[5]   H. Gressmann, *Der Messias*, 1929, p. 173. Cf. also Amos 9.13; Joel 3.18; Jer. 33.12–14; Ezek. 34.25 f.; Isa 51.3; Ps. 103.17

In the new Garden of Eden again the wolf and the lion will still be there, though now eating straw like the ox. It is important to recognize that that new state will have occurred only *after* they have torn and destroyed upon this earth. Could any philosophical terms express more clearly than does the above familiar picture the belief that the effect of all the pain and sorrow and sin of God's created world will have been woven into the pattern of the final End and into the content of God's ultimate *shalom*? With such a hope, then, lying before its saints, no wonder the OT has been called the book of joy.

(2) The second aspect of God's ultimate *pele'* has to do with Israel herself 'For as the new heavens and the new earth, which I will make, shall remain before me, saith the Lord, so shall your seed and your name remain' (Isa. 66.22; cf. also 51.16). The zeal of the Lord must perform this, despite all Israel's sin and apostasy, since God can do no other than be faithful to his Covenant. Two hundred years before Trito-Isaiah made this great declaration of faith, Hosea had had the insight to look forward to *two* marriage covenants still to come. He had looked for God's final marriage covenant with the land, and he had looked for the consummation of God's marriage with his chosen Bride, Israel. 'In that day will I make a covenant for them with the beasts of the field, and with the fowls of heaven, and with the creeping things of the ground: and I will break the bow and the sword and the battle out of the earth (or "the land"), and will make them to lie down safely' (Hos. 2.18). After speaking of the covenant that God will make with the land, Hosea then went on to refer to Yahweh's marriage to Israel: 'And I will betroth thee unto me for ever; yea, I will betroth thee unto me in righteousness, and in judgement, and in loving kindness, and in mercies. I will even betroth thee unto me in faithfulness: and thou shalt know the Lord' (Hos. 2.19–20. We need not now pause to analyse any of Hosea's great terms, all of which we have examined earlier). Then finally Hosea links the two covenants together in a great and majestic passage: 'And it shall come to pass in that day, I will hear, saith the Lord, I will hear the heavens, and they shall hear (answer) the earth: and the

earth shall hear (answer) the corn, and the wine, and the oil; and they shall hear Jezreel (meaning "whom God soweth"). And I will sow her unto me in the earth; and I will have mercy upon her that had not obtained mercy; and I will say to them which were not my people, Thou art my people; and they shall say, Thou art my God' (Hos. 2.21–23).

Here then we have the answer to the question whether Israel ever really entertained a resurrection hope, and we find the answer by discovering the place that the People of God had in God's plan for his whole creation. We are to remember that throughout the whole OT period, Israel's corporate relationship to God remains a vital factor in the thought of her prophets and historians (cf. 'Thou art *my* God' Hos. 2.23 above). Although composed of many individual men and women, each of whom God had made, in some sense, in his own image, yet Israel, the People of God as a whole, was in reality one great corporate *nephesh*. It was the people as a whole who had been called to be the Son, so that in the last analysis it was they who were made in the image of God as a corporate entity. But as Son of God (Ex. 4.22) Israel was also Son of man. We have seen in detail how the 80th Psalm, written from within the travail of the Exile, brought together more than one of the images which describe the unique relationship that obtained between this Son and his heavenly Father. In this psalm Israel is the Vine (v. 8), the Son (v. 15b), the Man of God's right hand (v. 17a), and the Son of man whom God didst rear (make strong) for himself (v. 17b). The renewal of Israel 'on that day' must therefore refer to her renewal as a corporate entity, or corporate Body. And as the Body of Israel comprises both *ruah* and *basar*, both spirit and flesh, in the one *nephesh*, so her renewal must necessarily be realized in both realms of 'heaven' and 'earth' at once. On the other hand, this corporate Son is not necessarily to be identified at all times with empirical Israel after the flesh, nor is the true Remnant of Israel likely to comprise merely the lineal descendants of Abraham. Once the Exile was a thing of the past, the People of God had come to realize that they were the People of God by grace alone.

Then we have also seen how the doctrine of the Remnant was integral to the heart and soul of Israel's faith over many centuries of her history, and how that doctrine was firmly bound up with the doctrine of her election. Thus there is no reason to reject the thesis that, one day, in fact, 'on that day', all Israel might possibly be represented and summed up in one man alone. If such should ever be, however, then, according to the genius of Hebrew thought, that one man would still be the Lord, the *'adhon*, the *ba'al*, who would sum up in himself all that the whole People of God was ever meant to be (Part One, chap. 2).

We come then at last to the final vision of empirical Israel which the OT has to give us. It is a vision of Israel as 'the People of the saints of the most High', now identified with the figure of the Son of man, whom the author of the 80th Psalm called also 'the man of thy right hand' (v. 17); and it is to Daniel, the last book of the OT to be penned, that we owe this significant vision.[6] 'I saw in the night visions, and, behold, one like the Son of man came with the clouds of heaven, and came to the Ancient of days, and they brought him near before him. And there was given him dominion, and glory, and a kingdom, that all people, nations, and languages, should serve him: his dominion is an everlasting dominion, which shall not pass away, and his kingdom that which shall not be destroyed . . . I beheld, and the same horn made war with the saints, and prevailed against them; until the Ancient of days came, and judgement was given to the saints of the most High, and the time came that the saints possessed the kingdom. And the kingdom and dominion, and the greatness of the kingdom under the whole heaven, shall be given to the people of the saints of the most High, whose kingdom is an everlasting kingdom, and all dominions shall serve and obey him. Here is the end of the matter' (Dan. 7.13–14; 21–22, 27–28a).

---

[6] For a discussion of the various images, see R.H. Charles, *Commenentay on Daniel*, 1929, p. 187; Wm. Manson, *Jesus the Messiah*, 1943, p. 176, etc.; T.W. Manson, *BJRL* 'The Son of Man in Daniel, Enoch and the Gospels', 1950, Vol. 32, No. 2. See also Part Four, chap. 18 (3).

The people of the saints of the most High are thus finally become the man of God's right hand, or, in other words, they are now 'sitting at the right hand of God'. It is the zeal of the Lord of hosts alone which has performed this.[7]

---

[7] Cf. Matt. 22.44 = Mark 12.36 = Luke 20.42; Matt. 25.33, 34; 26.64 = Mark 14.62 = Luke 22.69; Mark 16.19; Acts 2.34; 5.31; 7.55–56; Rom. 8.34; Col. 3.1; Heb. 1.3; 1.13;8.1; 10.12; 12.2; I Peter 3.22; Rev. 1.20; 2.1.

The question of the relationship of the Son of Man in the Gospels to the Heavenly Man of the contemporary Redemption Myth is no longer a problem when seen in the light of the words of the 80th Psalm. [William Manson, in *Jesus the Messiah*, 1943, presents the problem of that relationship in two useful and succint Appendices, pp. 171–190.] The inter-dependence of the Gnostic concept of a 'heavenly man' and I Enoch 37–71 and parts of IV Ezra is apparent. In these and other extra-canonical works in Son of Man is no longer to be understood in terms of the historical people of God, Israel, but as a pre-existent heavenly being, who has been hidden with God from before the creation of the world. According to this Gnostic thinking, it is a purely spiritual Son of Man who is to come at the End in the clouds of glory. Even the LXX, at Dan. 7.13, departing from Hebraic thought, identifies the Son of Man with the Ancient of Days rather than with empirical Israel. Speculation on the existence of a non-historical heavenly man shows a fear of taking history seriously, and departs in essence from the OT conception of the nature of God as one. It leads to a non-Hebraic separation between matter and spirit, and is thus the virtual denial of the relevance of the concept of incarnation. On the other, in the NT we find Jesus declaring that 'at that day', when there would take place that apocalyptic transformation of which the OT speaks and all things would become new, 'then shall appear the sign of the Son of Man in heaven . . . and they shall see the Son of Man coming in the clouds of heaven with power and great glory' (Matt. 24.30). By this he means that as human Son of Man upon earth, and as epitome of historical Israel, the work which he was performing on earth must necessarily be valid for all eternity, that is to say, for the realm of the spirit as well as for the realm of matter. In other words, the eschatological significance of his work on earth must inevitably be revealed 'with power and great glory' when, in the End, he comes with all the host of the redeemed *in* him, and takes his seat in triumph at the right hand of God.

Appendix

Israel and the Church

The Church continuous with Israel

The NT writers are aware of an essential identity between Israel of old and the Church which has come into existence through Christ (Acts 7.38; 15.14; Rom. 9.25–26; 11.16 ff.; Gal. 3.7, 29; 6.16; Phil. 3.3; Heb. 4.9; I Peter 2; Rev. 7.9). They hold firmly to this belief, despite the paradoxically opposite corollaries which result from such a faith. These corollaries are (*a*) that the Church is still Israel, is the *continuum* from the OT People of God;[1] and (*b*) that the Church, being a community of grace, is marked at the same time by discontinuity with that same Israel of old.

(*a*) Nowhere in the NT do we find it suggested that our Lord had to 'found' a Church on earth. Christ accepted the fact that God had already done so more than a thousand years before (Acts 1.6). We recall that every one of the first disciples was an Israelite after the flesh, as was our Lord himself. We recall that St Paul was proud of the fact that he was born of the tribe of Benjamin (Rom. 11.1; Phil. 3.5). We recall that when Christ first sent out seventy disciples (Luke 10.1), all of that seventy were Jews. The Jew, of course, had a peculiar position of responsibility as the People of God, over against the 'seventy' nations which traditionally peopled the earth (Gen. 10). The twelve Apostles, again, certainly

---

[1] Nowhere in the NT is the Church called 'the new Israel'. We should therefore refrain from doing so too.

represent by their very number the twelve tribes of the sons of Israel (Matt. 10.5; 19.28; Mark 6.43, etc.; James 1.1; Rev. 21.14)[2] Rightly, then, Eph. 2.20 can declare that the Church, continuous with the OT People of God, is 'built upon the foundation of the apostles *and prophets*'.

(b) Yet discontinuity marks the origin of the Church as well. The Church was born, not of the flesh, but of the Spirit, on the memorable day of Pentecost (Acts 2). The Church is thus also regarded as the Community of the Resurrection, whose day of rest is no longer the Jewish Sabbath, but the first day of the week, the day on which its Lord rose again from the dead.

Both elements thus need equal emphasis, if we are to seek to understand the nature of the Church, both the 'institutional' and the 'spiritual', the so-called catholic and so-called protestant.[3] The child of Christian parents is both born into the Christian heritage, and must needs be 'born again' in Christ. This 'discontinuity', to which the Pentecostal experience of the Church points, is none other than an aspect of the 'death-and-resurrection' motif, which we have seen to be characteristic of the whole OT revelation, and which represents the continuing power of God to bring good out of evil, life out of death. The People of God of old had to die, in the death of Christ on the Cross, before they could be reconstituted on the day of Pentecost in the risen Christ.

The Uniqueness of Christ

Although Christ is the Remnant of Israel in himself, yet there is total discontinuity between him and the People of God in the OT. In the OT, Israel had been adopted by God as his Son and Servant, but yet remained a sinful and rebellious people. Though the Son of the NT, on the other hand, epitomized in his own life, death

---

[2] Cf. W.D. Davies, *Paul and Rabbinic Judaism*, 1948, chap. 4; and H.H. Rowley, *The Biblical Doctrine of Election*, 1950, pp. 144 ff.

[3] Jean-Louis Leuba, in *New Testament Pattern*, translated by H. Knight in 1953, outlines these two strains as he finds them in the NT.

and resurrection the whole experience of the Israel of OT times, and thus was the 'End' of God's choice of Israel, yet he was 'from above' (John 8.23), was sinless (John 8.46), was conscious of his unity with the Father (John 17.21), and his work was thus unique, ἐφάπαξ (Rom. 6.10; Heb. 7.27). Central to the whole work of Christ was his death on Calvary. Not one member of the 'old Israel' followed him as he moved forward to take the cup and complete his act of substitution for all men: 'All the disciples forsook him and fled' (Matt. 26.56). It is because of his unique act that Christ is in consequence regarded as *Lord* of his Church. He rules the Church in the same manner as God has set him to rule all things in both heaven and earth (Eph. 1.22). Christ cannot thus be identified with Israel, whether old or new, *simpliciter*. The Pauline imagery depicts Christ as the Head of the Body, since it is from the Head that the whole Body is fitly joined together (Eph. 1.22–23; 4.15–16; 5.23; Col. 1.18). The Johannine imagery likewise regards him as the *whole* Vine, of which those who are 'in him' are the branches (John 15.1–8). He is not merely the 'stem' of the Vine, he is the whole Vine himself, inclusive of the branches. In like manner also he is the whole Rock (I Cor. 10.4), in fact the Rock on which all other rocks can repose (Matt. 16.18).

On the other hand, Christ is certainly regarded as the 'inclusive representative' of Israel, both old and new. We have studied the significance of this conception in the case of the OT messianic king, of the Suffering Servant of Deutero-Isaiah, and in the case of other figures as well. Thus while Christ is indeed the Head of the Church, yet the Church is equally certainly his very Body (cf. I Cor. 12.27: 'You are the Body of Christ'). We have seen that the Body of Israel, the Bride of God, is one day to be united as one flesh with her divine Husband. Such an expectancy was surely actualized in the event which we call the Incarnation. There we see the validity of the OT image of the union of the divine and the human as one flesh. Moreover, he who was both God and Israel at once undertook to fulfil the calling of Israel the Servant, and to pass through the Fire that is to usward the Wrath of the living God himself. It is the Church, however, that is now the Body of this same Christ. That is why the Church 'must suffer, as it is

written' (Mark 8.31, etc.), must take up her cross daily if the
purposes of God, who uses suffering to that end, are to work out
through her extraordinary relationship with her Lord.[4] The believer in Christ also must so be incorporated in Christ that he is
prepared to be 'buried' with Christ (Rom. 6.4), having been
'crucified' *with* him (Rom. 6.6), thus having 'died' with him (Rom.
6.8). Then follows the great correlative. Then shall he be enabled
to '*live with* him' (Rom. 6.8).

It was of the Son of man, of course, that the words 'must suffer'
were originally spoken (*v. supra*). We have now seen how the
whole OT People of God bore that significant name, yet how, in
terms of OT thinking, all Israel could still be summed up in one
individual inclusive representative who might bear that very
name. That is why, in Christ, the Son of man, the Church, all
Israel, will also one day be seen sitting at the right hand of the
power, and coming in the clouds of heaven.

Pentateuch and Gospels

The parallel nature of the literary criticism of the Pentateuch and
that of the Gospels reveals that God's purpose in making an initial
redemptive act through his Son is declared in common by both
our Testaments. NT scholars have recognized that it is both
difficult and rash to declare categorically that the Gospels always
present us with the *ipsissima verba* of the Lord. It has become
evident that both the 'supernatural' element and the factual core
of the Gospels have been overlaid by the various levels of interpretation that were made in apostolic and sub-apostolic times. In
other words, the analogy of the onion which we employed in the
case of Pentateuchal criticism in Part Three, chap. 13 is one that
could be adduced just as well in the case of the Gospels. The NT
witnesses to the mighty acts of God in Christ. But those witnesses
are themselves the very layers that comprise the Christian com-

---

[4]   Cf. Vincent Taylor, *The Names of Jesus*, 1953, 'Servant', p. 32. Also
R.H. Fuller, *The Mission and Message of Jesus*, 1954, p. 102, 108.

munity in the first century of our era. The action of God in Christ (the 'supernatural' element in the Incarnation) comprises the core round which the layers are wrapped. We recall how, in the case of the Pentateuch, the 'core' action of God was known to be a nexus of events which could indeed be reported upon, but only by a community that had been called into being by the very reality and factuality of that core activity itself. The Church is thus just as much a mystery in its origin as is the Israel of the OT. In both cases we meet with a community which witnesses to an event which cannot finally be assessed by scientific methods, but by faith alone. The People of God in the OT was a people called into being by God's initial act under the hand of Moses, and was thus a people that lived in direct dependence upon the grace of the God who had chosen them. The NT People of God is therefore similarly a people that has been called (so we have the word ἐκκλησία by God, in Christ, to be the new eschatological community with the same profound significance as Israel of old.

The Unity of the People of God

Because of the oneness of Israel, through Christ, from the OT People of God to the NT People of God, we discover that the Church too must be one. It is true that God had at times to break up the essential unity of his people for his own purposes, even while he worked through them and through their rebellious nature. Passages such as I Kings 12.25–33; 14.16; 15.30 speak of the 'sin of Jeroboam, wherewith he made Israel to sin', when he forced the division of the People of God into two camps. 'So Israel (the northern camp) *rebelled* against the house of David' (I Kings 12.19). Sinful as this rebellion was, however, it fell into place in the purposes of God. 'Thus saith the Lord', came the Word of God through Shemaiah the prophet to Rehoboam, king of Judah, 'Ye shall not go up, nor fight against your brethren, the children of Israel; return every man to his house; for this thing is from me' (I Kings 12.24).

The mercy of God, however, is from everlasting to everlasting. His purpose found fruition not only through judgement, when 'the two houses of Israel', each in turn, were consumed in the flames of God's refining Fire (722 B.C. and 587 B.C.). We saw that God's mercy and God's justice were one. It was to the two quarrelling houses of Israel together that the words 'Comfort ye, comfort ye, my People', were addressed (Isa. 40.1). It was the two houses of Israel which were once again united as the one stick (Ezek. 37.19) at the end of the Exile to become once more the one and only People of God. An appreciation of the theological significance of God's purpose for his one, united people in OT times is obviously our best guide for discovering his purpose for the Church in the twentieth century.

Israel and the Jews

St Paul makes it clear that his own people after the flesh possessed all the necessary qualifications to become the eschatological People of God that had been spoken of by the interpreters of Israel in the Scriptures of the OT. 'In this the NT stands alongside the OT, for it concedes to the Jews that their election by God gives them not only their existence, but also a unique and lasting dignity' (Matt. 21.33 ff.; Luke 13.16; 19.9; John 8.37).[5] Of this people St Paul said: They are 'my brethren, my kinsmen according to the flesh', and to them 'pertaineth the adoption, the glory, and the covenants, and the giving of the law, and the service of God, and the promises; whose are the fathers, and of whom as concerning the flesh Christ came' (Rom. 9.4–5). But all that significant heritage, as Paul so clearly saw, had never been 'transfigured'. The Jewish people of St Paul's day had not realized the eternal significance of their own unique calling and relationship to God. This was because, in their understanding of what it meant to be the People of God, the Body of Israel had never been wed, in

---

[5]   Karl H. Rengstorf, 'The Jewish Problem and the Church's Understanding of its own Mission', in *The Church and the Jewish People*, 1954.

Christ, to the ultimate meaning and purpose of the 'promise' which God had made to Abraham of old (Rom. 9.8). Just as a single man remains incomplete and unfulfilled if he does not wed 'an help meet for him' (Gen. 2.18), so the Jewish people, as a race, had remained unwed, and therefore incomplete, and their destiny unfulfilled. In the light of the study we have now made, we recognize that their incompleteness resides in their refusing to become 'one flesh' by faith with that Suffering Servant who would have united their sufferings, and the meaning of their very existence, with the sufferings of God and the purposes which God is working out through those sufferings, not only in this world, but throughout the whole cosmos. The Jewish people have never discovered the significance of the unique event which transformed the People of God of the OT period into the Church of God of the NT period. They have never recognized the significance of the Resurrection of the Son, and so they do not know the power of the Pentecost which followed it. The Bride's perfect marriage with God, of which Hosea spoke in eschatological language, has never in their case been consummated. The Jewish people are therefore no longer the *eschatological* Israel of God, even though, paradoxically enough, they are still the People of God. The Jews of today are not the Church of God as God means the Church to be. They are the shadow Church. On the other hand, the Gentile Church of the present day has no more right to be called the Israel of God than Jewry has, unless she allows herself to be truly identified, body, soul, and spirit, with that Servant who has represented her already, and who, on her behalf, has given himself and all that he had and was to the flames of the Fires of God. It is only at that moment when she does indeed identify herself with the Suffering Servant, and truly and humbly accepts the sacrifice which he has already made on her behalf, in and through the Body which they both have in common, it is only then that the Church really shares in all the benefits of his work, and is most truly the People of God.

Jewry still waits, however, for her *raison d'être* to become apparent, still possessing the adoption, the glory, and all the other elements of her unique heritage. Her Body, the Body which, historically speaking, she has already shared with the Body of

Jesus, is also still in existence in this world as an empirical fact of history. The one thing needful, for lack of which Jewry remains isolated from the Church of Christ, is an act of faith in that Suffering Servant who has himself sprung from Jewry 's loins. It is the self-sufficiency of modern Jewry, as a deeply religious people, that prevents them from committing themselves in faith to one whom they are not willing to identify with their own Body. It is the self-sufficiency of Jewry which blinds their eyes to the ultimately paradoxical truth that it is only he who loses his life who will save it, so that it is only when Israel, the Servant, shares in the sufferings of the other Servant *for* the world that both the world and the Servant can be saved (Mark 15.31, etc.).

Now, no one but the most incorrigible anti-Semite doubts that Jewry knows to the full the meaning and profound significance of suffering, especially when he learns something of the history of the Jews since their expulsion from Palestine by the Romans 1800 years ago. Thus it is not the natural human fear of suffering which prevents Jewry from understanding the claims of the Suffering Servant of old. On the other hand, Jewry has not been able to discover in its own sufferings any relationship to the meaning and purpose of the suffering that was inherent in the crucifixion of Christ upon the Cross. In other words, the modern Jew does not believe, in his present self-sufficiency, that he needs to be 'saved' by any act of Christ or of any other mediator in earth or heaven. There is no place for the Fall in his interpretation of his own OT literature.[6] The Jew believes that man was created by God to live through and in God as a free and independent being. As Leo Baeck explains,[7] man is called upon to act ethically in life by the exercise of his own free-will. The faith of the modern Jew is an idealistic one, and one that is optimistic about human nature and its possibilities for self-reformation. Man, says the modern Jew, is essentially good at birth, and is therefore *able* to rise to the heights of God. There is, of course, a gulf fixed between man and God; but 'it is a gulf that can be bridged by man's prayers and study,

---

[6]   Yet see Will Herberg, *Judaism and Modern Man*, 1951, p. 73.

[7]   *The Essence of Judaism*, 1936, p. 151.

by his thought and his actions'.[8] Yet if Jewry could but make the necessary act of faith in one who offers to do for man what man is not able to do for himself, and commit itself to the Suffering Servant whose action, under God, has been and ever is effective in the realm of the disrupted relations that obtain between God and man, then Jewry would find its own cross and its own history of suffering and rejection illumined and given the ultimate meaning and significance which we recognize actually belongs to the People of God throughout all history – this people which still possesses the promises, and whom God has never cast away. And so we may well ask in the words of Paul: 'What shall the receiving of them be, but life from the dead'? (Rom. 11.15). That day must surely dawn, the day when Jewry will become one with the whole Body of the saints. For without that people whom we know as Jewry the Church cannot express in its own Body the full meaning of service and obedience in the Servant who is Christ.

How near Jewry actually comes to a full and joyous understanding of her true calling as the Israel of God is frequently noticeable in her literature throughout the ages. We see it in the early centuries of the Christian era. 'God has bound up his name with the name of Israel in an indissoluble bond', runs *Numbers Rabbah*. A similar belief is enshrined in *Exodus Rabbah* 51, where we read that Jewry compared the giving of the Law on Mount Sinai to the marriage of Israel with God. The well-known words of *Sanhedrin* 37a, too, echo the faith of the Synagogue at that early period, the belief that it is the Jewish people as such who are the essential element on earth in the eschatological purposes of God: 'All Israel has a portion in the world to come'.

The individual Jew seems to possess a racial memory. When the challenge of the Person of Christ comes home to the consciousness of the modern Jew, it does so frequently with the clarity of

---

[8]   O. Lazarus, *Liberal Judaism and its Standpoint*, 1937, p. 86. See also M. Waxman, *A Handbook of Judaism*, 1947, p. 168; I.M. Wise, *Judaism and Christianity*, 1883, p. 62; *KzNT*, 1, pp. 8 ff., IV, pp. 4 ff.; and Th. C. Vriezen, *Die Erwählung Israels nach dem Alten Testament*, 1953, *passim*.

blinding light. This is because the whole long, and hitherto, meaningless story of his race seems to fall into perspective and to shape itself into a meaningful pattern. Not only does many an individual Jew then see his own personal sufferings taking on significance in the light of the Cross, but such a Jew also sees, as in a flash, the meaning of the sufferings of his race. It is when he sees Christ as the Suffering Servant that he knows the significance both of the Fall of Jerusalem in 587 B.C. and of the gas-chambers of A.D. 1944. All the sufferings of his people, both past and present, now fit into the biblical pattern of God's activity, a pattern which had been irrelevant to him before. He now relates the sufferings of his people to the five 'moments' in the story of the People of God in OT times. The Gentile convert to Christianity certainly sees the significance of the five 'moments' in his *own* experience of God's grace and redeeming love. But the Jewish believer sees much more than the significance merely of his own individual salvation. If he is biblically literate at all, it is the historical and the cosmic significance of God's grace and love that he grasps at once, for the reason that these are now newly epitomized in his own experience of grace. The 'adoption, the glory, and the covenants, and the giving of the Law, and the service of God, and the promises, whose are the fathers . . . ', phrases which may be fundamentally irrelevant to the thought and experience of the Gentile believer, all become illumined and meaningful to the Jew who finds the key to them in Christ. Therefore it is that his new discovery can provide him with an exhilaration and a joy beyond what is normally experienced by the mere Gentile Christian. The latter joys in his own personal salvation. But the Jew exults in finding more than a mere 'personal Messiah' in finding Christ. The individualism characteristic of modern, western Christendom seldom envisages the depth of understanding which the Jew may obtain in Christ. The Jew so often sees what the Gentile believer seldom even seeks to understand, viz., the place of the Servant People of God in the whole cosmic purpose of the Almighty.

It is at its peril, then, that the Church in its pride arrogates to itself alone the place and function of Israel. The Church has been engrafted into the stock of Israel from without by the grace of God alone. The whole biblical conception of the *Una Sancta* is impossible of attainment if it does not include within its scope that People of God 'of whom as concerning the flesh Christ came' (Rom. 9.5). The Christian approach to the Jew must therefore of necessity be the primary and fundamental activity of the modern Church as it explores its ecumenical duties. A Church which does not take seriously the biblical order of evangelism (cf. Matt. 15.24; Rom. 1.16, etc.), ought not to imagine that it has the right to pursue ecumenical ends. Such a Church too easily tends to be concerned primarily with the conversion of individuals, and with the attainment of an individualistic ethical life of which the NT does not speak. It tends too easily to forget that its roots go back to Abraham, and that it was not just born at Pentecost; and too easily it dismisses the essential insight of those central words of John 3.16: 'God so loved the *cosmos* . . . ' It is the continued existence of the shadow Church alongside of the Church Catholic which is the ever present reminder to the latter of the meaning and significance of a high doctrine of Israel. 'It may well be that the question whether the promises given to Israel are actually fulfilled in Jesus Christ will be decided for the Jews if they recognize in the Church, which claims to be the Body of Christ, the traits of the Messiah of the chosen people of God, Israel'.[9]

---

[9] Rengstorf, op. cit., p. 45.

Index of Subjects

Index of Biblical References

2.6 337
2.10 255
4.2 44, 133

Micah
1.4–5 124
1.15 87
3.8 24, 74
4.1 307
4.4 342
4.5 164
4.6–8, 10 323, 329
4.9–10 255
5.2–7 304
5.3 329
5.7 184
6.1–3 327
6.8 223
7.4, 7 191
7.15 312
7.18 44, 130

Habakkuk
1.12 277
2.3 191
2.4 334
2.6 145 n.
2.14 87
3.3, 8 151
3.10 152

Zephaniah
1.2 341
1.2 ff. 134
3.12 f. 254
3.14 320

Haggai
1.13 250
2.5 85
2.23 299

Zechariah
1.9 63
1.12–13 66
2.4–5 308
2.7 319
3.1–7 128, 256
3.2 128, 178, 199, 274
3.6–10 66
3.8 298, 311
3.9 66, 178
3.10 342
4.6 85
4.7 179, 221
4.9–10 178
4.10 303
6.5 61
6.8 85
6.9–15 310
6.12 298, 300, 311
6.15 179
7.12 85
8.4–5 342
8.6 343
8.7–8 328
8.21 308
9.8 66
9.9 320
9.9–10 304
9.11 215
10.11 312
11.15–17 327
12.1 23
12.3 177
12.10 162
13.1 306
13.2–6 317
13.4 235
13.7 327
14.4 306

Index of Hebrew Words

Index of Greek Words